The World of African Music

The World of African Music

Stern's Guide to
Contemporary African Music
Volume 2

Written and edited by
Ronnie Graham

Pluto **\| |\|** Press
Research **\|\|\|** Associates

First published 1992 by Pluto Press
345 Archway Road, London N6 5AA

Paperback published in the U.S.A. by Research Associates
751 East 75th street, Chicago, Il. 60619

Distributed in the U.S.A. by Frontline Dist. Int'l
751 East 75th street, Chicago, Il. 60619
Tel: (312) 651-9888 Fax 651-9850

British Library Cataloguing in Publication Data
A CIP catalogue record for this book is available from the British Library

ISBN 0 7453 0552 0 hardback
ISBN 0 7453 0657 8 paperback
ISBN 0 94839 003 4 paperback (USA only)

Library of Congress Cataloging in Publication Data
Graham, Ronnie.
    The world of African music / Ronnie Graham.
    235 p. 26 cm. – (Stern's guide to contemporary African music ; v.
2)
    Includes bibliographical references, discographies, and index.
    ISBN 0-7453-0552-0 (cloth).
    1. Popular music–Africa–History and criticism. 2. Folk music–
Africa–History and criticism. 3. Musicians–Africa–Biography.
I. Title. II. Series.
ML3502.5.G73 1992
780'.967'09048–dc20   92-9308
                                                        CIP
                                                        MN

Designed by Ray Addicott

Typeset by Archetype
Printed in the United States of America.

Contents

Acknowledgements

My interest in African music has, if anything, increased over the five years since I was researching for Volume 1 of the *Stern's Guide* and as my circle of friends and contacts has grown so too has my debt to them. In this respect, my first and biggest acknowledgement is to those friends who kindly agreed to contribute their specialist knowledge to this book – Graeme Ewens, John Collins, Trevor Herman, Pieter Hoefman, Nick Dean, Harry Roseboom, Musa N'Joh, Lucy Duran, Kofi Grey, Charles Easmon, Vince Luttman, Martin Sinnock, Klaus Frederking, John McLaverty and Lois Darlington.

Office space and technical support was generously offered by my friends at Stern's, Robert Urbanus, Don Bay, Dave Atkin, Scott Lund, Dominic Raymond-Barker, Ian Thomas, Rosalie Stockman, Basile Dakey, Ruth Abrahams, Rene Williams, Wouter Rossing, Kenny, Chantal Bougnas, Stewart Scotney and all other staff over the last few years. Thanks also go to Jumbo Van Renen, Iain Scott, Ben Mandleson, Charlie Gillet, Jo Shinner, Gunter Gretz, Kofi and Susie Grey, Fleming Harrev, Big Joe Asiedu, Ruth Abrahams, Maggie O'Toole, Eric Coull, Kevin Curley, Joe Sambo, Bridget O'Connor, Chibs, Paul Tanton, Herman Striedl, Graham Skinner, Stuart Lamb, Mr Khuswayo, Doug Bloom, Andy Palacio, Joe Palacio, Charlie Harrowell, Egbert Higinio, Zoila Ellis, Bev Swasey, Matt Mariano, Gus Ashdown, Richard Trillo, Rick Glanvill, Ian Peedle, David Nkhata, Roger Harris, Andrew Tracey, Donald Clarke, Andrew Kaye, Roger van Zwanenberg, Phillip Doner, Roger Armstrong, Keith Summers, Kitenge, Roger Thomas, Debbie Golt, Stuart Lyons, Bob George, Bert Spliff, Henk Tummers, Stan Rijven, John Gray, Tellef Kvifte, Josephine Zagbeli-Thomas, the late Edmund Collins, Pat Collins, Simon and Nora Collins, Nick Van Hear, Thomas Paquette, Bobby and Bernadette Leslie, John McGill, Clare Sampson, Colin Burns, Bunt Stafford-Clark, Myra Green, Priscilla, Nigel, Diane, Melinda, Leland, Aubrey, Anne, Donald, Sandra Hawke, Sean, Joyce, Meryl, Dennis, Helen, Jo, Sarah, Colin, Martyn and Maggie Anderson, Hugh, Brian, Stuart Sutton-Jones, Robin Miller, Steve Wood, Nick Carnac, Bev and Wim, Marylyn Alexander, Quentin Henderson, Ran Deb, Terry and Mary Lacey, Kwabena Fosu-Mensah, Herman Asafo-Agyei, Lynette Aitken, Richard Bradley and my many friends at VSO, in the WPA and amongst Stern's customers.

Thanks also, once again, to Paulyn De Fresnes, 'artiste extra-ordinaire' and designer of the ethno-linguistic maps.

Thanks, as well, to Justin Dyer, who copy-edited the manuscript.

For institutional support over the last five years, I would like to thank VSO, SOAS, NSA, BBC and Cooperation For Development.

For generously offering their time to answer many of my questions, I would like to thank E.T. Mensah, King Bruce, Nsimba Foguis, Paterson Mutebi, Fred Zindi, Mwana Musa, Abdul T-Jay, Herman Asafo-Ajyei, Samba Mapangala, members of Orchestre Maquis, Sam Mangwana, Gideon Mulenga, Konimo, Frank Williams and Russell Herman.

Finally, thanks of a more personal nature go to my wife, Mivvi, and to Ebony, who both tolerated the unsociable hours spent researching and writing this book.

Ronnie Graham
London, 1991

Using this Guide

NOTE ON THE MAPS

In Volume 1 great emphasis was placed on the importance of good ethno-linguistic maps and I believe they helped many readers identify the main ethno-linguistic groups referred to in the text.

Volume 2 includes a similar selection of maps, carrying the same provisos as Volume 1. In the first place, they only direct readers to areas of origin. The modern ethno-linguistic map would be considerably more complex given the dual impact of internal migration and urbanisation. Secondly, it should be made clear that while the maps follow the boundaries established by colonialism and accepted by today's nation states, they often mean little in terms of cultural, linguistic or musical configurations. Indeed, as this volume makes abundantly clear, for several countries the centre of musical production is no longer in Africa at all as recordings are often made in the metropolitan capitals and cassette reproduction takes place in the newly industrialising countries of the Far East. In this respect, at least, the last five years have seen the globalisation of manufacturing African music.

A good map can be worth a thousand words and I hope that these enhanced maps will enable both old and new readers to identify correctly where certain styles originate and how they have been spread across Africa. Space alone precludes the provision of a map for every African country but I am confident that the twenty-five maps contained in this volume will satisfy most readers.

NOTE ON SPELLING

The information appearing in this guide has been drawn from sources in a variety of European and African languages. This inevitably raises problems when it comes to standardisation of spelling. Wherever possible, I have tried to present information in its English usage, but where information has been taken directly from an original source (with no comparative or supporting information), I felt it was better to use the original spelling.

KEY TO PREFIX CODES OF MAIN LABELS SPECIALISING IN AFRICAN MUSIC

The following abbreviations cover international labels specialising in African music. The list does not include African companies distributing inside the country of origin. In terms of availability, most material from these companies can be found through specialist shops.

360	Sonodisc (France)
380	Syllart (France)
AAER	Anti-Apartheid Enterprises (UK)
AFRI	DisqueAfrique (UK)
ASLP	Polygram (Kenya)
AT	Touré Jim (Cameroon)
BM	Bareinreiter Musicaphon (Germany)
CBS	Columbia (US/Nigeria/Kenya)
CEL	Celluloid (France)
COOK	Cooking Vinyl (UK)
DWAPS	Decca (West Africa)
EMV	Earthworks (UK)
ESP	Disques Esperance (France)
ESPERA	Espera (Belgium)
EVVI	Verckys (Zaïre)
FE	Folkways (US)
FMSL	Rogue (UK)
GALP	Gallo (South Africa)
GEN	Genidia (Zaïre)
HNBL	Hannibal (UK–USA)
HQ	Harlequin (UK)
ILPS	Island (UK)
JIP	Jimmy (France)
KAZ	Kaz Records (UK)
MLPS	Mango (Island – UK)

MON	Demon (UK)
MOTO	Moto (UK)
NAK	Nakasi (Ghana)
NEMI	EMI (Nigeria)
OCR	Ocora (France)
OMA	Original Music (US)
ORB	Globestyle (UK)
PAM	Popular African Music (Germany)
PIR	Pirhana (Germany)
POLP	Polygram (Nigeria/Kenya)
RETRO	RetroAfric (UK)
ROUND	Rounder (US)
RMU	Rythmes et Musique (France)
RWLP	Real World (UK)
SAF	Son Afrique (France)
SHA	Shanachie (US)
ST	Stern's (UK)
SYL	Syllart (France)
TAN	Tangent (France)
TERRA	Triple Earth (UK)
V	Virgin (UK)
VDA	Voix d'Afrique (France)
WCB	World Circuit (UK)
WOMAD	World Of Music And Dance (UK)

NOTE ON THE DISCOGRAPHY

Volume 1 listed approximately 3,000 albums from the period 1955–85. This volume adds a further 2,750 items drawn mainly from 1986–91. However, where important early items have recently come to light they have been added to this discography. Secondly, where musicians and bands have established a major reputation over the last five years, I have sought to include their earlier works in this discography. Excluding these two exceptions, this volume does not repeat discographical information available in Volume 1 and readers are referred to Volume 1 for such information.

Introduction

During 1985–6, I conducted extensive research into the world of contemporary African music, drawing on seven years' residence in West Africa, two years' research at Stern's African Record Centre and countless interviews with African musicians. This research was subsequently published as *Stern's Guide to Contemporary African Music* (Pluto Press, London, 1988) and *The Da Capo Guide to Contemporary African Music* (Da Capo, New York, 1988). The intention was to document commercially available LP recordings of African music in an effort to support that growing market. A subsidiary aim was to provide a context for this music by combining elements of history, biography and economics to help explain where the music had come from, how it had evolved and where it stood at that moment.

Despite the book's shortcomings, the critics were generous in their assessment of its value. However, the commercial situation was changing rapidly in the world of African music and as time moved on the discographies became less and less useful as material was deleted and new recordings were released. For example, we can estimate that between 1986 and 1991 albums were being released at the rate of more than 100 a month – over five thousand in five years. Secondly, not only was interest in African music growing but that interest was changing. The music of Ghana and Nigeria, for example, became unfashionable while interest in the music of the Sahel and Southern Africa grew enormously. Finally, while the established stars largely retained their audiences, many new stars rose to prominence as musical and business interests began to coincide. For these reasons, it was decided to publish a companion volume; bringing discographies and biographies up to date; expanding various chapters to take account of musical developments since 1986; and analysing recent changes in the African music industry. In this respect, the current volume is an update on Volume 1 and should complement, rather than replace, the information provided in it.

A second major difference between Volumes 1 and 2 is that I no longer believed it possible for one author to cover the entire continent in terms of the specialised research required, and the sheer quantity of new music and the changing socio-economic climate in over fifty different African countries.

I also realised that several other writers were better equipped to deal with specific areas and subjects. Their contributions are warmly welcomed, although on several occasions I have taken the liberty of editing their text to conform to the overall style of the book. The rest of the book was researched during 1990–1 and is based on extensive archival work, many more interviews with musicians, research trips to the Caribbean, Zambia, Tanzania, Zimbabwe, Zanzibar, France, Holland, Germany and the USA, and, finally, many, many hours of listening and discussion with other aficionados.

In terms of geographical scope, historical perspective and commercial availability, it was decided to retain the same approach as Volume 1. However, it was also necessary to take account of two new factors arising directly from the growth of interest in African music – increasing research specialism and a fragmentation of the market. All five criteria are discussed in greater detail below. But above all, I felt it necessary to give much greater prominence to changes occurring within Africa which had the greatest direct impact on African culture. For while the availability, appreciation and enjoyment of African music increased considerably in Europe, the USA and Japan during the 1980s, the material conditions under which Africans lived and worked, for the most part, deteriorated quite dramatically (and often quite tragically) during the same decade.

The structure of the book is identical to that of Volume 1 and is divided into five regional sections, each subdivided into country chapters. Within this framework, biographical and discographical entries may appear to be somewhat haphazardly arranged. None the less, I have tried to follow a coherent policy based initially on style and thereafter on a combination of criteria which are, at one and the same time, chronological, musical and alphabetical. Unfortunately, the analysis of African music is not amenable to either a strict linear or geographical analysis and I have tried desperately to avoid the somewhat clinical and impersonal approach associated with dictionaries and catalogues. The book is comprised of almost entirely new material including hundreds of new and enlarged biographies; over two and half thousand new discographical entries; several important original essays; and more detailed ethno-linguistic maps. When occasion demands, important information from Volume 1 has been summarised and updated. Otherwise, it was not felt necessary to reproduce all the historical and sociological information appearing in

Volume 1. Where appropriate, the reader is referred to that volume.

As with the first volume, I have done my best to avoid passing personal, subjective opinions about musicians and their work. Having said this, while the structure of the current volume is identical to Volume 1, the balance and emphasis are different. For example, we have reflected changes in popular taste (hence commercial availability) by enlarging the entries on countries like Senegal, Mali, Guinea, Zambia, Zimbabwe and Madagascar. At the same time, major sources and influences like Zaïre, South Africa and Nigeria have been suitably expanded from their already large entries in Volume 1. Sadly, comparatively less has been heard from countries like Gabon, Ghana and Cameroon while others, like Chad, Somalia, Equatorial Guinea, Botswana and Malawi, have produced so little commercial music that it is difficult to say anything significant about them. On the other hand, small but important entries now appear on Lusophone Africa, the islands of the Indian Ocean, Niger, Ethiopia and Burkina. Volume 2 is a more comprehensive attempt to deal with all of sub-Saharan Africa and to reflect the current situation than was Volume 1 with its clear introductory and historical perspective.

The scope of this volume therefore remains basically the same as Volume 1 and is delineated by several criteria discussed in greater detail below.

Geographical. The scope of this book remains firmly focussed on sub-Saharan Africa. Friends have argued, with a great deal of justification, that by omitting Morocco, Algeria, Tunisia, Libya and Egypt, I am denying the underlying political and geographic unity of Africa. My response, then as now, is to argue that the music of North Africa is more closely related to the Middle Eastern musical tradition and that history and culture combine to make sub-Saharan Africa a more suitable focus of attention. Similarly, several friends have urged me to include a chapter on zouk from the French Antilles. And while wistfully agreeing that chapters on rai and zouk would undoubtedly enhance the commercial appeal of the book, I have decided to resist the temptation and retain a resolutely African and Afro-centric perspective. Secondly, it is increasingly apparent just how meaningless national boundaries are in terms of cultural and musical development. The current interchange between musicians from different countries but playing within the same basic style makes a nonsense of current political borders. Manding music in West Africa, taraab along the Swahili coast, rumba throughout East and Central Africa and the Paris studio scene all involve a great deal of musical exchange and experimentation.

Historical. In Volume 1 it was possible safely to predict that the era of vinyl in Africa was drawing to a close, although it will survive in one form or another for a few more years. However, the early 1990s more or less mark the end of the vinyl era in Africa as record companies close down pressing plants and re-invest in high speed cassette duplication.

In the west vinyl has largely been replaced by the compact disc, and although the appropriate hardware is beginning to appear in Africa (with over 1,000 African titles now available on CD), the market remains dominated by the ubiquitous audio-cassette.

For these reasons, given the unfortunate historical conjuncture of music manufacture and production in Africa, this volume continues to list vinyl productions and only to allude to material on cassette and CD when the vinyl product is not available. The discography is also more closely focussed on the period 1986–91, although where appropriate I have introduced definitive discographies for bands whose continuing success merits more than a retrospective glance.

Commercial availability. This has emerged as the most difficult and arbitrary of all criteria. Essentially, the African music industry is organised on a national basis with comparatively few records crossing over into neighbouring markets. Thus to begin with, we are dealing with more than fifty different countries of origin, even before we start to consider the various companies operating within these countries. Secondly, while music has a longer shelf-life in Africa than in the west, it seldom arrives in the UK in sufficient time to satisfy those enthusiasts always demanding something new from Africa. Thirdly, while most good titles eventually arrive in the west, they seldom arrive in sufficient quantities to satisfy everybody. For example, some extremely popular titles can be imported in quantities of fifty or less. At this level of trade it is simply not worth entering such productions into the back-catalogue. Finally, dozens of record companies exist for only one or two titles, making it highly unlikely that their products will remain available for any great length of time. Against this rather negative overview of availability it is necessary to mention two positive developments. The first is the emergence of major African record shops in the metropolitan capitals capable of, and willing to carry, extensive back-catalogue. Stern's, for example, keep over three thousand titles in stock. The second positive development (at least with regard to availability) has been the growth and consolidation of a dozen large independent record companies specialising in African music. Companies like Stern's, Earthworks, Mango, Original, Rounder, World Circuit, etc., have released a growing number of African titles ensuring that they remain available for several years at least. Unfortunately, none of these companies has seen fit to seek the assistance of Africans either in the selection or arrangement of repertoire, so while the issue of availability is at least partially resolved by these western independents, the criteria for selection remains quite arbitrary and occasionally quite questionable. We shall explore this controversial issue of selection later in this book.

While availability of material has become less of an issue over the last five years, this is not to say that all records can now be guaranteed. Those released on UK/US labels will remain in stock longer than others, but for French imported material and records direct from Africa the advice is to buy when you see and not complain too much when a much sought-after item becomes permanently unavailable. However, given the growth of interest in African music, it is not difficult to predict the imminent development of a thriving second-hand market where elusive albums will exchange hands at two or three times the recommended retail price. Finally, on the subject of availability, it is worth reflecting on the deep irony of a situation whereby a greater selection of African music is available in London, Paris and Tokyo than in Africa itself!

Research specialism. Since 1986, the increased sales of African music have been paralleled by a phenomenal increase in research into the recent African musical past. Some of it represented ongoing work but the great bulk stemmed directly from the growing involvement of western companies in African music as more obscure items were released, necessitating more thorough research into the music. In this respect, and for obvious reasons, African music released outside Africa tended to be accompanied by a great deal more background information than music released inside Africa. The focus of this new research was placed firmly on post-war urban popular music – not only was it easier to research than traditional music but it produced the kind of information which was required to support the commercial exploitation of African music. For these reasons, few new studies of traditional music appeared to complement the classic texts of Nketia, Bebey and Kebede. On the other hand, the post-war period was particularly well served by the continental surveys of Graham, Stapleton and May, Lee, Bender, Gray, Ewens and Manuel (see Bibliography).

At the same time, an enormous amount of original research was conducted into the evolution of individual national styles. Readers are therefore referred to the Bibliography for the research of Harrev on the West African Gome tradition, Bender on Sierra Leone, Collins on Ghana, Duran on Mali and Senegal, Coplan on South Africa, Zindi on Zimbabwe, Lonoh on Zaïre, Ben Mandelson and Anderson on Madagascar, and the excellent interviews with individual musicians by journalists like Glanvill, Ewens and Prince appearing in popular magazines such as *Folk Roots* and *World Beat*.

Individual stars also received growing attention with the appearance of important biographies of Miriam Makeba, Franco, Manu Dibango, E.T. Mensah, Mbaraka Mwinshehe and Youssou N'Dour to add to the earlier studies of Fela and Le Grand Kalle.

Taken together, all this original research and impressive journalism served to deepen the constituency of African music as thousands of new fans began to develop an understanding of what it was and how it had developed. The work of the last five years has done a great deal to present a positive image of Africa towards the end of a decade dominated by popular images of famine, drought, civil war and natural disaster. This work should not stop and we can anticipate even more thoroughly researched band histories and individual biographies in the future.

Market fragmentation. With the overall growth in interest in African music came an increasing fragmentation of the market as consumers became more informed and started to exercise greater personal preference. A marked difference lay between African and European consumers – Africans tended towards dance music while Europeans (mostly in the 20–40 age bracket) tended towards the more sedentary styles of the Sahel Region. As consumer preference became more marked so it became less easy to manipulate taste towards a certain style or artiste. In this respect, while the overall market doubled in size, it is debatable whether many musicians fully benefited, as more good music appeared on the market than ever before with a consequent dimunition in individual sales.

Of course several top stars like Clegg, N'Dour and Alpha Blondy gained, with sales often approaching half a million. But the core, global market remained between 5,000 and 10,000 units divided fairly evenly between rumba, jit-jive, mbaqanga, mbalax, fuji and the various styles of Francophone West Africa.

I conclude by restating the proviso appearing in Volume 1. This is not and cannot be a definitive guide to African music for many of the reasons outlined above and it is not Stern's current catalogue.

This guide only scratches the surface of African music, concentrating as it does on those musicians who have enjoyed a recording career and are widely regarded as the most popular or influential. Volume 1 attempted to survey the contemporary scene and I must thank those readers who wrote with additional discographical information. Fortunately, no one complained that a major star had been omitted so I feel confident that both Volume 1 and Volume 2 can be considered comprehensive, if not yet definitive.

A great deal more work remains to be done – on the crucial transitions from traditional to urban music, on the role of women in African music, on company histories and on a number of specific counties like Cameroon, Gabon, Uganda, Namibia and Guinea. Once again I would ask readers to get in touch with any complaints and suggestions for subsequent volumes.

Two more volumes are planned over the next ten years. By the turn of the century it is our hope to have put at your disposal a comprehensive guide to recorded African music in the twentieth century.

Introduction to Africa – the Compilation Album

In a sense, the compilation album is music in limbo – few of them provide a coherent introduction to African music and fewer still are bought by seasoned buyers. Given the fact that African music has, in general terms, beeen badly presented to the western consumer, many compilations add insult to injury through their curious criteria for inclusion, juxtaposing old and new, acoustic and electric, trance and dance. Yet over the last decade and growing in intensity over the last few years, virtually every western company in the business has seen fit to release a compilation album. A great deal of African music has been misrepresented in the process, misleading consumers and musicians alike. Worst of all, western compilations seldom really represent what is popular in Africa.

Yet despite all this there are good compilations which can entice listeners into the world of contemporary African music. They tend to be country-specific or style-specific in which case they are referenced under country headings. Otherwise, readers are advised to treat continental compilations listed below very carefully. Outstanding compilation albums must include the two Island samplers of 1982.

1982	802 551 928	Sound D'Afrique Vol. 1
	802 552 928	Sound D'Afrique Vol. 2
1985	ST 1015/16	African Moves (Double) – Recommended
	OMA 108	African Acoustic – Recommended
	TSA 1003	African Sounds For Mandela
1986	CICIBA 8401/2	Bantu (Double) – Recommended
	F 37986	African Roots Vol. 4
	CEL 6761	Tropic Tonic
	MUSIC 2	New Africa
1987	8260	Africa Oumba Vol. 1
	CEL 6110	New Africa Vol. 1
	OMACD 001	African Acoustic – Recommended
	OMACD 002	Africa Dances – Recommended
1988	CEL 6119	New Africa Vol. 2
	CELCD 6139	New Africa Vol. 3
	KL 033	Découvertes 88
	KLV 03	La Musique Africaine
1989	ST 1029	African Moves Vol. 2
	CDORB 907	Compact D'Afrique (Zaïre)
	66828	West African Connection Vol. 2
	CSLP 5003	Women of Africa
	CEL 6798	Tropic Tonic Vol. 2
1990	66876	Africa Oye – Recommended
	CDVA 011	Voix D'Afrique
	79524	Africolor
1991	CD 52910	30 Ans de Musique – Recommended
	LYRCD 7328	African Rhythm and Instruments 1 (Live recordings from the 1969 Pan-African festival in Algiers)
	LYRCD 7308	Sounds of West Africa (Lobi and Dagarti from Ghana & kora from Gambia)

PART I

The Music of Africa

1   The Political Economy of African Music: 1985–91

Africa Political

Africa Linguistic

AFRICA AND THE WORLD ECONOMY

The 1980s are now described as a 'lost decade' for Africa as development ground to a halt under the combined burdens of debt repayment, drought, civil war and, it must be said, misguided economic policies and often massive corruption. At the same time adverse macro-economic trends conspired to increase the cost of imported goods while reducing the value of primary exports. From this point of view, Africa as a whole was forced to contend with reduced national and personal income during a decade of often rapid population growth, which was only partially mitigated by increased migration to Europe and North America.

The second half of the decade in particular witnessed a serious downward turn in the spiral of underdevelopment as the continuing tragedies in Sudan and Ethiopia were joined by new catastrophes unfolding in Mozambique, Somalia, Liberia and Angola. By 1990 it was estimated that almost 30 million people were at risk either from drought and famine or from civil war and external aggression. Elsewhere, the new scourge of AIDS was cutting a swathe through the sexually active population with infection rates of over 30 per cent being reported from some East African countries.

The political response to a declining economic situation invariably involved the maintenance of military and one-party states, often degenerating into particularly useless and barbaric personal dictatorships. There were, of course, exceptions to this sweeping generalisation but in general terms few would argue with this characterisation of contemporary Africa with its consequent attributes of an absence of political freedom and an alarming incidence of human rights abuses.

However, towards the end of the decade, partly as a result of events in Eastern Europe, partly because of the end of the Cold War and partly because these political systems were increasingly incapable of maintaining themselves in power, a new drift towards western-style multiparty democracy was apparent in many African countries. Some regimes willing acquiesced in the process and new political forces came to power; but others proved more reluctant to forgo the panoply of personal power and at the time of writing it is still not clear whether countries like Zaïre, Madagascar and Kenya will in fact introduce the political freedoms demanded by their people. On the other hand, Robert Mugabe in Zimbabwe argued forcibly for the extension of the one-party state in a move guaranteed to antagonise opponents both at home and abroad. Finally, in South Africa, the entire political process was revolutionised by the unbanning of the ANC, the release of leading political prisoners and the dismantling of the legal apparatus of apartheid. However, while this apparent progress led to the lifting of sanctions and the partial reintegration of South Africa into the community of nations, the process is by no means irreversible and recent disclosures provide worrying evidence of the determination of the regime to subvert the democratic process at home as well as in neighbouring Namibia and Angola.

There are those who detect some signs of hope in the situation of Africa as we enter the 1990s. I am afraid that I do not share this optimism. There are precious few signs that African economies are going to improve. Indeed, with the current western fascination with Eastern Europe and the Soviet Union, there is every indication that Africa is being increasingly marginalised in terms of trade, aid and investment. Without an improvement in the economic situation it is difficult to see how recent political advances can be maintained, far less extended. Secondly, it is now apparent that many African societies need to be rebuilt given the collapse and destruction of infrastructure. Indeed, it could be argued that Africa's needs are as much social as political or economic. This being so, it is difficult to see how the end of the Cold War and the apparent victory of market-forces philosophy will actually assist those already trapped in a downward spiral of poverty, disadvantage and discrimination.

It will be difficult to find solutions to these many problems and it is increasingly clear that as continental and regional groupings fail to deliver the goods the onus will undoubtedly fall on each country to devise its own development plan. In the past, the west was able to develop largely at the expense of the Third World. It is now the case that the Third World, and particularly Africa, will have to develop at its own expense.

CONSOLIDATION AND CONTROL – GROWING POWER OF THE MAJORS

With global sales exceeding $20 billion in 1990, there can be no doubt that the international music industry is a lucrative area of capital investment and accumulation. As such, it is governed by the same rules which apply to all fields of multinational capitalism and cannot be regarded as in any way different to other multinationals operating in Africa in terms of ownership and control, structure and policy, research, development and technology.

Ownership

Over the last five years, the industry has witnessed an unprecedented increase in the size and number of takeovers as predominantly Japanese companies seek to complement their lead in hardware development with access to American-owned repertoire. In 1990, for example, Sony gained control over CBS in the largest media takeover in history, thereby combining Sony's dominance of the electronic sector with CBS's vast music repertoire. The implications are clear – Sony can now dictate what music will be available and on which format. Phillips, the Dutch-based electronic company, responded with an 80 per cent stake in Polygram, one of the five record majors. Matsushita took over MCA, another major, leaving EMI and WEA as the two remaining majors without a Japanese hardware partner.

Outside the five major companies, the remaining 30 per cent of the market was led by large international independents like Island and Virgin and by thousands of small independents.

Technology

As part of the increase in leisure time, the 'leisure industries' have experienced enormous growth over the last three decades, driven by rapid technological change. Up to ten years ago, the hardware for reproducing music was limited to record turntables (a basic technology suitable for several formats – shellac 78 r.p.m.s and vinyl 45 r.p.m.s and 33 r.p.m.s) and the audio-cassette player. However, by 1990, the concentration in ownership and the pace of technological change had combined to produce up to half a dozen different hardware formats for reproducing music. The vinyl LP was rapidly becoming obsolete with companies threatening to cease the manufacture of turntables by the mid-1990s. On the other hand, the audio-cassette had, within two decades, become the most popular global format until the compact disc (CD), first introduced in 1982, started to make vast inroads into western markets towards the end of the decade. Meanwhile, the DAT (digital audio-tape), another new format introduced by Sony, had largely failed to make an impact with the public (although it proved of enormous benefit to the record companies). The DCC (digital compact cassette) was able to combine a new technology with an old software while the mini-disc combined CD technology with an appeal to the portable music market. However, while the existence of six formats guaranteed consumer confusion and a potential drop in demand, many observers regarded the confusion as a temporary phenomenon until the next great technological leap forward – the storing of sound on computer chips. Diagram 1

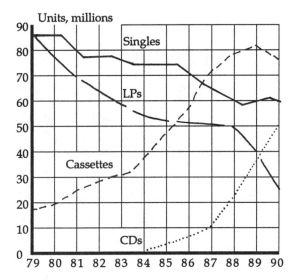

Diagram 1 (Source: BPI surveys/*Sunday Times*, 2 June 1991)

illustrates the changing fortunes of the most popular four formats over the last decade.

Motive and Policy

The majors have no real interest in African music beyond local sales (see Sony-CBS in Nigeria and Kenya) and the outside possibility that, one day, they will discover another Bob Marley lurking somewhere in their copyright back-catalogue. The five majors have demonstrated little understanding of Africa and seldom appear to know what local subsidiaries are doing. It appears as if their priority is to sell western repertoire to Africa rather than sell African repertoire to the west. Of course, the production and importation of vast amounts of western pop not only limits the market for local music but provides a strong and pervasive influence on the development of African music. Finally, when the majors do exhibit some kind of interest in African music, their own bureaucratic confusion and overall disinterest severely limits the impact which the music could make. Indeed, the last decade is replete with examples of African stars being given a very rough ride by the multinationals. Yet, in an era of an increasingly globalised culture, the prospect of Africa producing a million-selling star is as likely now as ever before.

MUSIC IN AFRICA: 1985–91

In Volume 1, the period 1975–85 was characterised as a decade of crisis in African music as the general deterioration of the position of Africa within the wider world economy became increasingly accentuated and as cassette piracy increased to such levels as to put at risk the very livelihood of African musicians. Some idea of current levels of bootlegging can be gauged from a 1991 incident in Togo when 1.5 million pirated cassettes worth in excess of 1 million dollars were seized on arrival from Singapore.

However, it was also accepted that cassette technology was a double-edged sword which could make or break the production and reproduction of contemporary African music. While on the one hand this analysis has proved tragically correct in terms of the continuing and intensifying crisis in Africa, a more positive and creative response to the problems of cassette piracy has proved that in certain sectors, despite the increasing dominance of western capital in Africa as a whole, it is still possible to maintain and indeed develop a specifically African response to the problems of the world. More specifically, the proliferation of cassette copying facilities in Africa has enabled many musicians to enjoy vastly increased sales, with the help of forward-looking producers and entrepreneurs like Ibrahima Sylla. Unfortunately, while legitimate cassette sales in Africa have increased phenomenally, western companies are reluctant to import African-produced cassettes, fearing consumer resistance to shoddy packaging and the possibility of sub-standard quality. The implications of this disrupture, whereby Africa produces music almost exclusively on cassette while the west increasingly turns to CD, are clear. In the not-too-distant future, there is every possibility that Africa and the west will be listening to different kinds of 'African' music.

Over the last five years, the music industry in Africa has responded in a variety of ways to the problems of creating and maintaining a viable and vibrant culture and it is worth stating that the least of these has been the way in which the west has been able to 'validate' certain styles and musicians through the process now understood as 'World Music'. If anything, evidence suggests that a closer approximation to western tastes and standards has inevitably involved a drop in domestic popularity (see Sunny Ade, Youssou N'Dour, Bhundu Boys, etc).

None the less, the problems caused by cassette piracy largely remain unresolved. By 1991 many countries in Africa still had no real policy regarding culture or renewable cultural resources such as music. In several countries (Liberia, Sudan, Mozambique, Angola, Somalia, Uganda, Namibia, Chad, Central African Republic and Rwanda) civil war, drought and warlordism had conspired partially to cripple any embryonic music industry. Music was enjoyed, if enjoyed at all, mainly in a traditional setting with very few urban pop bands surviving intact. In other countries such as Malawi, inability was replaced by general indifference to popular urban culture. In the great majority of countries official lip-service to the cause of culture failed to manifest itself in anything other than rhetoric. In such countries, the music business looked after itself in time-honoured fashion through an ad hoc mixture of patronage and entrepreneurship. Finally, a few countries (Ghana, Zambia, Nigeria, Kenya, Ivory Coast, Zaïre, South Africa, Zimbabwe, Senegal, Mali and Cameroon) managed to combine successful international entrepreneurship (Sylla, Shed, Khuswayo, Helwani, Toure, Mayala, Verckys, etc) with a lively domestic market for local music.

AFRICAN MUSIC IN THE WIDER WORLD

While the development of the music industry in Africa has been uneven at best, and tragically ignored at worst, the commercial development of the industry outside Africa has been steadily gathering pace over the last five years. In a purely geographical context, more and more countries have opened their ears to the contemporary music of Africa as first Scandinavia, then Italy and Spain started to import records, establish specialist magazines and radio programmes and even start to promote and produce musicians. The US market also started to fulfil its obvious potential while by the late 1980s Japan had emerged as a major market. In France, Britain, Belgium and Holland, earlier interest was maintained as more and more musicians took up residence and the independent companies were able to establish a viable network of shops, promoters, DJs, journalists and TV programmes. Further afield, African music continued to make considerable headway in the Caribbean (although not always to any great commercial gain), while Asian and Latin American markets proved difficult to penetrate, largely, it must be said, for the very same reasons which limit the market in Africa itself – poverty, piracy, poor facilities and government indifference.

This geographic spread of interest was matched by steadily rising sales figures as new markets were established and older ones maintained. Occasionally a single star or record could command sales in excess of 100,000, as in the cases of Mory Kante, Johnny Clegg, Alpha Blondy, Youssou N'Dour etc., but such figures proved to be the exception rather than the rule. It is always difficult to quantify sales (companies are reluctant to discuss such things) but we can consider the following figures to approximate the truth. These 'guestimates' relate to sales outside Africa. Inside Africa, it is even more difficult to estimate sales but Sylla reputedly sells in excess of 100,000 copies of cassettes while similar figures were fairly normal for Ade and Obey in the early 1980s juju music boom.

1983	Island	Sunny Ade	50,000 +
1984	Celluloid	Toure Kunda	100,000 +
1986	Pathé	Alpha Blondy	100,000 +
1987	Stern's/ Mango	Salif Keïta	100,000 +
1988	Barclay	Mory Kante (45)	250,000 +
1987	CBS	Paul Simon	6,000,000 +
1988	WEA	Johnny Clegg	100,000 +
1989	Virgin	Youssou N'Dour	100,000 +

Of course, just as these leading stars could occasionally sell into six figures, then just as easily could lesser luminaries fail to sell the few thousand copies regarded as the industry minimum. None the less, we can safely conclude that over the last five years the market for African music outside Africa has at least doubled. Supporting this trend is the growing number of small western record companies who have developed their own African labels, originating or licensing new material from Africa, as more and more musicians have arrived in Europe. By 1991 several companies in France, the US and the UK had released over 100 African titles, with many more smaller labels reaching double figures. We could estimate that somewhere in excess of 5,000 new African albums have been released in Africa or Europe over the last five years. If we were to include cassette-only releases then the figure would swell to over 10,000 new recordings. To conclude, over the last five years more African music has been reaching larger audiences in more countries than ever before, producing one or two household names along the way. Let us now turn our attention to a more detailed look at how African music has been bought and sold around the world.

France

Outside Africa, African music is most solidly established in France. Historically, France was the centre of an enormous empire including various Caribbean islands and vast swathes of the African continent. Unlike Britain, France retained close ties with its former colonies through the Franc zone, the French language and quite often the use of military force. By the 1970s Paris was emerging as a crucial nexus in the development of African music and by the 1980s hundreds of gifted musicians were based in France as part of a 4 million-strong Afro-Caribbean and North African community. Although the communities were often victims of rising French racism, the official policy of strengthening the use of the French language and the development of concepts such as 'Francophonie' also served to provide a more hospitable environment for music to flourish in than, for example, was the case in the UK. In 1981 the socialist government of Mitterrand took power, and although France was eventually forced to conform to the pro-market policies prevailing elsewhere in the industrialised world, some acknowledgement should be made of a progressive official policy towards culture and of the role of Jack

Lang as Minister of Culture. Musicians arriving for the first time were often assisted personally by the Minister, government funding was made available for African musicians to tour (both in France and in Africa), the radio stations were deregulated allowing more African music on the airwaves, while throughout the decade the country pursued a positive cultural aid policy. The private sector, with a large black domestic market, access to African markets through the Franc zone and a history of involvement in the production of African music for the former colonies, responded with a flood of new labels and companies to add to the well-established outfits like Sonodisc, Melodie, Pathé Marconi, Son Afrique and Barclay. Important new-comers include Syllart, Celluloid, Gefraco, Mayala, Ngapy, Cobalt, Wotre Musique, FNAC, Touré Jim, Jimmy's, Rythmes et Musique, Disques Esperance and Son Afrique. What is important is that many of these new labels are owned and managed by Africans, most notably Ibrahima Sylla, the Senegalese boss of Syllart; Kaluila, the Zaïrean behind Gefraco; Alhadji Touré's own Touré Jim's Records promoting native Cameroonian sounds; and Zaïrean Mayala with his impressive soukous catalogue. Yet, although the quality of the music and the recordings was consistently high, by the end of the 1980s a certain ennui had entered Afro-Parisian music-making. Many people felt that there was simply too much soukous and makossa on the market while others started voicing complaints about the overuse of studio formulas in producing music. Many musicians took the complaints to heart and, with a rising tide of French racism to contend with, started moving out of Paris to other European countries and the USA. The Afro-Parisian pop scene will inevitably survive these temporary hiccups but it may well be that the glorious days of the mid- to late 1980s are over.

The UK

Like France, the British involvement in African music has been heavily concentrated in the capital. In Volume 1 we presented a case study of the African music scene in London up to 1985. Since then Chris Stapleton's excellent essay, 'African Connections: London's Hidden Music Scene', has added greatly to our understanding of the crucial role of London in the dissemination of African music around the world. The years since 1985 have seen several important changes in the role played by London in developing African music. Not all of them have been either healthy or helpful and it may be useful to look at the various new companies on the scene before attempting any conclusions about the evolution of African music in the UK.

By 1985 a number of small independent companies specialising in African music had appeared in the UK, including Earthworks, Stern's, Oval, Globestyle, OTI and DiscAfrique. (See Volume 1 for details.) Since then, and with a growing intensity towards the end of the decade, a number of new companies have appeared,

some cashing in on the 'World Music' boom, others adopting a more considered and sympathetic approach.

Mango. A giant amongst pygmies, Mango, under the direction of Jumbo Vanrenen, is a brave attempt by major independent, Island, to keep in touch with the tropical scene following their ground-breaking efforts to promote reggae internationally. With a bigger budget to promote artists than any other London based outfit, Mango can cream the best off the top of contemporary African music and have over the last few years released material by Salif Keïta, Ray Lema, Baaba Maal and Thomas Mapfumo.

Real World. This company is a partnership between Peter Gabriel (ex-Genesis) and the WOMAD organisation. They started in 1989 with an eclectic selection of material including Ugandan Geoffrey Oryama and soukous star Tabu Ley. They attempt to recreate the excitement of a live show by recording artists in a live 'one-off' studio session, utilising the highest quality equipment. However, like Globestyle, Real World have Africa only in partial focus and have yet really to hit the nail on the head.

World Circuit. Formed in 1986 by Anne Hunt and Nick Gold, World Circuit grew out of the government-funded organisation Arts Worldwide, which had been active in promoting music, including several African stars, in the mid-1980s. Since then, with partially subsidised travel, they have explored many a rich vein of African culture, displaying a good understanding of both new and older material. Recent releases included Ali Farka Toure, Abdel Aziz El Mubarak, Shirati Jazz, Jali Musa Jawara and the incomparable Orchestre Baobab. In 1991 they were able to pull off one of the coups of the year in obtaining permission to re-issue the all-time Ghanaian classic *Hollywood Highlife Party*. However, by that time, funding was drying up everywhere and the touring arm of the business found itself in financial difficulty.

Triple Earth. Owned and run by Iain Scott and Bunt Stafford-Clark, Triple Earth grew out of a mail-order business and was formed in 1984. In 1985 they started with two gentle releases from Tanzania. An eclectic label with no known criteria other than a taste for the good, Triple Earth has been responsible for some of the most exciting sounds around over the last few years, including Ethiopian chanteuse Aster Aweke, the first international Rai release and the Guinean stars M'mah Sylla and Sona Diabate.

RetroAfric. Formed in 1986, this backward-looking company, specialising in the re-issue of African classics, kicked off with compilations from E.T. Mensah and Franco. In 1991 they burst into life again with a second Mensah album and a CD collection of the late Alick Nkhata, the enormously influential Zambian star.

WOMAD. Compilation specialists whose label grew out of their world music festivals. More recently they have started working with individuals, including the impressive Remmy Ongala. They now operate closely with the Real World label.

Rogue. In-house label of *Folk Roots* magazine. They have tended to favour West African acoustic material, reflecting the *Folk Roots* audience, although they also released Abdul T-Jay.

Hannibal. A joint UK–US label run by Joe Boyd which joined the World Music boom in 1987 with a string of Bulgarian releases. Since then, their attention has drifted to Africa, re-packaging Kanda Bongo Man for western consumption as well as several Senegambian releases. In 1991 the label collapsed and was eventually incorporated into the US Rykodisc catalogue.

Kijima. A now defunct label with South African releases.

Cooking Vinyl. Another Zimbabwe-oriented company releasing The Real Sounds and The Four Brothers. Also picked up S.E. Rogie from Sierra Leone.

Anti-Apartheid Enterprises. The commercial wing of the AA movement established in 1987 and responsible for the first international Angolan releases by Kafala Brothers and AKA Trio.

Mondeca. A rise and fall story. Established in 1988 as an off-shoot of Demon Records, Mondeca brought out three Zambian releases before disappearing in the depression of 1991.

These are the companies, what then has been the record of their involvement in African music? The first point to be made is that although several companies have profited from the growth of interest in African music, not one has yet been able to claim any significant level of profitability enabling them to undertake a direct investment in Africa. Secondly, there has been little or no involvement in supporting African artistes resident in the UK since Stern's early involvement with Hi-Life, Somo Somo and Kintone; Rogue with Abdul T-Jay; and Oval with various Ghanaians. In this respect, many African musicians based in the UK have a very low opinion of UK-based African labels and have struggled to put out generally very good material through their own efforts. Thirdly, there has been a general tendency for UK companies to follow trends rather than innovate. In the heady days of the 'World Music' boom it was not at all unusual to find company representatives rushing across Africa with microphone in one hand and contract in the other, 'discovering' musicians and raising totally unrealistic expectations.

The most common approach, however, was to contact various middle-men and license material. Stern's adopted this approach with great success in their dealings with the Senegalese producer and businessman Ibrahima Sylla, Earthworks (and many others) through Serengeti; Kijima through South African studios; and Globestyle through the Paris nexus. While this tactic undoubtedly served to bring much of the best of contemporary African pop to a wider audience, it also served to remove the need really to understand the music and the musicians. This 'gatekeeping' function also applied to efforts by DJs and critics to publicise African music without any direct experience of the music. The selection of material thereby became quite arbitrary and often quite questionable, reflecting personal enthusiasms until market forces stepped in to separate the sheep from the goats.

The USA and Japan

Over the last five years, both the US and Japan have emerged as major players in the African music scene. Of course, the US, with its substantial African-American population, had always been seen as a likely area of interest, but although a number of companies have attempted to sell into this market, no one has really succeeded and the market for African music remains predominantly white. For those companies brave enough to tackle the marketing of African music, the biggest problem remains that of distribution. Early pioneers include Shanachie and Rounder, who each succeeded in licensing a number of hot albums. Original Music lived up to its name with an exciting collection of early material, while more recently Celluloid (US), the African Music Gallery in Washington and, most recently, Stern's (US), Mango (US) and Real World (Virgin) have all joined the race to try to crack what is probably the most lucrative market in the world. As interest spread in the second half of the decade so too did the supporting infrastructure develop with dozens of radio shows devoted, at least in part, to African music. Many more retail outlets appeared and top African musicians became more regular visitors for one-off shows and tours. Several musicians in fact took out residency in the US with Zaïreans, Nigerians, Ethiopians and Ghanaians in the vanguard. Yet despite its enormous apparent potential, African music still has a long way to go in establishing a niche in the American musical consciousness. Various reasons have been offered for this apparent paradox given African-American fascination with their African ancestry. Yet while stars like N'Dour, Black Mambazo, Fela, Dibango and Makeba are almost household names, the scene remains small, white and middle class.

Japan, on the other hand, seems to have taken to African music in a serious way with some estimates putting the size of the Japanese market at between one-third and one-half of the total global market for African music. From 1985 onwards top attractions like Papa Wemba, Sam Mangwana and Zaïko Langa Langa all toured Japan to enormous audience acclaim. Initially, most of the records were imported but by the late 1980s Japanese companies were licensing some impressive recordings by top African stars for re-distribution around the rest of the world. (See Kanda Bongo Man.) At the macro-level, major Japanese hardware manufacturers took a major stake in the American music companies, although it remains to be seen whether their dominance of the global music business and their apparent openness to African music can be translated into a more dynamic approach to subsidiaries actually working in Africa.

WORLD MUSIC

The 'World Music' debate which so exercised the minds of many people involved in the African music business in the late 1980s could easily be dismissed as irrelevant were it not for the fact that the reality behind the debate significantly influenced the commercial direction African music was to take in the 1990s. Secondly, it can be argued that the switch in signifier from 'African' to 'World' tended to dilute the market for specifically African music when all along it had been African music which had spearheaded interest in non-European pop music. Finally, when the commercial value of the term 'World Music' declined in 1990, it had already served to limit and constrain popular perceptions.

The expression 'World Music' first emerged in 1986 when eleven UK-based independent companies met to discuss marketing problems for their various products. The common problem was that while African music had been enjoying a high media profile since at least 1984, it had proved difficult to persuade high-street outlets to stock the records. Potential customers appeared to be confused about what the music was and where it came from while the major stockists had themselves little idea of how to display or market the music. The response was to bring all non-western music under a convenient title so that shops would know where to put such material and customers would know where to look. The scheme was launched in 1987 and proved to be an enormous commercial success for the companies involved as sales rose 'exponentially' for African, Asian, Latin and Caribbean music. Media coverage was enormous, in print and on TV, and the tired palates of western consumers were sufficiently stimulated to embark on a post-*Graceland* record buying boom. The popular music of the non-western world had been successfully categorised and codified with the help of massive and misleading media overhype.

During the next few years, companies were able to confirm popular tastes along certain lines as the entire musical output of Africa jostled for space alongside Bulgarian, Indonesian and Columbian releases in the over-crowded World Music racks of high-street stores. By reducing the categorisation of music to its lowest common denominator, the instigators of World Music had paradoxically succeeded in bringing proportionately less African music to the general public than they had before. Other significant criticisms arose from the fact that no London-based, African-owned company had been invited to participate, producing the situation whereby no African was involved in the crucial decisions concerning repertoire, artistes or indeed overall direction. Worse still, the 'World Music'

bandwagon encouraged many opportunists to enter the business with some shoddy packaging of dubious material and inferior product. By the time 'World Music' had become obsolete a great deal of damage had been done; African music had to start rebuilding its constituency; African musicians and businessmen in London had been almost completely marginalised; while public taste had been largely manipulated along selective and somewhat arbitrary lines.

A second important issue arising from the 'World Music' debate concerned those musicians who had been playing and experimenting in world music before the term was commercially hi-jacked. Don Cherry, for example, had long been involved in cross-over and fusion as had Guy Warren, Foday Musa Suso and many, many others. By re-defining the term away from its original significance and meaning, further confusion was thereby created. At the same time, the 'World Music' phenomenon encouraged many more western musicians to attempt collaborative efforts with African musicians. However, given the market power of someone like Paul Simon compared with Miriam Makeba, it was clear that this approach was often a one-way street whereby African stars were reduced to the role of sidemen. Willie Colon, the salsa superstar, referred to this process as 'a cross-over nightmare' whereby the public identified latin with David Byrne and Africa with Paul Simon. The feeling that African stars wanted real exposure for themselves (and not through a white benefactor), as well as some of the mega-bucks flowing into western companies, was wide-spread. In strictly musical terms, this process involved Ry Cooder with Ali Farka Toure, Peter Gabriel and Youssou N'Dour, Carlos Santana and Salif Keïta, Paul Simon and Ladysmith Black Mambazo, David Essex and Afrigo, Housemartins and the Real Sounds, etc., etc. These were all laudable efforts but inevitably working more to the benefit of the western artists than the Africans. In this respect, the 'Rainbow Coalition of Music' failed to transcend existing power relationships between north and south within the record industry.

For the foreseeable future, it would seem that African music will remain in the close and suffocating grip of western music companies – whether they be multinationals or small independents. The ability of Africa to renew itself through culture and music will be sorely tested over the next decade as governments make up their minds to support music or remain in benign indifference to its universalistic potency. As it stands, the most popular music in Africa is reggae – an African form re-defined in the New World (despite the protestations of Toure Kunda, Thomas Mapfumo and Tera Kota to the contrary). Traditional music inevitably runs reggae a close second as deteriorating economic conditions enforce a return to cheaper and more rural forms of recreation.

ONE WAY FORWARD

There is an enormous irony in the popular perception of African music and the position actually occupied by Africa in the public mind. Music, for example, generates such immense acclaim that one could easily forget that millions of Africans are dying with millions more at risk. Indeed, an analysis of the language used to describe African music in the west invariably utilises the language of the positive image, although a racist subtext is clearly discernible amidst the general euphoria. Thus we have African music most commonly being described in the following terms – energetic, colourful, raw, hot, fresh, timeless, authentic, infectious, hypnotic, tropical, exuberant, exhiliarating, bewitching, magical and ecstatic. On the other hand, the adjectives used to describe Africa itself are far less romantic and exotic, and, while promoting a completely negative image, also reinforce the racist subtext apparent in even the most positive reporting.

The development of the music industry in Africa has suffered the same general fate as other industries in Africa over the last decade, with an almost total absence of investment inhibiting progress and, in several instances, producing a serious deterioration of existing facilities. It is indeed a sobering thought to consider the simple fact that the entire continent of Africa probably has fewer recording and manufacturing facilities than a single European capital city. Given this enormous imbalance, it is necessary to consider how best facilities can be improved, given the marginalisation of African music by both majors, who lack vision and flexibility, and the independents, who lack capital and expertise.

The first prerequisite remains a more open and supportive approach by African governments, in terms of reducing import duties on equipment and material, strengthening and updating copyright legislation and recognising that musicians provide the most potent and popular expression of the African personality. A second requirement is rooted in the clear understanding that audio-cassette technology (and quite possibly video) is likely to remain the cornerstone of the business in Africa for at least the next decade. Finally, every effort must be made to support a number of grass-roots, appropriate-technological initiatives currently being worked out in various parts of the continent. These vary from small-scale entrepreneurs experimenting with new equipment, through individual western initiatives to more substantial aid and development projects undertaken by multi- and bi-lateral development agencies. Local enterprise appears too concentrated in the spheres of production and distribution with little local investment in either studio facilities or musicians themselves. Small-scale, external involvement in African music largely attempts to redress this imbalance by seeking to establish 8–16-track studios in a number of countries. John Peel, for example, has initiated such a process in Sierra Leone; the Globestyle team are far advanced in their development of modular studio systems for installation in several countries while the saxophonist Gail Thompson is currently seeking assistance for a small studio in Gambia. Older, more established projects are run by John Collins in Ghana and Herman Striedl in Zambia. At the next level, that of institutional funding, we find organisations like the Norwegian DDD project attempting to finance equipment and training in various countries; the Finnish Institute of Workers' Music recording radio archives in Malawi; Wolfgang Bender persuading the German Government to transcribe the radio archives of Sierra Leone; the UK-based Cooperation for Development exploring means to supply recording and duplication equipment to Angola and Mozambique; and SIDA, the Swedish agency, supporting the transcription of radio archives in Zambia. Doubtless, there are many other similar initiatives currently under discussion or indeed under way. But what seems clear is that Europe is starting to respond in a positive fashion to the statement of intent regarding African culture appearing in the 1990 Lomé 4 Agreement between the EC and the ACP (African, Caribbean and Pacific countries). Of course there are those who would argue that institutional funding has no role to play in African music and that development is best left to the private sector. And while this argument does contain an element of realism, it actually collapses when we look at the past record of foreign private involvement in African music. Another argument raised against this type of development is that the provision of appropriate technology – usually an 8-track studio – is an insult to professional musicians wanting to work in the best studios available. However, once again the sad truth is that very few African musicians have access to any studio at all, far less a 48-track facility. Personally, I find it a greater insult to deny musicians the opportunity to record than to suggest that only the best will do.

The coming decade will provide as many problems for African musicians as it will offer solutions. The way forward remains unclear, but a growing western appreciation of African music should not be allowed to dictate how and where it develops. In Volume 1 it was suggested that the production and reproduction of music in Africa is part of a vital process of creation and recreation, 'growing endlessly from within the pulse of a people's life'. While this remains as true as ever we also need to be aware that in certain parts of Africa this 'pulse' is undoubtedly weakening.

PART II

Anglophone West Africa

2   Nigeria

(ECONOMY AND SOCIETY. Pop.: 100–120 million. Area: 924,000 sq. km. Capital: Lagos. Independence: 1960. Currency: Naira.)

Nigeria, 'The Giant of Africa', defies easy generalisation. Population, for example, has not been counted since 1961 and many people now suggest that Nigerians make up one-quarter of the entire African population. Historians now suggest that people have been living in the area since 5000 BC, passing through the Nok culture (300 BC) and establishing settled states by the seventh century AD. Islamic Hausa states flourished in the north between the eleventh and fifteenth centuries, while in the south the forest empires of Ife, Oyo and Benin flourished up until the nineteenth century. The Ibo east, meanwhile, developed a unique system of independent city states. Europeans first appeared in the late fifteenth century, but by the seventeenth century the British had replaced the Portuguese as the main exporters of slaves. Millions of Nigerians were thereby transported to Brazil and Cuba while Nigeria itself suffered from depopulation, military instability and economic regression. At the same time, northern Nigeria was equally exploited by the less-publicised but equally brutal trans-Saharan slave trade.

By the nineteenth century British interest had switched from slaves to raw materials to supply the Industrial Revolution and throughout the century missionaries, explorers and traders opened up the interior to Christianity, commerce and colonialism. In 1900 Britain declared two protectorates, of Southern and Northern Nigeria, and in 1914 combined both with the colony of Lagos to establish a unified Nigeria. By the 1920s opposition to colonial rule was growing, led initially by Azikiwe, although pressure on the British increased dramatically after the Second World War with various consitutions offering slow legislative progress towards independence. Unfortunately, however, by the 1950s, opposition to the British was coalescing along largely ethnic lines with the conservative north as the most likely successor to the British. Independence finally arrived in 1960 but over the next few years the country slid slowly into political anarchy with the various antagonisms finally bursting into the open with the military coup of 1966 and the rapid descent into Civil War.

The Biafran War lasted for three years, pitting the north and the west against the Ibo secessionists, inflicting serious wounds on the body politic from which (many would argue) Nigeria has not fully recovered. The war ended with Federal victory and the onset of a decade of military rule (Gowon, Murtala and Obasajo) before the country returned to democracy in the short-lived Second Republic of Shehu Shagari (1979–83). By this time, religious tension had been added to ethnic tension and in 1983 the Army intervened again through Generals Buhari and Babangida. By the early 1990s Nigeria was again contemplating a return to civilian rule through an imposed two-party system. Post-war Nigerian history is a complicated and convoluted affair, punctuated by military coups, religious rioting, civil war and an uneven economic performance. It remains enormously difficult to govern but is also one of the most vibrant and vital countries on the African continent.

TRADITIONAL MUSIC

Traditional music continues to play an important role in Nigerian life – new urban styles spring directly from traditional idioms which themselves maintain close recreational and ritual links to Nigerian society. With over 400 different ethnic groups and languages, Nigeria offers perhaps the greatest diversity of traditional music on the entire continent. Unfortunately very little crosses over from one group to the next, with even less appearing on western markets. Those readers interested in pursuing the subject further are referred to the enormous literature on traditional music and are advised to make a personal visit. (See Volume 1 for further discographical details.) By the mid-1980s virtually all traditional music was appearing on low-quality local cassettes.

Shata, Alhaji Mamman Shata. Hausa superstar, vocalist and goje player.

1972   NEMI 0066   Umaru Dan Danduna

Sokoto, Alhaji Dan Anache and his Group. Sokoto-based Hausa star.

1972   NEMI 0051   Shago

Sahara All Stars. Big band from Jos, Central Nigeria.

1974   NEMI 0188   Freedom for Africa

Dan Maraya. Alhaji. Goje player, praise singer. The most famous performer in this genre.

1977   NEMI 0360   Gar Gajiya

1978   NEMI 0418   Wakar Yansiyasa

MODERN MUSIC

The size and variety of the indigenous market has meant that Nigerian musicians have seldom wanted or been obliged to compromise their music. Juju, fuji, apala, waka, highlife, afrobeat and Ibo Blues remain vibrant, living idioms with clear and identifiable roots in traditional styles. Yet we should not take this to mean that indigenous styles are all that Nigerians enjoy. Reggae, for example, has become a powerful force on the contemporary music scene while guitar band highlife appears to be in gradual decline. Hip-hop, rap and ragamuffin have thousands of adherents, while many older styles are slowly but steadily dying.

For this reason, this chapter on contemporary Nigerian music complements as well as updates much of the information appearing in Volume 1. All the major stars seemed to have survived the decade intact – Fela, Ade, Obey, Barrister, Kollington and Osadebe – but many lesser luminaries of the early 1980s have almost disappeared from view. Sonny Okosun, for example, has drifted into a quiet obscurity while highlife stars like the Ikengas, the Orientals, Warrior, Prince Nico and the Imo Brothers have similarly failed to match the prolific outpourings of the early 1980s. Little is now heard of the Lijadu Sisters, Kubarat Alaragbo, Victor Uwaifo, Mike Ejeagha, or

Onyeka. Against this, the last five years have witnessed the growing power of fuji and the emergence of new stars like the reggae crew, Sir Shina Peters, Femi Kuti and a cluster of new afropop stars.

In a purely business sense little has changed over the last five years. Piracy remains endemic with massive bootlegging of local and imported music. Companies threaten to track down the pirates and deal with them but these are empty threats with no real legal muscle. Today, the market is almost totally dominated by cassettes with very little vinyl on sale, although hundreds of records are still released each year. Perhaps there are enough pirates in Nigeria to make it worth pressing records for them alone! Videos are also growing in popularity, although the CD has still to make a real appearance on the Nigerian scene.

Given the power of the pirates, most modern Nigerian musicians have come to rely on live shows for income, not through gate fees but through the custom of 'spraying' whereby a rich individual is mentioned in song and in return 'sprays' the forehead of the musician with as much money as status demands. The major stars – Obey, Ade and Barrister – can also augment their incomes through the ownership of clubs and the occasional overseas tour and licensing arrangement. On the macro-level, major changes have been taking place with the 1990 Sony takeover of CBS. It is too early to see if company policy will change but it seems reasonable to assume that Sony will continue trying to sell western music to the Nigerian market while attempting to exploit their Nigerian repertoire rather more than did CBS. Most top artists now own their own label, relying on an excellent selection of studios to work in and EMI for record pressing.

Juju

By the late 1980s juju had lost considerable ground to fuji as the main recreational music of the Yoruba, although the Lagos region was still estimated to support over 200 juju bands. Sunny Ade remains the best known international exponent of the style, although, in Nigeria, veterans Dairo and Obey compete for supremacy with relative newcomers like Adewale and Peters. With over twenty musicians to support and a constant pressure to introduce new 'systems' – either musical or technical – juju bands are expensive to run. Yet despite an unjustifiable neglect by western audiences, juju is still capable of converting new fans to its unique qualities – intricate percussion, sweet vocals and masterful guitar lines. It is also immensely capable of renewal and, while it may have peaked in the mid-1980s, it is still too early to write it off completely. Shina Peters, for example, ignited a new juju craze in the late 1980s and it remains a style in close social articulation with Lagos life. Recently, several new juju 'systems' have trimmed down the classic guitar style and have emphasised percussion and vocals instead. This may be partly due to the expense of maintaining all-electric bands, but it seems more probable that the sparser sound is an attempt to recapture some ground from fuji. Similarly, many fuji bands have started adding sound effects and new instruments indicating a growing convergence of the two styles. Volume 1 explored the roots of juju in some depth and since then Waterman has produced his splendid study of the genre (see Bibliography). The following section updates the biographies and discographies provided in Volume 1.

Dairo, I.K. With over forty albums to his credit and a career stretching back to the 1950s, I.K. Dairo is rightly regarded as the 'Father of Juju Music'. Volume 1 charted his career from the early days to the mid-1980s and should be consulted for biographical and discographical material. He maintained momentum throughout the 1980s with early hit compilations also continuing to sell well. In 1991 his music appeared on CD for the first time.

1980s	MOLPS 110	I'm Free
	MOLPS 112	Ma F'owuro Sene
	MOLPS 113	Late Papa Obafemi Awolowo
	OHRLP 18	Mo Fara Mi Fun O
	OHRLP 37	Dr G.I.M. Otubo
	OHRLP 38	Concord Holiday and Health Farm
	OHRLP 40	Ero Kun Soso Lenuwa
1989	DWAPS 2269	Original Dairo Hits
	DWAPS 2284	Yoruba Solidarity
1991	CDC 212	I Remember

Obey, Ebenezer. The 'Miliki King' reigned supreme on the domestic juju scene throughout the rest of the 1980s only launching a new system in 1990 with *Formula 0-1-0*. His twenty or so titles since 1985 accurately reflect the social and economic transition of Nigeria from oil-rich state to austerity. The titles alone indicate the characteristics required to survive in modern Lagos – from patience and determination, through ambition and security, to eventually find satisfaction in life. Lyrically, Obey has seldom been harsher, turning his attention to the young girl-lecherous millionaire-jilted lover scenario on *Aimasiko*, and the need for determination in Nigeria 'as a tranquilliser to our nerves which, at the moment, are at breaking edge'. In 1989 he commented on the *Formula 0-1-0* LP on the current mood of the nation 'where it is increasingly becoming a social trend to have just one meal a day'. That same year Obey signed a deal with the Dutch company Provogue, which saw his first CD release. In 1990 he started releasing new sounds on video as

well as vinyl. They are highly recommended for a Nigerian-produced, domestic market-oriented snapshot of current Lagos life. The discography presented below fills in a few gaps from Volume 1 and brings the story up to date.

1974	WAPS 218	Motun Gboro Agba De
1975	WAPS 258	Eda To Mose Okunkun
1979	WAPS 436	Obey in the 60s Volume 2
	WAPS 478	Edumare A De
1983	OPS 002	Thank You
1984	OPS 003	The Only Condition to Save Nigeria
	OPS 005	Peace
	ST 1005	Solution
1985	OPS 006	Security
	OPS 007	My Vision
	SHAN 43031	Juju Jubilee
1986	DWAPS 2252	Gbeja Mi Eledumare
	OPS 008	Satisfaction
	OPS 009	Providence
1987	OPS 010	Aimasiko
	OPS 011	Immortality
	OPS 012	Victory
	OPS 013	Patience
1988	OPS 014	Determination
	OPS 016	Vanity
1989	PRD 70012	Get Your Jujus Out (CD)
	OPS 018	Formula 0-1-0
1990	OPS 020	Count Your Blessings
	OPS 022	On the Rock (Also on Video)

Ade, Sunny. From 1986 onwards Ade released nearly all his new material on his own label. Older material was still available from the early 1970s. Although he seldom toured internationally he retained his domestic market with a series of fine juju albums. By the late 1980s the African Beats had swollen to 25 musicians and, like Obey's band, should really be considered more of a juju orchestra. But towards the end of the 1980s Ade seemed to retire to Lagos to lick his wounds after the adventures of the mid-1980s and the struggle for global success. He had been the first major star to break through in the west yet after three LPs Island had dropped him. Perhaps reflecting his personal experiences in trying to crack the global market, his lyrics increasingly turned to personal themes such as jealousy, rumour, truth, authority and destiny. Nonetheless, in 1990 he was awarded a new title when fans dubbed him 'The King of World Beat'; a suitable signifier for the man who had opened so many doors a few years earlier. He had reappeared briefly on the international scene with a couple of shows in London in 1988 where his tight arrangements and guitar virtuosity served as a reminder of his potent talent. The following year he ventured once again into the international market-place with a CD-only release from the Dutch company Provogue, who, almost alone against the tide of disinterest, also put out a juju CD of Ebenezer Obey.

Then, in 1990, a strange story emerged from the USA concerning the Ade–Onyeka collaboration on *Wait For Me*. Fans had already voiced some discontent about the change in style on the title song and a second cut entitled 'Choices'. Then it emerged that the album had been totally funded by the USAID Office of Population as part of a $30 million family planning project. None of this information appeared on the album and when the story finally emerged outraged African-Americans condemned Ade and Onyeka 'as accomplices to an attack on African cultural traditions and religious beliefs' – a sad attack on the Christian Ade who already had twelve children. In an interesting footnote, it also emerged that USAID, through their health programme, had also contributed to the recording of Franco's attack on AIDS in the 1987 LP *Attention Na SIDA* and had funded Zaïko Langa Langa to urge caution in sexual matters. The overall publicity was not helpful to Ade's career given his more usual advice about children. Then, early in 1991, the business was shocked by reports of Ade's sudden death. Of course the reports proved untrue but he was clearly in poor health after collapsing on stage in Lagos. He travelled to London for rest and recuperation with the best wishes of fellow-musicians and his thousands of fans.

1983	IVA 014	Live at Montreux
1986	APLPS 1	Sweet Banana
	APLPS 2	My Dear: New Direction
	APLPS 3	Let Them Say
1987	APLPS 4	Jealousy
	APLPS 5	Merciful
1988	APLPS 6	The Child
	APLPS 7	Destiny
	APLPS 8	The Good Shepherd
1989	APLPS 9	Wait for Me
	PRD 7022	Long Live Juju (CD)
1990	APLPS 10	Authority (Also APVC 1)
	APLPS 11	Get Up

Adewale, Segun. Since his international breakthrough in 1985–6, Segun's output has been inconsistent and sporadic, leading up to a major change in personnel in 1989, a personal blow to those who had served so well for so long. He also launched into battle with fuji music with his 1990 LP *Cash and Carry* which he claimed represented 'the long-awaited innovation to further enhance the dominance of juju music in society'. The claims were unfounded, and although he has diversified into video productions, he has failed to maintain his earlier momentum in the juju world, far less challenge the dominance of fuji.

1988	JLPRS 001	Yours Forever
1989	NEMI 0633	Omnipotent
1990	IVR 003	Cash and Carry (Also on video)

Abiodun, 'Admiral' Dele. Abiodun seemed to coast through the late 1980s with a series of good but not quite great recordings. Those listed below are in addition to the more substantial back-catalogue listed in Volume 1.

1975	ORPS 23	Abanijie
	MOLPS 30	You Told Me That You Love Me
1977	ORPS 60	Ile Ola
	ORPS 66	Original Super 8
1978	ORPS 79	Awa O Ni Legba
	ORPS 117	G'Esin Ni Kese
	ASLP 07	Sound of the Moment
1987	ASLP 08	Message of Joy
	ASLP 09	E Soko Ijo
1988	ASLP 010	Busy Body
	ASLP 011	Ring My Number

Adekunle, General Prince. Highlife–juju veteran of the 1970s and 1980s.

	AALPS 002	Orin Erin Tani Yio Fi We
1987	MOLPS 004	Ope Ni Fun Oluwa
1989	MOLPS 116	Survival
	MOLPS 118	People!!!

John, Monday (b. Monday Olufemi John, Lagos, 1940s). Monday started his professional life as a fine-art illustrator playing guitar in his spare time. However, in the early 1960s he moved to music on a full-time basis as guitarist with Roy Gabriel's Highlife Band. He then switched to the legendary Bobby Benson's highlife outfit, recording a solo album in the late 1960s backed by Benson's band. In 1968, in the middle of the Biafran War, he sensed which way the wind was blowing and switched to juju, joining another seminal bandleader, Tunde Nightingale, as guitarist. He toured widely with Nightingale and it was during a 1971 UK tour that he was spotted by Ebenzer Obey and invited to join forces with the up-and-coming juju king. He stayed for eight years, starring on an amazing total of 26 albums during that time. Obey and Monday parted company in 1978 but it was not until 1984 that Monday reappeared with his own new group – The New Wave Juju Band. He then moved to the USA carrying many musicians with him to set up home in Chicago as America's only resident juju outfit. His music reflects his skills and experience in over three decades of popular Nigerian music and has been described as a blend of highlife, jazz and juju. Judge for yourself on the 1990 release *Evil Cabal*. (Supporting vocals by Lijadu Sisters.) Other musicians in the 20-strong outfit glory in such names as The Genius Jerry, Goldfinger, The Sweet Tokunbo, Big Honest Setonji and Willie Bestman.

1960s		Emuagbon
1970s		Solo guitar on WAPS 48–WAPS 428
1984		Eyin Terije (The Rich)
1990	MRVC 001	Egbe-Kegbe (Evil Cabal – also on Video)

Ajao, Professor Y.K., and the Professional Brothers Band. Veteran of the Lagos scene, 'The Perempere Sound Creator' tried to update his basic juju system with both the 'perempere' style and, more recently, makossa.

1990	AR 001	Juju Makossa Series 1 (Also on video)

Peters, Sir Shina (b. Lagos, 1958). Stalwart of the Lagos scene, Shina finally hit the big time towards the end of the 1980s with a new 'system' dubbed 'afrojuju'. After years of playing with both Segun Adewale and fronting his own juju band, Shina recorded *Ace* in 1989. The response was immediate with the album selling 150,000 copies in the first few months. The bootleggers were not far behind and

soon all of Lagos was gyrating to *Shinamania*. The market seemed limitless and overnight Shina emerged as juju's newest and brightest star. Promoters rushed to him and booked him solidly until the middle of 1992. He also embarked on a 30-state US tour following up with a sold-out show in London for which he was reputed to have received £45,000 sterling, a record sum made up of £10,000 fee and the rest from generous on-stage donations, a typically Nigerian and typically extravagant feature of Lagos superstardom. With a dynamic stage show and with every effort made to maintain a frenzied momentum, Sir Shina revealed his secret, 'It is the start that is difficult. But once you get them into the groove, they are all yours.' Shina is an old hand at the game and has participated in all the major changes on the Nigerian juju scene for almost twenty years. He believes that his new sound, drawing on familiar juju elements enriched with bursts of western pop and performed by a 30-piece band of many years' experience, can last for a few more years at least. This remains to be seen but Shina certainly understands that to keep ahead on the juju scene, the secret is make sure the fans cannot predict the music.

1984	SPLP 001	Way To Freedom
1989	CBS-N-1002	Ace
1990	CBS-N-1006	Shinamania: Afro-Juju Series 2 (Also on video)

Owoh, Orlando, and His African Kenneries. He has continued to hit the top with powerful music and relevant lyrics including obituaries to Awolowo on ORLPS 002 and Sam Okwaraji on ORLPS 007. The 'King of Toye' has long been associated in the public mind with various forms of drug abuse, earthy lyrics and a reluctance to use hi-tech instruments in his rootsy Lagosian style. He was imprisoned during the 1980s, which led to a more mature approach to life on his release. He still complains of police harassment but has the satisfaction of knowing that he is now accepted as an important part of the Nigerian music scene, so much so that in 1991 he played in the UK for various Nigerian communities.

1986	SOS 216	Taboo
1987	ORLPS 002	Message
	ORLPS 004	'E Get As He Be
	ORLPS 005	Who No Know Go Know
	ORLPS 007	Kangaroo

Adeboye, Kengbe (a.k.a. Alhaji Pastor Oluwo), **and the Funwuton Organisation.** The highly polemical pioneer of 'Oduology' whose music fuses orthodox juju with modern fuji. His fused Christian–Islamic title alone gives an indication of what he is trying to achieve.

| 1985 | GARLPS 002 | Kengbe Oro |
| 1991 | OKLP 179 | Prince Kengbe Adeboye Funwuton |

Ogontodu, Dapo and His Oyemekum Stars Band. Classic mid-1980s juju.

| 1987 | NEMI 0613 | Aseni Serare |

Oladapa, Olatunbosum. A Yoruba-speaking Ewi star utilising strictly Christian, as opposed to Islamic, backing vocals in a memorial album for Papa Awo (Western Nigerian political leader Obafemi Awolowo).

| 1987 | NEMI 062 | Awo Si, Awo Lo |

Oni, Chief Brigadier Olu, and His Marathon System. Light-fingered juju from a rising star.

| 1988 | SP 2169 | Juju Marathon Vol. 1 |

Fayemirokum, Fabulous Olu, and His Standard Stars International. A full juju orchestra led by Fab with an unusual juju–samba opening track.

| 1991 | MOLPS 122 | E Get Cover |

Fuji

Sikiru Barrister is generally credited with fronting the fuji boom. Yet by the early 1970s, Lagos was throbbing to any number of fuji bands, led by singers who failed to maintain their early success. Inevitably, their failure has led to more attention being paid to the three fuji giants who today dominate the genre. But it was not always the case. The 1970s and early 1980s witnessed a proliferation of fuji bands, giving early warning to the juju stars who dominated the scene. If only for the historical record, it is worth paying a belated tribute to those early fuji stars. They included Adigun Adelani and the Oriade First International President, Sikiru Lawoyin and His Fuji Group, Alhaji General Monsuru Akande and His Fuji Reformers, Alhaji Sule Adeiku and His Group, Alhaji Ayinde Kamar and His Fuji Commodores, Rasheed Adio and His Fuji Moderniss-ers, King Ganiyu Kuti and His Fuji Group and Ayinde Rashidi and His Original Fuji Group. Virtually all these fuji pioneers recorded for Decca or EMI and their records may occasionally appear in second-hand bins. They are certainly worth a listen for a sparse and rough

treatment of what has now become a sophisticated style. Volume 1 provided a lengthy discussion of the roots of fuji and more recently Akin Euba has provided a near-definitive analysis of the style (see *Essays on Music in Africa, Vol.2* in Bibliography). Today, fuji has become one of the truly great African styles, described as a percussion orchestra of enormous power and stamina. Western listeners may occasionally be put off by the Islamic vocal inflexions but on no account should the style be ignored.

Barrister, Sikiru Ayinde. Barrister continued to ride the crest of the fuji wave and with twenty years' experience started to break into the international market in the early 1990s while retaining pole position at home. He was awarded a Ph.D. from the City University, Los Angeles, in 1988 and in 1989 was voted musician of the year in Nigeria. In 1990 he turned up in London where, in a number of privately organised shows, he thrilled almost exclusively Nigerian audiences with the 'Fuji Garbage' phenomenon. The band stayed on for a new recording with the London label Globestyle. During a 1990 interview with Graeme Ewens, Barrister revealed the origin of the term 'fuji'. 'I inherited that word fuji from the mountain in Japan. That is the mountain of love … something nice. When I create [sic] fuji music in 1965 I think I want a name that would be easy for everybody to pronounce. And I think four letter words is good.' Barrister estimated his total output at 52 LPs and was anxious to get involved in CDs. On his delicate relationship with namesake and fellow fuji master Wasiu, Barrister has this to say: 'He was working with me as a member of my group for about fifteen years. So when he starts for himself, I know that he is okay by himself, I make sure I do everything I can to help. So it's no threat. I am there as the father, he is there as the son.' Over the years Barrister has also cultivated a cordial relationship with the third fuji giant, Kollington. Musically, Barrister is more than ready to try to penetrate western ears and markets by westernising the sound while maintaining the percussive base which gives fuji so much momentum. By the late 1980s fuji's popularity could no longer be doubted. By appealing to a lower-class audience (an issue about which Sikiru is clear), fuji is not so much in competition with juju as simply appealing to a different market. However, in terms of actual sales, fuji has come to dominate completely. Barrister, for all his market appeal, has now entered the Yoruba élite as not only an immensely wealthy man but also the recipient of innumerable traditional chieftancy awards. He is now, as he redubbed his band, an international music ambassador, carrying contemporary Yoruba culture to the wider world.

Volume 1 carried the discography of Sikiru from 1982 to 1985 stopping at Cat. No. SKOLP 32. Clearly, if Barrister has released over fifty albums then this listing represents only those which became available outside Nigeria. The 1991 Globestyle CD represents the future direction of fuji and should be regarded as one of the top half-dozen recordings of the 1990s.

1984	SKOLP 026	Appreciation
1985	SKOLP 032	Fertiliser
1986	SKOLP 033	Okiki
	SKOLP 034	America Special
1987	SKOLP 035	Ile Aye Ogun
	SKOLP 036	Maturity
	SKOLP 037	Barry Wonder
1988	SKOLP 040	Barry Wonders at 40
	SKOLP 041	Fuji Garbage
1989	SKOLP 042	Fuji Garbage Series II
	SKOLP 043	Current Affairs
1990	SKOLP 045	Extravaganza
	SKOLP 044	Fuji Garbage Series III
1991	SKOLP 046	Fuji New Waves (Also on video)
	CDORB 067	New Fuji Garbage (CD)

Barrister, Wasiu. The Golden Talazo Fuji Messiah and the Royal Talazo Fuji Londoners. Wasiu served his apprenticeship with Ayinde Sikiru Barrister before emerging as a serious rival in 1984. His early material (see Volume 1) marked a major step forward for fuji but since then his 'system' has settled into the same basic groove as his rivals.

	OLPS 0268	Mecca Special
1985	OLPS 1323	Talazo Disco 85
1986	OLPS 1325	Elo Sora
	OLPS 1331	Ori
1987	OLPS 1333	Tiwa Dayo
	OLPS 1337	Baby Je Kajo
	OLPS 1338	Erin Goke
1988	OLPS 1341	Aiye
	OLPS 1351	Talazo in London
	OLPS 1352	Fuji Headlines
1989	OLPS 1356	Sun Splash
	OLPS 1357	My Dear Mother
1990	OLPS 1358	Achievement
	OLPS 1359	Fuji Rapping
	OLPS 1361	Jo Fun Mi: Dance For Me
1991	OLPS 1364	American Tips (Also on video)

Kollington, Ayinla. Kollington entered the last half of the 1980s as the third member of the fuji triumvirate. By the end of the decade he was introducing Hawaiian guitar, thereby adding a slightly lighter touch without sacrificing percussive power. The band, by then, numbered twenty: four talking drums, six vocalists, three sakara, organ, guitar, clef, calabash, sekere and gong. In the annual PMAN (Professional Musicians' Association of Nigeria) 1991 awards Kollington scooped the top fuji award from close rivals Wasiu and Sikiru Barrister.

1976	NEMI 0145	Ibi Eri Kigbe Mi Lo
1977	NEMI 0205	Ebami Dupe
1986	KRLP 013	Se Boti Mo
	KRLP 15	Oki Mi Gbe Mi
	KRLP 17	E Ba Mi Dupe
1987	KRLP 18	Second Tier
	KRLP 19	I Kilo
	KRLP 20	Late Obafemi Awolowo
1988	KRLP 21	American Yankee
	KRLP 24	Message
	KRLP 26	Quality
1989	KRLP 27	Blessing
	KRLP 29	Nigeria
	KRLP 32	Megastar
1990	KRLP 33	Fuji Ropopo (Also KRVC 1 on video)
1991	KRLP 35	Ijo Yoyo

Adepoju, Lanrewaju. A late convert to the drawing power of fuji. Known as the Ewi King (after his 'system'): 'The Alasa of Ibadanland'.

1986	LALPS 134	Eto Omoniyan
1987	LALPS 136	Iku Awolowo
	LALPS 137	Isokan Nigeria
1988	LALPS 138	Ede Aiyede
	LALPS 139	Itan Anabi

Other current fuji stars to watch out for include Alhaji Chief Isiaka Iyande Sawaba and His Fuji International and Alhaji Chief Sir Shina Akanni and His Current Fuji Natural Kings. But while fuji dominates the Western Nigerian neo-traditional scene, there are a number of other associated styles – waka, were, apala, etc. – which retain a strong appeal to the Yoruba. Volume 1 dealt at some length with the origin and development of these styles and should be consulted for details. Unfortunately, very little of this music now appears outside Nigeria and what follows is simply an update on the leading female performers.

Omoge, Madam Comfort and Her Asiko Ikale Group. Madam Comfort leads a 17-piece percussion orchestra and is reluctant to include any western instrumentation or effects in her music. She enjoyed massive success in the 1970s and early 1980s but her recorded output dropped considerably towards the end of the decade.

1989	SDP 117	Ari Ma Bo

Abeni, Queen Salawa. The current Queen of Waka, Salawa maintained her appeal and popularity throughout the 1980s, moving forward in a way her competitors failed to match. She records on Kollington's label – a straightforward relationship in a fuji–waka world of musical, political and sexual intrigue.

1985	LRCLS 44	Adieu Alh. Haruna Ishola
1986	KRLPS 16	Mo Tun De Bi Mo Se Nde
1988	KRLPS 22	Abode America
	KRLPS 28	I Love You
1989	KRLPS 30	We are the Children
	KRLP 31	Maradonna
1990	KRLP 034	Candle
1991	ALAD 005	Experience (Also on video)

Alaragbo, Kubarat. One of the rising stars of the mid-1980s, but her star faded towards the end of the decade.

1987	LRCLS 70	Come Let's Dance

Alake, Alhaja Chief Batile.

1986	LRCLS 55	Iwa: Manners
1987	LRCLS 59	Aje Onire

Highlife

Although I am reluctant to admit it, it now appears that Nigerian highlife is slowly dying. Created in the 1950s by blending the dance band styles of top Ghanaian bands with local guitar and drum traditions (see the various forms of native blues), Ibo highlife, as it became known, flourished in the 1960s and 1970s in Eastern Nigeria. The dance band variation soon disappeared to be replaced by the distinctive guitar band styles of Celestine Ukwu, Osita Osadebe and the Oriental Brothers. In such hands, highlife proved itself immensely capable of establishing tight and hypnotic dance grooves whose closest rival remained the classic Asante guitar bands of the 1970s – City Boys, Ashanti Brothers, Okukuseku, etc. But by the mid-1980s, the Ibo heartland of Nigerian highlife was undergoing a change as more imported music arrived. Key developments in the demise of highlife would include the arrival of reggae in a big way, the development of home entertainment, the growing insecurity of daily (and night) life and the death or retirement of leading musicians. Yet the style is not entirely dead, with Oliver de Coque and Osadebe continuing to produce high-quality highlife albums. However, a retrospective release of classic Oriental Brothers' material by Original Music proved to be the best-selling highlife of the early 1990s, perhaps indicating that the best highlife now lies in the past. If this is the case then fans who missed the highlife heyday are advised to look out for material by Warrior, Ukwu, Orientals, Osadebe, Seagulls, Peacocks, Oliver de Coque and Prince Nico.

Professional Seagulls. Formerly the backing band of Cardinal Rex Lawson (see Volume 1 for further details). The band reformed as the Professional Seagulls in 1976 following Lawson's untimely death, and continued to play the sweet highlife for which he was famed. One of the few highlife bands to survive in Western Nigeria. The title track from their second album became an enormous Nigerian hit in the early 1980s. The band is currently led by Prince David Bull.

1979	NEMI 0464	People's Club of Nigeria
1981		Soko Soko
1985	NEMI 0596	Our Lord's Prayer

Idahosa, Sir Patrick, and His African Sound Makers. Prolific highlife band active in the 1970s. Their music is probably not available anywhere now, but may turn up in second-hand stores.

1975	WAPS 230	Wa Gunmwen Gborue
	WAPS 265	No Gha-Ma Uba Gbon
	WAPS 292	Idahosa
1976	WAPS 345	Agbon-Do
1977	WAPS 370	Okhan Gbe Ro-Mo
	WAPS 383	Rio-Ubi-Mwen Rio

Osadebe, Osita. The evergreen highlife star clinched top highlife musician award in 1991. Consult Volume 1 for career and early discography of this seminal musician.

1986	POLP 144	Ndi Ochongonoko
1987	POLP 159	Onye Lusia Olie
	POLP 165	Ife Onye Metalu
1988	POLP 184	Nigeria Go Better
1989	POLP 194	Ana Masi Ife Uwa
	SPOSA006	Unubi Top Special
1990	POLP 232	Ezi Oyi Amaka

Coque, Oliver de. Oliver continued to delight fans with his brisk highlife workouts and lyrical content. The 1989 LP *Naira Power* concerned itself with the perilous state of the economy and an exhortation to revive what was left. His next LP became a tribute to Sam Okwaraji, who tragically died while playing for the national football team against Angola.

1987	ORLP 01	Engerigbo
1988	ORLP 02	
1989	ORLP 03	Naira Power
	ORLP 04	Sam Okwaraji Special
1990	ARLP	Born Singer

Mbarga, Prince Nico. The 1987 LP was sweet, light and lyrical; an excellent return for the *Sweet Mother* star.

1987	ROUND 5011	Free Education (Re-issue)
	RASLPS 095	Sweet Family

Orientals. Not much new material from the Ibo highlife stars but the US-released compact disc *Heavy on the Highlife* should guarantee a new generation of fans. Featuring material drawn from classic Orientals repertoire plus a Dan Satch and Warrior contribution, this was one of the best highlife compilations of the 1980s. An excellent place to start.

1988		Na Kwa Echeki
1990	OMA 116C	Heavy on the Highlife

Peacocks. One of the best Ibo highlife outfits. Prolific recording stars of the 1970s and 1980s.

1972	NEMI 0007	Uba Awuu Nwa
	NEMI 0092	Abiriwa Chapter Two
	NEMI 0252	Unbeatable Abiriwa

	NEMI 0566	Ije Nde Mma
1978	HNLX 5096	Smash Hits
	HNLX 5099	Egiogwu

United Brothers International Band. Five-piece guitar band led by Bukana T. Ogudoro. Based in Imo State and playing some of the best recent Ibo highlife.

1987	ARS 002	United Brothers

Chimezie, Bright (a.k.a. Okoro Junior), **and His Zigima Band.** Roots highlife band whose recent work strays into the 'Ozzidi' area charted by Sonny Okosun.

1987	POLP 172	Oyibo Mentality

Onwuandibe, Onwerri (a.k.a. Ala-Onwerri), **and His Emekuku Brothers International Band.** Excellent mid-1980s highlife.

1985	TRL 262	Onwerri Ndewonu

Azaka, Queen, and Her Ebologu Abusa Mma. A bit unusual to find a woman fronting a highlife band. This brand is known as Ukwani highlife and is slightly faster than classic Ibo highlife, with the band providing a sound base for Azaka's fine vocals.

1987	SODEC 001	In London

Wesco, Ade. Vocalist and 'Captain' of, first, the Destiny Band, and, subsequently, the New Super Sound. Fine Yoruba highlife enriched with traditional percussion and distinctly Yoruba vocals. The highlife lies in the guitar work with the Yoruba percussion permitting the occasional foray into a distinctively fuji groove.

1985	ORLS 001	Tribute (To Papa Awo)
1987	ORLS 005	Man of War
1989	ORLS 010	Na So You Be

Ibo Blues

Ibo Blues remains a powerful force in Eastern Nigeria but is seldom heard elsewhere. Prince Morocco Maduka and His Minstrels remain the most prolific outfit but they are by no means alone in this fascinating idiom. Indeed, there are so many bands working in the style that we can only scratch the surface. And it is not only Ibo Blues which has emerged as a distinct style. Enthusiasts are also charged with checking out Yoruba Blues, Bini Blues, etc. From time to time the outstanding Ibo highlife band, Imo Brothers, drifted off into Ibo

Blues. Similarly, Sir Patrick Idahosa would often return to roots Bini Blues.

It is highly improbable that much, if any, Ibo Blues will appear at the commercial level. One recommended Ibo Blues LP which has been available is referenced below. Also watch out for albums by Ogboli Ibusa, Gold Convention, and Nnadozie Ogbumba and His Odinala Supersonic. For Bini Blues look out for the Esigibie Cultural Troupe, Dandy Od Boy and the Jumbos Band, The World Eghudus, and, of course, Sir Patrick.

| 1988 | NXLP 011 | Ibealaoke Hukwukeziri & His Anaedeonu |

Oti, Sonny, and His Group. A more modern approach to Ibo Blues and a strong personal favourite. Sonny Oti tends to favour longer songs with social messages. A six-piece guitar band, their LP *Late Nite Husband* is a classic in its own right, featuring Nelly Uchendu on backing vocals.

| 1975 | NEMI 0194 | Detribalised |
| 1979 | HCE 013 | Late Nite Husband |

Afrobeat

Kuti, Fela Anikulapo. Of all African musicians, Fela probably needs the least introduction. Now fifty years old and with over fifty albums to his credit, he has become a rallying point for the Nigerian underclass and political prisoners everywhere. Controversial, innovative, stubborn and outspoken, Fela has been able to maintain a creative momentum unparalleled in West Africa. His career, now spanning three decades, has been consistently interrupted by government violence against his music, his band, his family and his person. Records have been banned, his nightclub destroyed, his mother killed and himself imprisoned, yet still he fights on against the corruption, brutality and inhumanity of successive Nigerian regimes.

A great deal can be explained by Fela's personal biography; the full story up to the early 1980s can be found in C. Moore's *Fela Fela: This Bitch of a Life*, one of the best biographies to date of an African musician (see Bibliography). Other information is easy to come by in the weekly Nigerian magazines where his every move is the subject of close inspection. Fela was born into an élite Lagosian family with a history of anti-colonial protest. His father was a celebrated composer and his mother a nationalist leader. In the late 1950s he moved to London where he encountered British racism of the most virulent kind, working, incidentally, in the Post Office to subsidise his music studies. A short spell in the USA in the late 1960s introduced him to the potent messages of the Black Power Movement.

Meanwhile, Nigeria was suffering terribly from political instability, military intervention and, by the late 1960s, the horrors of the Biafran War. As the plight of the poor worsened and the country threatened to pull itself apart, Fela sharpened his wit and honed the musical revolution which he was to dub afrobeat. He started slowly with a couple of inconsequential albums but hit a purple patch in 1972 with a series of well-constructed and powerfully delivered afrobeat classics. Almost any album from 1972 to 1978 will deliver the goods as Fela launched into a series of stinging critiques of everything from military government to skin bleaching, Lagos traffic, arbitrary arrest and, above all, the political and economic system which produced and reproduced such grinding poverty.

In 1984 the Government finally nailed him on spurious currency charges and sentenced him to five years. In December of that year the sentence was confirmed by the new military government and Fela was locked away in the notorious Kiri Kiri prison. Early in 1985 he was transferred to hospital with an ulcer, but after he had given an interview to the French magazine *Libération*, soldiers stormed into the hospital, plucked him from his sick bed and transferred him to another prison in Maiduguri – one of Nigeria's furthest-flung corners and an extremely hot and dusty place. (I know – I lived there for three years.) In mid-1984 the military government of Buhari was swept away in yet another military coup and soon afterwards the chairman of the tribunal which had sentenced Fela visited him and apologised for the sentence which he said had been imposed after the military had pressured the tribunal. He was unconditionally released in April 1986, having served eighteen months of the five-year sentence.

News of his release spread like wildfire and thousands greeted him when he touched down at Lagos airport. Throughout the country record shops played his records non-stop to celebrate his release. Traffic in Lagos was brought to a halt as thousands mobbed his house. Unrepentant, Fela vowed to continue his political struggle and to relaunch his presidential campaign when the military stepped down. His prison experiences left him physically weakened but entirely unbowed. His son Femi had stood in for him and kept The Egypt 80 going and by 1988 Fela was back in charge and on the road again, playing Brixton Academy and the Glastonbury festival. Musically, he returned stronger than ever with a powerful diatribe against apartheid and its supporters, singling out both Reagan and Thatcher for specific abuse on the excellent *Beasts of No Nation*.

Accompanied by his 40-strong backing band – The Egypt 80 – Fela has never been an easy star for the western media to deal with and a great many journalists were more than ready to write him off altogether. He has been accused of racism, extravagant sexism and overwhelming egoism. His

26

music has never been dance-oriented and his lengthy polemics, haranguing captive audiences, are legendary. Yet the miscomprehension has largely been one way. He retains a mass following inside Nigeria and his albums are treasured throughout the continent for their forthright criticisms of the failure of governments everywhere to resolve the very real problems affecting the continent. A committed pan-Africanist, consummate musician and a thorn in the flesh of successive Nigerian governments, Fela enters the 1990s as arguably Africa's conscience.

Volume 1 contains a more detailed assessment of Fela's career and lists all his recordings up to 1985. This contributon is more in the way of an appreciation, bringing his recording career up to date and mentioning the availability of two excellent videos of the afrobeat master at work. Through his contracts with major companies, Fela's music is easy to get, while some exciting back-catalogue CD releases help fill in the gaps. However, there will always be those elusive albums which may never be seen again. My own money for a succesful re-release would go on *Noise for Vendor Mouth* and *RofoRofo Fight* (both 1975).

1986	PH 2001	Zombie/Suffering and Smiling/Monkey Banana/ Everything Scatter
	PH 2003	No Agreement/Dog Eat Dog
	PH 2005	Jenwi Temi
	DWAPS 2251	I Go Shout Plenty/ Why Black Man Dey Suffer
1988	JD 160229	Black Man's Cry
	JD 160230	Fela & Roy Ayers: 2000 Blacks
	JDEUR360153	Beasts of No Nation/Just Like That
	JDEUR360229	Black Man's Cry (Double)
1990	JDEUR360442	ODOO/Overtake Don Overtake/ Confusion Break Bones
	K 010	Confusion Break Bones/ Which Head Never Steal
	WM 160 443	Fela Vol. 1: 1975–1978
	WM 160 444	Fela Vol. 2: 1981–1984
	WM 160 445	Fela Vol. 3: 1985–1986

Videos

1984	HEN 2 090	Teacher Don't Teach Me Nonsense
1984	HEN 2 091	Fela Live

Kuti, Femi Anikulapo (and The Positive Force). Son of Fela who manfully stood in when the 'old man' was in prison. In 1990 he starred at the WOMAD festival. His band plays in pure afrobeat style and features a full line-up of horns, percussion, guitars and the almost obligatory female chorus. Huge potential but may need to escape from his more illustrious father's shadow. His 1989 debut album featured heavy afrobeat rhythms but was marred by weak vocals.

1989	POLP 201	No Cause For Alarm?

Allen, Tony. An uneven and vaguely disappointing effort from former Fela drummer and afrobeat master percussionist. Assisted on one or two excellent tracks by Ray Lema.

1989	PM 264	Afrobeat Express

Jato, Jimmy. A joint Ghana–Nigeria afrobeat outing from Mr Jato. Slightly overambitious in his attempt to blend funk, juju, reggae and rock into an acceptable afrobeat.

1990		Who Will Save Nigeria?

Reggae

Fashek, Majek (b. Majekodunmi Fasheke, Lagos). As a child, Majek grew up in a religious/musical environment. As a youth he was strongly influenced by both Bob Marley and Fela – a double-barrelled radicalism of impeccable pedigree. He picked up guitar and starred in a TV special in the early 1980s. The rest of the decade was spent touring Nigeria with RAM, before departing in 1987 to pursue a solo career – as Nigeria's foremost reggae star. In 1988 Majek's rapid rise to stardom was acknowledged by his peers when he was awarded an unprecedented six awards at the annual PMAN ceremony. From this solid base he moved on to greater things with the first international release on CBS Nigeria.

From there he signed to Mango, an international subsidiary of Island. Success seems almost certain but African reggae is a notoriously difficult concept to sell (witness Alpha Blondy) for reasons discussed in the Introduction. On the Island release Majek covered Marley's 'Redemption Song' – sufficient tribute but a step behind Blondy who had actually recorded with the Wailers in Jamaica.

| 1989 | CBS-N 1003 | I & I Experience |
| 1990 | MLPS 1030 | Prisoner of Conscience |

Kimono, Ras. Ras is no stranger to the music business, having struggled to make an impact for almost two decades before his 1989 breakthrough. Backed by the Massive Dread Reggae Band, Ras leapt to stardom with the song 'Rum-Bar Stylee', the best reggae song of 1989, taken from his first LP. His brand of reggae has been adequately described as 'upbeat and rousing' while his politicised lyrics, in a sense typical of reggae, follow on directly from some of Fela's mid-1970s classic attacks on the Nigerian polity. His appeal lies directly with the Nigerian underclass, with whom he communicates directly in the same pidgin/Jamaican patois favoured by Fela. His first album sold over 60,000 units in the first two months of release but it was the second album, *What's Gwan* which shot him to stardom. By then he had refined the ideology of his attack to embrace pan-Africanism, the use of pidgin/patois as a universal black language, the legalisation of marijuana, the need to decolonise the mind and the need to abandon the principle of nationhood in Africa. Controversial stuff, particularly when added to the target of earlier attacks, namely, the role of African leaders as stooges for western interests. Kimono's ability to mirror the frustrations of Nigeria's teeming urban underclass points to a major international breakthrough as reggae increasingly becomes the universal language of resistance. In a 1989 interview he voiced his deep frustrations and commitment to finding solutions: 'There is nothing to smile about in this society. There are so many problems. People older than me go hungry. There are graduates living wretched. It hurts me. I prefer to die than see all this inhumanity to man in Africa.'

| 1989 | | Under Pressure |
| 1990 | POLP 240 | What's Gwan |

Kota, Tera (b. Gboyega Femi). The first major Nigerian reggae star, Tera claims reggae to be of Nigerian origin being derived from 'ere-ege' – a century-old form of praise music. His stage name claims equally distinguished ancestry, being a corruption of terra cotta – 'an ancient artifact that has been preserved for the purpose of tomorrow'. Quoting the end of the Nigerian oil boom and a decade of austerity as the context for his switch to reggae, Tera refers to reggae as the voice of reality. His first album, in 1982, shot to the top of the Nigerian charts, staying there for four months and selling over half a million copies. His second, appearing in 1985, was dedicated, in part, to Fela, still incarcerated in a Northern Nigerian jail. Over the next five years he toured the country and claims to have single-handedly turned the youth away from

disco towards roots reggae. He has been criticised, like all the other reggae stars, for failing to point the youth in a specifically Nigerian direction. His response is simple – reggae is African, it is universal and it is relevant.

1982		Lamentation in Sodom
1985		Solitude and Shackles
1987		Peasant Child

Mandators. Led by Victor Toni Essiet and Peggy Imanah.

| Mid-1980s | | Crisis |
| | | Rat Race |

Kole-Man Revolutionaire. Another new arrival on the reggae scene who favours patois as the medium of communication.

| | Tribulation |

Ogholi, Evi-Edna. Dubbed the Queen of Nigerian Reggae, Evi-Edna plays a lighter style of reggae and continues to sing in her native Isoko. She started her career in the late 1980s, recording her first album in 1989. Within the space of three years she had released three more albums, split with Polygram, established a massive reputation throughout West Africa and received Pepsi sponsorship for a national tour of Nigeria.

| 1989 | POLP | Happy Birthday |

Zitto, Alex. Rising reggae star.

| 1988 | | Tickle Me |

Okosun, Sonny. The 1980s proved to be a steady rather than spectacular decade for the Ozzidi King after the international success of the late 1970s. He maintained a steady appeal at home and a growing audience in the USA. His 1989 release was a mixed bag of social comment, political critique and ecumenicalism, recorded and mixed in the Caribbean, London and New York.

1980s	MFR 120714	Message
	HMV 058	Happy Days
1990	IVR 001	Wind of Change

Maha, Yvonne. A young female singer, helped by Sonny Okosun who wrote the songs and produced the album. Weak ballads sung by a weak voice, only 'Diocha' shows Ozzidi at full belt.

1983 GR 100 Child For Sale

Pop stars

Nigerian pop music, drawing on various black American styles as well as British rock, first emerged as a force in the early 1970s and, despite the wealth of traditional influences at the disposal of young musicians, has remained a popular route to the top. However, by working in essentially foreign styles, such musicians risk being left behind as western tastes and productions change. For this reason, no Nigerian pop star has been able to maintain a successful career, while Nigerian consumers will in the longer term revert to buying western imports rather than local imitators.

Bolarin (b. Bolarin Dawodu). Hi-tech, electric afro-pop which produced a series of Nigerian hits in 1989.

1990 ARR 001 Water Music

Soberekan, Neneba. Up-and-coming female vocalist with a pleasing brand of afro-pop.

1989 POLP 133 Seki Saki Lale

Cooper, Ogbe Jerry. Paris-based, afro-pop vocalist. On his debut LP he utilises some of the best Cameroonian musicians in a disappointing yet sophisticated recording.

1989 JECO 002 Everything For A While

Bruce, Don, and the Angels. Singing in Isoko and English, Don Bruce occupies an interesting position in popular Nigerian music, fusing Nigerian rhythms with straightforward reggae and western pop.

1990 NEMI 0274 Mind Your Business

Christian tradition

Please consult Volume 1 for background and discography.

Tobo, Prophet A. Ogbuo. A nine-piece Yoruba percussion group with Christian vocals and excellent percussive support.

1985 TRL 283 Obeche Ozena

Achilike, Anthony. Beautiful female vocals to accompany classic Ibo religious highlife.

1981 ERLP 4 Uwa Siri Ike

Others

1986 GCR 004 Brother Bannerman Embiowei

   GCR 003 Patsy: Thank You Lord

Yoruba theatre tradition

Ladipo, Duro (b. 1931, d. 1978). Actor/playwright who established his own theatre company combining folk traditions, Yoruba opera and drama to produce a truly popular Nigerian theatre. His mixture of music and drama are seen to best effect in *Eda* (1970), *Moremi* (1967) and *Oba Ko So* (1968).

1971 NCR LP Eda (Univ. of Ibadan)

Ogunde, Hubert (b. 1916, d. 1990). Seminal actor/playwright responsible for the transition from concert-party to folk theatre.

Ogunmola, Kola (b. 1925, d. 1973). Actor and theatre director responsible for staging *The Palm-Wine Drunkard* in opera form in 1967 as well as *Love of Money* in 1954 and various other folk operas.

Nigerian art music

'Art' music, or the acculturated music of Nigeria's educated and westernised élite, is often neglected in studies of African music, presumably due to its close approximation to western classical music. This exclusion is unjustified, and although several countries have produced many fine composers (Nigeria, Ghana and South Africa have gone further than others in this respect), very little 'art' music is currently available on disc. In Nigeria, the most respected composers would include Samuel Akpabot (b. 1931); Ayo Bankole (1935–76; Lazarus Ekwueme (b. 1936); Akin Euba (b. 1935); Adams Fiberesima; Okechukwu Ndubuisi (b. 1936); Josaiah Ransome-Kuti (1855–1930); Fela Sowande (1905–87) and Ikoli Whyte (1905–77). Many of their compositions involve adapting folk songs and traditions to western classical arrangements and instruments.

Nigerians overseas

Lawal, Gasper. The reclusive master drummer, a musician's musician, grew in reputation towards the end of the decade. The year 1989 was an extremely busy one involving stage and studio work with a variety of Irish and British pop artistes including the Pogues, UB40 and Robert Palmer. That year also included a major tour with Zaïrean superstar Papa Wemba and a Royal Command Performance before the Queen and President Babangida. By the start of 1990 he was looking for time off to get started on his third album. It was finally delivered to Globestyle in 1991 and was to enjoy immense critical acclaim. Buy it (and his two earlier records *Ajomase* and *Abiosun'ni* – if you can find them).

| 1991 | CDORB 071 | Kadara |

Olatunji, Babatunde (b. Michael Olatunji). Legendary teacher-drummer, the US-based Nigerian master-drummer signed a two-CD deal with Provogue in 1989. In some respects this sealed a thirty-year career in the business of African drumming. Along the way Babatunde had played with such stars as Bob Marley, Carlos Santana and Art Blakey. The 1986 album features, as an example, musicians from Santana, Airto and the Grateful Dead – an early and truly embryonic 'World Music'. The 1986 recording includes a reworking of the track 'Akiwowo' from the second LP, *Drums of Passion*. By the early 1990s, given western interest in working with master musicians, Olatunji was very much in demand, thereby somehow vindicating his decision to strike out and work from an American as opposed to a Nigerian base.

1970s	R 25274	Drums, Drums, Drums
	CS 8210	Drums of Passion
	CS 8434	Zungo-Afro Percussion
	CS 8666	Flaming Drums
	CS 9307	More Drums of Passion
1986	BLU 706	The Beat of My Drum
1989	PRD 70022	Drums of Passsion: Digital Remix (CD)
	PRD 70024	The Invocation (CD)

African Juju Music Stars. Washington-based juju orchestra formed in early 1991 by Itunu Abariko, formerly drummer with Orlando Owoh. He recruited other juju musicians who had decided to stay in the US after touring with Owoh, Abiodun, Dele Ojo, Prof. Ajao and Fela. These experienced musicians formed themselves into a cooperative and, with an estimated 20,000 Nigerians in Washington alone, seem set for at least local success. Whether they can record and compete with the home-grown product will be the true test.

Juwon. London-based keyboard maestro who has played with the cream of London session musicians as well as taking his own small combo on the road – a prodigious talent.

Leo, Bukky. A Nigerian-born sax player who arrived in the UK in 1982 following work with Tony Allen. Helped found the popular London-based band Farenji Warriors. His first jazz-funk album was released in 1989.

| 1989 | JAZID 7 | Rejoice in Righteousness |

3   Ghana

(ECONOMY AND SOCIETY. Pop.: 15 million. Area: 238,540 sq. km. Capital: Accra. Independence: 1957. Currency: Cedi.)

A great deal of research still needs to be done on the pre-history of Ghana but we know that most of the area was already inhabited by the eighth century, with further, major migrations into the region between the thirteenth and the seventeenth centuries leading to the establishment of the Akan states of the central forest region. The first Europeans to arrive were the Portuguese towards the end of the fifteenth century, establishing a fort at Elmina to tap into the legendary gold trade of ancient Ghana. In time, slaves replaced gold as the main European interest. Inevitably, the European presence was concentrated on the coastal region, with various European powers vying with each other to control the slave trade from the interior. Further inland, the Asante empire was steadily growing in power and sophistication, producing a threat to European interests. By the nineteenth century, the coastal settlements, and particularly the Fante, had produced a new local élite of lawyers, businessmen and teachers which found an early nationalist expression in the Fante Confederation of 1868. Inland, however, the Asante proved much more stubborn in

their dealings with Europeans and it required several armed expeditions finally to conquer them. However, by 1900, most of modern Ghana was under colonial control, although Ghanaians were resolute in their defence of land rights. For this reason Ghana never became a settler colony, although the prolonged exposure to European culture did play an important role in the political and cultural development of the country.

By the 1920s resistance to colonial rule was growing, although it was really the impact of the Second World War which stimulated a more militant nationalist movement, led by Kwame Nkrumah. During the war, many Ghanaians served overseas while thousands of American and British troops passed through on their way to the Middle East. The war shattered for ever the cosy colonial isolation of Ghana and, with a healthy economy based on cocoa, gold and diamonds, there seemed every likelihood that the country would move quickly towards self-sustaining independence. This duly came in 1957 and for the next few years Ghana enjoyed an enormous reputation under the dynamic leadership of Nkrumah as the first sub-Saharan African country to attain such a status. Yet Nkrumah retained a wider vision, of a United States of Africa, and by the mid-1960s many were arguing that the progress of Ghana was being sacrificed on the altar of pan-Africanism. But perhaps more to the point was the growing radicalism of Nkrumah, which was only halted by the US-supported coup of 1966. Over the next 15 years Ghana staggered from one regime to the next with politicians and soldiers alternating in a merry-go-round of ideology, policies and personalities. This instability, which had brought the economy to the brink of ruin, was temporarily halted by the 1981 coup of Jerry Rawlings – his second attempt to instil some discipline into political and economic life. By 1991, Rawlings was considering ways of returning Ghana to civilian rule.

MUSIC IN THE 1980s:
LESSONS FOR A CONTINENT

In Volume 1 enormous emphasis was placed on the historical and contemporary importance of Ghanaian music, which had been at the centre of the modern African music scene for over three decades, producing such musical giants as E.T. Mensah, E.K. Nyame, the

Ramblers, Nana Ampadu and the African Brothers, and the Sweet Talks. In their hands, highlife became one of the great sources of contemporary African music, influencing developments throughout West and Central Africa.

However, since the late 1970s the commercial development of Ghanaian music has suffered greatly from the widespread and well-documented collapse of the national economy. Economic difficulties fed into social life as nightclubs and dancehalls closed. The supply of beer dried up, equipment broke down and gradually musicians began to move abroad, at first only as far as Nigeria. But when Nigeria also entered a period of national austerity Ghanaian musicians began to turn up in ever-increasing numbers in London, Hamburg and Toronto.

The great majority of these self-exiled stars tried to adapt highlife to the styles they found overseas and it is fair to say that they seldom succeeded in their quest for an acceptable cross-over sound. A reputation established overseas was occasionally translated into success at home, but, in the main, Ghanaian music slipped into the margins of the African music boom, offering only eclectic little hybrids, a proliferation of tiny labels and one or two dubious wheeler-dealers.

At home in Ghana the situation was not much better. In 1981 Jerry Rawlings seized power for the second time and launched the second phase of the Ghanaian Revolution. The absolute impoverishment of the country could, of course, not be reversed overnight and in 1982 the Rawlings Government bit the IMF bullet and launched the country on a programme of economic recovery. But these were still hard times, with the legacy of past mismanagement combining with drought and the return of over a million refugees from Nigeria to produce tremendous material hardship in 1983 and 1984.

Ghanaians responded in a number of ways. Many, as we have seen, moved out of West Africa entirely, while many others turned to various Christian sects trying to compensate spiritually for what was denied them materially. Inevitably, given the close relationships between economy and society, and society and culture, musical developments mirrored social changes. The Ghanaian entrepreneur, hitherto the mainstay of the music business, found it increasingly difficult to operate in a system which could not maintain the infrastructure necessary for music to flourish. Beer remained in short supply, discos replaced live music, import duties restricted the flow of new instruments and equipment, and recording stuios failed to meet new technological challenges.

Yet we should not paint too bleak a picture. For if one thing is sure it is that the creative genius of the Ghanaian people will in time throw up a response to the difficulties created by these turbulent times. As we have mentioned, one response has been to turn towards religion whilst another has been migration overseas. But a third response has been directed towards the existing organisation of the music business and an adaptation to the new technology of production and distribution.

John Collins, the respected writer on African, and particularly Ghanaian, music, who was very much part of the reconstruction of the Ghanaian music scene, offers a personal account of the music business in Ghana during the 1980s. But his comments also hold a wider interest in that many of the problems he outlines were very much apparent in other African countries and as such he also provides a wider context.

Some of the changes in the Ghanaian music industry stemmed directly from Government policies. For example, the PNDC's 'cultural revolution' which was launched in 1982 not only included the decentralisation of the National Arts Council and the recognition of the Musicians' Union (MUSIGA) but also, in 1985, introduced PNDC Law 110, which made royalty infringement a criminal rather than a civil offence.

One immediate consequence was that the local GBC radio had to start paying out air-play royalties to local musicians for the first time. This strengthening of the Copyright Law also involved the creation of the Copyright Association of Ghana (COSGA) which made several attempts to bring the 'spinners' (DJs) under control. For as the nightclub and live scene had largely collapsed, dozens of mobile sound systems had been set up with high-fidelity equipment and fancy light shows. Outfits such as Willie Chii's, the Skyhawks, Mobisco and Studio 44 contributed to the decline in live music, pushing the bands off the urban dance floors and forcing them back to the villages on long rural treks. By the mid-1980s COSGA was beginning to tax the 'spinners' so that some performing royalties could go back to the musicians.

Another fight which COSGA became involved in was that of cassette piracy. Vinyl production had disappeared in Ghana by the early 1980s and the vacuum thus created had been filled by hundreds of small kiosks duplicating from records. In a creative response to a powerful enemy, COSGA and the National Phonogram Producers' Association (NPPA) began to quasi-legitimise the pirates by collecting levies and issuing licences. The pirates responded by creating a two-hundred-strong Ghana Tape Recordists' Association which cooperated with the NPPA.

This situation of coexistence based on mutual benefit lasted for three years until in 1989 a rival producers' association called the Phonogram Producers' Society of Ghana appeared, arguing that all attempts to legalise piracy be stopped and all kiosks closed down. This new association, seeking to turn the clock back, was partly financed and encouraged by the International Federation of Producers of Phonograms (IFPA), a European organisation representing CD, vinyl and video producers opposed to cassette technology. Their opposition was predictable since in Africa the decentralised system of cassette production was quickly replacing the centralised pressing plants with their international connections and massive import requirements.

The objective and conflicting interests of both sides seemed to indicate a stalemate but towards the end of the decade Ghana again appeared to have found a way forward. Suggestions were made that the Government now impose a levy on imported cassettes as they arrived in the country. Part of this levy would be collected by COSGA, who would distribute royalties to composers, performers and producers of both local and foreign music.

This move would in turn make the duplication of cassettes legal as royalties would be in effect pre-paid, thereby unlocking the full potential of a decentralised and local cassette-based production system. The introduction of DAT technology would enhance this process, producing exact clones rather than inferior second-generation copies. Once established this system would expand to incorporate a network of small cottage industry DAT duplicating kiosks as opposed to one or two large-scale record manufacturing plants.

So what has happened to the recording scene in Ghana over the last decade? Sadly, with the exception of the state-subsidised 8-track Ghana Film Studio, all the other studios from the heydays of the 60s and 70s had collapsed by the early 1980s. In their place emerged a new generation of smaller studios run by musicians rather than businessmen. First off the mark in 1982 was my own Bokoor studio, which by the end of the decade had produced almost 200 full recordings. This was followed in 1986 by guitarist Nat Fredua's 8-track Black Note Studio and in 1988 by Oko Ringo's 16-track Elephant Walk studio. In 1990 two more studios were opened by musicians, first A.B. Crentsil's 16-track business in Tema and then the 40-track (24 digital and 16 analogue) Overdrive Studio in Kotobabi run by Ralph Casely-Hayford.

During the 1980s, the Ghanaian music industry underwent some dramatic restructuring caused both by technological change and economic hardship. The Government generally supported the musicians' case unlike many other governments in Africa which continued to play lip-service to culture. Perhaps it was because of this period of transition that so little Ghanaian music reached the rest of the world. Musicians were forced to turn inwards in an effort to make a livelihood, and, anyway, without decent facilities where was there to record? With the new technology in place perhaps the 1990s will see a long overdue resurgence in Ghanaian popular music.

TRADITIONAL MUSIC

The traditional music of Ghana has been particularly well researched by Professor K. Nketia and others. Of particular interest is the study of Dagomba music by John Chernoff, an exquisitely written book by a meticulous participant-observer (see Bibliography). Unfortunately, very few new recordings of traditional music have been made in the last decade and readers are therefore referred to the substantial discography in Volume 1 for more information on what is likely to be available.

Acquaye, Saka. It may seem strange to classify Saka as a traditionalist but over the years this gifted individual has consistently worked in the middle ground between modern dance styles and older, pre-electric urban sounds. He is also a teacher, performer and playwright of considerable stature. Furthermore, he is well-known as the composer of several Ghanaian musicals, including *Obadzeng* (1961), *Bo Mong* (1962) and *The Lost Fisherman* (1968).

1960s	CREST 805	Drum Fever
1970s	H 72026	Voices of Africa: Highlife and Other Popular Music

Nua, Onipa (b. Amada Jebre, Northwest region, Ghana, 1940s). Blind since the age of two, Onipa learned to play the Ghanaian thumb piano (kalimba) as a child. He travelled widely as a youth before settling in Accra in the mid-1960s. He had previously acquired his nickname, Onipa Nua (The People's Brother), whilst working in Kumasi as a nightwatchman (an unlikely occupation for a blind man!). Popular but poor, Onipa remained very much a street musician, entertaining at social functions as well as purveying his Hausa songs at street corners. In 1980 promoter Faisal Helwani encouraged him to perform in more formal settings in an effort to turn his evident star quality into something a bit more tangible. His voice ranges over three octaves and has been described as 'Gravelly, gruff and sweet.' He made a cassette for the Ghanaian market and in 1990 performed to rapturous applause in Paris. He has also been experimenting with more modern fusions and has been enhancing several new recordings on Helwani's label. Audiences outside Ghana await an international release.

Others

1986	KB 001	New Juabeng Kete Troupe
1989	Bop Cass.	Kpanlogo: George Dzikunu

1987	ACFH 100	Roots of Highlife: Bamaya to Bosoe

Roots of Highlife is an introduction to the rhythms of Ghana in a traditional-dance bandmix featuring the Edikanfo Band led by trumpeter Osei-Tutu and the National Folkloric Company of the Arts Council of Ghana. Recorded at Faisal Helwani's Studio I in Accra, the musicians run through regional styles such as Dagomba bamaya, Asante adowa, Fanti ompeh, Ga kpanlogo, Ewe borborbor, Brong bosoe, Kasisina nagla, an agbadza from the Volta region and the Akan asafo rhythm from Akwamu.

Addy, Mustapha Tettey. Mustapha was born just outside Accra in 1943 into the Addy drumming family, of which he was to become the most famous member. His father was a Ga fetish priest who initiated Mustapha, as well as his brothers, into Ga ritual drumming and dancing. When his father died, Mustapha became 'dadeafoiakye' – head of the ritual drummers. During the 1960s he was loosely attached to the Institute of African Studies at the University of Ghana and was a full-time member of the Ghana Dance Ensemble – one of the best cultural troupes in Africa. During the early 1970s he travelled widely in West Africa, enriching his knowledge of other styles and techniques. In 1974 he formed his own group called Ehimono with whom he toured Europe on several occasions. He returned to Europe in the 1980s working mainly as a teacher. In 1990 he returned to the studio for the first time since the Tangent albums to record a CD with his son, Abdul Rahman Kpany Addy, and two German musicians. The CD was designed not only for enjoyment but with a secondary, pedagogic, purpose – to break down complex rhythms so that listeners could drum along.

1972	TGS 113	Master Drummer Vol. 1
1980s	TGS 139	Master Drummer Vol. 2
1990	WW 101–2	Come and Drum

Addy, Obo (b. Accra, Ghana, 1936). One of the celebrated Addy Brothers (Yacub and Mustapha Tettey are the others), Obo has perhaps travelled further than most in his endeavour to publicise Ghanaian music and to establish a viable life-style for a Ghanaian musician in the 1990s. His father was a Ga fetish priest and as a child Obo was constantly surrounded by the drumming, dancing and singing which accompanied his father's work. He was soon assisting his father, learning to drum and how to understand rhythm. Like most 'small boys' he started on the gong gong before progressing to drums, playing at ritual occasions and later at wider social gatherings.

In 1954 he joined Joe Kelly's Band, learning to play western music for highlife audiences in the new hotels and nightclubs. In 1959 he switched to the Builders' Brigade Band, one of Nkrumah's state bands, with whom he toured the entire country. Two years later he was approached to join the Farmers' Council of Ghana, whose band toured the country educating farmers through drama, music and cinema. This experience encouraged him to put traditional music on stage; a step away from both its traditional community context and from the syncretic highlife music he had hitherto been playing. He was able to put his ideas into practice with the unveiling of the show *Edzo* before Nkrumah himself.

By 1962 he was deputy leader of the Farmers' Band and leader of the traditional troupe which operated within the framework of the band. By operating in two different mediums, Obo was amongst the first actively to promote the idea of a return to roots without losing sight of the changes occurring in music and society. Then, in 1966, the year Nkrumah was overthrown, Obo formed a band to perform at the newly opened Continental Hotel, a tourist-oriented establishment near the airport. Once again he was able to combine popular music with traditional drumming. This was followed by a brief stint with the Ghana Broadcasting Band before he made a conscious decision to go back and retrieve some of the older drum and dance traditions of Ghana. He took a job at the Arts Council and began to develop his composing skills once again, mixing tradition and popular music. He was instrumental in forming Anansi Krumian Soundz using exclusively traditional instruments.

In 1972 he went to Israel on an Arts Council tour and on his return joined up with his brothers to form the highly acclaimed Obuade (Ancient). They were invited to perform at the 1972 Munich Olympics, which led in turn to invitations to perform in Europe, the USA and eventually as far away as Australia and Japan. The next three years saw Obuade perform widely and well, establishing a reputation as teachers as well as performers. Then in 1977 Yacub and Obo settled down in Seattle, USA, forming a new group called Ablade shortly after arrival. Radio and TV work augmented an income based on teaching and performing. In 1981 Obo formed his own group, which he called Kukrudu, as a vehicle for his compositions, and released two LPs in 1983 and 1984 on the Avocet label. In 1986 Obo repeated the operation by releasing two collections – a cassette of original traditional-style material and another, contemporary album appropriately entitled *African-American*. By the late 1980s all this hard work was starting to pay off as he became a frequent performer on the North American festival circuit. He also continued teaching and by the end of the decade his career seemed both stable and creative. In 1988 he formed a smaller performing group called

Okropong in response to growing demand for the music and dance of Ghana.

1970s	TAN	Kpanlogo Party
1983	AVO	Obo Addy and Kukrudu
1984	AVO	Obo
1986	SAN	Born in the Tradition
	FH	African-American
1991	EB D2500	Okropong: Traditional Music of Ghana
	EB D2602	Born in the Tradition (Re-issue)

MODERN MUSIC

Once again, readers are referred to the lengthy introduction to highlife which appeared in Volume 1.

Mensah, E.T. (b. Emmanuel Tetteh Mensah, Accra, 1919). Trumpet player, sax player, composer and bandleader, E.T. Mensah is known throughout the world as the 'King of Highlife' and is without doubt the single most important figure in the history of the style. Volume 1 presented a short but precise essay on E.T.'s career and the full story may again become available through a paperback reprint of Collins's *E.T. Mensah: King of Highlife* (see Bibliography). His career really took off in the early 1950s and for over two decades the King reigned supreme. His career dipped in the 1970s and he returned to pharmacy, but in 1986 E.T. (in the UK for medical treatment) returned to the headlines with the launch of his biography, the release of *All for You* and two special shows in London and Amsterdam. In 1988 he was awarded an honorary Ph.D. and in 1990 received the highest accolade of all when the Government of Ghana awarded him the title 'Okunini' – 'A Very Famous Man'. His health continued to fluctuate as he enjoyed the golden years of his life at home in Accra. In 1991 several key tracks appeared on the Original Music compilation CD (OMA 114CD) but it was the second volume on the RetroAfric label which really produced the goods. Both RetroAfric collections are highly recommended.

1986	RETRO 1CD	All for You
1990	OMA 114CD	+ Ramblers & Uhurus: Giants of Dance Band Highlife
1991	RETRO 3CD	Day By Day

Ghanaba, Kofi (b. Guy Warren, Accra, Ghana, 1923). Now known as Ghanaba – the Divine Drummer –

Guy Warren remains one of Africa's great enigmas. Volume 1 outlined his career up until 1985 but it was in 1986 that Ghanaba made a triumphant return with a powerful performance at the Royal Albert Hall. That year saw the publication of a complete boxed set of his music with copious notes, reviews and assessments. However, this collection remains as elusive as single copies of his albums. I have seen the sleeve notes but not the boxed set. Further details would be welcomed. In the meantime, try to find anything by Ghanaba, the man described by Max Roach in 1974 as being 'So far ahead of what we were all doing that none of us understood what he was saying.' Also see Volume 1 for discography.

King Bruce. Bandleader, music entrepreneur and star of the 1950s and 1960s. The publication of his long-awaited biography and a compilation of his classic songs are both due in 1992.

1992	RETRO 5CD	Original Black Beats

Ramblers International Dance Band. Top highlife dance band of the 1970s and the only big band formation which survived into the 1980s, playing residencies at the major Accra hotels. Led by Jerry Hansen (ex-Tempos) for over two decades, the Ramblers resurfaced in 1990 under the leadership of Jerry Junior. That year also saw the re-release of their 1970s' highlife classic *The Hit Sounds*.

1990	DWAPS 25	The Hit Sounds of the Ramblers
1991	OMA 114CD	Giants of Dance Band Highlife

Uhurus. The Uhuru Band grew out of a 1950s orchestra, the Broadway Dance Band. From 1965 the band was being run by guitarist Stan Plange and by then had become one the most popular dance bands in the country. By the mid-1970s they had reformed as the Great Uhurus, recording a single album for Faisal Helwani and playing regularly at his Saturday night shows at the Apollo Night Club. They enjoyed a minor revival (on CD) with the re-release of cuts from an early 1970 LP.

1970	WAPS 31	The Professional Uhuru Dance Band
1991	OMA 114CD	Giants of Dance Band Highlife

Nyame, E.K. Although one of Ghana's brightest stars, E.K.'s music is seldom heard in the West and has, for all intents and purposes, never been available outside Ghana. It is believed that the

Ghanaian producer Faisal Helwani recorded E.K. shortly before his death in 1977 but sadly these recordings have never been made available. In addition to the four LPs referred to in Volume 1 a few more albums have been spotted in private collections.

1970s	PN 02	Kae Dabi
	JNA 16	Wiase Mu Yeya
1974	SRLP004	E.K.'s Professional Band
1979	SRLP012	Gethsemani

African Brothers International Band. Led by the indefatigable Nana Kwame Ampadu Third, the African Brothers remain Ghana's top band, true to the guitar highlife tradition but never afraid to incorporate new elements and styles. They remain as prolific as ever, recording principally at Ambassador Records in Kumasi. Now almost an institution, they are the only major band in Ghana to have survived the ups and downs of the last thirty years. The LPs listed below help fill in the full discography of the band and bring up to date their recent recording history, although I have not included very recent Ghana-only cassette releases. In 1991 they returned to the UK for their first shows since 1984.

1973	PAB 03	Highlife Time (Also PN06)
1974	JN 022	Tribute to D.K.
	PN 10	Osekufuo
	PN 12	Emaa Bekum Mmarima
1976	JNLP10	Odaano Traditional Highlife
1978	6354020	Obiara Wo Nea Otumi No
1979	ABLP05	African Feeling
1988	AB11202	Oman Bo Adwo
1989	ABI1204	Odo Me Nsee

Mensah, Kwaa. The 'King of palm-wine music' died suddenly in early 1991 aged 71. Several cassettes of his late 1980s output are known to be available in Ghana but not outside the country. Surely some enterprising entrepreneur will try to rectify this situation.

Konimo (b. Daniel Amponsah, Fuase, 1934. a.k.a. Koo Nimo). Volume 1 provided an extensive biography of Konimo, again wondering why so little of his music had reached the wider market. Since 1985 Ko's profile has been considerably raised with the re-release of his mid-1970s material on compact disc and several overseas tours. Backed by his group Adadam Agormomma (the Roots Ensemble), which

features his son, Little Noah, on various drums and long-time accompanist Kofi Twumasi on guitar, Ko's lilting palm-wine guitar style has made many new converts over the last few years. The repertoire of the group is enormous and their mastery of styles and instruments impressive. Occasionally, they feature the six-stringed Asante lute – the seperewa – perhaps the only outfit thus to integrate the instrument in a live performance. In 1988 Konimo played a prestigious Broadway show at which a limited edition of 1,000 cassettes were sold. This cassette is now the only 1980s recording of the group available, although it will be extremely difficult to find. Since then, Ko's reputation has continued to grow both at home and abroad.

1987	ADC 102	Osabarima
1988	Cass. only	King of Up-Up-Up

Mann C.K. In 1988 C.K. Mann, one of the brightest highlife stars of the 1970s, re-emerged with the instant classic *Hi-Life Salsa*. Recorded in the UK with the help of British, Colombian and Ghanaian musicians, the LP demonstrated C.K.'s enduring talent in a creative and entertaining blend of highlife and salsa. True to tradition, C.K. devotes the second side to the Osode Medley, reminding fans of his powerful 1970s rhythm, the Osode Beat. Sadly, this highly popular musician suffered a personal tragedy in 1989 with the death of his son and bass player, Kwabena. However, he was back on the road in 1990 entertaining the growing Ghanaian community in Canada.

1988	KB 01	Hi-Life Salsa/Dance Time 88

Ackah, Jewel. See Volume 1 for early career and discography. Over the last few years, Jewel has been working out of Toronto, releasing a series of high-quality albums. For his 1991 release he renamed his band the Butterfly Six. He remains one of Ghana's most accomplished vocalists and bandleaders.

1988	JVK 01	You Better Fly High
1989	HW 2020	My Dear
1991	BAS 004	Pull Him Down

Ashanti Brothers. Top guitar band of 1970s and early 1980s. Lay your hands on anything you can find. The record listed below was omitted from the discography in Volume 1.

1978	6354025	Kill Me and Fly

Diamond 3. Led by Asare Baffour and Obiri Yeboah, the Diamond 3 are that rare commodity – a Ghanaian band still playing classic guitar highlife. Currently in Nigeria, where they record, their 1988 album must be one of the highlife highlights of the past decade.

1988	NEMI 0638	Home Sweet Home

Okukuseku. One of the finest guitar bands ever, who came to prominence in the 1970s before departing for Nigeria, where they produced much of their best material. Returned to home-base in Koforidua in the mid-1980s as the Nigerian oil boom came to an end. Still an active force but with limited recording opportunities.

1987	RASLPS 100	I Need Work

Konadu, Alex (b. Kumasi, Asante). In Volume 1 it was suggested that 'The One-Man Battalion' was on the verge of international acclaim. It was particularly satisfying to see Alex arrive in London in November 1987 for a series of shows promoted by Arts Worldwide. Konadu, like very few others, has remained true to the highlife idiom and has even been characterised as a 'purist'. What is obvious is that his music has not been influenced by other styles and that it has succeeded in taking palm wine guitar music from the informal and usually rural drinking bars to the nightclubs and dancehalls. He works on the basis of a fixed guitar melody around which other instruments improvise. His lyrics, dealing with love, personal strength, dilemmas, fears and tragedies, are extremely important. Sung in Twi, the rest of the band drop in volume when he approaches the microphone. His recording career is a mix of US releases on the Makossa label of material otherwise only available in Ghana. His 1987 tour produced the outstanding highlife album of the year, *One Man Thousand*. In 1990 Konadu toured Canada making and releasing the excellent *One Man Thousand in Toronto*.

1988	WCB 009	One Man Thousand: Live in London
1990	RTPLP 001	One Man Thousand in Toronto

Dede, Amakye, and the Apollo Kings International Band (b. Dan Amakye Dede, Agogo, Asante, 1957). Joined Kumapim Royals in 1975 as composer and treble vocalist but moved to Nigeria. Nicknamed 'Expensive Boy', Amakye Dede enjoyed a rapid rise to fame in the late 1980s inside Ghana. By 1990 he had recorded a succession of top reggae–highlife albums in Ghana, Germany, Holland and the USA

and entered the new decade as the singing sensation of the 1990s. His early career was with the famous Kumapim Royals before striking out on his own in 1980 with the Apollo Kings. They were based in Nigeria for several years enjoying reasonable success, particularly with the pidgin-English hit 'Jealousy'. In 1986 he scored his first Ghanaian hit with 'Kose Kose'. His career is clearly on the rise, and although his albums have never been distributed properly outside Ghana, they can usually be found in small Ghanaian shops in the UK and the USA.

1981	CYLP	To be a Man Na Wah
1982	CYLP 014	Jealousy
1989	KBLS 0104	Okyena Sesee
	COLP 665	Kose Kose
1990	OP 001	Odo Mfoni Special (USA)
	DP 002	Dabi Dabi Ebe Ye Yie (USA–Holland)
	JOM 001	Live in Europe (Germany)(Cass.)
1991	KAK 002	Magye Me Girl (Repackaged material including 'Kose Kose')

Cutlass Dance Band. A traditional highlife outfit with strong gospel influences. They produced half a dozen LPs in the late 1970s and early 1980s.

1980	LS 35	Osenkafo I.K. Annin Vol. 1
1981	LS 36	Vol. 2

Tuffuor, Nana. A gifted vocalist who emerged to some local and overseas prominence in the mid-1980s. His second album was recorded at Elephant Walk in Ghana and completed in Germany.

1989	ALP198929	Abibi Nsa
1990	KAM 1004	Nana Tuffuor

Crentsil, A.B. Another recent Toronto visitor. Has produced some excellent 'exile highlife'. I include the catalogue number for *Adjoa* missing in Volume 1. In 1989 Crentsil and virtually every other major Ghanaian star of the 1980s were brought together by Big Joe Asiedu in an excellent compilation album entitled *Party Time with the Stars*. Featuring Crentsil, Ackah, Pat Thomas, George Darko, Lee Duodo and Ben Brako, this LP should be the starting point for any newcomer to modern Ghanaian music.

In 1991 World Circuit (assisted by Gunter Gretz)

were finally able to obtain the rights to *Hollywood Highlife Party*, one of the finest highlife albums ever by the Sweet Talks led by A.B. Crentsil. With a seductive soukous rhythm built on the highlife framework, and saucy, entertaining lyrics, this must be the most welcome re-release of 1991.

1980	LS 53	Adjoa
1983	PAM 11	Moses (Re-release)
1985	WAZ 101	Toronto by Night
1987	DPLP 8801	Kofo Mpo Dzidzi
1988	PRO 01	Abrokyiri Abrabo
	RAP 002	Highlife in Canada
1989	NAK 008	Party Time with the Stars
1991	WCB	Hollywood Highlife Party

Ambolley, Gyedu-Blay. Another stalwart of the Ghanaian music scene, Ambolley scored, and not for the first time, with *Bend Down Low*.

1984	EBL 6133	Simigwa
1989	SIMIGWA	Adwoa Amissah
1990	SG06 9015	Bend Down Low

Pinado, Bob. One of Ghana's great musical showmen, Pinado has enjoyed periods of immense popularity in Ghana over the last two decades. In 1963 he received the Arts Council Award as the country's most talented musician (a very high accolade) for his song 'Sonobete'. In 1976 he travelled to the UK and recorded his first LP *Showmaster of Africa*. Back in Ghana he continued to entertain with his own variety show, mixing music, dance and an explosive sense of humour. In the 1980s he endured a spell in the UK and little was heard of him. In 1990 he returned to the Elephant Walk Studio in Ghana to record *Love is Love*.

| 1990 | PAD0025 | Love is Love |

Agyeman, Eric. Master guitarist with impeccable pedigree in many of Ghana's leading bands, Eric's last recorded work appeared in 1987. Where has he gone?

| 1987 | ASR6010 | Nananom |

Thomas, Pat. The final member of Ghana's trio of top vocalists, Pat Thomas, like both Crentsil and Ackah, touched down briefly in Canada where a collective of Ghanaian businessmen and musicians provided ample support for recording and live shows. After a couple of quiet years he struck back in 1991 with an outstanding new recording and live

shows in London, Paris and Amsterdam – belated recognition for an outstanding talent. Dubbed the 'Golden Voice', Pat has done as much as any other Ghanaian star to develop a modern highlife style, rooted in the past but tastefully modern. See Volume 1 for early career.

| 1988 | NAK 007 | Me Do Wiase |
| 1991 | CFR 001 | Sika Ye Mogya |

Jon K. (b. John K. Poku, Accra, 1956). Best known as a session and studio specialist, Jon is a fine young bass and keyboard player now based in London. Best known as producer of Ben Brako and Thomas Frempong, he also released a couple of albums in the late 1980s which were well received by the resident Ghanaian community and back home in Ghana.

| 1987 | VILL008 | Adowa |
| 1989 | NAK 009 | Asaboni |

Asafo-Agyei, Herman. Ghanaian bass player and law graduate, Herman cut his teeth with several fine bands in Ghana before joining Hi-Life International in London. (See Volume 1.) By the late 1980s he was a much sought-after session bass player and toured widely with the legendary Osibisa. In 1989, having formed his own band, Native Spirit, Herman moved to Toronto, taking Canadian audiences by storm with riveting live shows and a successful eponymous debut album. The six-piece band specialise in highlife fusion.

| 1990 | | Native Spirit |

Brako, Ben. Yet another long-time London resident, Mr Brako had been on the fringes of the African music scene for several years before going into the studio in 1987. He was able to put together a revue band and built a strong reputation for live shows. In 1989 he released a video of *Baya* recorded in Ghana and featuring local scenes and live stage shows.

| 1987 | MCL0801 | Baya |
| 1990 | MCL0902 | Everybody |

Darko, George. The original Burgher King (see Volume 1, pp. 102–4, for a discussion of Burgher Highlife). With three high-quality highlife albums from the mid-1980s, George remained in charge with the 1989 release *Soronko*. That year he finally left Germany and returned to Ghana. He followed up a successful London gig from 1988 with another in 1990.

| 1989 | 09030135 | Soronko |

Amoah, Charles. Yet another graduate from the German Burgher Highlife University. Funkier, heavier and a real production job, *Fre Me* was a genuine hit in Europe and Ghana.

| 1986 | 0118957V | It's a Love Story |
| 1987 | KAM1001 | Fre Me |

Aquai, Khodjo. US-based Ghanaian singer, Khodjo made a minor impact in 1984 with his first LP *Africaribe*, an appropriately named album mixing highlife with Latin and Caribbean beats. In 1989 he produced his second effort in the same cross-over vein. The title track features Pat Thomas on vocals and the whole album was put together in New York.

| 1989 | AQ 1004 | Nhyira |

Bafy, Frank. Born in the Volta region, Frank moved to London in the mid-1980s. An accomplished singer and keyboard player, Frank is highly respected by his peers for his sophisticated cosmopolitan sound which encompasses rap, reggae highlife and even house in the appropriately entitled track 'Highlife in the House'. He has released one LP to date and several cassettes for the local market.

| 1989 | MRA 001 | Sambra |

Mensah, Tony. His first LP, featuring George Darko, was put together at Accra's Elephant Walk Studios and polished in London.

| 1989 | MRA 002 | Maame |

Budjei, Nana. Talented Ghanaian-born, London-based vocalist who makes good use of the best London-based Ghanaian musicians. His 1988 LP featured an exciting attempt to blend the old and the new – highlife and zouk. Sadly it didn't quite come off.

| 1988 | ARLP 015 | Afrikaman |
| 1989 | KBN 0248 | Awoda Pa |

Hayes, Pozo. Long-time stalwart of the Ghanaian music scene. Travelled to Benin in 1988 to record his first LP. This album features the seldom heard but never forgotten Ignace De Souza on trumpet. Recorded at Studio Christiana with several top Beninois stars.

| 1988 | SATLP 192 | Looking Over There |

Korsah, D.Y. A rare highlife album recorded in Ghana and available outside.

| 1991 | KV 01001 | Starlite: Roots Highlife 2 |

Kumbi Saleh. Dutch-based Ghana band playing a loose blend of soukous and highlife. Formerly led by 'Sloopy' Mike Gyamfi, ex-leader of the Adinkra Band.

| 1988 | TORSO33066 | Be a Good Samaritan |

Lumba Brothers. Led by Daddy Lumba, the Brothers are based in Germany and made a substantial impact in the late 1980s with two well-received albums. They enjoyed impressive cassette sales in Ghana. *Sika Asem*, their third LP, probably best demonstrates the band's new 'burgher' style.

1989	NR 1964	Obi Ate Meso Bo
1990	TWV 10445	Yee Ye Aka Akawantoum
	NR 007	Sika Asem

Aban. A cultural fusion group led by KoNimo Jnr and featuring guitar, vocals, bass, keyboards and percussion. Their first LP was dedicated to those living back home in the hope they might understand 'the basic factors preventing some Africans from going home as expected. Those abroad, after listening to this album, will feel that they are not alone in the struggle.' Sadly, the music does not live up to the sentiment. The LP was recorded in Texas.

| 1987 | KOB 001 | Efie Ne Fie |

Schall, Alfred. Talented keyboard player who served an early apprenticeship with the Ramblers, Black Beats and Blue Monks. Now based in Toronto, his first solo album was yet another ambitious attempt to blend highlife with reggae and funk.

| 1985 | WAZ 100 | In Perspective |

Talata, Lady. Lady Heidi Talata, currently Ghana's foremost female vocalist. Her 1988 outing to the studios in Benin resulted in *Meko*. By 1990 she was in USA, recording the *In New York* album.

| 1988 | 3902 | Meko |
| 1990 | LT 003 | In New York |

Tutu, Osei Jnr. Paris-recorded dance album with help from Cameroonian guitarist and Paul Simon sideman Vincent Nguini.

1988	PH 1334	Hi-Life Nite in Paris

Ayesu, Little Joe. US-based Ghanaian singer of the old school. In 1987 he teamed up with calypso giant Lord Kitchener for the unusual *Trighana* album.

1987	TRACCS 001	Trighana: Haunting Melodies

Various

1987	ANM 1228	Kofi Busia: Oh Africa
	AKA 004	Wilson Boateng: Mabre Agu
	HRF1004	Kumapim Royals: Ehye Wobo
	COPAM11	McGod & The People: Hi-Life Ago-go
1988	BBFH200	Kwabena Okai: Highlife Festival
	AV0010	Andy Vans: Beautiful Collection
	170650.1	Sir Roberto: The First Album
	SUG 001	Sugumugu 80s: 24 Hour Drumming
1989	LP 016	Sam Yeboah: Hi-Life Sensation
	DWAPS2278	Wofa Akwabena Akwaboa Slim Ali: Bisa
1990	FP 001	Nana Addo: Edan Entese Adaka
		Elvis Sakyi-Donkor: Osofo Mako
	BIG 001	Captain Afriyie: Ye Re Bre

Gospel highlife

The emergence of gospel highlife has been one of the major developments in Ghanaian music over the last decade.These modern guitar bands with a full line-up of electric equipment and basic highlife style are identified by their use of Christian lyrics. They started to emerge in the early 1980s as secular bands went bankrupt and only the churches, usually separatist,

apostolic and evangelical, had the money to support them. The churches had always made use of clapping, drumming and singing so it was not very difficult to augment this sound with electric guitars. One leading church to enter music in a big way was the Christa Asafo Mission, a 15,000-strong body led by Prophet Kwadwo Safo. By 1980 they were running seven guitar bands including the Genesis Gospel Singers, who appeared on the excellent early 1980s compilations entitled *Guitar and Gun*. Other leading bands, many of whom have the resources to record, include the Advent Heralds, the King's Stewards, the Golden Gates, the Gospel Sowers, the Metallic Singers and the Blessed Elim Singers. Many western listeners may initially be put off by the religious tag but while quality is uneven, it is worth checking a few out for some of the best guitar band highlife around. Please consult Volume 1 for discographical details of early 1980s gospel highlfe.

1987	NAK 003	Merciful Lights
1988	NELIM001	Nelim Gospel Band: Osoro Akwantuo
	AA 1001	Kwane Anokye-Toku and His Paradise Gospel Band: Obere Yi, Beko Awiee
1989	NGBLP 1	Nazareth Gospel Band (Formerly the New Light Gospel Band, still led by Pastor Seth Boah): Ahenfo Hene
1990	DP 001	Bishop Bonsu's Asafo Healing Voices: Onim Me
	NGBLP 3	Nazareth Gospel Band: Nhyina Nka Nea

Ghanaian reggae

Ghana, like the rest of Africa, continues to enjoy reggae music to an enormous extent. Early pioneers must include the Tempos, who claimed to be the first band to have introduced reggae, following their London shows of 1968. By the mid-1970s the music of Bob Marley was everywhere and by the early 1980s not only had tastes in imported reggae diversified but many Ghanaian musicians had turned to reggae full-time. Alpha Blondy, from neighbouring Côte D'Ivoire, made an enormous impact in the mid-1980s, bestowing a new level of respectability and obvious commercial appeal on what for many was still regarded as an alien musical form. By the late 1980s reggae, either live or through the ubiquitous sound system, had become a fixture in Ghanaian musical life with new idioms and styles emerging to match the original Jamaican masters.

Classic Vibes. One of the earliest Ghanaian reggae bands, now based in Denmark. Led by Kojo Antwi, the band played to regional audiences in Côte D'Ivoire before touring Europe supporting such reggae giants as Tosh, Isaacs and Burning Spear. Antwi returned to Ghana in the late 1980s and started the new decade with a new blend of roots reggae.

Roots Anabo. Popular roots reggae artistes, credited with the development of 'Sunlife' music. The band was formed in 1982 and hit the big time in 1984 with a performance at Jamaica's annual Reggae Sunsplash.

Bell, Felix. Popular reggae singer with several local cassettes on the market.

Nframa. Up-and-coming reggae group, formerly based in Nigeria.

CONCLUSION

Many, many names have been omitted from both Volume 1 and Volume 2 for reasons of space; because their music has enjoyed only marginal success; and because, on occasion, they have decided to operate within a largely non-Ghanaian musical frame of reference. However, it would be an injustice not to refer to such fine musicians as Sidiku Buari (funk-disco artiste with two mid-1980s albums); Joe Mensah (now resident in the US and originator of the 'African Hustle'); Kiki Gyan (ex-Osibisa keyboard player with reggae inclinations); Eddie Quansah (extraordinary trumpet player now resident in Australia – had a major cross-over hit in the late 1970s with *Che Che Kule*); Kris

Bediako (hard-rock specialist with late 1970s success in Ghana); members of Hedzolleh (mid-1970s fusion band who later toured with Masekela); and Ben Badoo, (Accra-born drummer, long-time UK resident and drum teacher – responsible for Steel and Skin and Lanzel troupes).

By the early 1990s there was every sign that Ghanaian music was on the way up with a bustling local scene and some excellent re-releases to remind listeners of what they had missed. Popular current groups include several government and army bands – Pink Five, Police Band, Prison's Band, the Sweet Beans (veterans of the Cocoa Marketing Board) and the Sappers. The Ga roots music pioneered by Wulomei also maintained its popularity with the continuing success of Wulomei and that of relative newcomers Naa Amanua's Group and Kyirem. On the guitar band side, African Brothers, A.B. Crentsil, Kumapim Royals and Safohene Djeni all maintained their appeal and were joined by newcomers like Paa Bobo, Abebe and Nokoko.

Ghana remains a country where music is taken seriously – from the early days of Nkrumah's personal support of musicians through the state-supported bands of the 1960s, 1970s and 1980s to the creation in 1990 of a PNDC (People's National Defence Council) band featuring the musical talents of various ministers and officials led by Kofi Totobi Quakyi, the Secretary for Information. Highlife, as one of the proto-urban dance styles, has taken many different directions (both musical and geographical) over the last two decades and the search for the perfect synthesis seems unlikely to slow down. However, as the economy gradually recovers and a new sense of confidence emerges, we can expect many exiled musicians to return home and enrich Ghanaian music with the lessons learned overseas.

4   Sierra Leone

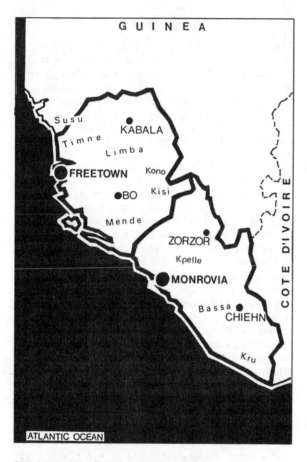

(ECONOMY AND SOCIETY. Pop.: 4.1 million.
Area: 71,740 sq. km. Capital: Freetown.
Independence: 1961. Currency: Leone.)

Originally inhabited by Temne and Mende people, together comprising about 30 per cent of the population, and other smaller groups such as the Lokko, Sherbo, Limba, Susu, Fulani and Kono, the modern territory of Sierra Leone came into existence in the early nineteenth century, following the resettlement of former slaves and the declaration of British colonial authority in 1808. These former slaves came in various waves, including groups from Britain (1787), Nova Scotia (1792) and Jamaica (1798). Throughout the nineteenth century these doubly transplanted settlers were reinforced by the settlement of various other West

Africans, freed by the British, until, by 1900, Sierra Leone could boast one of the most cosmopolitan societies in Africa with over 100 different languages spoken. Almost inevitably, despite much intermarriage, a privileged group emerged from the resettled community distinguished by education, language and religion, supported by the colonial ruling class and known as the Creole community.

During the early twentieth century deep divisions emerged in local society between the Creoles and the indigenous inhabitants on the one hand and the Creoles and the British on the other. But by the 1930s efforts were being mounted to overcome the divisions between Africans and Wallace-Johnson established the West African Youth League as a unifying, anti-colonial movement. The Second World War interrupted progress but thereafter things proceeded reasonably smoothly towards independence in 1961 under Sir Milton Margai. Further peaceful progress was interrupted briefly between 1967 and 1969 with several military coups seeking to establish stability before Siaka Stevens returned from exile to take power in 1969. Yet stability and economic development proved elusive and the next decade was marked by student riots, attempted coups and assassination attempts. In 1978 Stevens established a one-party state and held on to power for another seven years until he unexpectedly stood down to be replaced by his nominee, General Momoh – an army man in charge of a civilian regime.

TRADITIONAL MUSIC

Very little traditional music is currently available. Those listed below are little more than introductory albums to the wealth of traditional Sierra Leonian music.

OCR 558 549	Sierra Leone: Musique Traditionelles (Lute, guitar, flute, harp, drums, vocals, xylophone. Recorded by Jean Jenkins)
ETH 4330	Music of Sierra Leone
ETH 4332	Music of the Mende

MODERN MUSIC

Volume 1 introduced the modern popular music of Sierra Leone in a short essay. While recent research has done nothing to challenge the main conclusions it is imperative to point readers in the direction of *Sierra Leone Music*, an excellent compilation cassette and disc put together by writer/researcher Wolfgang Bender. The source of this selection was the Sierra Leone Broadcasting Service Gramophone Library which was persuaded to transfer all their 78 r.p.m. recordings on to tape for security and preservation. The project was funded by the German Ministry of Foreign Affairs in an imaginative and creative approach to international diplomacy and understanding. Both record and cassette are accompanied by an informative booklet containing short biographies, song texts and an overview of Sierra Leone in the 1950s. The music ranges from maringa to calypso, traditional to church choir and is an essential introduction to the more modern music of the country.

| 1988 | GEMA ZS 43 | Sierra Leone Music |

Calender, Ebenezer. As a singer and guitarist, Calender became the country's brightest star during the 1950s. Very little of his music is still available but one definitive track, 'Double Decker Buses', appears on the Bender compilation. Please see Volume 1 for full biography.

Pino, Geraldo and the Heart Beats. Founder of one of the country's first 'pop' bands and a seminal influence in both Ghana and Nigeria as a regional soul star. See Volume 1.

| 1974 | NEMI 0059 | Heavy, Heavy, Heavy |

Afro-Nationals. A large dance band who peaked in the 1970s with their unique brand of rumba-influenced pop. A personal favourite and prime candidates for re-release.

| 1983 | LPM 2328 | Tropical Funkmusic |
| 1984 | AME 9103 | Swinging Freetown |

Rogie, S.E. Volume 1 contained an introductory biography of the man who, although now in his fifties, has become the most prominent musician from Sierra Leone. The entry concluded by noting that by the late 1980s Rogie's career was more firmly established than ever with several international releases and a growing audience for his soft and relaxed 'palm-wine' style.

| 1975 | ROGI R1 | African Lady |

1976	ROGI R2	The Sixties Sounds of S.E. Rogie
1987	COOK 010	Palm Wine Guitar Music
1989	PLAYLP 9	The King of Palm Wine Guitar Music
1991	PLAYCD 18	The New Sounds of S.E. Rogie

Oloh, Doctor. Pioneer of the 'Milo Jazz' style with roots in the earlier Gumbe (Goom-bay) tradition popularised by Calender. Oloh was responsible for many early developments in the 'Milo' tradition, introducing new drums in the basic percussion ensemble and adding a harmonica. He himself played the lead drum and composed most of the material. During the 1960s and 1970s, Freetown reverberated to his lively 'Milo' Jazz with tours to the US and Cuba. He has released several local cassettes and established his own 'college' which can now provide several ensembles for local functions. His contribution to the national music scene was acknowledged by the government in the late 1980s and in 1991 he played a spectacular show in London to the Sierra Leonian community.

Dean, Aki. Sierra Leonian producer responsible for Bunny Mack's success, which he followed up with a string of material on the appropriately named Discalypso label. Released as maxi-45s, he was able to bring many top musicians of the early 1980s into the studio, providing a family feel to all the recordings. Participants included Miatta Fahnbulleh, Prince Nico Mbarga, Teddy Davis, Ade Forster-Jones and Leon Charles. The best of the singles were subsequently released on *Tumba*, an excellent compilation album from 1980, occasionally seen in second-hand racks.

Mack, Bunny. Cross-over star of the early 1980s who has since slipped into obscurity. See Volume 1 for biography.

Others. With a few notable exceptions, the music of Sierra Leone is notoriously difficult to track down and is becoming increasingly so as local cassettes come to monopolise the music scene. On the other hand, so many talented musicians are now working overseas that there is no reason for western audiences to feel starved of what remains one of the most vital and productive musical traditions in Africa.

| 1975 | NEMI 0137 | Various: Music From Sierra Leone |
| 1980 | | Big Fayie & Sierra Leone Band: OAU |

1980		Various Artistes: Tumba
1982		Sabanoh 75: Woman
1983		The Godfathers: Papa You Go Know
	M 2374	Fanga Alafia: Drum Dance

The London scene

London has remained the favourite destination of Sierra Leonian musicians wishing to advance their musical careers, and by the mid-1980s it could boast half a dozen bands led or influenced by Sierra Leonians, including Orchestra Jazira, African Connexion, Sayinoh, African Culture, Masala Kotoko and Super Combo. The musicians involved were all articulate advocates of African music with specifically Sierra Leonian references as a key part of their repertoire.

Musa, Mwana. Guitarist, composer and singer, Mwana remains one of the most active and imaginative musicians working the London scene. He helped formed African Connexion in 1983, releasing three impressive singles over the next two years – 'C'est La Dance', 'Dancing on the Sidewalk' and 'Tell Mandela'. Musa is one of music's great innovators, and although drawing principally on Zaïrean sources, his policy is constantly to introduce new patterns and rhythms. The band eventually collapsed in 1986 with musicians going their separate ways and Musa striking out on his own to produce the exciting 1988 LP, *Welcome*.

| 1988 | MUSALP 88 | Welcome |

T-Jay, Abdul (b. Abdul Tejan-Jalloh). Over the last decade Abdul has become one of London's (if not Africa's) finest all-round guitarists, much in demand on the live circuit and for session work. Having parted company with Musa in 1986, he quickly established African Culture as a vehicle for his explosive guitar work and rootsy approach to the Sierra Leonian musical tradition. He had already recorded two impressive singles, 'Salima' and 'Agooda Medley', which were less influenced by soca and soukous – two favourite reference points for Sierre Leonese – than the session work which he undertook for Aki Dean. By the late 1980s Abdul was digging deeper in the past, reviving the milo jazz tradition and experimenting with palm-wine music. Meanwhile he was building a rock-solid reputation for dynamic live shows on the UK African circuit. In 1990 he released his first LP, the critically acclaimed *Kanka Kura*, on the *Folk Roots* house label, Rogue Records. In 1991 he was in the studio with British pop star David Essex working on a charity album for Voluntary Service Overseas as well as on his own second album with his band Rokoto.

| 1990 | FMSL 2018 | Kanka Kura |

Fyle, Hilton. BBC presenter of Network Africa and as such a household name on the London African scene and throughout the continent. Now trying to establish a reputation as a musician.

1984	ANS 8414	I Love Mama Africa
1986	NADLP 1002	Fresh
1988	FIN 401	Salut Africa

De Champ. London-based pianist.

| 1990 | CHAMP 1 | Feeling Good |

5   Liberia

(ECONOMY AND SOCIETY. Pop.: 2.5 million. Area: 111,369 sq. km. Capital: Monrovia. Independence: Never colonised. Currency: Liberian dollar.) For map, see p. 42.

Little is known of Liberian pre-history prior to the arrival of African settlers, repatriated from the USA, in 1822. By then the area was occupied by three principal groups: a Mande-speaking group including the Mandingo, the Kpelle, the Mende and the Vai; a Kwa-speaking group including the Kru; and a West Atlantic linguistic group comprising the Gola and the Kissi. Black settler society was first established under the rule of light-skinned mulattos until they were replaced in 1869 by darker-skinned members of the True Whig Party. Yet despite their own ancestry and the much-vaunted ideals of the American republic, the new Liberian ruling class behaved no differently from neighbouring white colonialists, introducing a system of forced labour which caused an international scandal as late as the 1930s and which somehow survived until the 1960s. Unfortunately, the black settlers proved unable to develop the local economy and became reliant on foreign investment. During the 'Scramble for Africa' in the late nineteenth century the weakness of the Liberian state ensured that parts of Africa's first republic were lost to European colonising powers.

By the twentieth century Liberia was stagnating in a vicious cycle of dependence and underdevelopment with a highly privileged local élite depending on revenues arising from massive foreign investments – most notably from the Firestone Rubber Company. Indeed, far from regarding Liberia as an independent country surrounded by the vestiges of European colonial power, it was really an American colony using the US dollar, dependent on American capital and, later, the site for the powerful Voice of America radio station. Between 1944 and 1979 the True Whigs ran the country very much as a personal fief under the presidencies of Tubman and Tolbert until, following rice riots in 1979, the entire ruling class was overthrown in a coup led by Master-Sergeant Samuel Doe. Since then, the country has slipped slowly and inexorably into political and economic bankruptcy climaxed by the civil war of the late 1980s, the capture and execution of Doe and the arrival of a joint West African Peace-Keeping Force (ECOMOG). At the time of writing, Liberia was facing famine on a massive scale as various warlords struggled with both ECOMOG and the international community for control of the benighted country.

TRADITIONAL MUSIC

FE 4465	Folk Music of Liberia
BM 30L 2301	The Music of the Dan

MODERN MUSIC

Little research has been conducted into the popular music of Liberia and readers are referred to Volume 1 for a summary of post-war developments. Records were produced between 1960 and 1980 but by then cassettes were taking over. By the late 1980s, with a shattered economy and political chaos, no new music was being recorded, although Liberia remained one of the biggest sources of pirated music in Africa.

Fahnbulleh, Miatta. Formerly Miss Liberia who broke into the music scene supporting Makeba on her 1977 West African tour. Now based in London and occasionally asked to contribute her vocal talents to studio sessions. She is perhaps best known for her late 1970s single on the Discalypso label, 'Kokolilo' – a reworking of a well-known West African folk song.

Others

1970s	KR 25	The Africanas: Music of Liberia
	LPM 2345	Afro Disco Band
1981	US 0081	Kapingbdi: Don't Escape

PART III

Francophone West Africa

6   Senegambia

SENEGAL

**(ECONOMY AND SOCIETY. Pop.: 7.7 million.
Area: 196,192 sq. km. Capital: Dakar.
Independence: 1960. Currency: CFA franc.)**

Senegal has been inhabited for over 15,000 years but recent history begins with the Ghana empire in the eighth century and the Mali empire of the fourteenth century. Senegal was part of both and had been Islamicised by the Almoravids from the ninth century onwards before a large part of modern Senegal came under the control of the Djolof empire, which did not collapse until the sixteenth century. By then a number of European powers were vying with each other for control of the lucrative slave trade and by the seventeenth century Senegal was one of the main centres of that trade.

When the trade was abolished in 1848, the French turned their attention to groundnuts but had to overcome several religious uprisings by El Hadj Omar and Amadou Chekory before they could finally 'pacify' the area and start on the construction of the railway inland to Mali. By the end of the nineteenth century the French had conquered the entire region and set about organising an administrative and commercial structure. Senegalese politicians had been

sitting in the French Assembly since 1848 and it was therefore not too surprising that local politics were much more sophisticated in Senegal than in other parts of Africa. Between 1933 and 1948 local politics were dominated by the Senegalese Socialist Party (with an important Communist Party further to the left), which, in 1944, nominated Leopold Senghor to sit in the French Assembly.

As an academic, poet and consummate politician, Senghor remains one of the key figures in twentieth-century African affairs. Between 1944 and 1960 he worked actively to secure the independence of Senegal, and in a lively political scene with a variety of parties he eventually led Senegal to independence in 1960 after a short-lived, French-inspired union with Mali. Thereafter, Senghor drifted steadily to the right, maintaining close ties with France and suppressing local opposition by incorporating all opposition parties into the UPS. Senghor held power until 1981 when he stood down in favour of heir apparent Abdou Diouf. He thus became the first African president to hand over absolute power through a peaceful process. But he had already started recognising new political parties and during the 1980s Diouf had to fight several elections, although state power ensured that he would not be seriously challenged. But although Senegal could afford a limited version of democracy, little could be done to reverse the economic decline or to resolve the problem of the Casamance separatists. By the late 1980s more trouble for the country appeared in the form of border clashes with neighbouring Mauritania.

GAMBIA

**(ECONOMY AND SOCIETY. Pop.: 814,000. Area:
11,000 sq. km. Capital : Banjul. Independence: 1965.
Currency: Dalasi.)**

Gambia, a tiny slither of land on either side of the River Gambia, is entirely surrounded by Senegal. Inhabited since the first century AD, the area came under the control of the Mali empire before it disintegrated into small local kingdoms which gradually came under the control of the Islamic Manding. The Portuguese arrived in 1455 and were soon joined by the British and the French, with the area occasionally being administered from Dakar. However, despite alternating political interests, all the European powers were interested in slaves and Gambia became a centre for the trade until it was finally abolished in 1807. British influence spread steadily throughout the nineteenth century, first establishing a protectorate over the area and then declaring it a colony in 1888 with a boundary settlement with France in 1889 settling the territory's borders. Political parties began to emerge after the Second World War with the rural PPP led by David Jawara capitalising on the majority Manding vote and bringing the country to a peaceful independence in 1965 after a decade of discussion about the relationship between Gambia and Senegal.

Initially, there were doubts about the viability of the tiny country – it shared a common history with Senegal and had on occasion been ruled from there. Yet Gambia was able to survive, and when a tourist industry took off in the wake of Alex Haley's *Roots*, the future seemed more secure, despite the problems which tourism created and the hostility of the Muslim majority. Then, in 1981, the country was shaken when Samba Sanyang took over in a short-lived coup which was crushed by Senegalese forces and the SAS, both invited in by President Jawara. Jawara immediately set about establishing an integrated army with his Senegalese saviours and throughout the rest of the year the two countries explored other aspects of union before announcing the creation of Senegambia in February 1982. The new Confederation moved steadily towards deeper union but found it difficult fully to integrate the two economies. Tension between the partners was mounting and by the mid-1980s both parties were keen to delay any further progress towards union. Meanwhile, Jawara was able to retain personal power and comfortably won the last elections in 1987.

TRADITIONAL MUSIC

1950s	FE 4462	Wolof Music of Senegal and the Gambia (Vocals, percussion, sabar, lutes)
1960s	FE 4323	The Music of the Diola-Fogny of Casamance (Vocals, percussion)
1969	LRLP 12	Musique du Senegal et du Mali (Female vocals and percussion)
1970s	OCR 15	Senegal: La Musique des Griots
	SNG 001/002	La Voix du Senegal
1975	FW 8505	Ousman M'Baye and His African Ensemble: Songs of Senegal (Vocals, guitar)

The kora tradition

For many newcomers to African music, kora music marks the starting point. It is not hard to see why, given the basic familiarity of the sound, the fact that one or two musicians proved to be commercially viable in terms of flights and other costs and the way in which a number of influential DJs also opened their African account with the kora tradition. Inevitably, kora music has generated a great deal of academic and journalistic coverage, initially through the efforts of Anthony King and subsequently through Lucy Duran. For a critique of recent efforts to promote kora music in the west see Galina Chester and Tunde Jegede, *The Silenced Voice* (Diabete Kora Arts, London, 1987). The majority of those kora records listed below can be found without too much difficulty.

1960s	920 043	Mamadou Seck & Boubacar Diabate: Chansons Africaines D'Hier et Aujourdhui (Guitar and kora)
	LIST 7308	Sounds of West Africa: Koras and Xylophones of Ghana, Gambia and Senegal (Includes Foday Musa Suso)
1977	SON 8208	Mamadou Seck & Boubacar Diabate: Deux Authentiques Griots Africaines (Guitar and kora)
1982	VX 1006	Konte Family: Mandinka Music
1986	ST 1010	Malamini Jobarteh & Dembo Konte: Jaliya
1987	HQ 2060	Hot Music in the Gambia 1984 (Field recordings of a dozen kora, balafon and vocal ensembles)
	ENC 9027	L'Histoire du Cora (Cass.)

Suso, Jali Nyama (b. Bakau, Gambia, mid-1920s, d. 1991). Kora master, teacher and composer who did more to promote the kora tradition outside Africa than any other player. He grew up in a kora-playing family and was a fluent performer by the age of eight. However, when he was sixteen a bad fall cost him a leg – a double blow for someone who made a living by travelling around and entertaining people at weddings, births and other ceremonies. He started recording for the radio in 1956 and by the mid-1960s had become a true national star, favoured by President Jawara and appointed arranger of the national anthem, 'Fode Kabba'. However, by the time he fell from favour, he had already started work with two visiting musicologists (Knight and King), which later led to a year's teaching in the US, where he recorded his first album for Ocora. In 1973 he worked with Sam Charters on 'African Journey' and played on an album of the same title. He had earlier worked with Alex Haley, author of *Roots*, recording 'The Kinte's Tune' to accompany the series. By the late 1970s he was playing regularly to devoted Swedish audiences, although his touring and playing had failed to make him any real money. By 1986 he was suffering from tuberculosis, from which he died in 1991.

1972	OCR 70	Mandinka Kora
1973	SNTF 666	African Journey: Roots of the Blues
1975	FE 4178	The Griots: Masters of the Spoken Word (Double LP)
1977	SNTF 729	Songs from the Gambia

Konte/Kouyate. Dembo Konte (b. Gambia) and Kasau Kouyate (b. Senegal) toured the UK on several occasions in the late 1980s to massive acclaim from everyone from *Folk Roots* to pop journalists.

1988	FMSL 2009	Tananle
	FMSL 2011	Simbomba
1990	FMSL 2020	Jali Roll

Jobarteh, Pa (b. Gambia). Son of Malamini Jobarteh and grandson of acknowledged kora master Alhaji Bai Konte (see Volume 1). Pa Jobarteh has been in and out of the UK since 1987 and is featured on the compilation/sampler SPM 1009.

1970s	R 5001	Alh. Bai Konte: Kora Melodies from the Gambia
1979	EDM 101	Amadu Bansang Jobarteh: Master of the Kora
1982	VX 1006	Mandinka Music. Konte Family: Kora Songs and Music from the Gambia

1985	ST 1010	M. Jobarteh & Dembo Konte: Jaliya
1987	WWCD 005 (CD)	D. Konte & M. Jobarteh: Baa Toto
1988	SPM 1009	Great Moments of Vinyl History

Koite, Sourokata (b. Tambacouda, 1955). Born into a griot family, he learned to play kora and balafon as a child. In 1975 he travelled to Dakar, where he played for several years in a tourist hotel band. In 1977 he signed a six-month contract with a French company and spent the time performing, again for tourists, in a club in northern France. In 1978 he moved to Paris, once more playing the club and restaurant circuit. His career blossomed and by the 1980s he was a regular on the European festival circuit. His first LP, in 1985, was cut in Holland. In 1987 he teamed up with Diombe Kouyate on balafon for his third album.

| 1985 | | En Hollande |
| 1987 | JND 05105 | Les Griots |

Jamaneh, Bubacar (b. Gambia, 1948). Born into a Muslim family, Bubacar grew up in traditional fashion in a farming and fishing community. He finished school in 1963 and, although heavily discouraged by his father, took up music, joining Ambiance Jazz of Bakau before moving on to the Gambian Police Band in 1965. However, this did not last long and by 1967 he was a sailor on a Greek ship tramping up and down the West African coast. He then turned his hand to mining, working in the diamond fields of both Sierra Leone and Liberia. The early 1970s found Bubacar in Spain before finally settling in Berlin in 1975. He quickly put together a number of bands to support his electric/acoustic guitar playing, forming the Afro-Combo Band, Banjulos Band and Jajang Band in quick succession, linking up with ex-Vedette Jazz and ex-Gulewar musicians for the 1982 album. To date, this is his only release and introduces another variety of electro-manding pop.

| 1982 | JR 106 | Manding Beats from the Gambia |

MODERN MUSIC

The Second World War marked a turning point in modern Senegalese music with the gradual dissemination of Cuban music and its incorporation into the standard repertoire. However, French music remained very much in demand and it was not until the emergence of the Star Band in the early 1960s that the metropolitan musical influence was finally swept aside. During the 1960s and 1970s, the soft, melodic reworkings of Cuban themes dominated popular taste with Star Band and Orchestre Baobab leading the forward charge. But slowly the means to support these big bands was disappearing and by the late 1970s a slimmed down, more frenetic style associated with Youssou N'Dour and Diamono was gaining mass popularity. By the mid-1980s 'mbalax' (as it was now known) was popular not only throughout Francophone West Africa but was starting to impinge on western pop consciousness. Since the 1960s Senegal has produced hundreds of gifted bands and individual musicians and we cannot mention them all here. However, for those who wish to dig deeper into post-war Senegalese music, I can refer them to such stars as Canari de Kaolack, Diarama de St Louis, Diene Doumbia, El Hadji Faye, Idy Diop, Khar M'Baye Madiaga, Kine Lamb, Madiop Seck, Maahawa Kouyate, Madiodio, Moussa N'Gom, N'Diaga M'Baye, Ousmane Diop, Ousmane Seydi, Ouza and the Ouzettes de Dakar, Pape Djiby, Orchestre N'Dakaru, Royal Band Thies, Soda Mama Fall and Souleyman Faye.

Senghor, Sonar, et Les Siccos. The band was formed in 1947, one of the earliest Senegalese dance bands to combine traditional idioms with modern instruments. The three-volume *Anthology* set appeared on the Everest label.

1952	MC 20015	Musique et Danses de L'Afrique Noir
	3254	Anthology of Music Vol. 1
	3255	Anthology of Music Vol. 2
	3256	Anthology of Music Vol. 3
	ESO 513	Tribal Music and Dances
1976	OL 6121	Re-issue of ESO 513

Star Band. Formed at the Miami Nightclub, Dakar, by Ibrahim Kasse. Seminal band in the development of Senegalese pop. See Volume 1 for career and discography. Amazingly, given the current popularity of the Senegalese sound, no one has yet seen fit to re-release Star Band material.

1970s	IK 3020	Bamos Pa'al Monte
	IK 3021	Simbonbon
	IK 3022	Solla
	IK 3023	Daga Ndiaye
	IK 3024	With Orchestre Laye Thiam

	SAF 3025	Kaele
	SAF 3026	Salam Alekoum
	IK 3027	Adioupe Nar (With N'Dour)
	IK 3028	Mariama
	IK 3029	Ndeye Ndongo
	IK 3030	Birame Penda Vagare
	IK 3031	Sala Bique

Johnson, Dexter. Nigerian-born horn player, settled in Senegal in the 1950s and enjoyed enormous popularity with the Star Band and, later, the Super Etoile (Star) Band. In 1989 Laba Sosseh paid homage to Johnson on a locally released cassette.

1950s	PF 11601	Dexter Johnson et le Super Stars
	PF 11602	Dexter Johnson et le Super Stars
	PF 11603	Dexter Johnson et le Super Stars
	LPDS 790	Estrellas Africanas
1989	7418	Hommage Posthume à Dexter Johnson (Cass.)

Diarama, Orchestre de St Louis. Led by Baye N'Diaye, solo guitarist. A big dance band featuring three guitarists, tam-tam and a full percussion and brass section.

1977	SAF 50054	Folklore Senegalese

Goram, Orchestre. Big band formed in the early 1970s.

1977	SAF 50056	Authenticité 77

Koten Diming Jazz. Led by Conde Sekou. Sekou also led L'Orchestre Sini-Sigui, releasing three albums in the mid-1970s.

1970s	ASL 7013	Massire
	SA 300042	Elhadji Oumar
1977	SAF 50066	Koten Diming Jazz

Ouza (b. Ousmane Diallo). Started playing in the 1970s but despite a number of albums and countless cassettes has never been able to reach a wider audience beyond Senegal. Similar in style to Youssou N'Dour, Ouza's music is derived from Wolof rhythms and he remains more of a traditionalist than his younger competitors – even complaining that they mis-apply the tama drum. His music is seldom available but he was one of the first musicians to work with Sylla and in 1980 recorded an LP recalling the heroic anti-colonialist struggles of the late nineteenth century led by, amongst others, the man who provided its title, Lat Dior.

1980	JM 5003	Lat Dior

Tropical Jazz de Dakar. Led by Mady Konate.

1970s	MAG 101	La Ultima Rumba

Baobab Orchestre. (Formed 1970.) The original band members were Atisso (guitar), Baroune N'Diaye (sax), Sedat Li (bass), Laye Nboub (vocals), Rodolphe Gomis (vocals) and founder and current leader Balla Sidibe (vocals). In the early days, the band covered Star Band material before developing their own sound and reinforcing the line-up with Issa Cissoko (horn) and Peter Oudu, a Nigerian clarinettist. Thione Seck also joined in as an extra vocalist, as did Ndiouga Dieng, who shared vocals with Nboub.

The band took up residency at the famous Baobab Club and for seven years everything went well. Then the ownership changed and the new owner had little idea of how to run the club. In April 1977 the band resigned and moved over to the Djandeer (later the Kilimanjaro) where they stayed for over a year. It was during 1977–8 that the band recorded five LPs, poor quality recordings only available in the US and Senegal and hard to find. A residency at the Balafon followed but the business side soon degenerated and, despite reasonable wages, when they were offered the chance to play in Europe they were both happy to leave and anxious to show Europe what Senegal could offer. In June 1978 the band set off for Paris.

But things did not go well. No arrangements had been made, no advertising, no promotion, etc. They played a few shows in Paris and then switched to Marseilles, where at least there was a sizeable Senegalese community. They struggled to survive, unable to send any money home and desperate to leave. They recorded twelve songs which were pressed up, but by Christmas 1978 the band was back in Senegal with nothing to show for their efforts.

They were able to pick up another residency at the Ungalam but some musicians had become despondent at the lack of success in Europe, while others, like Thione Seck, were consciously looking back to the past. The musical tastes of the Senegalese were changing rapidly, away from the Latin-Cuban sound of Star Band and Baobab and towards the younger musicians like Etoile 2000 and Youssou N'Dour.

The early 1980s was a period of transition for Baobab, reluctant to abandon the Cuban sound completely yet keen to bring in new elements. These years also saw a fundamental change in instrumentation with the horns disappearing to be replaced by more guitars. Personnel turned over rapidly with only Balla Sidibe remaining from the original line-up. The band survived but a change of direction was required. So, in 1985, Sidibe called all the musicians together and with the help of TV and radio unveiled the new Baobab, incorporating tama drum, sabar and stronger, more relevant lyrics. A local cassette release indicated just how much the band had changed. Two female singers were added to the line-up and another cassette was released from which one song became a national hit.

The band saw out the 1980s in a state of marginal success. Poor studios, expensive studios, poor producers, etc., all conspired to limit the commercialisation of the new Baobab. In 1989 Gunter Gretz, the knowledgeable German musicologist, travelled to Dakar on behalf of World Circuit Records and arranged with Sidibe the re-release of the 1982 classic entitled *Pirates' Choice*. It was an immediate critical hit with such a smooth and timeless feel that it became a universal favourite. Charlie Gillet, the pioneering DJ, described the sound on the sleeve notes of WCD 014 in the following reverential terms.

> By turns inspiring and soothing, spell-binding and exhilarating, the album takes the listener to another time, back to a magical studio session, where the musicians fell effortlessly into relaxed rhythmic grooves over which the singers and soloists sang and played a few of their favourite songs. No pressure, no pretension; recorded straight onto two track; no overdubs, no second thoughts, no remixes.

But the golden era is now finished. Sidibe still leads a version of Baobab including original singer Rodolphe Gomis. Laye Ndoup was sadly killed in a car crash, while Thione Seck has gone on to stardom with his own band. Barthelemy Atisso, the guitarist on *Pirates' Choice*, now resides in Togo, while Issa Cissoko still plays with other Dakar bands. The whereabouts of the others remain unknown. As we go to press, it is rumoured that World Circuit have another Baobab LP ready for re-release.

1975	BRLP 001	'75'
	BRLP 002	Guy Gu Rey Gu
	BRLP 003	Senegal Senegal
	BRLP 004	Visage au Senegal
	BRLP 005	Adduna Jarul

1978	ASL 7001	Baobab à Paris Vol. 1
	ASL 7002	Baobab à Paris Vol. 2
1979	DARL 001	!Africa (Mon Afrique)
1980	JM 5000	Mohamadou Bamba
	JM 5004	Sibou Odja
1981	BS 15155	Sotante Xalat
1982	MCA 307	Ken Dou Werente (Also WCD 014)
	Bootleg	Valente
1989	WCD 014	Pirates' Choice

Boussou, Mama Diara. Ex-Baobab, cassette-only release.

| 1989 | ST 2000 | Mama Diare Boussou |

Seck, Thione. Mr Seck, a Baobab graduate, is a gifted vocalist and percussionist who started his career with the family-based traditional ensemble. As a young man he learned a great deal about traditional music and soon established a local reputation. He cut his teeth with Orchestre Baobab, joining them in 1977 at the tender age of 23. But Baobab was changing and in 1979 he left the group to go his own way. He had always been more comfortable with traditional material and together with his brother Mapenda formed Raam Daan. They released four cassettes entitled *Ballaago, Jongoma, Aida Soukue* and, finally, *UNESCO*. The best material was then re-recorded for Thione's third LP. On the second release, *Yow*, Seck utilised top Camerooninan session men like Guy Lobe, Dalle Penda and the increasingly ubiquitous Manu Lima to underscore his own drumming and vocals. On his third LP, with London label Stern's, he demonstrates the unusual and appealing combination of sad and serious lyrics and up-tempo, vital music. This LP was described at the time as a 'subtle blend of mbalax and reggae' featuring horns, guitars and percussion.

1980	VAL 002	Chauffeur Bi
1983	SYL 8398	Yow (Also 38771)
1984		Vol. 1
1985		Vol. 2: Jongoma
1986		Vol. 3: Aida Soukue
1987		UNESCO
1988	ST 1023	Le Pouvoir D'Un Coeur Pur
1990	38771	Yow

Guelewars of Banjul. Led by Baboucar Sadikh Dabo and later by Laye Ngom.

1970s	DARL 007	Warteef Jigeen
1980	VAL 001	Sama Yaye Demna N'Darr
	JM 5001	Tasito
1982	SAF 50110	Wolo

N'Dour, Youssou. Since Volume 1 appeared in 1987, Youssou has become a truly international star, playing with household names around the world. He has remained as creative and prolific as ever and now has an enormous discography running to over 20 LPs and over 30 cassettes, with a good number being pirate issues. He has had a book published about him as well as a detailed discography and has probably received more column inches than any African musician past or present. Nearly everybody likes his music, wishes him well and thinks they understand him. Inevitably, this vast output and enormous media coverage has thrown more light on his career than anything written in Volume 1 might indicate. The discography provided in Volume 1 remains basically correct but we can now provide a comprehensive and possibly definitive discography, drawn from the meticulous research of Fleming Harrev and Gunter Gretz. They are to be applauded for their work. For the story of Youssou's life up to 1988 please refer to Jenny Cathcart's *Hey You!* (Fine Line Books, London, 1989). For a more recent interview, see S. Coxson, *Folk Roots*, No. 13. In 1989, with much public fanfare, Youssou signed to Virgin, a giant step forward for all of African music, but in 1991 he was unceremoniously dumped by the same company only to be picked up by American film producer Spike Lee, in what might well be the most astute move of his career. It may also prove to be an enormous step forward for all African music if Lee can introduce African music to a wider African-American public.

Star Band with Youssou N'Dour

1970s	IK 3027	Adioupe Nar
	IK 3028	Mariama
	IK 3029	Ndeye Ndongo
	IK 3030	Birande Penda Vagame
	IK 3031	Sala Bique

Youssou with Etoile de Dakar

| 1979 | DA 001 | Xalis |
| | DARL 002 | Absa Gueye |

1980	ET 001	Toulou Badou Ndiaye
1981	MCA 302	Thiapathioly

Youssou with Super Etoile de Dakar

1982	MCA 304	Ndiadiane Ndiaye
	MCA 305	Diankarlo 83 (Also DS 8006)
	MCA 306	Panorama de Senegal
1983	ED 008	Mouride

Youssou N'Dour

1983	ED 0010	Show à Abidjan
	MP 122	Diongoma
1984	CEL 6709	Immigrés (Also EMV 10)
1985	240 4461	Nelson Mandela (Also ERT 1009)
1987	CEL 6809	Inédits 1984–85
1989	V 2584	The Lion
1990	V 2634	Set

Only a part of Youssou's enormous output was put on to vinyl. The rest appeared on cassette, and although this is basically a vinyl discography, we feel an exception needs to be made in the case of N'Dour simply because there is so much interest in his music and so much confusion about what was released where, when and how.

Youssou and Etoile de Dakar

1978	Touba	Vol. 1: Thielly
1979	Touba	Vol. 2: Thiapathioly
1980	Touba	Vol. 3: Lay Suma Lay
	Touba	Vol. 4: Xaley Etoile
1981	Touba	Vol. 5: Maleo

Youssou et Super Etoile de Dakar

1982	Touba	Vol. 1: Tabaski
	Touba	Vol. 2: Ndakarou
	Touba	Vol. 3: Independence
	Touba	Vol. 4: Bandjoly Ndiaye
1983	N'Dour	Vol. 5: Yarou
	N'Dour	Vol. 6: Djamil

	N'Dour	Vol. 7: Daby
1984	N'Dour	Vol. 8: Immigrés
	N'Dour	Honda: Live in Paris
	N'Dour	Vol. 9: Africa: Deebeub
1985	N'Dour	Vol. 10: Ndobine
	N'Dour	Vol. 11: Bekoor
	N'Dour	Live
1986	SAPROM	Vol. 12: Jamm (La Paix)
1987	SAPROM	Vol. 13: Kocc Barma
1988	SAPROM	Vol. 14: Gainde
1989	SAPROM	Vol. 15: Set
	SAPROM	Vol. 15b: Jamm

Super Diamono. Highly rated manding-rock outfit featuring 'rock-hard guitars' and vocalists Moussaa N'Gom and bandleader Omar Pene. A prolific recording band, there are at least 12 cassettes/LPs from the late 1970s and early 1980s not listed here. One influential graduate is Ismael Lo (see below).

1983	MCA 303	Ndaxami
1984	MEL 8011	Mam
	MAG 105	Geedy Dayaan
1987	ENC 139	People
1989	08530–4	Cheik Anton Diop
1990		Adama N'diaye

Toure Kunda. One of the earliest and best bands to break through in Europe. Paris-based, they enjoyed enormous commercial success in the mid-1980s. Towards the end of the decade they seemed to go through a couple of lean years, blamed on sheer exhaustion after three world tours and hundreds of shows. They returned home in 1988 and recharged their batteries. They added yet another brother, Hamidou, to the line-up, hired a new manager and brought in Nabu Diop as dancer/animateur. They extended their repertoire with new songs each picking out a specific target – farmers, the elderly, etc. They also extended their range to five languages – Wolof, Soninke, Peul, Mandingue and Portuguese Creole, the last possibly with an eye on the market of neighbouring Guinea-Bissau. In 1990 they returned to the limelight with shows as far afield as Morocco and New Caledonia, a warm-up for a planned fourth world tour. In 1990 they set the ball rolling with the excellent album *Salam*, which enjoyed good media coverage and healthy sales in France.

1986	CEL 66804	Best of Toure Kunda (Material drawn from first five albums)
1990		Salam
1991	CEL 66779	1981–82 (Material drawn from CEL 6549 & CEL 6599 – CD)

Konte, Lamine. Highly gifted kora and guitar player equally at home in traditional or modern idioms. (See Volume 1 for complete biography.) His current anonymity in the midst of widespread appreciation for Senegalese music remains a mystery.

1975	ARN 33179	Les Rythmes, Les Percussion et La Voix de Lamine Konte Vol. 1
	ARN 33313	Vol. 2
	ARN 33701	Afrique, Mon Afrique
1977	SAF 50049	Tinque Rinque
1978	SAF 61002	Bako L'Autre Rime
1979	ESP 165530	Baara
	C 20000	Africa, Africa, du Senegal aux Amérique

Diatta, Pascal, and Sona Mane. Diatta, a guitarist, was raised in a mission orphanage. When he became interested in music he tried to build his own guitar, with mixed results. In a 1988 interview with Ian Anderson he revealed that the first effort involved an oil drum and strings made out of bicycle brake cables. The second effort involved a wooden packing case. Eventually he was given a guitar. There then followed a spell in the Army where he acquired the nickname 'Keno' (from the Kenyan athlete) for his athletic talent. On leaving the Army he decided to try to live up to his nickname by becoming the best guitarist in the country. Over the years he has evolved his own unique style, apparently uninfluenced by other local and international styles. He married Sona Mane, developing her vocal style around his own compositions. By the mid-1980s he had developed a considerable reputation in Senegal, playing on radio and the ceremonial circuit of baptisms and weddings. But he was reluctant to record following a bad experience when he agreed to do so for Lyrichord but received no royalties. In 1989 he was persuaded to record and the results can be heard on *Simnade* (Listen!). He also toured the UK with his wife to widespread acclaim. The 1989 recording was made in a Ziguinchor hotel room and

sounds just fine. Ian Anderson, in *Folk Roots* (April 1989), described their style in the following terms:

> This is utterly extraordinary music. Pascal plays guitar unlike any West African I've ever heard. He's got a completely unique two finger/thumb picking technique, pulling out fast, staccato notes and flurrys of runs and riffs . . . Sona Mane sings the lead, pitched much lower than the more Islamic vocals one is used to hearing in West Africa, and Pascal mostly sings harmony.

| 1989 | FMSL 2017 | Simnade |
| 1991 | | Amérique |

Xalam. Nine-piece band who enjoyed considerable international success in the mid- to late 1980s. See Volume 1 for early career.

1979	XPS 001	Festival Horizonte Berlin 79
1986	ENC 134	Apartheid
1988		N'Diguel

Lo, Ismael (b. Niger, grew up Rufisque, near Dakar, Senegal). Described on one set of liner notes as a 'precocious talent', Lo was performing on TV at the age of 15. In the late 1970s he joined Super Diamono, then enjoying a purple patch of creative activity. He then departed for Spain and returned to painting, one of his first loves, cultivated during his art school training. He returned to Senegal in 1984 and released three cassettes in quick succession – *Xalat*, *Xiff* and *Natt*. In 1989 he released his most ambitious set to date in the form of the Sylla-produced *Diawar* which was then licensed to Stern's as a UK release. Ismael handles the lyrics, arrangements, vocals and rhythm guitars but, being in Paris, he called on the special skills of Manu Lima on keyboards, Guy Lobe on drums and Ndjock on rhythm guitar. The result of this studio blend of Senegal and Cameroon was fine and *Diawar* can be considered one of the most finely crafted albums of 1989.

1981	BS 15155-03	Gor Sayina
1986	SYL 8314	Xalat
	CEL 8725	Xiff
1989	ST 1027	Diawar (Also 38759)
1990	38740	Natt (Double)
1991		Mbalax New Look

Maal, Baaba (b. Podor, N. Senegal). Born into Toucouleur society, Baba did not come from a griot family but his awareness of the specific Toucouleur contribution to Senegalese society is evident from the name he gave his band – Dande Lenol (Voice of the People). He started out as a law student but was soon involved with the traditional musicians who formed the group Lasli Fouta. In 1984 he recorded the cassette *Djam Leeli* with friend and guitarist Mansour Seck, supported by electric guitar, percussion and balafon. In 1985 he formed Dande Lenol to give a more electric presentation of his music and followed up in fine style with two Sylla productions. Regarded as a progressive intellectual, by 1990 Baaba Maal was considered to be second only to Youssou N'Dour in terms of popularity in Senegal. He then toured the US with Mansour Seck and Dande Lenol, following up with his third visit to the UK, feeling more comfortable every time. In an illuminating interview with Mwana Musa (*African Connection*), Baaba outlined his personal agenda.

I see the world differently. I have got to know and understand a lot of things we take for granted eg. about pollution, about the hypocrisies of Western nations, the idiocy of Africa's fancy politics, above all the bonds that hold everyone together. My band is more democratic . . . the music is more compact, a little of what people may say is reggae, jazz, the lot. Basically the bringing back of African music that my people took away to the new world all those years ago . . . . I have to do a lot of research about our music and African sensibility to diffuse an otherwise complex situation. . . . I am not interested in this social group or that social group. I am a Senegalese and an African and that is enough.

In 1989 Baaba toured the UK with Mansour Seck, performing a number of live shows and appearing on the acclaimed TV series 'Rhythms of the World'. His 1990 LP *Taara* was quoted as having surpassed the heights of *Wango* with Baaba supported on vinyl by Sidiki Youyate on bass and Patrick Ripper on lead guitar. In that same year Baaba Maal signed with Mango/Island, under the benign guiding hand of ex-Earthworks supremo Jumbo Van Renen. The band's attitude was one of, 'well we've done our bit, now it's up to you'. The first release was entitled *Génération Nouvelle*. Sadly, during the 1989 UK tour Mansour Seck was diagnosed as suffering from a hereditary blindness.

Baaba strikes audiences as being someone rooted in tradition but fully attuned to changes both in his own society and in Europe. His 1991 all-format release was a return to the acoustic style with the brilliant support of Mansour Seck. Baaba Maal has also released a number of local cassettes. They will be extremely hard to track down.

1970s		+ Mansour Seck: Danniige
		+ Mansour Seck: Elimaan Buurbarkan
		Vol. 2: Yela
		Vol. 3
		Vol. 4: Wandana
		Vol. 5: Yar Leeli
1984	FMSL 2014	Djam Leeli (With Mansour Seck, re-released 1989)
1987	ST 2007	Suka Naayo
1988	SYL 8348	Wanga
1990	SYL 8359	Taara
	MLPS 1061	Génération Nouvelle
	ST 2006	Ndilane
1991	MLPS 1061	Baayo

Diop, Idrissa. Master percussionist with the ability to play in a number of styles. The *Femme Noir* album, for example, is an electro-jazz fusion featuring percussion and electric balafon.

LK 0188	Femme Noir

Suso, Foday Musa. A personal favourite from the days when we were neighbours at South Legon in Ghana, Suso seems to go from strength to strength. After several fine albums on the US Flying Fish label, Suso entered the mid-1980s with an enormous reputation in the USA which led him to work with Herbie Hancock. They collaborated throughout 1984–6 and co-wrote the theme song for the 1986 Los Angeles Olympics, 'Junka'. In 1985 they also released an album together entitled *Village Life*. Then two countrymen – both musicians of high renown in Gambia – arrived in New York and contacted Suso, still based in Chicago. Suso told Flying Fish that the singer Tamba Suso and kora master Jarju Kuyateh were what they claimed to be and that recording time should be arranged for a real roots–kora collaboration. They went into the studio on New Year's Day 1986 and recorded the delightful LP listed below. His next studio outing came in 1990 when *Dreamtime* was recorded. More New York overdub than Gambian kora, Musa continues to sail in uncharted waters.

1978	FF 076	Mandingo Griot Society (With Don Cherry)
1980	FF 269	Mighty Rhythm
1984	CEL 6103	Watto Sitta
1985	CBS	Village Life (With Herbie Hancock)
	FF 318	Hand Power

| 1986 | FF 380 | Mansa Bendeng |
| 1991 | CMPCD 3001 | Dreamtime |

Adioa. Reggae-influenced big band, made a notable signing with Mango Records in 1989. This was the band responsible for the Sahel-Reggae epic 'Toubab Bile'. Led by Maxidilick Adioa on vocals and percussion.

| 1990 | MLPS 1013 | Soweto Man |

Soumono, Hadja

| 1988 | SYL | Hadja Soumono |

Kibwe

| | MO | Cassamance |

Lam, Kine (b. Dakar). Kine was born into a griot family and started performing as a child. In 1979 she joined the Daniel Sorano National Theatre as leading female vocalist and for the next few years performed at numerous official functions. She is now famous as the first female vocalist to challenge the men on their own ground.

| 1989 | 38764 | Cheickh Anta Mbacke |

Niang, Paap. Mid-1980s Senegalese reggae in the 'Lover's Rock' style. Ably supported by Rykiel and members of Xalam.

| 1986 | ENC 137 | Saxal Garap |

N'diaye, Ouzin. A very good singer who graduated from Le Super Etoile. Assistance on vocals from Youssou himself.

| 1988 | CEL 6812 | Autorail |

Rose, Dudu N'Diaye. Traditional percussionist with an enormous reputation and much in demand for studio work. Not content with a musical family, he directs the lives of an entire musical village.

| 1988 | ENC | Sabar |

N'Jie, Ousu. Veteran keyboard player and drummer who played with the Gulewars in the late 1970s before settling in Norway in the mid-1980s. His 1988 album features a Norwegian backing band for his afro-reggae music.

| 1988 | KKB 001 | Right Direction (With Kunte Kinte Band) |

Ifang Bondi. Meaning 'Be Yourself', Ifang Bondi grew out of the former Gambia band called the Super Eagles. As such they have been credited to be the true originators of the current 'Afro-Manding' sound as extemporised by stars such as Youssou N'Dour, Salif Keïta and Mory Kante – a trio who between them are representative of the 'Golden Triangle' as mined by Western record companies. The Super Eagles were formed in 1967 and toured Ghana in 1968, making an enormous impact with their very African sound in a country which was shortly to produce Osibisa. Their debut album came in 1972 featuring an exciting mix of cha cha chas, highlifes, pachangas, boleros, funk, soul, rumba and even a cover version of 'Hey Jude'. The band was enormously influential along the West African coast, transcending linguistic and stylistic boundaries. They disbanded in 1972 only to rise again from the ashes, as Ifang Bondi, in 1974. The name was new as was the sound, featuring for the first time indigenous Senegambian rhythms, melodies and instruments. Two LPs followed in quick succession as the band sought to consolidate the progressive African ground so recently developed. In 1990 Ifang Bondi toured the UK supported by London-based African Dawn. They received the anticipated critical acclaim.

1972	250 069	Super Eagles: Viva
1976	GR 7603	Saraba
1982	MAG 107	Sanio
1983	LPH 2366	Mantra
1991	CDDK 860017	Sanyo (CD release)

Senemali. Santana-influenced Senegalese rock group. First international release on Dutch label.

| 1989 | 1150221 | Africa |

Various. In 1989, Martin Scorsese, film producer, unveiled his latest masterpiece entitled *The Last Temptation of Christ*. Peter Gabriel scored the music, which duly appeared as an LP on his Real World label. The soundtrack featured music by both Youssou N'Dour and Baaba Maal.

| 1989 | RWLP | Passion Sources |

7   Mali

(ECONOMY AND SOCIETY. Pop.: 8.5 million.
Area: 1,240,000 sq. km. Capital: Bamako.
Independence: 1960. Currency: CFA franc.)

The independent country of Mali took its name from
the medieval Sudanic empire founded by Sundiata and
remains in the forefront of African countries who retain
a vibrant and fertile relationship with their pre-colonial
past. Independence came in 1960, after which Mali was
led by the charismatic president, Modibo Keïta until
his overthrow in a 1968 coup. Until then, Mali was
known as a proud but poor country, loosely aligned to
the Soviet bloc and prepared to play a leading role in
pan-African and regional affairs. The 1968 coup, led by
Lt Moussa Traoré, ushered in two decades of one-party
rule under the UPDM. It proved to be a system of
'imposition and endurance' until Traoré was himself
deposed in a 1991 army takeover following serious
rioting by pro-democracy groups. This was not the first
time that Bamako had been rocked by civil distur-
bance – the regime had been badly shaken in 1977 by
riots following the death of ex-president Keïta in
prison.

The Malian economy has always been one of the
weakest in independent Africa – landlocked, largely
infertile and resource-poor. However, the externally
imposed structural adjustment policies of the 1980s did
little to improve the situation and by the end of the

decade Mali was officially one of the poorest fifteen
countries in the world.

MUSIC AND SOCIETY

In few other countries does the concept of the
urban–bush continuum have greater applicability than
in Mali. Possibly because of the jali–griot tradition,
Mali has produced and continues to produce an
enormous number of musicians with complete mastery of instruments, styles and traditions. Inevitably
many have moved into more modern expressions of
tradition but almost without exception they have been
able to creatively incorporate more traditional idioms
into their modern repertoire. This sense of feeling at
home in either tradition has created space in the Malian
music scene for musicians to switch with consummate
ease from old to new. Thus Keletigui Diabate plays
with Salif Keïta, Kasse Mady switches at will and Ali
Farka Toure is comfortable with blues and rock stars
from well beyond the borders of Mali. An important
dimension of Malian culture revolves around the
Jatigui – wealthy patrons who over centuries have
assumed the responsibility of supporting traditional
musicians.

TRADITIONAL MUSIC

There are two basic styles of Malian music – Manding
and Bambara. However, there is also a deeper and
more significant division between male and female.
Essentially men are musicians and women are singers.
The boundaries are of course flexible but Lucy Duran
has argued that women, whether singing, clapping or
keeping time on the 'nege', are the real stars of Malian
music. They 'animate' the music, sell more cassettes
and are favoured for praise singing. During the 1980s
female singers working in a number of styles and
drawing on both Fula and Manding traditions rose to
prominence, although this was not reflected in western
markets until the end of the decade. Up until then,
observers could have been forgiven for assuming that
male stars and big dance bands dominated the
domestic scene. By the early 1990s over half a dozen
female stars had released albums which were widely
available outside Mali, reflecting a wider appreciation
of the emotive power of the female voice and the

59

growing appeal of all Sahelian styles and traditions. In response to this growing appeal, we have increased the size of the discography of traditional Malian music, incorporating titles listed in Volume 1 and including many additional titles which are unlikely to be available but may be useful for the determined collector of Mali music.

1960s	LDS 8246	Au Coeur du Sudan
	LDS 74596	Math Samba
	C 469	Avec les Seigneurs des Sables – Les Touareg
	VP 8326	Epic, Historical, Political and Propaganda Songs of the Government of Modibo Keïta Vol. 1
	VP 8327	Vol. 2
1970	BM 30L 2501	Le Mali des Steppes et Savanes
	BM 30L 2502	Le Mali du Fleuves – Les Peuls
	BM 30L 2503	Le Mali des Sables – Les Songoy
	BM 30L 2504	L'Ensemble Instrumentale du Mali
	BM 30L 2651	Troupes Artistiques
1970s	VOX DN2	Segou Bourama
	VOX VP1	Chants de Culture
	VOX GT3	Danses des Diables
	BAMLD 5750	Tombouctou la Mystérieuse
	BAMLD 5772	Folklore et Musique de Mali
	DAD 501	Brahima Daugoune/ Bintou Sarre
	DAD 503	Brahima Daugoune/ Bintou Sarre
	DAD 505	Brahima Daugoune/ Bintou Sarre
	360 059	Koni Coumare et Fotigui Diabate
	F 51270	Koni Coumare et Fotigui Diabate
	F 51271	Koni Coumare et Fotigui Diabate
	FE 4338	Music of Mali
	FE 4470	Taureg Music of Southern Sahara
	KO 770410	Soundiata, L'Epopée Mandingue
	KO 770411	Dah Monzon, L'Epopée Bambara
	KO 770412	L'Ensemble Instrumental du Mali
	KO 770415	Le Kanaga de Mopti
	KO 770418	Sidi Yassa
	OCR 33	Les Dogon
1980s	OCR 662/663	Ousmane Sacko/Yiakare Diabate
1988	SYL 8370	Koni Coumare: Bazoumanaba (Cass.)

For serious collectors, these exemplary early recordings appear on the following labels: Bareinreiter-Musicaphon, Africa Vox, Boîte à Musique, Chant du Monde, Disque Alvares, Djima, Albatross, Fiesta, Folkways, Konkan, Musidisc, Ocora, Son Afrique and Songhai.

Female vocalists

Damba, Fanta (b. Segou, 1938). Known to her many admirers as 'La Grande Vedette Malienne', Fanta was born into a well-known family of griots. Singing in Bambara, she started recording in the 1960s and soon became one of the leading interpreters of Mali's traditions. By the end of the 1960s she had released many singles and had become both a regional and national star. She formed her own group in 1975 and was often accompanied on stage by daughters Nana and Aminata. She has recorded with the cream of Malian kora and guitar players and, whether singing solo or accompanied, remains a legendary figure with a considerable recorded output. She appeared at FESTAC (Festival of African Culture, Lagos) in 1977, and has influenced performers as diverse as kora player Dembo Konte and Senegalese superstar Youssou N'Dour. With a stark and powerful voice, Fanta has been described as 'a singer's singer' with a vast repertoire of traditional songs. In 1985 she made a pilgrimage to Mecca and retired from public performance.

1960s	BM 30L 2506		La Tradition Epique
1970s	SON 8201		Loterie Nationale
	SON 8202		Hamet
	SON 8205		Ousmane Bamara
	KLP 1041		Mamaya
1980s	SON 8210		Samega
1982	CEL 6637		Bahamadou Simogo
1983	KS 099		Fanta Damba (Cass.)
1986	ESP 7518		Mamadou Magadji

Sacko, Fanta (b. Kankan, Guinea, into a Malian family with Gambian connections). Her father was an accomplished kora player related to both Sidiki Diabate and Amadu Bansang. As a child she maintained an interest in Guinean music and followed the early efforts of Fodeba Keïta and Kante Facelli to update traditional Guinean themes. She was also influenced by legendary singer Sory Kandia Kouyate (see Guinea) and began to extemporise around lyrics and melodies of Sory Kandia. By the early 1960s she had established a new trend in female singing – love songs. Her style was dismissed by older, more traditional stars but with her hit song 'Jarabi' she became a firm favourite of the masses. However, unlike her great rival Fanta Damba, Fanta Sacko found it difficult to reconcile a musical career with her large family and she has made only one record. In a 1986 interview with Lucy Duran she had this to say about that occasion in 1970: 'They came to my house to record me, and since it was the government, I trusted them and gave them my best. I sang Jarabi, Tita and Jimbe Wata Dabola, my most famous songs. I was promised that the royalties would be split between me and the government but to this day I have never received anything.' Twenty years later, her one and only recording is still available, testifying to the importance of her contribution and the timeless appeal of her music. She remained much in demand throughout the 1970s, singing locally for private and state functions, but her popularity waned towards the end of the decade and by the mid-1980s she had virtually retired from performing following an overdose of mercury-based skin bleach.

1970s	BM 30L 2551	Musique du Mali

Kouyate, Tata Bambo (b. Bamako, late 1940s). Born into a well-known family of Jalis (hereditary Manding musicians), she started singing as a child. In the 1960s she joined the Mali National Ensemble, travelling with them to the 1967 Pan-African Music Festival in Algiers. Her first big hit was 'Bamba', which provided her nickname. She was now one of Mali's most popular singers and travelled all over Africa at the invitation of homesick Malian patrons. During one of these trips she came to the attention of wealthy patron Babani Cissoko, who followed her to Paris in 1984 and for whom she recorded her greatest hit, 'Hommage à Baba Cissoko', assisted by Keletigui Diabate on balafon and violin. Her repertoire ranges from Manding classics to current praise songs of patrons and friends – the Jatigui who for centuries have sponsored Malian culture. Her voice has been aptly described as 'hot, gritty and full of passion'. The 1989 Globestyle album is a delightful re-issue of the 1984 Paris recording. She has also released a great deal of music on cassette only – a format which rarely arrives in western shops. On the 1988 release *Djely Mousso* Tata Bambo switches from traditional instrumentation and style to a more contemporary approach featuring synth, electronic drums and bass guitar to augment the traditional fiddle – ngoni. Produced by Boncana Maiga, the album succeeds in proving that in the hands of truly gifted musicians old and new can mix.

1988	SYL 8360	Djely Mousso
1989	ORB 042	Jatigui (Also Hommage)

Koita, Ami (b. Kirina, 1952). Contemporary of Tata Bambo, and born into a family of griots. Surrounded by music, she started singing in Mandinke with a slightly more modern feel than her rival. Both have worked in traditional idioms and modern studio settings, attempting hi-tech cross-overs towards the end of the 1980s. In 1991 Ami Koita toured the UK to great critical acclaim.

1983	KS 1461	Hire Mansa (Cass.)
1989	ESP 7517	Debe
	BM 89	Beny Mariko (Cass.)
	42079	Tata Sira
1990		Mory Jo
		Nakar

Diabate, Nahini (b. Mali, late 1960s). Nahini is equally at home with either a traditional balafon–kora accompaniment or with her own large dance band. In the same fashion, she is equally comfortable on stage performing electric Manding music or in more traditional settings performing praise songs at weddings, baptisms and other social functions. A fairly new arrival on the scene, she has yet to make solo recordings, appearing only on a local compilation cassette.

Doumbia, Nahawa (b. Bougouni, Sikasso Region). Nahawa has enjoyed a rapid rise to fame. Orphaned at an early age, her career blossomed after winning first prize in the 1982 Biennalle Artistique. In 1983 she followed up by winning first prize in Radio France Internationale's Découverte category. The following year she was entertaining heads of state at the France–Afrique Summit Meeting. In 1988 she released her first European LP with the help of producer Boncana Maiga. The Stern's release features the skills of Rigo Star and a clutch of Cameroonian session men, once again co-ordinated by Maiga. An astounding album, it will surely stand the test of time and fashion. Unlike many of her contemporaries, Nahawa is firmly fixed in the modern dance-orientated idiom – a change which occurred when she moved to Bamako in the early 1980s. Unlike the hereditary Jalis (Damba, Sacko, Tata Kouyate and Nahini Diabate), Nahawa operates in a different tradition – that of the Fula, where music is not a hereditary profession.

1980	AS 005	Vol. 1: Djankonia
1981	AS 006	Vol. 2: Sakoro-Mery
1983		Vol. 3: Korodia
1988	SYL 8337	Didadi
1990	ST 1033	Nyama Toutou

Sangare, Oumou (b. Wassoulou Region, 1968). In 1989 she travelled to Abidjan to record her first LP at the JBZ studio at the behest of top producer and promoter Ibrahima Sylla. The result was a cassette which reportedly shifted 160,000 copies in Mali and the rest of West Africa. Featuring traditional instruments and electric bass, the cassette-only (African) release stunned audiences with songs of life and love, jealousy, tradition and the position of women in contemporary Malian society. A circuitous licensing deal from Sylla to Stern's and on to World Circuit brought the album to UK audiences where initial sales were extremely good. The excellent *Diaraby Nene* was subsequently extracted to appear on Stern's *Women of Wassoulou* compilation (ST 1035).

| 1988 | Cass. | Djama Kaissoumou |
| 1990 | WCB 021 | Moussoulou |

Kouyate, Kandia (b. Kita, 1958). Born into a musical family, Kandia's powerful and beautiful voice became increasingly popular during the mid-1980s. She started her career singing with the National Ensemble before forming her own group in the early 1980s – one which included rising kora virtuoso Toumani Diabate and guitarist Bouba Sacko. With the ability to draw from classic praise songs and her own compositions, Kandia's music also varied from traditional Kita melodies to the kora music of Senegambia. In 1985 she recorded a cassette in Abidjan featuring the song 'Maimouna Sarama', which made her nationally famous and brought her to the attention of patron Baba Cissoko, who took over as her principal sponsor. Since 1987 most of her material has been devoted to the generosity of Cissoko. She became immensely wealthy, splitting her time between Mali, France and Gabon (where Cissoko lived prior to his loss of fortune).

| 1985 | Cass. only | Amary Dou présente K. Kouyate |
| 1987 | BM 88 | Project Dabia (Cass.) |

Sidibi, Coumba. Another new name for Maliphiles to digest. Cassette-only releases until two songs were extracted for the Stern's sampler.

| 1988 | SYL 8352 | Gnogonte |
| 1990 | | Tche Kan'wele |

Sidibi, Sali. Like Nahawa Doumbia, Sali operates in the Wassoulou 'Didadi' tradition without attempting the studio sophistication of Nahawa. None the less she experiments with new and traditional acoustic instruments, tackling contemporary social issues rather than the praise song tradition of the Jalis or the proverbs and metaphors of Nahawa. Little recorded output to date and what there is is seldom available outside Mali, with the honourable exception of two tracks on ST 1035.

1980	006	Vol. 1
1982	STA 835	Formidable
1988	SYL 8362	Toukan Magni (Cass.)
1990		N'Dia

Others

1985	IS 56	Oumou Kouyate: Kala Djoula
1987	SYL 8346	Sadia Kouyate: Madiou Bana
1988	SYL 8371	Ma Damba: Pory
	SYL 8365	Sadio Diabate: Djouba Kamale
1991	ST 1035	Various: The Wassoulou Sound (Excellent compilation featuring three Sidibes, Oumou Sangare and Dienaba Diakite)

Male instrumentalists

Diabate, Keletigui (b. 1930, Kita, Mali). Seminal balafon player who, as one of these rare master musicians who can also turn his hand to trombone, violin and saxophone, exemplifies the Malian ability to create genuinely stunning new sounds. Keletigui grew up in the musical town of Kita, second capital of fourteenth-century Mali empire. Inhabited by hundreds of singers, musicians, dancers and griots, Keletigui recalls seeing Balani Diawara perform in Kita with over 100 female singers responding.

As a child, Keletigui fashioned his own balafon before being taken under the wing of his first master, Bandiou, who taught him to play the instrument correctly. Having mastered the balafon, Keletigui moved on to modern European instruments, explaining that in modern situations like hotels he felt the balafon alone risked becoming boring to modern urban audiences. Over the years he added various new instruments to his armoury, learning them all by ear. Between 1957 and 1961 Keletigui was based in neighbouring Guinea where he first tried to mix old and new while working with the band of the National Guard. In time, the Orchestre de La Garde Republicaine became Guinea's top band, only relinquishing the title when the incomparable Bembeya Jazz appeared. By the 1960s he was back in Bamako and was immediately put in charge of the Orchestre National No. 1. He directly set about introducing both Bambara and Manding material to the modern electric band. 'At that time [the early 1960s] we received delegations from Europe, or other African countries, and at such occasions we'd perform our traditional ceremonies. Each time we received a European delegation . . . they couldn't dance our traditional dances. So we had to find international rhythms and put our traditional sound within that' (*Folk Roots*, August 1989).

During this period Keletigui was also involved with the National Ensemble Instrumental, which brought together musicians from all ethnic groups. In this way he widened his musical horizons and mastered a wide variety of styles. With the Orchestre National, he played guitar and arranged the horn parts. Years later he played with Lionel Hampton in Washington. They exchanged instruments, balafon for vibes: 'We played together like that. That night made a great impression on me. I'll never forget it.' Throughout the 1960s he remained in great demand and worked with a number of other bands and musicians, including Sidiki Diabate with whom he toured Africa. He also played with the various regional state bands and in the 1970s toured West Africa with the Ambassadeurs, including two later stars – Salif Keïta and Kante Manfila. By the 1980s he was playing and recording with Amy Koita, Tata Bambo, Toumani Diabate and Salif Keïta.

Diabate, Sidiki, et son Ensemble. The group was formed in 1987 to perform in the BBC Radio 3 documentary 'Music of the Royal Courts'. Sidiki was born in the Gambia in the late 1920s and grew up in Mali, home of his parents. A founder-member of the Instrumental Ensemble of Mali, he has been decorated by both Guinea and Mali. Featuring two koras, balafon and three female backing vocalists the Ensemble play in the cool Malian style described by one critic as 'stunning. . . . The interlocking rhythms and call and response between the instruments are seductive and the vocals are fiery.' Sidiki is considered to be Mali's greatest kora player.

| 1977 | SAF 50077 | Rythmes et Chants du Mali |
| 1987 | FMS/NSA 001 | Ba Togomba: Manding Music |

Kouyate, Sekou Batorou. One of the most famous of all Malian kora players.

1960s	BM 30L 2505	Cordes Anciennes
	KR 28	Keme Bourama
1976	KLP 1041	Mamaya

Diabate, Toumani. Son of Sidiki, Toumani was raised in a family of incredible musical pedigree. Born in 1965, Toumani listened to a wide range of music while growing up and later incorporated much of it into his kora repertoire. His first solo recording received enthusiastic reviews. In 1989 he returned to the UK and linked up with double bassist Danny Thompson and members of Ketama, the Spanish flamenco outfit, for a fruitful collaboration on stage and in the studio. The resulting LP – *Songhai* – was a critical success, 'a delight with the odd stunning moment'.

| 1988 | HNBL 1338 | Kaira |
| 1989 | HNBL 1323 | Songhai |

MODERN MUSIC

The modern music of Mali reached an early apogee with the popular success of the big state regional 'orchestres'. Six excellent albums from 1970 demonstrate the power and range of the regional bands. External influences included the Latin/Cuban sounds mediated through Senegal while Ghanaian horn arrangements emerged from the cultural diffusion spawned by the early regional grouping of Ghana,

Guinea and Mali – a pan-African political union brought into being through the foresight of Presidents Nkrumah, Toure and Keïta.

The 1960s were the highpoint of state-sponsored cultural development in West Africa and Mali seemed to go further than most in actually placing instruments in the hands of traditional jalis as well as up-and-coming youth groups. Out of this melting-pot of tradition, external influences and government support emerged one of the most vibrant musical scenes on the continent. Choice tracks from the five albums itemised below were later selected and re-released on an excellent introductory album sponsored by the Government of Mali and Stern's in 1988.

By the 1970s the state bands were at their peak, spawning many individual stars who later carried Malian music to the rest of the world. But by the 1980s the situation of the big bands was precarious, reflecting the decline of the economy and mirroring the experience of state-sponsored and big dance bands in Ghana, Tanzania and Guinea. The bands were expensive to support, they required regular injections of new equipment and, above all, they required viable venues. They remained popular but gigs were few and far between and most musicians had to take day-jobs to make ends meet. Malians returned to traditional styles for entertainment and the 1980s witnessed an enormous growth in popularity for both established traditional stars and dozens of new female singers.

1970s	BM 30L 2601	Orchestre Régional de Segou
	BM 30L 2602	Orchestre Régional de Mopti
	BM 30L 2603	Orchestre Régional de Sikasso
	BM 30L 2604	Orchestre Régional de Kayes
	BM 30L 2605	L'Orchestre National
1977	KO 770416	Kene Star de Mopti
	KO 770417	Mystère Jazz de Tombouctou
1988	ST 3001	Mali Music: Legendary Bands

Bamba, Sory (b. Mopti, 1941). Regarded as the moderniser of Dogon folklore, Sory specialises in setting folk traditions to modern instruments and arrangements.

1960s	P 79-098	Sory
1977	SON 8203	Faux Galant
	SON 8206	Yayoroba

1979	SAF 50097	Mayal
	360195	Sigui
1987	BP 15	Le Tonnerre Dogon

Toure, Ali Farka (b. Gourmararusse, Mali, 1939). Ali spent his early years in the village of his birth before moving with his mother to Nefenque near Timbuktou in 1946. He was enrolled in school but didn't quite fit in and switched to the more informal Koranic school. In 1949–50 he picked up the monocorde, the traditional guitar, but had no ambitions for a musical career and played simply for pleasure. Not for the first time in Africa, Ali's family objected to his musical interests and he was forbidden to play. He did not return to music until 1957 when he became interested in the guitar. He was given a few lessons by the local nurse and decided to make his way to Bamako for the bi-annual youth event, a musical gathering where each region demonstrated its unique sound. Ali now began to make a name for himself and over the next decade he became known throughout Mali. He also followed a variety of careers including a spell as a chauffeur and later as a sound engineer. In 1971 he was transferred to Bamako as a radio operator. During these years he was able to travel with his music and during the late 1960s and 1970s visited Bulgaria, Hungary, Czechoslovakia, Turkey, Finland and finally Paris. He also started recording, releasing six LPs between 1976 and 1985. The experience left him bitter about the music business with his full wrath being reserved for a particular French record producer. In a *Folk Roots* interview, he explained:

> I was made a fool of . . . he has been very well looked after out of all this. If I could see him today I'd change his skin into drops of water, cut his throat and make mincemeat out of him. But now he's doing fine in a country where I can't reach him. If he came to Africa he'd be eaten alive, in broad daylight! I've been abused and used in order to give them material wealth. It's the mafia, the world of the mafia.

Strong stuff but sadly such feelings and experiences are not unusual in the world of African music. None the less, Ali's records were gradually becoming available and several people began to pick up on the unique Toure style, always and instantaneously comparing Ali to the great blues guitarist John Lee Hooker. It was the affinity of the Toure sound to the blues which in turn stimulated radio play and in 1987 Arts Worldwide set off to Mali to track him down. In time he was located and duly arrived in London late in 1987 for some shows and another attempt to record; the first London LP was released in 1988. His music and his forthright style made him an instant success and he returned to the UK that same year for a further series of shows. In 1989 he was back again to record his second World Circuit LP, *The River*. More recently his name has been linked with various American guitarists in what could be one of the great musical cross-overs.

1970s	SAF 50013	Bandolobourou
1976	SAF 50016	Ali Farka Toure
	SAF 50020	Special
1977	SAF 50032	Biennale
	SAF 50060	Yer Sabou Yerkoy
1979	SAF 50085	Banga
1984	ESP 165558	La Drogue
1987	WCB 007	Ali Farka Toure
1988	ESP 8448	Sidy Gouro
1990	WCB 017	The River

Ambassadeurs. Big band from Mali formed in the early 1970s and now one of the legendary outfits in the African music world. Many gifted individuals have drifted through the ranks, including Salif Keïta and Kante Manfila. The band recorded prolifically and toured widely in Francophone West Africa, reaching a zenith of popularity and performance towards the end of the 1970s. By the 1980s, life was proving more difficult for large dance bands everywhere and, despite the change to Ambassadeurs Internationaux in the early 1980s, the band's fortunes were clearly on the decline. Please refer to Volume 1 for a more detailed history of the band.

1975		Live
1977	SAF 50014	Les Ambassadeurs du Motel
	SAF 50030	Yassoumouka Vol. 1
	SAF 50031	Vol. 2
	CEL 6635	Djougouya
	CEL 6640	Best of Ambassadeurs
	CEL 6717	Tounkan
	CEL 6721	Mandjou
1981	SP 002	Mani Mani
1984	DS 7986	Les Ambassadeurs Internationaux
1989	ROUND 5013	Re-release of CEL 6640

Rail Band. Formed in 1970 by the Ministry of Information, the incomparable Rail Band were (and still are) the most famous and most respected of the Mali big bands. With the help of the Hotels Division of the National Railway Company, the band secured their famous venue at the Buffet de La Gare, Bamoko, where they still perform on Saturday nights. They adapted traditional instruments and rhythms to the demands of modern urban pop music, singing in Bambara and reaching audiences far beyond Bamako. Like the Ambassadeurs, the Rail Band also acted as a training school and have seen many present-day celebrities pass through their ranks. The band, with state assistance and an international reputation, are one of the few outfits to have survived the economic ravages of the 1980s intact and are now generally regarded as a national cultural institution. Throughout the 1980s they continued to attract a new generation of admirers with music for the most part recorded in the 1970s. Some fans were simply digging deeper into the music of Keïta and Kante but in the main it was the timeless appeal of the band's music which lay behind their popularity. Neither were companies slow to cash in on the Rail Band's continuing commercial appeal. In 1989 Sylla re-released the 1977 classic *Wale Numa*, from the period when Keïta had left but Kante was there on balafon and guitar. A few of their best recordings are still available but personal favourites (HNLX series – recorded during a tour of Nigeria) are sadly seldom seen.

1970	BM 30L 3606	Orchestre Rail-Band de Bamako
1970s	RCAHNS 1582	Orchestre Rail-Band
	RCAM 013373	Rail-Band: Buffet Hotel
1975	HNLX 5146	Soundiata
	HNLX 5147	Rail-Band
	HNLX 5148	Rail-Band
	HNLX 5149	Rail-Band
	HNLX 5150	Rail-Band
	HNLX 5151	Rail-Band
	KLP 1040	Kandoun
	KLP 1042	Concert Rail Band
	KLP 1043	Melodias Rail Band
1979	LS 24	L'Orchestre Super Rail Band
	LS 25	Affair Social
1983	KS 223	Djali Madi Toukara & Rail Band (Cass.)
1985	ORB 001	New Dimensions in Rail Culture
1989	SYL 8378	Wale Numa Lombaliya

Keïta, Salif (b. Djoliba). Salif is now one of the top half-dozen African stars. Please consult Volume 1 for details of his early career. Following the massive success of *Soro*, Salif found himself in incredible demand over the next few years. He had been based in Europe since 1984 so was well placed to exploit his creative success. He toured the UK in 1987 and signed to the Mango subsidiary of Island Records the following year. In August 1988 Stern's released a 7" single taken from *Soro* and later that year Salif found himself in Greece, recording alongside Eleni Demas for her CBS Greece album. He also starred at the Montreux Jazz festival. In 1989 he released the follow-up to *Soro* – a slightly weaker effort entitled *Ko-Yan*. It had taken four months to record and sought to balance traditional elements with the hi-tech production of its predecessor. It was described at the time as pan-African music with a Manding feel, although Mango boss Jumbo Van Renen felt it to be 'too neat, too smooth and too rounded off'. But sales were good with 5,000 copies exchanging hands in the first few days. Salif toured extensively in support of the LP, including shows in London, before returning to the studio with a new all-African band. The critics were harsh with *Ko-Yan*, the general feeling being that Salif had become 'too western' in approach. Whether his return to a Malian band for support indicated that Salif took these criticisms on board, or whether he was simply continuing his search for musical expression, must remain to be seen. In 1991 the result of another lengthy studio effort was unveiled in the form of *Amen*, once more an eclectic collaborative collection, put together with the help of jazz men Joe Zawinul and Wayne Shorter with guitar work on some of the tracks courtesy of Carlos Santana. In an interview in *Folk Roots* (October 1991) Salif revealed that he may end up living in the US, having become disillusioned with Paris and unsure of the changes European unification would bring in 1992. He also appears unsure of his direction, wondering whether the failure of an African star really to succeed in the wider pop world was due to European indifference 'or the record companies not investing enough in the artistes, or whether it's the fault of the musicians themselves, because they are not open enough in artistic terms to other sounds to maintain a career. One year it's Manding, the next year it's South African. There is no cohesion.' Several years ago, in the first flush of Kante–Keïta enthusiasm, Salif was keen to recommend countrymen to various record companies. Now he states that 'A record company is like a sling shot – the artiste is the stone. If the stone isn't strong enough, it crumbles when it lands.'

1987	ST 1020	Soro (Also 240751)
1989	MLPS 1002	Ko-Yan
1991	MLPS 1037	Amen
	083 146	Salif Keïta Live (Video)

Super Djata. Led by guitarist Zani Diabate (b. 1947). Born into a griot family, Zani learned guitar/kora/balafon as a child. He joined the National Ballet du Mali in 1969 but soon moved on to form the Super Djata Band. A completely original guitarist, Zani has captured western attention with his unique style, transposing old into new, melodies into a new instrumental arrangements, almost at will. He toured the UK in 1989 and featured at length on the BBC 2 series 'Under African Skies'.

	ABC 1019	Black Power
1981		En Super Forme Vol. 1
1982		Vol. 2
1985	MM 851001	Super Djata
	ILPS 9899	Super Djata
1988	CID 9899	(Re-release of ILPS 9899)

Super Biton. Formed in 1952, the Bamako-based Bambara stars were regular prize-winners in music festivals throughout the 1960s. A big band featuring brass, guitars, drums, synths, they play up-tempo Bambara-derived rhythms to the obvious delight of listeners. In the early 1980s they toured Europe on several occasions under the leadership of trumpeter Madaou Ba. By the late 1980s they were one of the few big bands still in business.

1970s	38749	Taasi Doni
	38766	Nyangaran Foli
	KO 770413	Super Biton de Segou
	KO 770414	Super Biton de Segou
	TK 1167	+ M. Dumbiya: Nyeleni
1983	TAN 7008	Balandzan
1986	BP 13	Afro-Jazz du Mali
1988	BM 91	Folikan
	SYL 8358	Taasi Doni (Re-release)

National Badema. Highly regarded big band who acted as the official state band in the 1970s and who were an early home to Kasse Mady.

	38748	Tira Makan
1983	38767	Nama & Kasse Mady (Cass. KS 278)

Kasse Mady (b. 1955, Kasse Mady Diabate, Kela, S.W. Mali). Kasse Mady was born into the griot tradition and as a youth joined his first band in Kangama. Traditional instruments were provided by the village headman and the group began to perform at local fêtes and weddings. But the talent of Kasse had been spotted by powerful men in Bamako and although he had settled into a farming career he was eventually persuaded to give it up and join Orchestre (i.e. National) Badema as singer. In retrospect he has few doubts about the wisdom of his decision:

> You see in the beginning I was both; 50% farmer and 50% musician. So I said to myself, I can become a good farmer but there is no future in it for me or my family . . . with music, I was sure that one day it would work out better for me than to stay in the village. So I don't have any regrets. Now, I'm proud of being a musician. (*Folk Roots*, March 1990)

So in 1972, at the age of 17 Kasse moved to Bamako and for the next 12 years remained with Orchestre Badema as lead singer. They made several recordings, the last being *Nama* in 1983. Badema was a state-sponsored band which used modern electric instruments as well as the traditional instruments familiar to Kasse. There is a rumour that Kasse was obliged to join National Badema on the insistence of President Traoré. He departed Badema in 1983 determined to pursue a solo career and over the next few years put together a band which was able to blend past and present in what critics described as a truly cosmic fashion. By the late 1980s Kasse was ready to cash in on his enormous overseas reputation and duly arrived in Europe to make some of the best albums of the decade. *Fode* in 1989 set the stage; a stunning LP produced by the ubiquitous Ibrahima Sylla with Boncana Maiga as arranger. They roped in a number of top Cameroonian session men (Njock, Penda Lobe, Lima, etc.), and with the core of Kasse's own band (Mama Sissokho, Papa Kouyate and five vocalists) they effectively reworked basic ideas worked out in earlier years with Orchestre Badema. In 1990 Kasse Mady followed up the critical success of *Fode* with the outstanding *Kela Tradition*. Reputed to cost £40,000 to record, the new LP featured an all-Malian line-up including Mam Sissokho on ngoni and Moriba Koita

on lead guitar. Once again, Sylla took charge of production. The rest of the year was spent touring, including a repeat of his 1989 London show and a trip to the island of Reunion, where he came under the beguiling spell of the local maleya music.

1983	38767	Nama
1988	SYL 8355	With National Badema (Re-release)
1989	ST 1025	Fode (Also SYL 8385)
1990	ST 1034	Kela Tradition

Traoré, Baboucar. Singer/guitarist who started adult life as a teacher but by the early 1960s was performing regularly with Orchestre Régional de Kayes (see above). Together, he and the band won many prizes before he decided to follow a solo career in 1973. Over the next few years he toured widely both in Mali and beyond. Today he is a major star in Mali, singing in both Bambara and Kassake to increase audience size. His second international release, *Kar Kar*, is due out in late 1991 on the Stern's label.

| 1990 | ST 1032 | Mariama |
| 1991 | ST 1037 | Kar Kar |

Maiga, Boncana. Multi-instrumentalist who studied in Cuba and recorded with Los Maravaillas. More recently he has become one of the leading West African producers, working on Sylla material in Abidjan. His 1990 recording produces the expected tight arrangements and demonstrates his mastery of a truly eclectic range of styles.

1985	SON 79426	Keleya
1987	LS 90	Panache
1990	66877	Jingles Dances

Diabate, Abdoulaye. Vocalist.

| 1987 | SYL 8343 | Bobereni (With Koule Star) |
| 1989 | 38765 | Kassikoun (With Kene Star) |

8   Guinea

(ECONOMY AND SOCIETY. Pop.: 7 million. Area: 245,857 sq. km. Capital: Conakry. Independence: 1958. Currency: Guinean franc.)

The area now called Guinea has been inhabited since neolithic times, with modern history starting with the eleventh-century Ghana empire. By the fifteenth century most of the country was inhabited by the Manding, including the Malinke in the east, the Susu in the west and Dialonke in the centre. Subsequent migrations brought the Toucouleur and the Fulani (Peul) into the area. European encroachment into the area from the sixteenth century onwards was steadily resisted, reaching a climax in the late nineteenth-century efforts of the famous warrior Samori Touré. He was finally defeated in 1898, by which time the French were already claiming suzerainty over the area.

Resistance was resumed in 1947 when Sekou Touré established the PDG and by the mid-1950s he had started reorganising the state in preparation for independence. Then in 1957, when De Gaulle offered either independence or semi-autonomy within the French empire, Touré and the people of Guinea rejected any further links with the imperial power and became the first Francophone colony to achieve independence. Volume 1 graphically recounts the

situation existing in Guinea following the sudden French withdrawal as the embittered French did everything they could to undermine and isolate the new state. Sekou Touré immediately attracted good will from neighbouring countries and initially tried to follow a non-aligned foreign policy. However, confronted by western hostility, he soon moved to establish a one-party socialist state, although practising decidedly pragmatic economic policies with respect to the multinational mining companies involved in the exploitation of Guinea's rich mineral deposits. Yet, despite a positive international image as a Third World leader, Touré's domestic policies were aimed at removing opposition to the party, suppressing intellectuals, traders, businessmen and civil servants in turn. It is now estimated that up to a quarter of the country's population left during the 1960s because of political repression and an unimpressive economic performance.

By the late 1970s Touré had been obliged to change course, establishing relations with neighbouring countries and, most dramatically of all, with France. The economy was increasingly opened up to foreign capital and by 1980 Guinea was one of the largest recipients of French and Arab aid in Africa. Nevertheless, the apparatus of the one-party state was retained, with Touré being returned for another seven-year term in 1982. However, he was not to see it out and in 1984 was rushed to the US, where he died shortly afterwards in hospital. Three days later, the Army stepped in and seized power. They moved quickly to dismantle the one-party state and to speed-up the opening of the economy. At the time of writing the Army, under President Conte, remains in power, less affected by pro-democracy demands than other Francophone states.

TRADITIONAL MUSIC

While French remains the official language of Guinea, three local languages dominate daily life – Malinke (spoken by 40 per cent of the population), Fula (by 30 per cent) and Susu (by 23 per cent). Guinea is also a predominantly Muslim country with only 1 per cent of the population professing Christian beliefs. Volume 1 outlined the variety of traditional music in Guinea, listing 10 LPs, and should be consulted for further details. However that volume made little mention of the Guinean Ballet – one of the most impressive cultural troupes in Africa – so I have included a short study of this at the end of this chapter.

MODERN MUSIC

The modern music of Guinea was extensively covered in Volume 1 and there is no need to repeat the same material. However, mention should be made of the revolutionary folk song tradition of the late 1950s. Unfortunately, none of these songs were ever recorded. More recently, a few Guinean musicians, spearheaded by Mory Kante, have succeeded in attracting considerable international attention, although there are no indications that this success had been recognised by the Government, with most musicians still recording outside the country and complaining of poor facilities at home.

Bembeya Jazz. Formed in Beyla in 1961, Bembeya have been the foremost Guinean band for over three decades, playing some of the most sublime music on the African continent. They started out under the leadership of Aboubacar Camara, becoming the official national band in 1966. Featuring anywhere between 15 and 25 musicians, the band consist of electric guitars (most notably that of Sekou Diabate), horns, vocals and percussion, drawing on a mouthwatering range of sources including Guinean tradition, soukous and rumba. During the 1960s and 1970s, the band were somewhat constrained by the foreign policy initiatives of President Sekou Touré and were only able to tour the USSR, Cuba and neighbouring West African states. Their stately progress was only once undermined, by the sudden and tragic death of bandleader Camara in a 1973 car accident. However, by the mid-1980s, with Touré gone and more liberal regime in power, the band were able to visit Europe, recording a batch of fine albums and thrilling audiences with tours of France, Belgium, Holland and the UK. No newcomer to the world of contemporary African music should fail to acquaint themselves with both the classic recordings of the 1970s and the slightly sharper, slicker albums of the mid-1980s.

1970	SLP 4	Djanf Amagni
	SLP 24	10 Ans de Succès
	SLP 27	+ Horoya Band: Chemin
	SLP 39	Parade Africaine
	SLP 44	Spécial Recueil Souvenir
1978	SLP 59	Le Defi
1982	SLP 61	La Continuité
	SLP 64	Regard Sur Le Passé
	SLP 65	Mémoire de Aboubacar Camara
	SLP 66	Discothèque 76
1985	F 1014785	African Roots (Compilation)
	ESP 8418	Télégramme
1986	ESP 8430	Moussoukro
	ESP 8431	Yekeke
1988	ESP 8442	Sabu
1989	ESP 8460	Wa Kele

Diabate, Sekou. Nicknamed 'Diamond Fingers' for his virtuosity on the guitar, Sekou is lead guitarist with Bembeya with a couple of impressive solo albums to his credit.

| 1985 | ESP 8419 | Montagne (With Bembeya) |
| 1988 | ESP 8443 | Digne |

Les Amazones. All-female dance band formed in 1961 as the band of the Guinean Gendarmerie. Like Bembeya, they have undergone many personnel changes during the last three decades, although their recorded output has inexplicably been restricted to a single 1983 album. Again, like Bembeya, they benefited from a loosening of travel restrictions in the wake of Sekou Touré's death and made several highly acclaimed tours of western capitals.

| 1983 | SLP 76 | Au Coeur de Paris |

Diabate, Sona. Singing sister to Sekou 'Diamond Fingers' Diabate, Sona started her musical career at an early age, hardly surprising in such a famous family of griots:

> from a very early age we had to start learning to play instruments such as balafon and guitar. My father taught me to play balafon; then I moved on to guitar and it was my brother who taught me. It was my father who taught me to sing and how to compose songs. In the family, everybody can play instruments (*Folk Roots*, October 1990).

There was never any question of her future career and, as she explained to Ian Anderson, once she had mastered the rudiments, her real career started with an instrumental band called Faranah. Further studies followed before she met up with Miriam Makeba, a long-time resident of Conakry, who advised her on stage-craft and vocal techniques. Finally, in 1983, she joined Les Amazones. By the late 1980s she had become a familiar name to western audiences with three outstanding albums to her credit. In 1989 and

1990 she toured Europe with her brother Sekou, performing in the acoustic tradition and making plans for forming her own band. The 1989 LP is taken from a live Paris recording and features both her brother and Dembo Camara on acoustic twelve string guitar. Enchanting.

1987	SLP 77	Sons de la Savanne
1988	TERRA 106	+ M'mah Sylla: Sahel
1989	PAM 06	Kankele-Ti

Jawara, Jali Musa (b. 1961, Kankan). Born into a musical family of Jalis (hereditary musicians), Jali Musa started on kora at the age of six. He was taught by his equally illustrious brother, Mory Kante, and continues to be influenced by Mory's international approach to Guinean traditions. In 1979 Jali Musa moved to Abidjan to join Mory Kante's band – playing guitar – although he kept his acoustic kora and balafon band running at the same time. Jali Musa acknowledges the cultural role played by Sekou Touré in the development of Guinean music but personally found it difficult to reciprocate by singing praises of the Government. In this respect, he was attracted by the comparative freedom offered by Abidjan to take whatever musical route he wanted. In the early 1980s Jali Musa recorded one of the finest LPs ever to come from Africa – the timelessly perfect *Fote Mogoban*. The follow-up, on World Circuit, reinforced his international reputation but so popular did *Fote* become that it has remained available long after other LPs of its era have disappeared.

1983	TAN 7002	Fote Mogoban (Also OVLP 511 and GGLP 1)
1988	WCB 008	Soubindoor
1989	HNBL 1355	Yasimika (Fote Mogoban on the fourth time round!)

Kante, Mory. Singer, composer and multi-instrumentalist, Mory Kante is one of the few African musicians to have become a household name outside his own country. Volume 1 provided a comprehensive biography up to 1985 but it was in 1986 that his career moved into super-drive with the afro-pop dance-floor hit 'Yeke Yeke', of which any number of mixes now exist. In 1990 Mory re-appeared on the international scene with the long-awaited *Touma*. It was variously received, with one reviewer describing it as 'A blinding daylight disc of vibrant tunes', while others complained (again) of the distance Mory appeared to have moved from his Guinean roots in search of a cross-over hit. *Touma* featured Djanka Diabate on vocals and Carlos Santana on guitar and sold

reasonably well, although perhaps not well enough to justify the amount of time spent in various Parisian and American studios. By 1991 Mory's stage act had reached new levels of sophistication which, sadly, seemed to leave audiences transfixed by the sheer spectacle rather than dancing to the music.

1977	SYL 8378	Mory Kante & Rail Band
1981	MP 000123	Courougnegne
1984	LS 73	A Paris (Including Yeke Yeke)
1986	829 0871	10 Kola Nuts
1988	281 833	Akwaba Beach (Also 833119)
1988	7836	L'Ensemble Instrumental du Guinea avec Mory Kante (Cass.)
1990	843702	Touma

Manfila, Kante. (b. Kankan, 1947). Kante was born into a family of jalis and as a youth accompanied his parents on balafon. In the late 1950s he switched his attention to guitar and within a few years was a member of Les Ballets Africains. During the 1960s he moved to Bamako and joined the Rail Band, then also featuring the combined talents of Mory Kante and Salif Keïta. In the early 1970s he transferred his skills to the equally legendary Ambassadeurs, taking Keïta with him. Thus began almost a decade of brilliant collaboration before they split in the early 1980s to pursue solo careers. Part of Manfila's output can be heard on the three Ambassadeurs LPs listed below. By the 1980s Manfila was firmly based in Paris, pursuing a solo career but making use of top Guinean and Malian musicians when he wished to record. His later work finds him equally at home in the big band format of the Rail Band and the Ambassadeurs and with smaller, more traditional outfits.

1970s	EPL 7835	Echoes D'Afrique Vol. 1
	EPL 7836	Echoes D'Afrique Vol. 2
	EPL 7837	Echoes D'Afrique Vol. 3
	MEL 6717	Ambassadeurs & Kante/Keïta
	MEL 6721	Ambassadeurs & Keïta
	MEL 7640	Best of Ambassadeurs
1985	AICD 003	Mansa Coulon & Youssouf Kante

1986	TAN 7016	Musicale Mandingue
1988	ST 1021	Tradition (Also TAN 7017)
1990	ESP 8467	Diniya

Kouyate, Ousmane (b. 1952, Dabola). Like so many of his countrymen and contemporaries, Ousmane was born into a musical family – his father was an accordionist and 'ngoni' player; his mother a singer and dancer. As a child he was taught to play balafon but soon picked up the guitar and by 1966 had formed a youth band with friends. He continued to receive great encouragement from his father but serious study came first and in 1972 Ousmane went to university to read agriculture. However, this was not his chosen career and he left a few months before graduation to try his luck in Bamako. There he met fellow-Guinean Manfila Kante, leader of Les Ambassadeurs, whom Ousmane joined in 1977. He stayed for several years, striking up a friendship with Salif Keïta and contributing to what many consider to be one of the finest flowerings of Manding music. He toured widely with the Ambassadeurs, including a trip to the USA and various West Africa tours. When Salif Keïta quit the band, Ousmane moved with him and appeared as Salif's guitarist on both *Soro and Ko-Yan*. Meanwhile, he was also pursuing a solo career, releasing two albums, the second of which, *Kefimba*, drew critical acclaim. In 1990 he signed a three-album deal with London company Stern's, who released *Domba* the same year. Despite enormous studio costs and blanket media coverage, the album failed to generate significant sales. Perhaps the western market was satiated with Manding hi-tech cross-overs, perhaps western audiences balked at the way in which this new fusion was handled, but whatever the reason it proved to be an expensive and embarrassing exercise (expensive for the company and embarrassing for the many reviewers who praised it so highly). Praised for its eclecticism, condemned for its westernness, *Domba* remains an enigma in the modern world of African music. Ousmane has a great deal more to offer but perhaps the world is not quite ready for a sound which fuses George Benson, Wes Montgomery and Django Reinhardt on the one hand with the timeless kora, balafon and guitar music of Guinea on the other. Of the thousands of African albums released during the 1980s it is perhaps no coincidence that the two which have excited most heated debate are both from Guinea. *Domba* and *Touma* both break new ground; whether the soil is fertile is indeed another question.

1982	SACODIS	Beni Haminanko
1985		Kefimba
1990	ST 1030	Domba

Diabate, Djanka (b. Kankan). As a child, Djanka was influenced by her family to take an interest in music, but when her father died the family moved to Abidjan. She started singing locally and came to the attention of reggae superstar Alpha Blondy, who encouraged her to make her first recording with the production skills of Boncana Maiga. She soon became a celebrity in Ivory Coast and was dubbed 'La Divine'. In 1984 she moved to Paris to join her illustrious cousin, Mory Kante. In 1989 she recorded her first international release, simply entitled *Djanka*. The following year she consolidated her growing reputation with a series of shows with the Gypsy Kings, the Spanish flamenco outfit. Musically, her sound embraces a variety of influences including zouk, soukous and Guinean traditions.

1989	JDCOB360274	Djanka

African Soli

1988	UP 27003	Bamoule

Dadje. Fusion band whose first LP was recorded in Quebec.

1990	VA 001	Meeting

Fatala. Drum and dance troupe formed in 1981 by Yacouba Camara, a gifted percussionist who left Guinea in the early 1960s, travelling through West Africa and Europe before finally settling in Paris. He quickly established a reputation as a master drummer with groups such as Kaloum Tam-Tam, Forêt-Sacrée and Les Grands Ballets d'Afrique Noir. In 1977 he moved to Holland, establishing Africa Djole and releasing two hard-to-find LPs. He then returned to Guinea and recruited an ensemble of musicians and dancers who in 1981 metamorphosed into Fatala – the name of a river in Guinea. Featuring traditional percussion, balafon and kora as well as two electric guitars, Fatala draw inspiration from tradition and are against the introduction of European instruments and effects, arguing that 'Europeans invented computers and synthesisers and drum machines and so, when you hear those machines, even when they are playing a supposedly African rhythm, you're going to hear something European. It's baloney trying to copy African rhythms without African instruments.' During the 1980s, the group toured widely throughout Europe, performing at a number of prestigious events, including two shows in London supporting Peter Gabriel. Accordingly, in 1988, Gabriel invited them to record at his Bath studios and in due course WOMAD released the album listed below. It includes a version of 'Yeke Yeke'. In 1989 the band visited the US, performing to wild and enthusiastic audiences.

| 1990 | WOMAD011 | Timini |

Kouyate & Kouyate. Singing sons of Sory Kandia Kouyate. See Volume 1.

| 1989 | ESP 83109 | Faso |

Les Ballets Africains. Musical ambassadors for the people of Guinea, Les Ballets are a traditional ensemble who, over the last four decades, have developed a highly polished show suitable for the international stage. They were formed in 1959, a year after independence, although the core of the company had been working in Paris from 1952 as Les Ballets Africains de Keïta Fodeba. Fodeba had worked as a teacher with a dream of presenting African culture to western audiences. During the early 1950s he travelled through Africa, researching dances and recruiting members before establishing the ballet in Paris. For the next six years they toured the world to considerable public and critical acclaim. In 1958 Sekou Touré invited Fodeba to return home and help him implement his vision of cultural development. And although the country had been left bankrupt by the departing French, Touré somehow found the means to fund and equip the company. During the 1960s and 1970s the ballet became involved in a massive amount of touring, on the road for up to two years at a time. During one world tour they appeared in almost every capital in the world, playing 695 shows in the space of 730 days. However, Fodeba had by this time become Minister of the Interior, and after falling out with Touré, sadly lost his life. The ballet itself survived the 1984 change of regime, receiving consistent government support for their efforts, although world tours were no longer undertaken. The company remained together and in 1990 resumed their international travelling under the directorship of Italo Zambo, with strong encouragement from Bailo Telivel Diallo, National Director of Culture. The 1990 world tour saw the ballet perform in front of over 200,000 people. Unlike most other cultural groups, the ballet has been able to survive the vicissitudes of the last four decades, entering the 1990s with a legacy of top-quality artistry and a five-year plan to carry them towards the new century. This plan involves an internationally funded Institute of Music, Dance and Theatre which will bring all the elements of the Guinean cultural patrimony under one roof. This will include Le Ballet Djoliba, L'Ensemble Instrumental, Le Théâtre National and Les Percussions de Guinea, a group of drummers drawn from Les Ballet Africains and now touring in their own right.

1950s	MON 373	Keïta Fodeba & Mouangue & Facelli
	P 08 672	Musiker Des Keïta Fodeba Ensembles
1960s	BEL AIR 411043	Les Ballets Africains
1969	CLVLX 297	Les Ballets Africains Vol. 1
	MFS 373	Keïta Fodeba & Kante Facelli: The Voices and Drums of Africa
	SLP 14	Ballets Africains de la République Du Guinée
1990	DD 40001	Les Ballets Africains (Soundtrack from British 1990 documentary)

Others

| 1988 | | Hits de Guinea 88 |
| 1988 | | Hits de Guinea 88 |

9 Côte D'Ivoire

(ECONOMY AND SOCIETY. Pop.: 12.5 million. Area: 322,463 sq. km. Capital: Abidjan. Independence: 1960. Currency: CFA franc.)

Little is known of the early history of the area now known as Côte D'Ivoire. What we do know is that the main migrations into the area are comparatively recent, occurring in the fifteenth and sixteeenth centuries for the Kru and the Voltaic peoples, in the eighteenth and nineteenth centuries for the Akan and the nineteenth century for the Manding. These four major ethnic groups have since spawned over 60 different ethnic groups. Unlike neighbouring Ghana, relations with the Europeans were few and far between but by the mid-nineteenth century the French were gaining the ascendancy, being ceded the area in the 1884 Berlin carve-up and declaring a colony in 1893. French colonial policy was directed towards military control and the export of raw materials and they encouraged French settlement on plantations, making use of local forced labour until after the Second World War. By then nationalist parties were starting to emerge, the biggest being the PDCI led by Houphouet-Boigny. Following a brief period of repression, Houphouet-Boigny adopted a more conciliatory approach to the French, even campaigning to keep the country within the wider French community. How-

ever, French plans for a large West African Federation did not prove popular and in 1960 Houphouet-Boigny took the lead and declared the country independent. Since then, the country and the party have remained under the tight control of the President, proving to be a conservative force in regional and African politics through close links with France and the occasional flirtation with South Africa. After 1960 the country initially enjoyed an economic boom, based on an expanding cacao industry, but by the 1980s the chickens were coming home to roost and by the end of the decade Houphouet-Boigny was under considerable pressure to reform the political system.

TRADITIONAL MUSIC

The traditional music of Côte D'Ivoire is extremely rich and varied. It is closely linked with rural life and social events – an omnipresent part of African existence. As in the rest of Africa, Ivorian traditional music takes a number of forms – group music, individual, recreational music, the music of itinerant musicians, ritual music, etc. – and involves a wide range of instruments. The percussion family is perhaps the largest and most popular of all the instruments. With only rare exceptions, such as the Fedonon, a branch of the Senoufo family, whose women are allowed to use drums in initiation ceremonies, drumming remains a male preserve, with the drums themselves assigned special qualities according to their gender. Certain drums have specific functions, while types of drum vary from the slender Akan drum to the Agni-Baoule 'kettle' drums and the ubiquitous 'tama' of the Malinke. The balafon is also widely played, particularly amongst the Senoufo and Lobi of southern Côte D'Ivoire. Once again, these wooden xylophones can be played alone or, in the case of the Lobi, in large balafon orchestras accompanied by mass percussion – a truly awesome sound. Wind instruments include a huge variety of horns, flutes, fifes and whistles, utilised in various ways – from children herding cattle to important religious ceremonies. Stringed instruments play a less central role in Ivorian society than in neighbouring regions. However, there are instances of recreational mouth-harp music as well as more specific usages such as the Korhogo one-string harp and the Malinke three-stringed harp. More elaborate string instruments include the Guere 'duu' or lute-harp – a six- or seven-stringed affair which can also be heard in neighbouring Liberia. Finally, there are several instruments which do not fall into any of these three categories. These are the 'sanza' or hand-piano and the 'rhombe' – a whirling blade on a cord which replicates the cries of animals and is unique to the Baoule. Sadly, not a great deal of Ivorian traditional music is available outside specialised archives. Those listed below represent a starting point for further research.

1962	OCR 34	Musique Baoule-Kode
	OCR 48	Musique Gouro
	OCR 52	Musiques Dans
	SOR 6	Côte D'Ivoire – Musique Baoule
	BM 30L 2308	Music of the Senufo

The Ivories. Originally from Guinea, the three musicians in this traditional kora/balafon ensemble moved to Abidjan in search of patronage. Playing Manding music in timeless fashion, Sidiqui Jajo, Mori Jobarteh and Kalifa Kamara turned up on the obscure American label Worldwide Communications under the rubric 'The Ivories'. Compact disc only.

| 1987 | WWCD 006 | Bala |

MODERN MUSIC

Abidjan is without a doubt one of the main centres of the West African music business. It has some of the best studios which attract regional and even Zaïrois musicians to record and occasionally settle there; Sam Mangwana, Souzy Kasseya, Tshala Muana, BibiDens, have all at one time or another spent time in Côte D'Ivoire. It also has one of the liveliest and most chic nightclub scenes in Africa, providing plenty of opportunity for local musicians and visiting stars to show their paces. Finally, Ivorians enjoy good music and provide enthusiastic audiences. So why has the country consistently failed to produce a homegrown sound which could project Ivorian music overseas?

Perhaps its very status as a musical capital has inhibited local musicians, producing imitators and not innovators. Perhaps audiences prefer imported music, or maybe the musical heritage is so rich that any single style, for example, ziglibithy, can support only a limited market. What is certain is that Côte D'Ivoire produces many skilled musicians who find various outlets in the vibrant scene. Some become internationally respected producers – Boncana Maiga, Jimmy Hyacinthe, Paul Wassaba and Nguessan Santa. Others plough the fertile furrows of tradition, while a few experiment with innovative fusions and new mixes. As

if to prove the point that Côte D'Ivoire may be suffering from a crisis of direction, we only have to consider that the only true international star which the country has produced is the inimitable Alpha Blondy, who plays reggae. Rising stars to watch out for include Kati Loba, Jeanne Dah, Bony Castro, Johnny Lafleur, Monique Seka (who had a big Parisian hit with 'Missounwa'), Seyoulou Zombra, Virginie Gaudji and Pierre Amedee and Woya.

Blondy, Alpha (b. Seydou Kone, Dimbokoro, 1953). International reggae star perfectly at home in French, English or Dioula – a local language shared with neighbouring Burkina (where his mother came from). His early career – from Liberia to New York and Jamaica then back home – is now well documented, and by 1987, with four outstanding albums to his credit, massive media coverage and a constant tour schedule, Blondy was established as one of Africa's mega-stars with album sales regularly in excess of 100,000 units. However, having recorded with the Wailers on *Jerusalem*, Blondy put out the vaguely disappointing *Prophets* in 1989 and returned home to take a breather. In 1991 he launched his sixth album, *SOS Tribal War*, a short reminder of his potency, with tracks about AIDS, tribal war (possibly referring to the situation in Liberia) and Babylon. Backed by the Solar System, the second side stands out. It is too early to draw any firm conclusions but, with six LPs to his credit, it certainly seems as if the earlier material is stronger.

1983	38710	Jah Glory
1984	SGLC/1	Cocody Rock (Cass.)
1985	SYL 8312	Rasta Poue (Maxi 45)
1986	ST 1017	Apartheid is Nazism
		I Love Paris (45 r.p.m.)
1987	ST 1020	+ The Wailers: Jerusalem
1989	791793	The Prophets
1991	JIP 031	SOS Tribal War

Hyacinthe, Jimmy. Ace guitarist turned producer. Perhaps best known on disc for his modernisation of the 'goli' rhythm.

| 1987 | LS 89 | Retro |

Bezy, Beny. Gifted singer who worked with Naimro from Kassav in the mid-1980s to produce an impressive Afro-Caribbean synthesis. Thereafter, despite high expectations, little more was heard of Beny.

| 1985 | BB 003 | Amlini |
| 1986 | BMCA 8607 | Assi Assa |

Manfei, Obin. A student of music as well as a practising musician, Obin seeks in his work to bring the traditional strengths of Ivorian music into the modern mix. His research into the richness of the Ivorian traditional scene got off to a good start when, in 1979, he was awarded a two-year scholarship with L'ADEAC funded by the French Government. In 1980 he launched his first group, Bloanan, featuring a blend of old and new – harmonica, guitar, balafon and bass, drums, sax, violin and flute. Having moved to Paris he took up work with the PROCAP and was able to release several LPs.

1980	WEA 50566	Me Bitouo Nin
1981	WEA 58100	Migration People
1983	WEA 28254	Cheri Coco
	ERO 2534	Boton Le Lièvre

Modibo, Askia. Malian-born singer now resident in Côte D'Ivoire. Performs a kind of Wassolou-reggae. His first LP was released in 1990.

| 1990 | | Djiguiya |

Simplice, Sery (b. 1949). Chief exponent of 'gbegbe' dance rhythm, Sery learned guitar as a child before moving to Abidjan in 1966. He then teamed up with Pierre Amedee, attempting to blend folklore with the dominant rumba sounds. By the mid-1970s he was working with the late Ernesto Djedje trying to create a new synthesis which eventually saw the light of day in 1977 as 'ziglibithy' – one of the first home-grown Ivorian styles to make a major impact. In 1977 Sery established his own band known as Les Frères Djatys and over the next six years experimented with his 'gbegbe'-based fusions. He first recorded in 1978 and has since made more than a dozen albums, testifying to his local success. In 1985 he travelled further afield, touring Europe, but despite some positive publicity in the mid-1980s he has returned to Côte D'Ivoire and what he knows best – 'gbegbe'.

| 1979 | | Gbolou (2nd LP) |
| | | Atrikakou (3rd LP) |

Agnimel, Jeanne. Talented female singer with over a decade of recording and touring experience.

| 1985 | SAS 055 | Zoum |

Azney, B. Adu

| 1987 | STC 5601 | Pot-Pourri |

Big Sat. Female singer paying respects to the President's wife.

| 1988 | BS 0002 | Awoulaba |

Dallo, Fifi

| 1987 | BMCA 8702 | Behi |

Daouda. See Volume 1 for early career and discography.

| 1988 | 7354 | Les Femmes D'Aujourdhui (Cass.) |

Dickael, Liade Justin. Son of the great Ivorian singer Emile Liade Lago, Justin started singing as a child, later developing 'Le Zitho' – a new style combining the best of ziglibithy and 'tchouru'.

| 1990 | 010 H88 | Gblinadre |

Doh, Albert

| 1986 | RZ 014 | Comment Ça Va? |

Eponou, Catherine Agoh. Born in the western region, into the Akan ethnic group, Catherine sings in Agni with a massed percussion and vocal backing. She calls her style 'adjoss'.

| 1990 | | Danse Indenie |

Fatou, Mattha. Singer/composer.

| 1987 | LX 93033 | Yafama |

Frères Keïta et Ismael. Ivorian reggae band who enjoy enormous local popularity. Comprising the Keïta brothers – Hassan and Ousseyne – the band is often joined on stage and in the studio by Ismael.

1986	TAN 7013	Liberté
1987	CEL 6817	Tchilaba
1989	ESP 8463	Yatiman

Gozene, Dominique. Talented female vocalist starting to make an impression beyond Abidjan.

| 1988 | 52188 | Procès |
| 1990 | LP 52188 | Nayou |

Kaba, Baba Djan. Manding neo-traditionalist. The 1989 album was arranged by Kante Manfila.

| 1989 | AMP 112 | Feeling Mandingue |

Kamson, Jim. Backed by the Africa Star, Kamson purveys a fine brand of Ivorian reggae in a style similar to Blondy.

| 1990 | OK 0001 | Djakabo |

Kass Men

| 1987 | TAN 7012 | Kass Music |

Kone, Aicha. Female singing sensation known affectionately as 'La Diva Ivorienne'. On her 1989 outing she covered one side with Kwassa Kwassa and on the other reverted to more Ivorian material.

1983	WAM 793010	Aminata
1984	KS 434	Le Chanson de la Chance
1989	EMI	Tchaga

Leak, Jah Roy, and the Wadada Spirits (b. Aboisso). Smooth and vibrant reggae.

| 1990 | OK 007 | Cry Freedom |

L'Orchestre de L'Université d'Abidjan. Dutch recording.

| 1986 | 830 2931 | Oppression |

Lystrone, Kouame

| 1988 | KM 361 | Abissa Swing |

Liz, Ade

| 1988 | AD 130 | N'Se Man |

Lougah, François. A stalwart of the 1970s soukous scene but searching for local roots and inspiration during the 1980s. Enormously talented guitarist.

1976	SAF 50036	Au Zaïre
1977	SMP 6030	Bénédiction (Also JAM 001)
1991	FG 001	Ambiance Non-Stop

Makan, Djely

| 1989 | SA 300046 | Lonan Tcheni |

Meiway

| 1990 | EF 47301 | Ayibebou |

Modibo, Kone. Formerly a local reggae star switching to the sounds of Wassolou on his latest album, keeping some of the rougher edges missing on recent Paris productions.

| 1990 | OK 010 | Hommage à El Hadj Souleymane Doumbia |

Pajot, Eugène. New vocalist whose first album features Freddie Caracas on bass.

| 1988 | RD 109 | An Pointe |

Seka, Monique. Enjoyed enormous success with her 1988 Paris hit, *Missounwa*.

| 1988 | TS 88200 | Missounwa |

Sinclemen. Reggae band comprising four Ivorian Rastas from Treicheville. Inspiration drawn from Marley, U-Roy and Yellowman, the musicians are drawn from Côte D'Ivoire, Mali, Senegal and Burkina.

| 1990 | | Envol des Sinclemen |

Spinto, Bally. Veteran of the local scene, best known as moderniser of 'gbegbe'.

| 1987 | FRO 587 | Laisse Moi T'Aimer (Maxi) |
| 1988 | FRO 687 | Gnia Mama |

Tia, Thomas

| 1987 | G 2000 | Le Nouveau Tempo |

Tolio, Anatole. An Akan by birth, this fine young singer combines catchy soukous guitar lines with traditional rhythms. The 1990 LP was his third vinyl outing.

| 1990 | GDA 403X | Nolo Sobade |

Yeple, Abel, et le Yeple Jazz. Abel and the band all hail from the western region and are Gouro by birth. They came together in the late 1970s, recording several albums before slipping into obscurity in the mid-1980s. The 1990 LP finds them back on form with their unique 'Gahou' style, fast percussion-based music with fine guitar and keyboard work supporting Abel's vocals.

1990   NH 0013   Adji Aka

Woya. Adventurous afro-funk outfit formed by teenagers in mid-1980s.

1988   7299   Ewe (Cass.)

Zadje, Olive Guede. A young singer from the western region singing in the Bete language in a style known as 'polihet'. His first LP features

up-tempo dance music with guitars, horns and keyboards.

1990   MAILPS 1050   Hommage à Maman Ziallo

Zeze, Lavet (b. Ouragahio). Performs in the recreational 'Alloukou' style, fast-paced dance music in Bete.

1990   OK 008   Gouza

Zikalo. Norwegian-based, Paris-recorded, Ivorian afrobeat band.

1990   NR 001   Tata-Le

10 Burkina Faso

(ECONOMY AND SOCIETY. Pop.: 9 million. Area: 274,000 sq. km. Capital: Ouagadougou. Independence: 1960. Currency: CFA franc.)

The Mossi, comprising half the population of Burkina, dominated pre-colonial history. By the sixteenth century they were organised in a number of kingdoms which survived until the French conquest at the end of the nineteenth century. Other important ethnic groups include the Mamprussi (who extend into northern Ghana), the ubiquitous Fulani and the Bobo, Lobi, Senufo and Bissa who remained outside an organised state system. The French were particularly brutal in their conquest of the area, taking Ouagadougou in 1896 and declaring the area a colony in 1919. But by 1945 nationalist parties had appeared to challenge French rule, gaining independence under Maurice Yameogo in 1960. Yameogo retained close ties with France and soon established an autocratic style of government. In 1966 a united opposition appeared under the leadership of historian Joseph Ki-Zerbo, and although the party was immediately banned, a popular uprising in that year succeeded in toppling Yameogo.

The Army promptly stepped in under Col. Lamizana, who oversaw the return to democracy in 1970. But the politicians could not agree and it was no surprise when the Army left their barracks once again in 1974 to try to resolve some of the economic problems faced by one of Africa's poorest countries. Once again the Army ruled for four years before fresh elections in 1978 legitimised the rule of Lamizana. Yet stability was extremely hard to establish, with Zerbo taking over in 1980 and Ouedraogo in 1982 before the revolutionary Thomas Sankara rose to the top. He quickly established relations with Ghana and Libya and soon became a popular spokesman for the Third World, indicating his willingness to break with the past by renaming the country Burkina Faso in 1984 (meaning the Land of Incorruptible Men). Sankara did a great deal to restore respectability to Burkina, but when he tried to establish a one-party state and curb the power of the unions, his comrades assassinated him in a coup in 1987. Since then, Campaore has struggled to cope with the substantial underlying economic problems of the country.

TRADITIONAL MUSIC

Like many countries of the Sahel region, Burkina has a rich and varied traditional culture, some of which has been captured for posterity on disc.

	OCR 51	Musique Du Pays Lobi
	OCR 58	Musique Du Bisa
	SOR 10	Haute Volta (Mossi, Bambara, Peul, Lobi, Gan)
	ADE 670	Balafons, Percussion, Chant de Bobo-Dioulasso
	2C-62 11568	Les Griots: Rendez-Vous à Ouaga
1969	LYRCD 7328	African Rhythms and Instruments Vol. 1
1975	D 8006	The Fulani (UNESCO)
1976	CVD 010	Les Trésors du Mogho (Traditional Mossi group)
1979	ACCT 47904	Chantes et Musique Traditionels Haute Volta (Mossi, Senoufo, Peul, Gourounsi, Bissa, Samo)

1981	H 72087	Savannah Rhythms: Music of Upper Volta

MODERN MUSIC

Very little modern music (or traditional for that matter) from Burkina has reached either a wider African or international market. At the same time very little research on the contemporary pop scene has been conducted and I must thank Pieter Hoefman and MASK Productions for almost all the information in the following section.

The first major band to make an impact in the post-war era was L'Harmonie Voltaique, and during the 1950s and 1960s modern Burkina music was heavily influenced both by afro-cuban sounds and the ubiquitous rumba from Zaïre. During the 1970s a few stars, like George Ouedraogo and Bozambo, emerged to regional acclaim but otherwise the music scene remained somewhat parochial. More recently, Farafina have attracted wider international acclaim through their work with western pop stars, but despite enormous local talent and popularity the majority of musicians have been hampered by the absence of decent recording studios. The radio station operates a 4-track facility but it was installed in the 1950s and has not been upgraded since. There are also a couple of small commercial studios but they have been described as little more than rooms with instruments. This state indifference to music is somewhat surprising given that Burkina Faso hosts the annual FESPACO (African Film Festival) which on its own guarantees a cosmopolitan cultural jamboree. Secondly, former President and national hero, Thomas Sankara, was an enthusiastic amateur guitarist who, on one legendary occasion, linked up with Jerry Rawlings of Ghana for a short presidential jam. We can only hope that eventually the Government will realise the potential of Burkinabe musicians and either build or facilitate the development of reasonable recording studios.

L'Harmonie Voltaique. Founded in 1948. In 1960 they became the first Burkinabe group to receive official state sponsorship from President Yameogo. They started out as a military band playing a largely French repertoire. However, by the early 1960s they were experimenting with indigenous rhythms and languages under the leadership of Maurice Simpaure. Unfortunately, despite their long career, there are no extant recordings.

Volta Jazz. Founded in 1964 by Kone Idrissa who immediately changed their name from Tropical Jazz to Volta Jazz. Like most other bands of the 1960s, Volta Jazz played in a Cuban-influenced style but in time they began adding elements of their native Bobo traditions. The band featured many talented composers and singers, of whom the most celebrated was Tidiani Coulibali. They hit a peak between 1967 and 1972, making several tours to neighbouring countries, recording several singles and a solitary album which is now impossible to find. In 1977 they went into the studio for a second time with a new line-up. Coulibali was missing but the band remained under the overall direction of Kone Idrissa.

1977	SAF 50058	Orchestre Volta Jazz

Echo Del Africa National. Founded in 1965–6 by Outtara Basoungalo amongst others. Based in Bobo, the band survived until 1983 making six singles and the LP referenced below – an adventurous concept album recounting the history of Bobo Dioulasso. Their most acclaimed singer/composer was Youssouf Diarra (El Grand Ballake – 'The Great Porcupine', or 'A Man With Power'), who, prior to his untimely death in a car accident in the late 1970s, had recorded a solo album with the help of the group Super Saman.

1973	SHA 004	Y. Diarra et Super Saman: Rockstar
1976	SAF 50035	Echo Del Africa National: Récit Historique de Bobo Dioulasso

Dafra Star. Formed in 1975 by Tidiani Coulibali, who had quit Volta Jazz to follow his own roots-revival musical ideas. In this respect, he made a conscious return to the past, bringing in the balafon as lead instrument in his otherwise electric line-up. He did not have to wait long for his ideas to pay off and in 1976 he won first prize in the Burkina National Festival of Modern Music. Together with Dafra Star he recorded several singles and two LPs. The band toured regularly in neighbouring Mali and by the early 1980s had become one of the most popular outfits in Burkina. They finally split up in 1985 due to financial problems (indicating just how precarious the music business was – even for a relatively successful band). Tidiani then continued as a solo artiste, occasionally recording on to cassette while trying to put together his own traditional orchestra.

1975	MHLP 001	Dounian-Kogobe Kogobe
1976	DSLP 01	Recital Premier Prix

Léopards, Les. Army band from Bobo who played good copyright material in a variety of West African styles, although perfectly capable of turning their hand to specifically Burkinabe material.

2 BE 13	Les Imbattables Léopards

CVD, Orchestre. Formed in 1976 by Adama Ouedraogo, the group began as the house band of the record label Club Voltaique du Disque (CVD). The label had been around since the early 1970s and had provided an outlet for many Burkinabe musicians. The band covered all the popular styles of the time – rumba, soul and reggae – and although personnel changed frequently, they remained a solid outfit enjoying enormous popularity all over the country. They finally collapsed in 1979, having recorded several singles and two albums.

| 1976 | CVD 017 | Orchestre CVD Vol. 1 |
| 1977 | | Orchestre CVD Vol. 2 |

Super Volta, Orchestre. Founded in 1968 by To Finley, J.C. Bamogo and Moise Ouedraogo. The band enjoyed a brief two-year existence until instruments and equipment were seized by the owner.

| | CVD 042 | Mobutu |

Traore, Amadou (b. Kantiari, 1949). Outstanding vocalist nicknamed 'Ballake'. He started his career playing with a number of local outfits including Les 5 Consuls, Orchestre Super Volta and Les Dieux, with whom he recorded an album in 1976. By then he had also released ten singles on the same label. Playing in the modern Mandingue style, his music swings in a relaxed fashion. In the late 1970s he left Burkina to try his luck elsewhere and over the next decade travelled widely, recording in Mali, Abidjan, Paris and New York. One of the few international stars to have come from Burkina.

1976	CVD 008	A. Traore et Ses Dieux
1979	IS 11-79	Amadou Ballake Vol.3 (SACODIS)
1982	ZAMIDOU 1582	Afro-Charanga (New York)
1983	ABC 1135	Taxi Men
1987	SACODIS	In Paris

Bamogo, Jean Claude. A native of Ouaga, Bamogo (nicknamed 'Man') is famous for his modernisation of the Mossi 'Waraba' rhythm by introducing modern electric instruments. One of his first groups was the short-lived Super Volta. When the band collapsed he moved to Abidjan to broaden his musical horizons, staying several years. He returned home in 1975 and formed the Afro-Soul System with To Finley. He also played briefly with Orchestre CVD before forming his own band, Le Komenem Mogho, in 1983. He made several singles in Abidjan

but more recently has restricted his output to the occasional cassette.

Ouadraogo, Georges. Best known as the drummer with Burkinabe supergroup Bozambo. A Mossi by birth, the local 'Waraba' rhythm is easily identified in his drumming. He started his career with Volta Jazz in 1965, making several recordings with them. In 1966 he moved to Côte D'Ivoire and helped put together Bozambo with guitarist Jimmy Hyacinthe (see Côte D'Ivoire). Over the next few years Bozambo played in France and Germany in an effort to put Burkina on the musical map. In 1978 the group collaborated with guitarist/kora star Lamine Konte (see Senegal) on the soundtrack of the film *Bako*. By the early 1980s Georges was back home in semi-retirement. He made several new recordings, as yet unreleased.

1974	SHA 0010	George Ouadraogo in Paris
	DPX 806	Gnafou-Gnafou
1978	SAF 61002	Bako L'Autre Rime Bozambo: Spéciale Haute Volta
	60169	Mr Le P.D.G.

Ouadraogo, Amidou. Percussionist from Bobo who plays traditional music. In 1989 he toured Holland with the group Faso Tile, playing at the Africa Mama Festival in Utrecht. The live recording listed below is taken from that performance.

| 1989 | KOCH 322415 | Lamogoya Cole Bobo |

Ouedraogo, Hamidou (b. Dori). Moved to Ouahigoya in 1954, eventually settling in Ouaga where he found employment as a mechanic. A Peul (Fulani) by birth, Hamidou started his musical career gradually, graduating from harmonica to accordion. In 1970 he entered a music competition and grabbed the first prize. By this time he had gained a reputation for his skill in accompanying the 'Gumbe' dance on accordion. His first recording as made in the mid-1970s with Moise Ouedraogo on guitar.

| 1970s | SON 8204 | Le Vedette Voltaique |
| | SON 8207 | Le Chanteur Voltaique |

Ouedraogo, Eduard. Nicknamed 'Le Prince', Eduard first recorded in the late 1970s in Abidjan on the Disk-Orient label. Singing in Mori, his music was a conscious attempt to blend Mori rhythms with Ivorian pop.

| 1970s | DO 003 | + L'Orchestre Nakobisse: Bizamsse Poupele |

Malonga, Charles (b. Pointe-Noire, Gabon). He started his career as a musician at the age of nine in the local school band. In 1958 he joined Renove Jazz, but then moved on to lend his vocal and guitar skills to the more traditionally-oriented Madi Badio. In 1977 he moved and settled in Burkina, playing with several local bands including Les Quatres Black Brothers, with whom he achieved great local success. In 1990 he released his first solo cassette, only available on the Burkina market.

| 1980s | SAF 61003 | Les Quatres Black Brothers |

Cisse, Abdoulaye. Talented singer/composer rooted in Burkinabe tradition but with residual Cuban influences.

| | CVD 084 | Jeunesse Wilila |

Dembele, Bakary. As almost the only performing 'tiahoun' player in the country, Bakary occupies a unique position in the Burkina musical firmament. The 'Tiahoun' is a traditional reed instrument which sounds somewhere between a balafon and a kalimba. It was originally played as a portable instrument by farmers on their way to work. Extremely popular inside the country with several best-selling cassettes to his credit, he is unknown outside Burkina.

Yelbuna. Formed in Italy in 1981 by To Finley, T. Sawadogo and O. Kuiliga. The band stayed there for a year, recording their first LP in Rome. Their music has been described as a sophisticated mix of tradition and soul. The vocalist, To Finley, has an exceptionally clear and open voice. He graduated through the ranks of Super Volta, Afro Soul System and Orchestre CVD. Yelbuna lasted for just over a

year before the three friends returned to Burkina. Since then, To has recorded with friends but nothing has been released.

| 1982 | Pontaccio | Afro Juke Box |

Farafina. Formed in 1973 by Maham Konte as a four-piece percussion outfit, later augmented to eight. Operating from a base in Geneva, their neo-traditional music highlights the balafon playing of Mahama and the 'djembe' playing of Paco Ye. In the early 1980s they made a strong showing at the Montreux Jazz Festival, which produced their first (live) album. They travelled widely throughout Europe and Japan before re-entering the studio in 1988 with Jon Hassell and Brian Eno to record the experimental *Flash of the Spirit*. In 1988 they played at the Mandela birthday bash in London as well as at the Glastonbury Festival with Hassell (both events were televised) and in 1989 were invited by the Rolling Stones to work with them in the studio. They released the highly acclaimed *Bolomakote* the same year.

1980s		Live at Montreux Jazz Festival
1988	CDP 7911862	Flash of the Spirit
1989	VERABRALP 26	Bolomakote

Soubega, Edouard (b. Koudougou). A Mossi by birth, he moved to Paris in the mid-1980s and formed a short-lived reggae outfit.

Others. By the late 1980s there were quite a few bands and singers enjoying local popularity based on live shows and a thriving cassette market. Watch out for Jean Bernard Samboue, Kindiss, Jeremy Dim, Roger Wango, Desi et les Symatics, Les Frères Coulibaly, Vincent Sanou, Opportune, Dominique Valea, Aboubacar Soare, Faso Sira and Sami Rama.

11 Togo

(ECONOMY AND SOCIETY. Pop.: 3.5 million. Area: 56,000 sq. km. Capital: Lomé. Independence: 1960. Currency: CFA franc.)

A tiny country sandwiched between Ghana and Benin and occasionally referred to as the 'Switzerland of Africa', Togo was first settled by the Ewe in the south and the Kabiye in the north. Both were lineage societies linked by the cattle trade, but when the slave trade appeared in the sixteenth century, the Ewe became middlemen dealing with both Elmina to the west and Ouidah to the east. During the eighteenth century a number of ex-slaves from Brazil returned to settle in the area of Anecho, eventually becoming a wealthy élite known as the Mina. Other, smaller groups living in the north included the Moba, Losso, Lamba and the Kaye.

The area of modern Togo was only finally conquered by the Germans in 1902 but German colonial rule was short-lived and they lost all their African colonies at the end of the First World War. Thereafter, the colony was split between France and the UK under a League of Nations mandate, further adding to the confusion and disruption caused by the imposition of arbitrary boundaries. Throughout the 1930s and 1940s, nationalist demands were shaped by the desire for re-unification as well as independence. The first political party to emerge, in 1946, was the CUT, led by Sylvanus Olympio, arguing strongly for re-unification. Yet it was not to be, and in a UN plebiscite in 1956 British Togo voted for inclusion in Ghana, then rapidly approaching independence. The French then tried to force their own candidate on Togo but violent demonstrations led to new elections with Olympio becoming Prime Minister – a position he held until independence in 1960, when he became the country's first president. As a conservative businessman, Olympio failed to adopt the more progressive policies of the CUT's youth wing and in 1963 he was assassinated and replaced by Grunitzky, who, in turn, was replaced by General Eyadema in the 1967 coup. Eyadema moved quickly to consolidate power, establishing a one-party state in 1972 and clamping down on political opposition.

In economic terms, Togo made rapid progress in the 1960s and 1970s based on phosphate mining, agricultural exports, a small tourist trade and smuggling. But by the 1980s the economy was in trouble and by 1983, at the behest of the IMF, Eyadema was pursuing rigorous austerity policies. He also had to contend with several coup attempts, accusing the revolutionary regimes in Ghana and Burkina for assisting, if not directly organising, the coup plotters. By 1990 he was under renewed pressure to democratise the political system and reduce state control over the economy.

TRADITIONAL MUSIC

Please see Volume 1 for a brief survey of Togolese traditional music.

1970s	OCR 16	Musique Kabre du Nord Togo
1976	SNTF 667	Various: Ghana, Togo, Gambia Vol. 2 (Obscure recording of many styles including Ewe drumming and Ghanaian brass band)
1984	ROUND 5004	Togo: Music from West Africa (Excellent introductory compilation)

MODERN MUSIC

The music scene in Lomé seemed to die completely in the second half of the 1980s. The first 24-track studio in the region (Africa New Sound) had opened to great publicity in 1984 with international releases by Dr Nico, Abeti and Mayaula, amongst others. But such was the quiet and creeping censorship of the regime that by the late 1980s it had become virtually compulsory for local musicians to sing the praises of Eyadema. Many musicians were reluctant to do this and despite their great gifts the local recording scene more or less died as musicians moved overseas. Since then, very little has been heard from Togo until in mid-1991 the music press reported the seizure of 1.5 million pirate tapes in Lomé under the direction of the state trading company, SNIAD, Congo. Originating in Singapore, these cassettes consisted of African and French music, and although they had a street value in excess of one million dollars they represented only the tip of the bootlegging iceberg.

Mala, Afia. Talented female singer with a substantial regional following.

| 1984 | MI 1001 | Lonlon Viye |
| 1989 | ESP 8468 | Désir |

Agboti-Yawo. Singer/composer backed by Odiba.

Their 1989 LP demonstrated a fine blend of highlife and soukous.

| 1989 | LP 39502 | De Retour des USA |

Lala, Nimon-Toki (b. Lama-Kara, 1955). Female singer who took up music as a child, learning to play the guitar and to dance. Her early efforts were rewarded in 1982 when she was awarded the prestigious RFI (Radio France Internationale) Découverte prize. By this time she had been playing professionally for seven years, releasing her first single in 1978. Now based in Paris, from where she released her 1991 hit album *Ayele* with help from Shimita and Luciana on vocals plus assorted Soukous Stars and members of Loketo.

| 1984 | SYL 55 | Banind |
| 1991 | JIP 027 | Ayele |

Others

1984	ANS 8409	Deg-Dos: Right To Live
	FATAO 0113	Mamo Logbema: Laisses Couleur
1985	ANS 8417	Itadik Bonney: Save Africa
1986	18402	Koffi: Do'nku Djigne
1990	YD 49308	Fifi Rafiatou: Djofe

12 Benin

(ECONOMY AND SOCIETY. Pop.: 4.7 million. Area: 112,622 sq. km. Capital: Cotonou. Independence: 1960. Currency: CFA franc.) For map, see p. 82.

Little is known of the early history of Benin, another small country lying between Togo and Nigeria. The modern country contains three principal ethnic groups – the Fon in the south, the Yoruba in the south-east and the Bariba-Somba in the north. Political organisation occurred first in the south amongst the Fon, who had established a number of powerful kingdoms by the sixteenth century, including Allada, Porto-Novo and Abomey. All three acted as middlemen in the slave trade, acquiring guns which in turn were used to acquire more slaves. In fact so many slaves were shipped through Ouidah that the area became known as the 'slave coast', with early Portuguese contact being replaced by English and French interests. By the early eighteenth century, all the Fon kingdoms had come under the control of Abomey, a powerful state willing and capable of waging war with the Yoruba kingdoms to the east.

By the nineteenth century palm-oil had replaced the trade in slaves, although European competition continued with the French ousting the British in 1868 and establishing a protectorate along the coast. Opposition to French rule spluttered throughout the rest of the century but in 1894 the French seized control of the entire area and established the colony of Dahomey. The first decades of the twentieth century were characterised by further resistance (from the Holli, the Bariba, the Bogou and Sahoue) but the French were able to pacify the country and between the two world wars made some progress in terms of health, education, and infrastructure. Early political progress was made by a new class of 'évolues' and returned Brazilian slaves, but, as elsewhere in West Africa, full nationalism was very much a post-war phenomenon. The struggle for independence was generally peaceful and Dahomey became independent in 1960 under Hubert Maga. He did not last long and was overthrown in a coup in 1963 by Colonel Soglo. Yet political stability proved elusive and governments changed hands several times before Mathieu Kerekou seized power in 1972.

Kerekou represented the young progressive officer class and quickly set about radicalising Dahomean life, based on the teachings of Marx and Lenin. In 1975 he changed the country's name to Benin, marking a break with the colonial past. Over the next few years, Kerekou survived several coup attempts and a mercenary-led attempted invasion. He responded by adopting more pragmatic economic policies, having acknowledged that the west wanted to remove him and that by playing into their hands he might just survive. The 1980s proved a difficult decade for Benin despite the discovery of oil. The border with Nigeria was closed for several years, debt mounted and agricultural exports suffered on world markets. By 1989 Benin was undergoing structural adjustment with advice from the IMF. Politically, Kerekou retained the one-party state but the country was isolated in the region and by the late 1980s he was under considerable pressure from students and civil servants to democratise the system. This was duly done and in 1991 Kerekou stood down in favour of Nicephore Soglo – a former World Bank economist.

TRADITIONAL MUSIC

Volume 1 provided a brief outline of the traditional music scene, listing three LPs covering aspects of Beninois traditional music, and should be consulted for further details.

1960s	AMS 12017	Musica Sacra
1974	6586 022	Ceremonial Music From N. Dahomey
1976	EMI 064 18217	Dahomey: Musical Atlas

MODERN MUSIC

Volume 1 had little to say about the Benin music scene with the exception of a brief look at the career of sax player and bandleader Ignace De Souza, a true African star of the 1950s and 1960s. The other abiding force on the local scene has been Gnonnas Pedro, a veteran vocalist who has survived the vicissitudes of popular taste to remain a star attraction into the 1990s. One explanation of the absence of Beninois stars on the wider international stage lies in the autarkic policies of the left-leaning regime of Kerekou which had isolated the country for over two decades. A second reason may lie in the fact that Benin lies between two other powerful musical epicentres (Ghana and Nigeria), with local taste conforming as much to neighbouring styles as to more international influences. In 1990 John McLaverty travelled through the country with a keen ear for musical developments. The following account provides an excellent update on developments in Benin.

Entering the country from the north, the Malian 'djeli moussou' sound is favoured in the northern towns of Malanville and Kandi. Oumou Sangare's voice blasts from cassette players and her face beams from t-shirts and bar murals. Further south, in Parakou and Abomey, the pervasive sounds of Zaïre begin to take grip with Aurlus Mabele as the star – his record sleeves are faithfully reproduced on the walls of bars and hotels while his bright Paris pop springs from every taxi. Listening to the radio and visiting cassette stores adds to the musical confusion with even local bands in the national music competition heavily influenced by soukous, reggae, highlife and Nigerian pop. One begins to wonder whether there actually is a 'Beninois' sound. Orchestre Poly-Rythmo, for example, are one of the few Beninois bands to have released material outside the country and are still playing inside Benin, yet they have no recordings in the shops. The entire market is now cassette oriented but there were very few home-grown products for as well as a full range of Parisian productions, Benin also imports from Nigeria and Liberia.

The jack-of-all-trades remains Gnonnas Pedro, with recordings aiming to please the widest range of tastes and taking in soukous, Latin, highlife and ballads, including a recent hit in Spanish, 'Yo Prefero El Son'. With the Ewe in Benin listening to highlife and the Yoruba to juju there is simply not much room for a local style to develop. For example, Sagbohan Danialou plays an old-fashioned Ghanaian brass band style while Dossou Letriki, singing in Fon, lets loose with a distant cousin of fuji enriched with bass and guitar to produce a wild and exciting dance style. Even then, by singing in local languages, the cross-over appeal of such music to other Beninois is limited. Makossa, Kassav and rumba are all extremely popular raising the question of whether the recent opening up of the country will bring more external influence to bear on popular music or whether a more market-oriented economy can stimulate a commercial interest in local talent.

Early stars

1960s	PF 11565	Francis Aguessey
	PF 11566	Francis Aguessey
	PF 11552	Lemiel et Super Stars
	PF 11553	Lemiel et Super Stars

Pedro, Gnonnas. One of Africa's top vocalists, he has enjoyed limited success outside his native Benin.

1960s	231 227	G. Pedro y Sus Panchos de Cotonou
	231 306	G. Pedro y Sus Panchos de Cotonou
1979	ASL 7003	La Combinaçion
1980	ASL 7009	La Musica en Vérité
	ASL 7010	Atimawuin Dagamasi
1981	ASL 7022	Salsa
	ASL 7031	El Cochechivo
1984	SYL 55	Mimi Pinson
1985	SYL 8311	Les Femmes D'Abord
1989	7481	The Band of Africa Vol. 4 (Cass.)
	SS 73	Je Voudrais Te Voir (Cass.)

Poly-Rythmo, Orchestre. Large dance band formed in the 1960s and still playing around the country. The Tangent recording is the only one available either inside or outside the country.

ALS 038	Zoundegnon
ALS 048	Yehouessi
ALS 049	Agbaza Mimin
ALS 068	Vol. 7
LIR 23	Ambiance Africana
TAN 7007	Zero + Zero

Kidjo, Angelique. One of the newer stars, as a child Angelique grew up listening to both indigenous music and imported pop music. At the age of 10 she was singing in her brother's band and by 18 was a national star with various recordings and tours to her credit. She then moved to Paris to add an international dimension to her career, and after playing with a few other musicians decided to strike out on her own. Her current output has been described as fusing 'timeless Beninois traditions with melodic jazz-funk'. Married to a French bass player who doubles up on arrangements, Kidjo is fiercely independent and prepared to take full control of her product using the best available talent – never a problem in Paris with its coterie of African, Antillean and French musicians. She released her first international album in 1989, performed in London the following year and burst upon a wider audience with her 1991 Island release.

1989	848219/2	Parakou
1991	MLPS 1091	Logozo

Oliver, Nel (b. Noel Ahounoy). Nel started in music in the late 1960s singing with Ryda-Jazz. In the early 1970s he moved to Paris, searching for better recording facilities, where, in 1976, he released his first album. He then moved on to the US recording a second effort for CBS. In 1984 he was back in Togo as the engineer at the new 24-track Africa New Sound Studio, where he recorded his third album, *Tobolo*. He then toured in Cameroon, Gabon and Côte D'Ivoire. In 1988, he released his fourth album – a collection of greatest hits entitled *Wadjo*.

1976		Let My Music Take You
1980	CBS	In the Heart of the Ghetto
1985	ANS 8415	Tobolo
1989	VA 010	Wadjo

Ade-Oye, Prince. Juju star sharing a common Yoruba patrimony with better-known Nigerian stars.

1989	VA 012	Juju Music

Letriki, Dossou. Fuji-based star.

1990	SERLP 56	Adjarra Adovie Masse Couhoun (Cass.)

Tohon, Stanislas. Neo-traditionalist working in the field of Beninois ritual music. During the mid-1980s he developed his 'Tchink-system' of old and new instruments.

1984	AP 001	Koude
1987		Owhaou

Danialou, Sagbolin. Brass band stylist.

1990	LIR 27	Alouwe (Cass.)

Others

1980s	ALS 0133	Souradjou Alabi & Akpala: Music of Porto Novo, Benin
1981	MY 005K	Lemed Janvier et Les Volcans du Benin
1983	SOS 127	Various: Talents du Benin
	MAS 1001	Joel Lawani: Tata Li Baba

13 Niger

(ECONOMY AND SOCIETY. Pop.: 7.5 million.
Area: 1,187,000 sq. km. Capital: Niamey.
Independence: 1960. Currency: CFA franc.)

Northern Niger has been inhabited for over 4,000 years, with settlement dating back to the time of a fertile Sahara. By AD 1000 many groups had moved south, controlling the southern end of the trans-Saharan trade and, eventually, themselves coming under the control of the great Sahelian kingdoms of the Hausa, the Kanuri and the Songhai. Islam first appeared in the ninth century but failed to make much headway amongst rural people until the last century.

The area was first 'explored' by the British during the nineteenth century but it was to be the French who eased themselves into power by playing one group off against another. Between 1891 and 1911 the French consolidated their power through military force, putting down several violent revolts in the process. Thereafter, the French moved to curb the power of the traditional chiefs, although there were few agricultural resources to exploit beyond groundnuts. With little to exploit and no reason to hang around, the French acquiesced in early political activity and through the 1940s and 1950s Niger made steady progress towards independence, which duly came in 1960. For the next

thirteen years President Diori and the moderate PPN–RDA ruled the country, stifling radical opposition but unable to do much in the face of frequent drought and a resource-poor economy. They could not control the consequences of the great drought of 1973 and the Army stepped in under Lt Gen. Kountche. Two years earlier enormous uranium deposits had been discovered at Arlit, leading to foreign investment in the economy and two decades of steady growth to compensate for the loss of agriculture and livestock during the frequent droughts. Kountche retained power until 1987, when he died in a Paris hospital to be succeeded by his cousin Col. Ali Saibou, who continued the gradual policy of returning Niger to civilian rule.

TRADITIONAL MUSIC

The traditional music of Niger is by no means under-represented in terms of recordings by international companies and field recordings by ethnomusicologists now deposited in sound archives and music libraries around the world. However, little of it is currently available and most of it was never really released in the commercial sense. For this reason, we have tried to be as comprehensive as possible. The albums listed below appeared on the following labels – Albatross, BAM, Columbia, EMI Odeon, Folkways, Nonesuch, Ocora, SELAF, Sorafom and Tangent.

1959	BAMLD 353	Musique Touareg et Haoussa de la Région d'Agadez (Lute kountigui, vocals and one-string fiddle godje)
1960s	DR VOL1	Festival National de la Jeunesse Nigerienne Vol. 1 (Flutes, percussion, vocals)
	DR VOL2	Festival National de la Jeunesse Nigerienne Vol. 2 (Guitars, percussion, flutes, vocals)

1963	OCR 20	Niger: La Musique Des Griots (Vocals, godje, alghaita, lutes)
	OCR 29	Nomades du Niger: Musique des Touaregs et des Bororo (Vocals, percussion, flutes)
	SOR 4	Rythmes et Chants du Niger (Houassa, Sonrai, Tuareg, Griots)
1965	BAMLD 409	Africa Noire: Panorama de la Musique Instrumentale (Kountigui, godje, vocals)
1969	VPA 8256	Ritmi e Strumenti Africani (Trumpets, percussion, alghaita)
1976	BAMLD 5886	Les Nomades du Niger (Peul, Tuareg – vocals, percussion)
	CETO 723	La Mare de la Vérité: Musique Zarma
	ETH 4470	Tuareg Music of the Southern Sahara

MODERN MUSIC

In 1990 John McLaverty toured Niger researching several recent music developments. The following is his first-hand account.

As befits a country at the cross-roads of Africa, Nigeriennes enjoy a surprisingly diverse range of music. Every town has a cassette shop, market stalls and boys hawking cassettes from bicycles. If local charts existed they would be filled with local music, the 'djeli mousso' sound from Mali, soukous, reggae, zouk and funk – Bobby Brown rather than Michael Jackson. But almost anything could be a chart contender in Niger – from salsa to rai and from Thomas Mapfumo to lambada. Furthermore, Niger enjoys a good TV service and although not many people own their own set, people congregate outside shops and bars to watch zouk and soukous videos crammed in between other programmes. Through the radio station – Tele-Sahel – the latest Paris pop also reaches Niger. By comparison, local music is given scant coverage with the exception of 'Camera Au Village' – a half-hour magazine programme covering aspects of folklore but no electric dance music.

Nigerienne music is inevitably recorded at live shows for later cassette duplication. Even the most down-at-the-heel shop boasts a high-speed duplicator to produce copies as custom demands. Many customers order a bespoke compilation tape in the morning and call back later in the day to pick up a copy. This cottage industry exists alongside the distribution of official tapes from Mali, Senegal, Zaïre (via Paris) and Nigeria. All tapes, whether 'official', 'bootleg' or homemade, sell for the same price, although there does not appear to be much bootlegging of material already available on the 'official' market. In this respect, the ability of Syllart to distribute tapes to the most remote locations (and long before they arrive in Europe) has got to be admired. His biggest success has been 'Moussoulou' by Oumou Sangare, with her modern roots sound blasting from every bar, shop and taxi in town. In a similar groove, songs by Bintou Sidibe ('Samba Dian'), Coumba Sidibi ('Dounouyan') and Sali Sidibe ('Toukan Magni') are also immensely popular. If there was to be a modern Nigerienne sound then it would probably sound like the rasping vocal and staccato instrumentation of 'Dounouyan'. Zani Diabate and Super Djata are also popular, with their older material selling as well as newer efforts. The Ambassadeurs, and the smoother, more melodic styles of the 1970s, are still enjoyed but the market is small, with their cassettes, like those of Youssou N'Dour, gathering dust on cassette shop shelves.

Indigenous music, however, also plays a part in the scene with a great deal of activity flowing from the annual 'Damgourmou' competition, stimulating a round of cassette releases. Top attractions of the late 1980s included Groupe Carnaval (from Maradi), Super Tontoni (Niamey), Super Hske (Zinder), Gueze Band (Agadez), Azna (Tahoua), Assode (Agadez), Groupe Oyouwan (Agadez), Saguera (Dosso) and Groupe Marhaba (Niamey). All these musicians appeared on the 1990 cassette *Parade de la Musique Moderne du Niger*. The 1990 winners, Groupe Carnaval, later released their solo cassette entitled *Badossa* – a nationwide hit which inspired many spirited sing-alongs. However, by 1990, there was little sign of the 1989 stars – Orch. de Sahel, Orch. Super Sonni and the aptly named and blistering hot Acid Rock du Sahel.

The current stars, Groupe Carnaval, produce a rough and ready sound, partly the result of poor recording and partly the result of deliberate sound distortion. The guitars verge on feedback and jostle for space in the busy arrangements as the lyrics are spat out. The whole sound is energised by busy percussion, particularly in the 'animations', where they sound not too dissimilar to Super Djata from neighbouring Mali. Other bands draw on different influences. Super Tontoni mix Malian styles and rumba; Super Hske follow the reggae route; while Gueze Band take an acid guitar riff and polyrhythmic percussion above and beyond the call of duty. Groupe Marhaba, meanwhile, occupy the folkloric fast track.

But does the modern music of Niger have any unifying theme? It can be argued that the Nigerienne sound is very much in a process of formation, much as Senegal was in the 1970s. It takes influences from outside (Mali, reggae and rumba) and blends with traditional idioms with distinctly Hausa drumming and group singing appearing on several recent electric recordings. A number of guitarists also play in the Ali Farka Toure acoustic groove, adding neo-traditional riffs to modern guitar bands. Kasu Zurmi Kwata from the In Gall oasis plays another style of folklore accompanied by frantic percussion; Houmeissa plays a deep hypnotic Tuareg music reminiscent of raw rai; while the popular guitar style owes a great deal to Jimi Hendrix. If you were to take the sound of traditional stringed instruments and add the fuzz and feedback of the western rock tradition, then that might suggest the basis of Niger's unusually muscular guitar sound.

Niger music has a rough spontaniety, particularly in the vocals, which would perhaps be difficult to reproduce in a studio. Indeed, many Nigeriennes comment that they prefer the music to sound 'rough' and that much Malian music was too 'clean'. A distinctive Niger sound is emerging, and the fact that local stars like Carnaval already rub shoulders with Mali's best proves that the local scene has already come a long way. Yet many problems have to be overcome before Niger will be offering up another variety of electric Sahelian music to the rest of Africa. The government media appears indifferent, entrepreneurs seem content with things the way they are and the market is incredibly small with no large presence in France to pull the music along. Given the fact that bands can seldom stay together for long and the competition from Nigeria, Mali and Zaïre, the commercial future must remain uncertain despite the gradual emergence of a national sound.

By 1990, the Nigerienne domestic music market was exclusively cassette-orientated, having never really produced much in the way of vinyl in the first place. The majority of albums released were traditional in orientation, often recorded by ethnomusicologists working with international companies. However, in 1989, an organisation called 'Centre de Formation et de Promotion Musicale' was established in Niamey to promote the music of Niger. Directed by Dominique Pagani and Mahaman Garba, the Centre hopes to make the music of Niger more interesting to the people of Niger by teaching various aspects of music to school children; by promoting ethnomusicological research; by establishing a centre for relevant research materials;

and finally by providing a resource centre for musicians. The centre-piece of their efforts remains the annual music festival (established 1987) which awards the 'Prix Damgourmou' to the best band in the country. (The prize is named after the most celebrated Nigerienne musician). In 1987 the contest was won by Super Kossai de Moussa Poussy; in 1988 by Super Sonni; in 1989 by Arc en Ciel de Niamey; and in 1990 by Carnival de Maradi. For those really interested in digging deeper into this relatively unknown musical culture, the National Radio Station holds a collection of several local stars.

Orchestre Internationale de la Capitale

1988		Vol. 1: Ya Iya Allah
		Vol. 2: Nafissa
		Vol. 3: Yani

Acid Band Du Sahel

1989	Cass.	Prix 1

Super Sonni. Winners of the 1988 music contest with 'Inne Inne'. Led by Mahaman Garba of the Centre (they hold several recordings).

Taya, M'Elhaj. Pioneering moderniser of traditional Nigerienne music.

Ambassadeurs du Sahel, Les. A big dance band who recorded in 1975 for Radio Niger.

Caravanne de Niamey, Orchestre

Assode D'Agadez, Orchestre

Oyiwane D'Agadez, Groupe

Turji de Agadez, Groupe

Mariko, Fatima. Female singer with traditional accompaniment from Niamey region. Strong Sonrai influences.

Toukou, Moussa. Singer/guitarist from Niamey with the touch of Ali Farka Toure.

Guem. Europe-based drum band.

1988	VA 003	Voyage
1989	VA 006	Best of Percussion

Various

1990	Cass.	Parade de la Musique du Niger

89

14   Chad

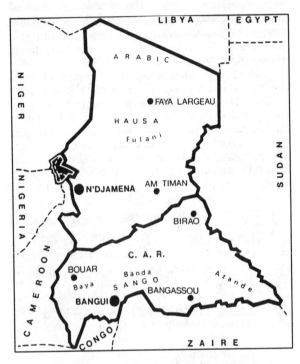

(ECONOMY AND SOCIEY. Pop.: 8 million. Area: 1,284,000 sq. km. Capital: N'Djamena. Independence: 1960. Currency: CFA franc.)

Chad's pre-colonial history revolves around the northern Islamic centralised states dominating the decentralised Bantu people of the south. The most powerful empire was that of Kanem–Bornu (ninth–sixteenth century) followed by the later Baguirmi and Ouaddai kingdoms. Towards the end of the nineteenth century, the brutal slave trader Rabeh was able to establish dominance over much of modern Chad, providing perhaps the most severe resistance to French advance anywhere in the Sahel. Rabeh was finally defeated in 1900, whereupon the French set about the subjugation of the rest of the territory, only completing military conquest in the 1930s. French rule, more firmly established in the south, served to reverse northern dominance until the appearance of the first political party in 1947 persuaded them to side with more reactionary northern forces as a way of retaining power. With the ethnic balance re-established, the French felt they could now safely withdraw leaving their strategic and military interests secure. Independence duly arrived in 1960 under François Tombalbaye.

Tombalbaye moved swiftly to consolidate personal power, forcing opposition into an underground movement which emerged in 1967 as FROLINAT, a fully fledged guerilla movement. Since then Chad has enjoyed no peace as FROLINAT split into two wings led by Hissen Habre and Goukouni Weddeye and embarked on a labyrinthine pro-Libyan policy with France militarily supporting the beleaguered regime of Tombalbaye. Tombalbaye was eventually removed in a 1975 coup but by then the Civil War was well under way, further adding to the economic catastrophe of drought and resource-poor, landlocked isolation. By 1979 events were reaching a climax with the arrival of Weddeye in the Chadian capital of N'Djamena and the renewed split with Habre. The sides were then redrawn with Libya supporting Weddeye and the French stepping in behind Habre. The French poured in men and matériel and by 1985 had established Habre as President in the war-torn capital. Few African countries have suffered so much as Chad over the last two decades. Infrastructure is almost non-existent, the country is one of the poorest in Africa, with a per capita income of under $150, while all the time it struggles with one of the harshest environments in the world, stretching from desert to tropical at its climatic extremes.

CULTURE IN CHAD

| LDX | Music of the Tibetsi (Lute and fiddle cermonial music) |
| LDX | Music of Kanem (Drums and reeds) |

15   Mauritania

(ECONOMY AND SOCIETY. Pop.: 2 million. Area: 1,030,700 sq. km. Capital: Nouakchott. Independence: 1960. Currency: Ouguiya.)

The earliest inhabitants of this region, at a time when the Sahara was considerably more fertile than today, were the Bafour, the ancestors of the modern Soininke. But by the third century AD the Sanhadja Berbers were moving southwards into Mauritania, establishing a unified state which by the eleventh century, and now under the control of the Islamic Almoravids, had defeated the Ghana empire and seized control of the trans-Saharan trade. By this time the region was thoroughly Islamicised, apart from the African minorities in the south (Toucouleur, Soininke, Wolof and Bambara). The Almoravid empire survived until the seventeenth century although it was never a solid administrative unit and eventually fell to the Maqil Arabs, a Bedouin group. However, by the sixteenth century various European powers were taking an interest in the trading possibilities along the coast; France was eventually to gain exclusive control in the early nineteenth century. Thereafter, Mauritania was more or less run from Senegal under a system of indirect rule which left considerable power in the hands of the traditional chiefs. By the early twentieth century the French were using Mauritania as a base in their attempts to subjugate Morocco, having crushed Mauritanian opposition in 1910.

Resistance to French rule reappeared after the Second World War led by Ould Daddah and the UPM. The UPM made steady legislative progress and was rewarded with full independence in 1960 after a joint French–Spanish force had crushed a pro-Moroccan uprising in the Western Sahara and northern Mauritania. Since then, Mauritania and Western Sahara have had to deal with the expansionist claims of a Greater Morocco, although Morocco did finally recognise Mauritanian independence in 1969. Ould Daddah soon established a one-party state but his efforts to Arabise the country met with considerable opposition from the African groups in the south. Economically, Daddah espoused a leftist ideology which led to the nationalisation of foreign mining companies and the creation of a national currency outside the Franc zone. In terms of foreign policy, the most decisive event of the 1970s was Daddah's decision to cooperate with Morocco in the partition of the former Spanish colony of Western Sahara. This sparked off the Polisario resistance movement whose efforts to establish an independent Western Saharan state continue until today and which have caused enormous problems for Mauritania despite the 1979 ceasefire.

Economically, Mauritania is characterised as a country of shifting agriculture with a few mining enclaves. The country suffered severely in the Sahelian droughts of the mid-1980s with around 35 per cent of the population urbanised by 1985, compared with just over 3 per cent at the time of independence. Throughout the 1980s Mauritania struggled to come to terms with IMF structural adjustment policies and despite ambitious irrigation and fishing plans remained one of the most vulnerable countries in Africa.

Recent political developments began with the overthrow of Daddah in 1978, a second coup led by Ould Louly in 1979, a ceasefire with Polisario in the same year and the mounting enmity of Morocco. The early 1980s saw numerous coup attempts until one finally succeeded in 1984, bringing Ould Taya to power. Taya repaired relations with Morocco, Algeria and Libya and seemed capable of establishing a degree of stability until the crisis with Senegal erupted in 1990.

MUSIC IN MAURITANIA

Mauritanian music, developed over centuries, is a creative mix of African and Arabic influences based on expressive vocals and complex rhythms. Moorish musicians have their own musical families – the 'Iggawin' – who pass on traditions, for which they act as repositories. Yet although tradition is important (and audiences know when errors are made), Moorish music is also open to innovation by skilled and highly trained musicians. More recently, with increasing urbanisation, the role of the Iggawin has also been changing from that of a praise singer to that of an entertainer and creative artiste. New electric instruments have also been introduced to the traditional line-up of the 'ardin' (a fourteen-stringed kora), the 'tbal' (a percussion instrument) and the 'tidinit' (a type of lute).

The music of Mauritania, briefly dealt with in Volume 1, is based on four modes of expression: El Karr depicts joy; El Faqhou depicts anger; El Signima depicts sentiment; and El Beygui depicts sorrow. Each mode is subsequently divided into thematic material derived from three genres – black, white and spotted.

Readers more interested in this fascinating tradition are referred to the excellently concise sleeve notes on WCD 019.

| 1970s | OCR 28 | Musique Maure |
| | 558532/3 | Anthologie de la Musique Maure |

Abba, Dimi Mint. Female singer, described by Ali Farka Toure as one of Africa's greatest vocalists, whose current popularity stretches across the Sahara to the Middle East. Her talent was recognised as a child, and since she had been born into a Iggawin family it was only natural that she should stay in music. As a child she was taught to dance and play percussion and by the age of 16 she was appearing on national radio, representing her country at a music festival in Tunisia the following year. She appears on the excellent World Circuit CD (WCD 019).

Eide, Khalifa Ould. Male singer and 'tidinit' (lute) player. Toured the UK in 1990 with Dimi Mint and recorded a CD-only release for World Circuit. The CD features both traditional material and Khalifa on electric guitar for more modern interpretations. It was also the first quality studio recording of Moorish music.

| 1990 | WCD 019 | Moorish Music from Mauritania |

Ba, Saidou

| 1983 | SAF 50062 | Mankayira Vol. 3 |

16   Guinea-Bissau

(ECONOMY AND SOCIETY. Pop.: 1 million. Area: 36,125 sq. km. Capital: Bissau. Independence: UDI – 1973. Currency: Peso.) For map, see p. 68.

A tiny country, situated between Guinea and Senegal, Guinea-Bissau is populated mainly by the Balante (32 per cent), the Fula (22 per cent), the Mandjak (14 per cent), the Mandinka (13 per cent) and the Pepel (7 per cent). The earliest known arrivals were the Naulu and Landuma people who arrived in the thirteenth century following the decline of the old Ghana empire. Between the twelfth and fourteenth centuries the area comprised part of the Mali empire, but by the fifteenth century the Portuguese had arrived in search of slaves. During the following four centuries the French, British and Portuguese vied for power and influence until the Portuguese finally established hegemony towards the end of the nineteenth century, with resistance to colonial rule continuing on in some areas until 1936.

Portugal was easily the most backward and poor of the European colonial nations and as such failed almost totally to develop its imperial possessions. This weakness meant that Portugal could never exploit its colonies efficiently and was forced to rely on military power long after other colonial powers had withdrawn. Of course this meant that the anti-colonial forces were obliged to turn to the armed struggle since there was little or no possibility of a peaceful, political advance. Resistance movements put down deeper roots than political parties producing a sophisticated radicalism, which in Guinea-Bissau operated as the PAIGC under the leadership of Amilcar Cabral. Formed in 1956, the PAIGC soon became one Africa's most respected political movements, militarily defeating the Portuguese and declaring independence in 1973, with the Portuguese finally withdrawing the following year.

The PAIGC immediately faced a number of problems, such as refugees and western hostility, in addition to the wider structural legacies of colonialism and war. Luiz Cabral (brother of Amilcar who had been assassinated in 1973) ran the country until 1980 when he was removed in a palace coup. The coup largely replaced the 'mestizo' leadership and led to a deterioration in relations with Cape Verde. The new President, Joao Vieira, moved quickly to consolidate his position within the PAIGC, surviving a coup attempt in 1985 and trying to establish better relations with the west. But Guinea-Bissau remains an incredibly underdeveloped country even by African standards, increasingly relying on the IMF and other western institutions to prop up the economy.

TRADITIONAL MUSIC

As far as I am aware, no traditional music has been released, although, presumably, a local cassette market exists for both traditional and modern sounds.

MODERN MUSIC

In 1990 the top band in the country was Super Mama Djombo, closely followed by other artistes such as Maio Cooperante, Manecas, Africa Libre, Dulce Mario, Justinio Delgado, Cobiana Jazz and Jetu Katem.

Super Mama Djombo. Bissau's top band have now been playing for over a decade with a clutch of albums to their credit.

1970s		Festival Vol. 1
		Pamaparera
1980	SMD 001	Na Cambanca
	SMD 002	Festival Vol. 2
1987		Super Mama Djombo

Ramirez, Naka (a.k.a. Naka Ramiro). Vocalist who enjoyed a growing reputation in the late 1980s.

1985	DYA 81055	Naka & L'Orchestre Guinea-Bissau: Je Viens D'Ailleurs
1986	SAS 039	Garde Ta Personalité
1986	RA 81065	Djunda Djunda
1991		Salvador

Mane, Kabe. Became successful at home then moved to Paris. Mane bases his music on his native Koussounde style, singing in Balante. His two recent albums feature stunning guitar work and solid brass arrangements. In 1989 he toured the UK.

1988	ESP 7519	Chefo Mae Mae			
1989	98560-1	Kunga Kungake			
1990	WCCM 1	Best of Kabe Mane (CD)			

Cobiana Jazz. Led by singer José Carlos Schwarz.

SAF 50071	Indicitavo

Others

	De Cancoes: Uma Cartucheira
SAF 50072	Paulo Nanque
779013	Sa'ba Miniamba

N'Kassa Cobra

750118	Unidade-Luta-Progresso

17 Cape Verde

(ECONOMY AND SOCIETY. Pop.: 382,000. Area: 4,033 sq. km. Capital: Praia. Independence: 1975. Currency: Escudo.)

The archipelago comprising Cape Verde remained uninhabited until the arrival of the Portuguese in 1456, but by the end of the century the islands had become a major entrepôt for the slave trade, with many slaves being forced to work on island farms before being shipped over the Atlantic. With an important strategic position and an excellent natural harbour the island of São Vicente had become a significant commercial centre by the nineteenth century. However, with the end of the obnoxious trade, the islands' importance declined and they suffered from repeated droughts which regularly decimated the population. Miscegenation had by this time produced an indigenous class of mestizos who forged a unique Cape Verdean nationality and culture based on the Crioula language.

In 1951 the status of the islands was changed from that of a colony of Portugal to that of an overseas territory. This provided easier access to education than was the case in Portugal's other African colonies, although the absence of job opportunities on the islands led Verdeans to take up jobs throughout the Portuguese African empire (hence the popularity of Verdean music in Angola). In 1956 Amilcar Cabral founded the PAIGC, and although Portuguese repression and the isolation of the islands prevented the growth of a strong anti-colonial movement on the islands, they did provide many early educated members of Cabral's movement. In 1963 open war broke out and when the Salazar regime fell in Lisbon in 1974 widespread resistance erupted in the colonies, obliging the Portuguese to withdraw. Independence duly arrived in 1975.

Since then the PAIGC (renamed the PAIGV) has been the sole legal political party, adopting socialism as the path to development and guided by the works of Cabral – one of Africa's pre-eminent political thinkers and leaders. However, a change in approach could do nothing to improve the climate and the islands continued to suffer from dreadful and regular famines. For many, escape from these famines has meant migration and there are now strong Verdean communities in the US (over 300,000!) and in Holland as well as Portugal. With an economy based on sugar and coffee, and thus vulnerable to the vagaries of the international market, it is difficult to see how Cape Verde can make any substantial progress. Economic viability now depends on remittances from relatives living abroad. Politically, Cape Verde has remained stable with early efforts to unite the islands with Guinea-Bissau under the banner of the PAIGC failing to transcend two rival nationalisms and almost 500 miles of Atlantic Ocean.

TRADITIONAL MUSIC

In an interesting section in *Popular Musics of the Non-Western World* (see Bibliography), Manuel outlines the key developments in the evolution of a specifically Cape Verdean sound. Essentially, Cape Verde developed a unique musical culture through a blend of African, Portuguese and Brazilian influences. The African retentions remain the most important element, although it is difficult to pin-point exactly where they came from given 500 years of imported slave labour. From this perspective, there is no indigenous tradition to draw from and all Verdean music is acculturated to a greater or lesser extent. Specifically Portuguese elements emerged in the form of 'morna' – a musical poetic rendition accompanied by a stringed ensemble comprising the violin, guitar and the 'cavaquinho' (a ukele-like instrument). The 'morna' is believed to have Luso-Brazilian origns and emerged in the early nineteenth century with additional influences from Italian salon music. It remains popular and can be performed in either the older 'classical' style or with a variety of modern instruments. A second important style to emerge in the nineteenth century was the 'coladera', which is believed to be influenced by the polka and is now a faster, pop style drawing on various local roots such as the 'morna', black American music, Antilles pop and local folk traditions.

MODERN MUSIC

However, while 'morna' and 'coladera' remain popular, they have been overtaken in terms of popularity by two modern styles with a more distinctive African feel – the 'batuco' and the 'funana'. Both styles are drawn from the island's black underclass and have become up-tempo, polyrhythmic dance styles. Both were denounced during the colonial period but emerged in the 1970s as basic elements in Verdean dance band repertoire.

The modern music of Cape Verde is an intriguing mix of afro-Brazilian, Portuguese and Casamance influences. Current stars, in addition to those listed below, include As Estrelas, Rene Cabral and Cocktail des Iles.

Evora, Cesaria. Known on the islands as 'La Diva aux Pieds Nus', Cesaria is the undisputed queen of Cape Verdean song and still lives on the islands, unlike many others. She draws exclusively on 'mornas' and 'coladeras' for her music.

1989	LA 5901	La Diva aux Pieds Nus (Brandao Label)
1990	82484	Music de Cap Vert

Morais, Luis. Highly respected elder statesman of the local scene whose name appears on many recordings as arranger and/or reed player. His latest solo album is an attempt to apply modern studio technology to older styles. He spent some time in Holland (where quite a few Verdean albums are recorded).

1980s	LP DLS 1001	Broadway (La Do Si Discos label)
1989	79523	Lagrimas (Lusafrica/ Melodie label)

Cabo Verde Show. Perhaps the best known Cape Verdean band, led by vocalist Cabral.

1984	AP 026	Bem Danca
1985	JM 9001	+ John Matias
1989	38778	Beijo Cu Jetu

Matias, John. John doubles up on sax and clarinet.

1985	JM 9001	+ Cabo Verde Show

Mendes et Mendes. Two brothers from Cape Verde but long resident in Senegal where they were involved in the big band Cabo Verde Show. To date they have only made one LP, poor profit for ten years' travel and experience in France, Holland and Senegal. They specialise in Afro-Brazilian rhythms.

1984	AP 023	Mendes et Mendes

Son of Cap. Strange name for a young group who

emerged in the early 1980s. Playing typical island rhythms, the music is both danceable and calm.

1984	AP 025	Maldita

Jovino. Vocalist at home in many different styles and languages.

1985	DPX 813	Afro Bump

Black Show, The

1985	AP 1782	Black Show
1986	13384	Solucao

Os Tubaroes. The band moved to Lisbon in the 1980s and enjoyed a short spell of intense popularity towards the end of the decade when they crossed over into Portuguese mainstream pop with a blend of Verdean styles, funk and rock.

	T 003	Djonsinho Cabral
1990	7943001	Os Tubaroes (Valentim de Cavalho label)

Finacon. One of the most popular dance bands from the islands, whose 1990 album (in addition to two earlier releases in 1987 and 1989) was a brave attempt to introduce a new tropical dance craze to succeed the lambada and soca. They played to a rapturous crowd in Paris in 1990 but the style largely failed to take off. The 1990 LP contains tracks from previous recordings plus two new songs produced by Ray Lema.

1990	CBS-467227	Funana

Lima, Abel. Vocalist and pianist who recorded his 1990 album in Abidjan with the help of Hekimian, Maika and Seba.

1990	AL 011	Canta Afrika Nostalgie

Manix

1990	38754	Tanguy

Various

1970s	VJ S1	Musica Cabo Verdiana: Protesto e Luta
1989	DS 48201	Various: Show de Cabo Verde

18　Cameroon

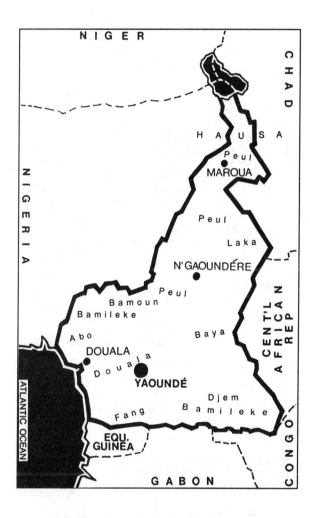

(ECONOMY AND SOCIETY. Pop.: 12 million.
Area: 475,000 sq. km. Capital: Yaounde.
Independence: 1960. Currency: CFA franc.)

Named after a type of large pink prawn, modern
Cameroon is a true colonial creation. Prior to the
twentieth century, the area was occupied by a variety
of groups practising different forms of socio-economic
organisation. The north of the country lay on the
periphery of the Northern Nigerian feudal empires
and reflected their central organisation; central
Cameroon, occupied by the Bamileke, supported a
number of independent chiefdoms; while the south

and the east were occupied by Bantu people organised
in both patrilineal and matrilineal societies. By the
sixteenth century the Europeans had arrived on the
coast, and with them an expansion of the slave trade,
while the north had long been in contact with North
Africa and the Middle East through both Islam and
trade.

With the abolition of the slave trade the Europeans
turned to a trade in agricultural products, steadily
being drawn into local politics. The British seemed to
have established a protectorate by the mid-nineteenth
century, but when Victoria refused to deal on equal
terms with the king of Douala the kingdom turned to
Germany, which established a protectorate in 1884 as
a prelude to full control over the entire country by the
early twentieth century. German control did not last
long and when Germany lost its overseas possessions
after the First World War the League of Nations
divided up the colony, awarding the west to Britain
and the east to the French. For the next three decades
the country remained split with different official
languages and different systems of justice and education. Then in 1948 the UPC was set up, arguing, like the
Togolese, for both national unification and national
independence. Both colonising powers moved quickly
to crush the movement, eventually forcing it underground and pushing it to the left. Meanwhile a more
moderate party, the Union Camerounaise, led by
Ahmadou Ahidjo, proceeded to follow parliamentary
procedures and approved of the great repression of
1958 when over 300 UPC activists were killed. Ahidjo
then seized control of events and set about transform-
ing the northern-based Union into a national party.
Independence duly arrived in 1960, sparking off the
Bamileke revolt, which was brutally suppressed by
French ground and air forces. (A state of emergency
was imposed on the Bamileke area which lasted well
into the 1970s.) In 1961 Cameroon was finally reunited
through a referendum and Ahidjo proceeded to
impose a one-party state on the country. Unification
was now the main priority, with economic development taking a back seat. Ahidjo finally stood down in
1982 after two decades in power during which much
had been done to provide an enforced stability on the
country. He nominated Paul Biya as his successor,
who, despite recent pro-democracy activity, has ruled
the country with the same iron grip as his mentor for
most of the last decade.

97

TRADITIONAL MUSIC

See Volume 1 for a brief introduction and nine-item discography.

MODERN MUSIC

During the late 1980s the music of Cameroon lost much of its popular appeal due to over-saturation of the market by a Paris-based coterie of studio musicians led by Alhadji Touré, Toto Guillaume, Manu Lima, Jules Kamga and female vocalists Tity Edima, Florence Tity and Charlotte Mbanga. Volume 1 covers the development of modern urban music in Cameroon from the early years of the twentieth century to the mid-1980s and should be regarded as an essential introduction. However, by the late 1980s the makossa movement was steadily losing steam with neither Sam Fan Thomas, nor Moni Bile able to replicate the dance-floor success of earlier years. Dibango continued to explore new paths while the only other major innovation came from Les Têtes Brulées and their up-tempo bikutsi.

Dibango, Manu (b. Douala, 1933). One of the true giants of modern African music, Manu stands head and shoulders above most of his compatriots. Sax player, pianist and composer, his enormously varied and influential career has now spanned five decades, without any apparent dimunition in momentum. In 1989 he entered the pantheon of African musicians when, in addition to his enormous musical output, he collaborated with D. Rouard on the excellent autobiography entitled, somewhat mysteriously, *Trois Kilos De Cafe* (Lieu Common, Paris, 1990). Volume 1 also provided a summary of his earlier career and a long but incomplete discography.

Since the mid-1970s Manu has continued stretching the sound of music in several new directions. The late 1970s found him working with Sly and Robbie in Jamaica; the mid-1980s found him in Paris with Martin Messonier for *Abele Dance* and in New York for *Electric Africa* with Bill Laswell. Most recently he has been in the studio with Working Week producer Simon Booth on the 1991 Dibango classic *Polysonik*. Live shows maintained the Manu myth with packed houses in Europe and the Antilles (1989) and a starring role at the annual SOS Racisme gig in Paris. Despite his many musical incarnations, the Dibango sound is instantly recognisable – surely the highest accolade for any musician working out of Africa in an era of stereotypes and bland imitation. He has been described as possessing an Afro-Euro-sensibility grounded in a 'Négropolitaine' philosophy. Now approaching 60, he remains in the vanguard of efforts to put African music on the map. In 1991 his autobiographical film *Silences* appeared on European screens, further cementing his global reputation.

1988	SP 8701/2	Seventies (Double)
1989	82427-1	Happy Reunion (Double)
1990	85900	Afrijazzy
1991	LP 63703	Soft and Sweet (Re-release from 1983)
	850 420	Polysonik

Bebey, Francis. Academic, journalist and eclectic musician, Francis Bebey approached the end of the decade in fine form with a clutch of new albums and his first CD-only release. The two 1989 releases reveal just how wide his scope is with *African Woman* featuring hi-tech synth sounds while *Baobab* provides a rich, neo-traditional instrumental outing. With a truly global appeal, Bebey is now at the peak of his creative powers. In 1989 he played the prestigious Francophonie festival in Martinique and appeared in London several months later at the African Music Village in the delightful setting of Kew Gardens. By the 1990s Bebey was producing (exclusively on CD), generously lengthy LPs mixing a variety of styles and sounds from original bikutsi and film scores to mbira, keyboards, sax and jazz. Only Bebey could possibly carry it off. See Volume 1 for early career and discography.

1987	8229	Si Les Gauloises Avaient Su
1988	OZIL 3312	African Sanza (Re-issue)
1989	FB 88318	African Woman
	FB 88319	Baobab
1990	13901 CD	Paris-Dougou
1991	13902 CD	Amaya

Tala, Andre Marie. One of the most influential Cameroonian singer/guitarists. Originator of the 'tchamassi' rhythm. See Volume 1 for details.

1974	SAF 360057	Hot Koki
1975	SAF 360060	Lomdie
1976	SAF 360069	Djamena
	SAF 360084	Black Woman
	SAF 362010	Super Tchamassi
	SAF 362011	Special Tchamassi
	SAF 360019	Notre Fille
1981	AND 33801	Tala 81
	AND 33802	Tu M'as Ment
	AND 33803	Binam

	AND 33833	Mother Africa
1984	AND 33855	Je Vais à Yaounde
1989		Qui Saurait Me Dire

Thomas, Sam Fan. One of Cameroon's truly great stars, his recent LPs are of a consistently high quality but a repeat of the massive success of *African Typic Collection* proves as elusive as ever. The song itself received another outing on the Earthworks compilation; as good a place as any to start with the music of Cameroon. In 1988 he toured widely, cashing in on his global reputation with tours of the Antilles and Reunion. Towards the end of the year he played several gigs in London. The following year saw a switch to a major label when he signed to Mango, the World Music label of Island Records. In 1990 he played several disappointing shows in New York, hampered by the absence of a good support band. In 1991 he was back in the studio in the hope that a change of label could help him escape from the well-worn 'Typic' groove.

1986	MS 5004	Makassi Plus
1988	NE 5002	Makassi Again
1989	EWV 12	Various: African Typic Collection

Manga, Bebe. Some songs never die, and although Bebe continues her career in relative obscurity, the mega-hit 'Amie' came in for its third re-release in 1990. See Volume 1 for career details.

1990	425001	Amie

Ngoh, Misse

1988	EP 010	Yoya
	WEI 597	Vol. 1

Guillaume, Toto. Omnipresent guitarist and producer. He released half a dozen albums in the early 1980s but since then has concentrated on studio and session work.

1985	TN 591	Elimbi Na Ngomo

Touré, Alhadji. Omnipresent bassist and producer. Played one successful show under his own name in New York, 1990. Owner of Touré Jim's record label.

Decca, Ben. Check his contribution to Hilarion Nguema's 1989 smash, *Turbo Hits 89*. In 1990 his sister Grace, already an accomplished session singer, burst forth with her first solo LP, *Besoin D'Amour*, written and produced by brother Ben with extra help

from Toto Guillaume, Geo. Bilong and Gilly Doumbe.

1988	MH 106	L'Amour à Sens Unique
1989	MH 110	Réconciliation
	MH 112	+ Ngeuma & Bell: Turbo Hits 89
1990	SNFL 1001	Grace Decca: Besoin D'Amour

Brilliant, Ekambi

1987	JMA17724	Ayo Mba Ebolo

Bell, Dina. Vocalist with half a dozen early 1980s LPs to his credit. Recent output is uneven.

1988	MH 108	Muendi Mu

Lottin, Eboa. See Volume 1 for early career and discography. A true giant of modern Cameroonian music, his act gets classier and classier by the year. A talented multi-instrumentalist (guitar, harmonica, bass, keyboards), he is highly regarded by his peers. His 1988 recording (TSHI 005) includes tributes to various local and international stars including James Brown, Nyanka Bell, Dibango and Cameroonian football star Thomas Nkono. On TCHI 007 he followed up with a tribute to another grand old man of Cameroonian music, Francis Bebey.

1985	TSHI 002	Disque D'Or (Double)
1988	TSHI 005	Musique Anti-Crise Vol.1
	TSHI 007	Sodome et Gomorho

Kemayo, Elvis. Nothing new from the studio master but Elvis seemed happy enough putting together and producing bands in neighbouring Gabon.

Bile, Moni. Makossa master from the mid-1980s found it extremely difficult to follow up early hits. Played shows in London 1988 and New York 1990. Returned to UK in early 1991 as promoters sought to cash in on the publicity generated by the Cameroon–England football friendly. In early 1991 Moni released the *Best Of* LP and listeners are advised to compare these reworked versions with an original sampler released at the same time by Sonodisc (CDAT 501). The latter CD is an excellent place to start a makossa collection.

1985	MB 112	Nasi Lingui (With Ben Decca)
1986	MB 113	African Melody

	MB 114	Makossa Ambiance
1988	MB 115	Affection
1991	MB 52711	10ème Anniversaire: Best of
	CDAT 501	Chagrin D'Amour

Tim & Foty. Often regarded as the best session horn section in Cameroon if not in Africa. The pair have been together for over a decade, releasing a clutch of excellent albums in-between session demands.

1975	ESP 165509	Eda
1976	ESP 165519	Ddo Lam
1979	DWAPS 2113	Loba Loba
1989	TF 48901	Zoulou
1990	AIRTF 560	Help

Tezano, Johnny. Johnny, following his massive success in 1986, has managed to maintain momentum, partly through his own talents and partly through surrounding himself with the very best musicians of the Paris scene. His 1989 LP, *Carreau Magique*, featured Manu Lima and Rigo Star on guitars, Lokassa on rhythm, Alhadji Touré on bass, Dally Kimoko and Guy Bilong. The style of music on the LP is a Cameroonian strain of Kwassa Kwassa, subtitled Ma-Kwassa. In 1990 he followed up with *Soukous Boogie*, another dance-floor hit, with the help of Touré, Bilong, Ngouma, Lokassa and Tchekou.

1985	TAM 14	Missile 85
1988	TG 3306	Circuit Court
1989	AT 078	Carreau Magique
1990	AT 088	Soukous Boogie

Hekimian, Denis. Omnipresent Paris-based drummer. One of the earliest and most consistent of the African–Antillean cross-over artistes, now in incredible demand as a session drummer. In 1989 he released his first solo album, accompanied by brother Dada on percussion and vocals.

| 1989 | DDH 01 | Entre dans la Danse |

Moussy, Pierre De. The master of smooth and lyrical makossa was able to build on successful albums from the mid-1980s.

| 1987 | MOU 011 | Douala City Dibi |
| 1988 | MOU 012 | C'Est Ma Wa |

| 1989 | MOU 015 | O-Bolane Mba |
| 1990 | | Reviens Moi Fatimatou |

Mbanga, Lapiro de. Like so many stars, Lapiro found it difficult to emulate the success of his earlier hit, in 1986. In 1990 he turned to a makossa–bikutsi blend with the help of other luminaries such as Manu Dibango, Toto Guillaume and Willie Nfor, with more than a nod in the direction of afrobeat.

1985	MB 0101	Pas Argent No Love
1986	TSHI 003	No Make Erreur
1989	TG 3303	Surface de Réparation
1990	NE 5003	Ndinga Man

Bikutsi

A Yaounde traditional rhythm given strong government support towards the end of the 1980s as the ethnic music of President Biya. Bikutsi is now an up-tempo dance style which enthusiasts either like or dislike; Cameroonian music dancing to a different drummer.

Vétérans, Les. Appropriately named bikutsi pioneers – a sophisticated twelve-piece dance band formed in the 1970s and making their commercial breakthrough in 1983. A roots revival band of the highest order.

1986	STC 010	Traditions (Vol. 4)
1987	TC 0007	Au Village
1988	DTC 024	Les Vétérans Présentent Ahanda

Têtes Brulées, Les. Formed in Cameroon in 1980 and led by former journalist Jean-Marie Ahanda. Ahanda was brought up in Cameroon before moving to Paris to study in the late 1970s where he played with Toure Kunda and cut a few tracks with Antillean superstar Jacob Desvarieux and Zaïrean keyboard star Ray Lema as The Bwana Zoulou Gang (see Lema for details). But Ahanda, by now a student of publicity and advertising, was having second thoughts about how African music was presented to the public. In due course he returned home and after an initial refamiliarisation with traditional instruments – the balafon and the mvet – he formed Les Têtes Brulées (Burnt Heads). Ahanda had clear musical and cultural ideas and set out singing in both Beti and street French. Culturally, the aim was to create a new current of expression for Africans and others in the wider Francophonie. The new image was based on up-tempo, frantic bikutsi rhythms and a new eccentric look involving shaved heads, painted bodies, day-glo uniforms, sunglasses and a general air of pyschedelia. Little is known about the band until they resurfaced in 1988 as stars of a French documentary following up in 1990 as mascots of the Cameroonian World Cup Team. That same year they exploded on a jaded African music scene as a bolt from the blue, playing several well-received shows in Europe. Les Têtes Brulées are in many ways the first packaged African act, although this does nothing to detract from their musicianship. In 1990 the band suffered the loss of lead guitarist Zanzibar who died after a short illness.

It remains to be seen whether the band can retain their commercial momentum or whether they will simply disappear as an interesting and eccentric African act. Whatever happens, they have succeeded in putting the bikutsi rhythm on the musical map and by the early 1990s reports from Cameroon indicated that bikutsi was taking over from makossa as the people's favourite dance rhythm (although whether this reflected popular taste or presidential preference remains unclear). In mid-1991 the band returned to the studio to record their long-awaited follow-up LP.

| 1988 | ML | Zanzibar et Les Têtes Brulées: Révélation Télé-Podium 1987 |
| 1990 | ST 9001 | Les Têtes Brulées |

Drakus, Gibraltar. Têtes Brulées clone. LP produced by the aptly named Mystic Jim. First LP dedicated to deceased Brulées guitarist Zanzibar.

| 1990 | | Hommage à Zanzibar |

Bekono, Roger. Another foray into bikutsi featuring Gibraltar on vocals.

| 1989 | IDS 890513 | Jolie Poupée |

Mbala, Bonny (b. Mballa Omgba Isidore). Vocalist and guitarist jumping on the bikutsi bandwagon.

| 1990 | BM 005 | Bikutsi Non-Stop |

Nkodo, Si Toni

| 1988 | PMI 870002 | Ace de Bikutsi |

N'Joh, Bella. Mid-1980s star vocalist who turned to bikutsi in the early 1990s. Also doubles up on drums.

1986	GME 010	Mambo Penya
1987	ASS 1374	L'Ascenseur Est Bloqué
1991	49909	Belle Mere

Mekongo, President. Keyboards and vocals.

| 1990 | MHK 116 | Bikutsi Koba |

New wave makossa

Lobe, Guy. Enormously gifted composer/singer. Starting to make a name for himself towards the end of the 1980s. On the 1990 album he is backed by a veritable 'Who's Who' of the makossa scene. An experienced session singer, in 1989 he successfully fused zouk and makossa, featuring bright horn arrangements and solid guitar lines. Had one of Cameroon's biggest Paris hits with *Coucou*. In 1990 he teamed up with Ndedi Dibango and Manulo for a brisk makossa offering under the T.J.R. Trio label. Featuring half a dozen covers of classic makossa cuts, the Trio carved a dance-floor niche in what was becoming a very crowded makossa scene. In 1991 Lobe struck gold with *Malinga*, featuring twin vocalists Epee and Koum, with Ringo and Gille Doumbe on guitar.

1980s	AT 066	Esele Mba
	AT 068	Mon Amie et Moi
1988	AT 071	Aye Mba
1989	AT 075	Solitude
	TG 3304	Union Libre
1990	AT 080	Coucou
1991	ACP/CG 007	Malinga

Epee and Koum. The twin brothers produced one of the biggest makossa hits of the early 1990s with their makossa–soukous cross-over. They acknowledged the key role played by the Cameroonian soccer team in the 1990 World Cup finals in bringing the national sound to global attention, describing football and music as 'sisters'. Their first LP was released in 1990 to tremendous acclaim. It was characterised by typical makossa key changes, lush arrangements and ringing soukous guitar courtesy of Toto Guillaume. They followed up with *Makossa Collection* – a medley of virtually every Cameroonian international hit since 1985.

| 1990 | AT 90 | Soukoumakossa |
| 1991 | ATO 83 | Makossa Collection |

Ddam, Claude. New-wave singer.

| 1988 | DTC 008 | |
| 1991 | DTC 028 | U Ngue Ya |

Petit-Pays. New style vocalist supported by the cream of session men – Touré, de Majunga and Doumbe.

1988	EP 015	Sala Malekum
1989	EP 010	Ça Fait Mal
1990	AT 087	Trouver La Vie

Seba, Georges. Top-drawer guitarist who surrounds himself with other leading stars, including Jules Kamga and Yves Ndjock.

| 1985 | 79417 | M'Aye Bo Aya |
| 1990 | 88271 | Freedom |

Emerent, Ange Ebogo

1985	NNM 184	Experience
1987	DTC 019	Nge W'ayem
1990	BTC 027	Explosion

Eyango, Prince. Vocalist.

| 1989 | TG 3302 | You Must Calculer |
| 1990 | AT 082 | Soul Botingo |

Douleur, Jackie. Prime-time vocalist who scored heavily with his 1988 LP.

| 1986 | TN 592 | Wake Up Africa |
| 1988 | KL8702 | Beneground |

Nelson, J.R. Backed by the usual Cameroonian crew. Up-tempo makossa.

1985	TN 590	Nyam'am
1986	TN 593	Ba Iyo
1990	TN 599	Dia

Manulo. Vocalist whose 1990 LP was a major hit in France.

| 1989 | AT 081 | Bombe 'H' |
| 1990 | TG 3301 | Fundament |

Mouyenga, Pierrot. Cameroonian singer who, against the migration to Paris, records in neighbouring Lagos. His début album reflects this with a more open approach to makossa than that favoured by other Cameroonians. Perhaps spoiled by drum machines but still a varied LP with several ballads as well as more up-tempo numbers. This was

the first release on the WireWise label set up Mike Odumosu, ex-Osibisa.

| 1988 | WIRE 1 | Ugulongo |

Doumbe, Gilly. Extremely talented guitarist starting to make his mark with this solo LP and numerous session appearances. When on form he can hit one of the heaviest makossa grooves around.

| 1990 | AT 086 | Makossa Syndrum |

Black, Djboue. Vocalist.

| 1988 | GME 009 | C'est Pas Sérieux |
| 1989 | DB 47901 | Les Roses de la Vie |

Perriere, Charlie. First solo LP in 1990 featuring the guitar skills of Master Mwana Congo and a curious yet somehow appealing big-band reworking of traditional Pygmy music.

| 1990 | BM 8601 | Koubourou |

Mbanga, Charlotte. One of the brightest new female vocalists to emerge from the Parisian profusion of session singers. Her first LP, *Nostalgie*, featured the very best of the session men, songs composed by the great Dina Bell and a hit medley 'Makossa Non-Stop'. Followed up with a big hit in 1989, *Konkai Makossa*.

1988	AT 072	Nostalgie
1989	AT 075	Konkai Makossa
1990	AT 076	Makossa New Form

Golden Sounds. Makossa group.

| 1986 | DTC 014 | Zangalewa |
| 1987 | DTC 021 | Vol. 2 |

Esa. Two-piece group, using good back-up men.

| 1986 | THUA 1218 | Muto |
| 1988 | VAW 007 | Eyaye |

Dalle, Penda. Gifted vocalist with a steady rather than stunning track record. Nicknamed Jeandall.

1983	AOLP 004	Tadi
1985	DR 784	Langwe Yo Te Mbo
1987	WEI 586	Na Beli Na Wodi

1988	WEI 595	Nyonga Muleme
1989	WEI 599	Alea Mba

Batcho, Sam (b. Samuel Tchomagni). Solo singer who toured widely with Sam Fan Thomas at the height of his success – from the French Antilles to Reunion in the Indian Ocean. Recorded his first LP in 1985 with the help of Sam Fan.

1985		+ Tamis D'Or: Nadia No Tondi
1990	NE 5001	More Makassi

Baba, Ali. Multi-media performer who first struck gold in 1985 with the unusual album *La Démon de la Danse Africaine*.

1989	MH 014	On Ne Tape Pas La Femme

Masso, Georges W. His first LP produced the monster hit 'Lolita', the biggest Cameroonian hit since *African Typic Collection*.

1989	GME 012	The Greatest

Mbarga, Manga. Gifted singer, helped out on the 1990 album by Vincent Nguini, Zanzibar and Ange Ebogo. By 1991 he was known as Mbarga Soukouss.

1987	DTC 018	Brigitte
1990		Congolees
1991	DTC 028	Essamba

Mouna, Solo. Vocalist with two late 1980s hit albums.

1988	GME 006	Ma Doudou
1989	GME 008	Confirmation

Mouna, Axel. Vocalist who scored in 1991, supported by Guillaume, Bilong and Naimro.

1991	49910	Time Ni Time

The Best of the Rest

1987	MS 5005	Etienne Ohandjo
	KL 8701	Sam Mbende: Mauvais Chasseur

	PET 007	Peter Makossa
1988	TC 005	Minsy: Ma Ben
	T 0006	Ottou Marcellin: Ou Va Afrique?
	TC 009	Samson: Petit Papa
	PL 217	M. Fragile: Tropical Swing
	YM 2187	Moussa Meicadre: Egalité
	66848	Janet Ndiaye
	GME 010	Bella N'Joh: Mambo Penya
1989	350201	Edgar: Ca Déménage
	NDM 003	Francis Manga: Mutaka Mwam
	PV 9366	Moise Thezenes: Honoré L'Amour
	GME 011	Tchaya Stoppeur
	WEI 596	Ebanda Manfred: Lolo
	OK 46401	Sammy Tokoto: Nataka
	ACA 101	Chikado: Makossa Collection
	SP 121	Jo Bayi: Conscience Professionelle
	82446	Jack Djeyim: Dansez Dansez
	KAR 8812	Sam Alpha: Doudou Caramel
	MA 400027	La Wass: Immigré
	AT 084	T.J.R. Trio: Tchoki Dance
	DTC 022	Govy: Naya Naya
	DTC 023	Essindi Mindja: Salade de France
	PS 4001	Kilama: Secouez
	BK 47101	Blacky's Koum: Doudou
	AT 077	Maele: Abom
	MN 662	Hoigen Ekwalla: Chat Botte
	AT 085	Hoigen Ekwalla: Femmes Il Faut
	SDD 001	Nkoti François: Na Dedi Mbaki

	SDD 002	Hommage aux Createurs du Makossa
	SDD 003	Black Styls 89
	AT 075	Ndedi Dibango: It's All Right
1990	C 4010	Djene Djento: Pompe
	TP 50744	Tonye et Son Groupe Wenawe
	PS 48001	Kilama: Africa-Carnival
	OK 46402	Sexco Dibebe: Choose Me
	BT 1269	Ebeny Ngosso: Muna-Muto
	NST 1990	Jean Noel Sengat: Qu'est-ce Que?
	FK 501	Pierre Didy Tchakounte
	AT 089	Frank de Blaiso: Mandela
1991	ESPERA 29503	Alexia Waku: Chikida
	ACP/CG 005	Alex Fauchy: Maman Pas Plere
	53678	Pondi Kally: Minou
	8047 (CD)	Jeannot Louk: Coco

Others

Nguini, Vincent (b. Yaounde). Vincent had been around for years before deciding to cut what could have become one of the most embarrassing records of 1989. Instead, with his group Maloko, reinforced by Kass Kass star Jean Papy and Zaïrean guitar wizard Syran, his reworking of classic soul numbers became one of the big successes of 1989. Covering such songs as 'In The Midnight Hour' and 'Stand By Me', the album received considerable airplay and, amidst rumours of potential major deal, a 12" single of 'Midnight Hour' was put out by Charlie Gillet's Oval records. In 1990 Vincent was kept equally and successfully busy, featuring heavily on Paul Simon's long awaited *Graceland* follow-up, *The Rhythm of the Saints*.

1989   AMG 006

Collinet, George. Not often that a DJ rates an entry but in a studious, laidback and delightfully academic manner, Cameroon-born Collinet has been playing some of the best music around – on both sides of the Atlantic.

Milla, Roger. Outstanding Cameroonian football player of his generation who inspired all of Africa with his performances at the 1990 World Cup Finals in Italy. By 1991 he was in the studio recording his first LP. The result was *Saga Africa*, which, despite the involvement of Manu Dibango, was universally slated by the critics.

1991   Saga Africa

PART IV

Central Africa

19   Zaïre/Congo

A Burundi   B Rwanda

ZAÏRE

(ECONOMY AND SOCIETY. Pop.: 36 million.
Area: 2,344,855 sq. km. Capital: Kinshasa.
Independence: 1960. Currency: Zaïre.)

The early history of Zaïre was largely shaped by environmental factors which produced various types of society, from the communal organisation of the pygmies to more settled farming communities. By the fourteenth century the kingdom of Kongo had been established and so when the Portuguese arrived in 1482 they found a coherent political and economic structure in Central Africa. Other kingdoms in southern Zaïre (Luba, Kuba and Kunda) also flourished on the basis of their pivotal role in long-distance trade. However, the new relationships developing out of the slave trade served to weaken the Kongo Kingdom and by the nineteenth century the region had been considerably depopulated by both the trans-Atlantic slave trade and the overland slave trade to Sudan and Zanzibar. It is now estimated that the central African region lost over 13 million people in three centuries of slave trading.

In 1876 King Léopold of Belgium financed the exploratory journeys of Stanley, eventually claiming a vast area as a private estate, a claim which was somehow recognised at the notorious Berlin Conference in 1884. Between then and 1908, Léopold ran Zaïre as a personal fief, instituting one of the most brutal and ruthless forms of colonisation ever inflicted on Africa. Rubber was now the principal export, with an economy run by chartered companies and with the Catholic Church monopolising education.

Against this, early resistance to colonial rule first emerged in a distinctly religious fashion with the messianic movement associated with Kimbangu striking the first blows in the 1920s. Thereafter, nationalism developed in a more orthodox manner around a black middle class of évolues. By 1958 political parties were appearing with Patrice Lumumba and the MNC offering the only real nationally based option.

In January 1959 the Belgian Congo exploded into widescale rioting and by the end of the year negotiations were under way for a transfer of power. In June 1960 Lumumba took power as the country's first Prime Minister, only to face a secession in Katanga, encouraged and supported by western interests. In the ensuing months, amidst great political instability, Mobutu seized power, Lumumba was murdered and the country was plunged into four years of political confusion which only came to an end when Mobutu seized power for a second and final time in 1965.

Since then Mobutu has steadily concentrated power in his own hands, forming the MPR in 1967 and banning other parties in 1970 as he embarked on a policy of 'Authenticité' which saw the country and the capital renamed Zaïre and Kinshasa respectively. In 1974 his power became absolute with the introduction of Mobutuism. However, the economy continued to decline and throughout the 1970s and 1980s Zaïre faced growing external debt, falling export prices and massive state corruption. Security became the main pre-occupation of the regime as coup after coup was foiled and political opponents disappeared. By 1985 political opposition to Mobutu was growing more vocal and by the end of the decade Mobutu had accepted the principle, if not yet the practice, of multipartyism. Meanwhile, Belgium (Zaïre's main trading partner) was becoming increasingly critical of Mobutu's rule and in 1990 diplomatic relations were broken. It remains to be seen whether Mobutu can withstand the pro-democracy forces now emerging in Zaïre and whether the economy can survive the inevitable political crisis which will follow.

CONGO

(ECONOMY AND SOCIETY. Pop.: 2.2 million. Area: 342,000 sq. km. Capital: Brazzaville. Independence: 1960. Currency: CFA franc.)

The area of modern Congo contains various ethnic groups whose exchange-based lineage system was easily exploited by the slave trade. By the mid-nineteenth century, palm-oil and rubber had replaced slaves but by then depopulation had almost destroyed traditional society. In 1885 the area was explored by the Frenchman De Brazza, who paved the way for the imposition of French colonialism in 1886. For the next three decades colonisation meant recruiting forced labour to build the railway, punctuated by frequent massacres of recalcitrant citizens. Subsequently, resistance took two divergent forms, the first being recourse to religious messianism and the second being a fairly orthodox communism.

Independence arrived in 1960 under the leadership of President Youlou but despite the rigid orthodoxy of Congolese communism it was difficult to establish stability and Congo underwent several changes of government until Marien Ngouabi seized power in 1968. As a small country with a small population and a resource-rich economy, Congo remained a fairly prosperous country throughout the 1970s, which even the assassination of Ngouabi in 1977 failed to interrupt. Brigadier Yhombi-Opango ran the country for a couple of years until the current president, Nguesso, was named Head of State in 1979. He has remained in power since.

For the rest of this chapter Congo and Zaïre will be dealt with together, given their common musical traditions, the near impossibility of distinguishing betwen Congolese and Zaïrean rumba and the fact that musicians have been moving to and fro for over three decades.

TRADITIONAL MUSIC

The earliest known recordings from the Belgian Congo were made during the first decade of the twentieth century and include material gathered by Emil Torday between 1900 and 1909 and the collection of recordings made by the Starr expedition in 1906 and now held by Indiana University. Another major collection, prosaically called *Primitive African Music, Stirring Rhythms and Unusual Melodic Tunes as Played and Sung by the People of the Great Equatorial Forest*, was compiled by George Herzog in 1937 and released by the Reeves Sound Studios, New York. Finally, Hugh Tracey was actively recording material in both the Congos from the 1940s onwards; this was released as LPs in the 'Music of Africa Series', rarely available now but well worth the search. Other LPs, famous at the time, which are

also extremely hard to find, include the various Congolese masses – most notably the *Missa Luba*. The records listed below are in addition to the albums noted in Volume 1.

1950s	GALP 1017	No. 14. Music of the Congo Republic and Ruanda
	GALP 1252	No. 23. Music of the Northern Congo (Bantu)
	GALP 1251	No. 22. Music of Northern Zaïre (Sudanic)
	AFR 45 806	Masanga: African Musical Instruments, Guitars
1960s	PCC 606	Les Troubadors du Roi Baudouin: Missa Luba (Also 428 138 PE)
	840 432 BY	Les Petits Chanteurs du Kinshasa: Musa Kwango
	MFS 735	The Sounds and Music of the Congo
	LLST 7313	Sanza and Guitar Music of the Bena–Luluwa of Angola and Zaïre

MODERN MUSIC

For convenience, the post-war music of Zaïre/Congo can be considered in two parts. The first, from 1950 to 1970, was epitomised by the establishment, growth and consolidation of the large Congolese orchestras, and although several continued into the 1970s and 1980s, by the end of the 1960s a second phase in the development of the modern Congo sound was under way with the formation of smaller guitar bands led by Zaïko Langa Langa. To help illuminate these two periods, I am pleased to include two essays by Vincent Luttman and Martin Sinnock, both of whom have immersed themselves in the music of the period. The first, by Luttman, covers the years 1950 to 1970, while, later in the chapter, Sinnock introduces the music of the 'School of Zaïko'.

The era of the orchestras 1950–70

By the early 1950s a number of recording houses had established themselves in both Leo and Brazza. These houses utilised pools of musicians with artistes and ensembles frequently interchanging. Many of the most famous names from the 1950s and 1960s either had successful careers prior to the formation of the orchestras or were serving their apprenticeship backing popular artistes. These ensembles, apart from studio work, also played live most evenings in the bars of Leo and Brazza. Initially, both 'maringa' ensembles and the new-style orchestras flourished, much to the satisfaction of the bar owners who sponsored the musicians and cashed in on the extra profits to be made by offering live performances. The main labels of the early years included Ngoma, Ndombe, Olympia, Esengo, Voix de son Maître, Opika, Loningisa, Philips and Bantou Success. Each had its own pool of resident musicians. African Jazz, the most famous ensemble of the early years, was led by Kalle and it was he who recruited Tina Baroza, Albert Yamba Yamba, Georges Dula and Labola. Lead guitarist Nico was recruited soon afterwards, having already gained a formidable reputation by 'out-mastering' his guitar teachers – Dechaud and Jhimmy. Members of the Opika pool included Jhimmy, Malapet, Essous, Edouard Nganga (Edo), Daniel Loubelo (De La Lune) and Celestin Kouka. Other famous folklore stars of the early days included Paul Kamba, Rene Kisamuna, Antoine Kasango, Polidor, Vicky Longomba, Antoine Wendo, Henri Bowane, Lucie Eyenga, Camille Ferudzi and Jean Bosco Mwenda, the celebrated Katangan guitarist.

By 1954 both Edo and De La Lune had joined the rival Loningisa pool and were recording with Bowane, Lando Rossignol and other house musicians, including a young rhythm guitarist called Franco who was then developing his 'likembe'-derived folklore technique whilst also following the influences of his teacher, Henri Bowane, and the Belgian guitarist Bill Alexander. In 1956 Franco established his own orchestra known as OK Jazz. From the outset they played rumba in a style which was much more reminiscent of the maringa bands and more identifiable with the folklore of Zaïre than the Latin phrases being reworked by African Jazz. It was around this time that African Jazz also changed labels when Ngoma collapsed and they moved on to Esengo. Esengo already had a pool of musicians and it was they, in the persons of trumpet player Willy Kuntima and percussionist Antoine Kaya (Depuissant), who were absorbed into African Jazz. One member of the Esengo pool who proved to be a vital ingredient in the later African Jazz sound was the guitarist Paul Ebengo, popularly known as DeWayon. Primarily a guitarist, DeWayon had become the house 'cha cha cha' writer for Esengo but Kalle utilised his skills to produce many of African Jazz's most elegant works. DeWayon also forged a strong partnership with Nino Malapet. A fine testimony to their songwriting skills is the classic cha cha cha entitled 'Maria Valente' by Rock a Mambo Orchestre. Quite aside from writing songs for others, DeWayon also found time to lead his own orchestra, Conga Jazz, later Conga Success, of which he relinquished leadership to his brother, the guitarist Johnny Bokelo.

By the late 1950s the appeal of the maringa ensembles was waning. Many orchestras had followed the lead of African Jazz and incorporated electric guitars and punchy brass sections into their line-ups.

Orchestras such as OK Jazz, Negro Band, etc., had replaced the maringa ensembles as the new champions of folklore legend. These orchestras incorporated folklore-derived techniques into their styles such as the rootsy vocal melodies of Demon or Edo or the likembe-like soloing of Franco and Baguin. African Jazz on the other hand represented modernism with their sharp Latin style and mastery of such rhythms as cha cha cha, samba, merengue, etc. However, they also paid some homage to their Congolese roots in songs like 'Lemote'. The African Jazz rhythm section also utilised a variety of locally-made percussion instruments like tom toms, drums and cowbells. These instruments were played in a fashion directly inspired by traditional teaching.

During the late 1950s Radio Brazzaville began broadcasting four hours of Congolese music each day; because it had formerly been Radio Free France, it was equipped with extremely powerful transmitters which made it possible for people across Africa to tune into Radio Brazza, thereby exposing orchestras such as OK Jazz to a much wider audience than they would otherwise have reached. It thus allowed these artistes to play a key role in the promotion of modern Congolese music across Africa. During these years, bands like Rock a Mambo and Vedette Jazz produced a series of highly danceable merengues, cha cha chas and rumbas which served to promote Congolese music as the champion of 'La Danse Afrique'. Rock a Mambo were particularly important in the development of the Congolese sound, being a fusion of folklore and modern as characterised by OK Jazz and African Jazz. Towards the end of the decade, they became, in effect, the 'mother' of Orchestre Bantou. Rock a Mambo was formed by Lando Rossignol when he left OK Jazz. He then recruited clarinet player Nino Malapet. Malapet had been an early member of the Brazza-based Negro Band but had become a modernist through his love for New Orleans jazz. He had also studied Spanish at College and put his skills to good use through beautiful compositions such as 'Mi Cançion', a cha cha cha sung in Spanish by Rossignol and Kalle. The other crucial factor in the development of Rock a Mambo was the recruitment of several OK Jazz members who had returned to Brazza after the disturbances in Léopold-ville in January 1959. Leaving OK Jazz for Brazza were such luminaries as Edo, Essous, Pandy and De La Lune. The début line-up of Rock a Mambo therefore included Essous, Malapet, Tino Baroza, Roitelet, Pandy, Satan and Rossignol.

Within a short time, Rock a Mambo were recording for Esengo with a new line-up featuring Nedule (Papa Noel) on guitar in place of Baroza. Nico and Kalle were also involved, as members of the Esengo pool, and together all these musicians produced some of the most beautiful songs of the era including the stunning 'Balia' of 1960. Other influential members included the guitarist Honore Liengo and the female vocalist Lucie Eyenga who took the lead on such songs as 'Mabe Na Yo Moko' and 'Bridgette'. Between 1960 and 1962 Rock

109

a Mambo underwent some dramatic personnel changes including the loss of Malapet, Essous and Nedule to the Bantous (set up by Malapet). It was to be a deeply damaging loss from which the band never really recovered, although they struggled on into the mid-1960s.

As Congolese music became increasingly popular across Africa so some of the larger UK-based labels (HMV and Columbia) realised the business opportunities to be exploited by licensing the 78 r.p.m.s of Esengo and Loningisa which they re-pressed in London as 45 r.p.m.s for re-export to the West African market. By the mid-1960s, the Congolese music industry had undergone several major changes, with earlier labels disappearing and new ones taking over. In 1966 the leading Congolese houses included Vita, Epanza Makita, Congo Disque, Surboum African Jazz, Boma Bango, Matanga, Londende, CEFA, TCHEZA and Matata. To begin with, the most important of these labels was Surboum African Jazz, established by Kalle in 1960. He struck deals with European labels like Decca, ensuring good-quality recordings for the Francophone market. Kalle was also responsible for signing OK Jazz to Surboum. At the same time, he was leading the band to tour and record in Europe; as far as we know, the first European shows took place in venues such as Matiti and Wangata, African bars in Brussels.

Soon other labels were following the example of Kalle, and orchestras such as the Bantous were being whisked away to Paris to record for Pathé Marconi. These tours and recording sessions proved to be a hard slog with up to 100 songs being recorded in single sessions on the latest 2- or 4-track equipment. Live dates followed the studio sessions. During these years, a few musicians began to think about settling in Europe where they had access to recording studios, better equipment and also the chance to escape the post-Lumumba political turmoil in Zaïre. Other orchestras also started moving to East Africa, again because of the social unrest at home. Others, like Ry-co Jazz (who recorded over 20 EPs for the French Vogue label between 1960 and 1961), toured extensively in West Africa, writing songs praising the various nationalist movements they came across. See for example the famous 'Independence Senegal Cha Cha Cha' from 1961. Indeed Ry-co Jazz should now be acknowledged for playing a crucial role in the spread of Congolese rhythms throughout West Africa.

By 1963, when African Jazz split up, new recording houses were appearing with musicians like Roger Izeyidi becoming administrators behind labels such as Editions Vita, which he had formed with musicians from African Fiesta. When Fiesta split in 1965, Vita also folded and Rochereau and Izeyidi formed Editions Flash. Nico, on the other hand, formed his own record label with his brother Dechaud and called it Editions Sukisa. Kalle had also been busy since the African Jazz/African Fiesta split in 1963. He first travelled to Kampala with Papa Noel to re-acquaint himself with some former colleagues then playing with Vox Africa and in the hope that he could recruit a few of them to form a new band. Together they returned to Kinshasa and African Jazz soon recovered their old form, scoring hits for Editions Matanga with Jean Bombega compositions like 'Jolie Nana'. Yet despite this success, Kalle announced in 1965 that he was stepping down to reassess his position. He returned to action in 1966 with a series of concerts featuring guitarists Papa Noel, Damoiseau and Casino, Jean Balu on drums and Willy Bofomba on traditional percussion. The vocalists included Jean Bombenga, Matthew Kouka, Alex Mayukka, Rolly and Kalle himself. This was indeed a top line-up and African Jazz enjoyed continuing success until their eventual demise in 1969, marking the end of one particular era.

The early to mid-1960s was a period of great transition for the other top orchestra of the period, OK Jazz, as Franco moved away from the more 'tinseltown' Latin rhythms of African Fiesta and began to develop a solid rumba rhythm to replace the seemingly endless stream of boleros and cha cha chas of which Brazza and Kinshasa audiences were beginning to tire. In 1964 Franco and other members of OK Jazz launched their own label – Editions Epanza Makita – and over the next four years they recorded for this as well as for Boma Bango, Likembe, Editions Populaire and Viclong (run by OK Jazz vocalist Vicky Longomba). The evolution of the OK Jazz sound can be heard on the African 360 000 series while further background information can be found in *Luambo Franco and 30 Years of OK Jazz* by Graeme Ewens (see Bibliography).

The biggest competition to OK Jazz during the late 1960s came from the Orchestre Negro Success, led by singer Bholen and guitarist Bavon Marie Marie – a younger brother of Franco whose style was so similar as to be almost indistinguishable. The rivalry between the two bands was, however, as much tongue in cheek as real. It was rumoured, for example, that Franco would often be invited to guest at Negro Success recording sessions with Bavon being invited to return the compliment when OK Jazz entered the studio. The real threat posed by Negro Success was, however, that of age. By the mid-1960s most of OK Jazz were in their late twenties whilst Negro Success were much younger. While Franco still had his admirers, it appeared as if the eyes and ears of the younger Kinshasa women were now firmly fixed on Bavon and Bholen. Negro Success also created their own 'smart set' of Kinshasa friends and fans and helped develop the Kinshasa youth scene by living a fast high life, setting fashions and fads like wearing skin cream to bleach their complexions. Sadly, the band's life was soon brought to a sudden and premature end in 1970 with the death of Bavon in a car accident. A number of recordings by Negro Success were made for the Makita, Tchenza and Revellion labels and are still available on the African label. They provide a useful reference point for comparisons with OK Jazz for the same period.

However, a more persistent and tortuous pain for OK Jazz started in 1968 when saxophonist Georges Kiamuangana (Verckys) left the band and formed Orchestre Veve. Initially Veve relied on an OK Jazz sound, particularly in the brass arrangements, but, unlike OK Jazz, Veve were not content to operate exclusively in the rumba framework. Veve borrowed freely from other bands, bringing in the 'Kiri Kiri' from the Fiesta school. The band enjoyed enormous popularity, enabling Verckys to establish his own label and enter into the Kinshasa business world of promotions, sponsorship and management with new orchestras such as Zaïko Langa Langa.

During the 1960s an enormous amount of quality music came from Zaïre and it is worth recording the names of a few of the bands from the rumba heyday of that period. Top Kinshasa-based bands included OK Jazz, African Fiesta Nico, African Fiesta Rochereau, African Jazz, Jazz Beguen, Conga Success, Conga Negro, Conga Jazz, Rock a Mambo, Negro Band, Nova Boy, Nova Success, Con Bantou, OD Jazz, Rick Jazz, Negro Success, Diamant Bleu, Mexico Jazz, City Five, Begen Band, OK Band, Negro Fiesta, Jazz Venus, Casa Nova and Los Angels. The main orchestras based in Lubumbashi included Tino Mambo, VEA Mambo, Kit Jazz, Katanga Jazz, OD Negro, OD African and Jekokat. Kisingani offered the sounds of Rock N Band and Air Fiesta while over the water in Brazza the incomparable Bantous de la Capitale continued to hold sway.

Recommended

The following section of the discography covers the major orchestras of the 1960s. For Kalle, Nico, Rochereau and OK Jazz please refer to individual entries. The albums listed below were compiled by the African label from material originally appearing on various local labels like Esengo, Epanza Makita and Londende, etc. Where possible, I have supplied original recording/release dates rather than re-release dates.

Negro Success

1966	360 051	Succès D'Hier
	360 003	L'Afrique Danse Vol. 3
1967	360 153	Les Merveilles du Passé
1968	360 089	African Party Vol. 1
1968–70	360 013	Les Merveilles du Passé
	360 023	Bavon Marie Marie

Cobantou

1968	360 007	L'Afrique Danse Vol. 7
	360 090	African Party

1968–9	360 165	Les Merveilles du Passé

Conga Success/Conga 68

1966	360 001	L'Afrique Danse Vol. 1
	360 002	L'Afrique Danse Vol. 2
1968	360 007	L'Afrique Danse Vol. 7
1968–9	360 090	African Party Vol. 2

Kalle, Le Grand (b. Joseph Kabaselle Tshamala, Matadi, Zaïre, 1930, d. 1983). The first 'Grand Maître' of Zaïrean music and the man who dragged neo-traditional styles and influences into the modern pop era. Enormously influential on the careers of Dr Nico and Rochereau, who both played with him before moving on to their own orchestras, Kalle's recordings from the 1950s and 1960s with the seminal African Jazz should comprise the starting point for any assessment of modern Zaïrean music. Much of it is now being re-issued on CD. Please consult Volume 1 for a longer biography. By the time of his death in 1983, Kalle was widely acknowledged to be the 'father' of modern Congolese pop and fans can choose from over a half a dozen compilation albums.

1960–3	360 142	Hommage au Grand Kalle Vol. 1
1960	360 143	Hommage au Grand Kalle Vol. 2
1963–6	360 107	Authenticité Vol. 5
1966	360 002	L'Afrique Danse Vol. 2
	360 003	L'Afrique Danse Vol. 3
1967–8	360 089	African Party
1969	360 051	Succès D'Hier
	360 090	African Party
1969–70	360 017	L'African Team
1984	360 104	Kalle and the African Team
	360 105	Kalle and the African Team
1990	AMCD 01	Le Grande Kalle Vol. 1 (CD)

Dr Nico. See Volume 1 for biography and discography of this seminal guitarist who tragically died in 1984. Material from Nico continues to reappear, including the excellent *Dernière Mémoire* album from the 1982 Lomé New Sound Studio sessions.

1986	360 159	Les Merveilles du Passé (1967)
	360 160	Les Merveilles du Passé (1967)
1987	360 161	Les Merveilles du Passé (1963)
	360 162	Les Merveilles du Passé (1962–3)
	360 163	Les Merveilles du Passé (1962–3)
1989	AMG 008	Adieu
1990	VDA 013	Dernière Mémoire
	AMR 103	Nico & Vonga Aye & Deyesse

Franco (b. L'Okanga La Ndju Pene Luambo Makiadi, Sona-Bata, Zaïre, 1938, d. 1989). Only the second 'Grand Maître' in Zaïrean musical history and beyond any doubt the single most influential and popular musician in Africa. His tragic death in October 1989, following a short illness, left an unfillable gap in African music. No single musician will be more sorely missed by millions of admirers throughout the continent. Beloved by men and women, respected by Heads of State, Franco stood head and shoulders above all other African musicians for over three decades. During these years, Franco and OK Jazz released over 150 albums, countless singles and, more recently, more than a dozen CDs. The quality of the music, from the early acoustic rumbas, through the big band sounds of the 1960s and 1970s and the disco beat rumba of the 1980s to the late epics, never slipped. If anything, the music continued to gather momentum as the band proceeded on its all-conquering march through modern Africa and beyond. OK Jazz also acted as the most respected University of Zaïrean music, with hundreds of musicians passing through before establishing their own bands. The band roster from 1966 demonstrates the quality of just some of the musicians involved with Franco.

OK Jazz in 1966

1.	François Luambo (Franco)	Composer, Guitar, Vocals	Zaïre
2.	Victor Longomba (Vicky)	Composer/ vocalist	Zaïre
3.	Joseph Mulamba (Mujos)	Composer/ vocalist	Zaïre
4.	Isaac Dele Pedro	Composer/ sax/flute	Nigeria
5.	G. Kiamungana (Verckys)	Composer/sax	Zaïre
6.	Christophe N'Djali	Trumpet/sax	Zaïre
7.	Simon Lutumba (Simaro)	Composer/ guitar	Zaïre
8.	Antoine Armandos (Brazzos)	Guitar/bass	Zaïre
9.	Simon Moke	Drums/ maracas	Zaïre
10.	Nicolas Bosuma (Dessouin)	Drummer	Zaïre
11.	Michel Boyibanda	Vocalist	Congo
12.	Edouard Nganga (Edo)	Vocalist/ composer	Congo
13.	Daniel Loubelo (De La Lune)	Composer/ bass	Congo
14.	Jean Mossi (Kwamy)	Composer/ vocals	Zaïre
15.	Jean-Felix Puela	Tam-Tam	Congo
16.	B. Bitshoumanou	Guitar/bass	Chad
17.	Nestor Diangani	Drums	Zaïre

The last few years of Franco's life are perhaps the best-documented of his long career. By the 1980s Franco and OK Jazz were more frequent visitors to Europe, playing in France, Holland, Belgium and the UK. Africa was not neglected and the band toured East Africa and Zambia in 1987. During these last years, Franco proved as prolific as ever (see below), with several outstanding albums including *Ekaba Kaba*, *Attention Na SIDA* and *Mamou*. In 1989 Franco entered the studio for what was to be the last time, appropriately joining forces once again with his favourite vocalist, Sam Mangwana. These last two albums demonstrated that although Franco's health was failing, his skills were as sharp as ever. Indeed, the first indication that all was not well came from these albums with cover photos showing a much slimmer Franco. Rumours of AIDS quickly began to circulate, denied to the last, as Franco complained instead of liver problems. Then in mid-1989 Franco and OK Jazz were billed to play in London. The band went on stage briefly but Franco was now extremely ill, conducting interviews from his hotel bed – a shadow of his former self. He finally passed way in October 1989, at Namur in Belgium.

The world of African music was stunned as the news flashed across the continent. His body was quickly flown home, with Mobutu declaring four days of national mourning as Franco lay in state at the capital's Palais du Peuple. The radio station observed the occasion by playing the music of OK Jazz non-stop for four days. He was buried at Kinshasa's Gombe Cemetery on 17 October. And so passed away one of the all-time greats, the 'African Balzac', the 'Sorcerer of the Guitar'. He left behind several wives and seventeen children.

The items listed below are, firstly, additions to the extensive discography presented in Volume 1 and, secondly, material released since 1986. I am currently compiling a definitive discography of Franco and OK Jazz for publication in 1992 to accompany the forthcoming biography of Franco by Graeme Ewens. I am afraid real 'Francophiles' will have to wait until then for definitive listings. In the meantime, I would urge fans of Franco everywhere to start completing their collections now. There will be no more music from Franco but he could not have left a more magnificent musical legacy.

1962	2C064 15806	African Retro Vol.2 (Re-issued 1977)
	2C064 15959	African Retro Vol.4 (Re-issued 1977)
1981	POP 07	La Bon Vieux Bon Temps Vol. 1
	POP 08	Vol. 2
	POP 09	Vol. 3
1986	360 158	Les Merveilles Du Passé (1957–8)
	C 1026	+ Simarro: Testement Ya Bowule (7" – four songs)
1986	RETRO 2	Originalité (The first OK Jazz recordings from 1956)
1987	ASM 001	Attention Na SIDA

	ASM 002	+ Dalienst: Mamie Zou
	CHOC 008	+ Josky: Kita Mata Bloque
	CHOC 009	+ Baniel + Nana: Les On Dit
	ESP 8427	+ Jolie Detta: Massu
1988	POP 34	Retro Non-Stop
	ASM 003	+ Simarro: Coeur Artificiel
	360 168	Les Merveilles Du Passé (1962)
	360 001	+ Bokelo: L'Afrique Danse Vol. 1
	360 158	Motema Ya Lokasso
	8701	Live En Hollande
	9508	Ekaba Kaba
1989	CHOC 010	La Réponse de Mario
	CHOC 011	+ Nana & Baniel: Cherche Une Maison
	CHOC 012	+ Pepe Ndombe: Anjela
	RMU 850	+ Sam Mangwana: Lukoli
	38775	+ Sam Mangwana: For Ever

Soon after Franco's death, the various companies with whom he had dealt throughout Africa realised that there would be no more from 'Le Grand Maître' and began to look with fresh eyes at the back-catalogue. First off the mark was GMFLP (Kenya), who in 1990 released a series of ten compilation albums drawing, without any apparent thought, on tracks from 1965–75, including singles and album tracks. Francophiles are advised to check both the content of each LP and the quality of the pressing to avoid disappointment. The Dutch also jumped on the bandwagon with a sub-standard release entitled *Franco Still Alive* culled from the previous 'Live in Europe' sessions. It is possible that other material may still appear, particularly from the early days, and there are rumours of an unreleased late recording where Franco tried to silence those who suggested that he was dying of AIDS. Otherwise, it is surely everyone's hope that Franco's music will not be seen as a resource to be exploited and that any further re-releases will be more tastefully dealt with.

1990	GMFLP 001	In Memoriam Vol. 1
	GMFLP 002	In Memoriam Vol. 2
	GMFLP 003	In Memoriam Vol. 3
	GMFLP 004	In Memoriam Vol. 4

GMFLP 005	In Memoriam Vol. 5
GMFLP 006	In Memoriam Vol. 6
GMFLP 007	In Memoriam Vol. 7
GMFLP 008	In Memoriam Vol. 8
GMFLP 009	In Memoriam Vol. 9
GMFLP 010	In Memoriam Vol. 10
ASLP 458	Rétro
EMING 001	Le Temps Perdu
	Franco Still Alive

Finally, in 1989, Franco's music appeared on compact disc for the first time with Sonodisc's re-release of outstanding material from the last five years of his life. Once again, it will be necessary for Franco admirers to check the precise track listings on these CDs.

1989	CD 50382	20ème Anniversaire Vol. 1
	CD 50383	20ème Anniversaire Vol. 2
	RETRO 2CD	Originalité
1990	CD 8473	Testement Ya Bowule
	CD 8474	Kita Mata Bloque
	CD 8475	J'ai Peur
	CD 8476	Eperduement

OK Jazz. (Officially TPOK Jazz, the TP standing for 'Tout Puissant'. Commonly known as OK Jazz.) In October 1989 OK Jazz were left leaderless. While Franco's estate was being settled, it was made clear to the band that the Government expected a period of mourning during which live shows would be prohibited. But the core of the Orchestre remained intact and with over three decades at the top had a host of former members on whom they could call. The following section of the discography attempts to trace the studio history of OK Jazz since late 1989. Various leading members took turns in fronting the band, producing several mega-sellers in late 1990 and early 1991. On no account fail to secure copies of *Mizele* and *Belalo*. The 1991 *Heritage de Luambo* reunited all the top stars of the late 1980s including long-time 'Chef D'Orchestre' and would-be leader Simarro, Madilu System, Josky, Ndombe Opetum, Papa Noel, Jerry, Yuma and Djo Mpoy. The band numbered 27 musicians in total with the set purpose of 'faithfully perpetuating the genius of Franco'. This album was the first official recording from TPOK Jazz since the demise of the Grand Master. In terms of touring, OK Jazz did not travel far in 1990, observing a year's mourning for Franco, but in 1991

they embarked on an ambitious European tour, reminding fans of their power, potency and sheer musicianship in a series of impressive performances. In musical terms, the band seem perfectly capable of continuing to innovate within the spirit of Franco's music, with rich arrangements, sparkling guitars and honey-voiced vocalists combining to create and recreate some of the world's best dance music.

1990	ESPERA 29091	Madilu: Na Pokwa Ya Lolo
	KPS 001	Mayaula & TPOK Jazz: Mizele
	DEF 001	Dalienst & TPOK Jazz: Belalo
	ESPERA 26989	Les Champions du Zaïre: Hommage
	CVS 8477	Franco & TPOK Jazz: Live in Europe (Video)
1991	TMS 90002	TPOK Jazz: Héritage de Luambo
	EBS 001	TPOK Jazz & Josky: Les Mayeno A Gogo

Mayoni, Mayaula. Guitarist/vocalist who has flitted in and out of OK Jazz over the last two decades, producing exquisite albums on his own . The three LPs to search for are *La Machine à Tube*, *Fiona Fiona* and *Mizele*.

1960s	ASMLP004	African Sound of Music Vol.4 (Includes the all-time classic 'Cherie Bondowe')
1985	ANS 8417	La Machine à Tube
	ASLP 1002	Veya
1987	REM 80	+ Malage: Fiona Fiona
1990	KPS 001	+ TPOK Jazz: Mizele

Josky. Barrel-chested, front-line OK Jazz vocalist for most of the 1980s. One of the most remarkable voices in Africa.

1986	MA 4005	Josky & Rigo Star: Jotongo
1986	ASLP 1008	Josky & Dalienst: Médecin de Nuit
1987	REM 810	Telema Na Malembe

1988	SF 1001	Josky & Dalienst: Sans Frontière
1989	M I	Josky & Madilu: Destin
	SF 004	Josky: Chandra
1990	MUS 1001	Josky

Dalienst. Josky's front-line vocal partner in OK Jazz.

1985	REM 430	Iza Issa (Also TSV 02)

Malage de Lugendo. Another OK Jazz vocalist who has recently been recording with the other great Zaïrean musical institution, Zaïko.

1988	SYL 8359	Baiser de Judas

Madilu System. Widely regarded as Franco's favourite vocalist, Madilu joined the band in the mid-1980s, soon becoming a star in his own right. He left briefly after the Kenyan tour but returned to the fold in 1990. He can be heard on many late 1980s recordings and is much in demand with other bands, adding his unique vocal talents to recent albums by Nyboma, Mbilia Bel and Pepe Kalle.

Opetum, Ndombe. Veteran OK Jazz vocalist.

1987	REM 590	Djefano

Ley, Tabu (b. Tabu Pascal, a.k.a. Rochereau, Bundundu, Zaïre, 1940). Zaïrean and African superstar, ranked just behind Franco in terms of output and popularity. A precocious child talent, Tabu Ley has consistently maintained an exceptionally high standard with Kalle, Dr Nico and, from 1965, his own Afrisa. Volume 1 provides an extended biography and discography up until 1986. Since then (and coincidentally since the split with Mbilia Bel), Ley has remained an active force but has largely failed to scale the heights of the 1970s and early 1980s. In 1986 he played in the UK and in 1989 followed up with a US tour. He is by no means a spent force but certainly needs to assess direction. The discs listed below fill in a few gaps in early output and bring the story up to date.

1980	APM 001/2	Tant Que Je L'Aime (Double)
1983	DS 7989	Mpeve Ya Longo (Vol. 7)
	DS 7990	Kele Bibi (Vol. 8)
1986	GEN 119	Ley & Nyboma: Sacramento

	C 2021	Ley, Bel & Tess: Nadina
1987	GEN 121	Ley, Bel & Tess
	GEN 122	Ley & Bel: Contre Ma Volonté
	GEN 123	Ley & Tess: Le Monde à L'Envers
1988	GEN 124	Ley & Ciel: Ebouroumounkoue
1989	GEN 125	Ley & Tess: Moto Akokufa
	KL 038	Trop C'est Trop
	RWLP 5	Babeti Soukous
1990	GEN 126	C'est Comme Ce La Vie
	GEN 127	Soum-Djoum
	GEN 128	Tour Eiffel 100 Ans
	GEN 129	Ley & Tess & Ciel: Allo Paris
1991	083 148	Various: Zaïre Groove (Video)

Bel, Mbilia. See Volume 1 for early career. Mbilia Bel, christened Marie-Claire, rose to prominence in the mid-1980s as a protégée of Tabu Ley, performing alongside the old master on a number of classic albums as well as releasing a succession of successful solo LPs on the Genidia label. Following the birth of her first child, Mbilia stepped down from the constant touring to reassess her career. The result was a decision to part company with Ley and to concentrate on a solo career. In 1987 she finished off her years of collaboration with the best-seller *Contre Ma Volonté* and by 1990 she had become a solo performer of considerable stature. She started in 1988 with the strong-selling LP *Phénomène*, establishing a solid professional relationship with top Paris-based guitarist Rigo Star. Together they went on to release several more recordings of an exceptionally high technical standard but limited market power. Despite the enormous amount of gossip generated by her split with Ley, Mbilia Bel has put all such talk firmly behind her, inviting her fans to 'take her as she is'.

Now based in Paris and bemoaning the absence of good studio facilities in Kinshasa, Mbilia has clearly benefited from Rigo's experience in the French capital. She does not maintain her own band, relying instead on session musicians for support at live shows, not always too successfully. Like Tabu Ley, she is no stranger to innovation within the classic rumba framework, although her 1990 recordings demonstrated a return to the Makwundu Ku roots soukous style from Bandundu. Lyrically, Mbilia Bel has never been afraid to broach controversial subjects and her subject matter generally deals with mature love – love with rough edges. Issues like polygamy, jealousy, exile, cross-cultural marriage and neglect have all been covered in her songs. In 1989 and 1990 she toured in the US, the UK and West Africa, drawing large crowds of enthusiastic Zaïreans and whites alike. By the start of the decade she was looking for a major recording contract – something her popularity, talent and experience surely deserves. Just how highly she is rated can be seen from the fact that her Paris label judged it worthwhile to re-release all her recordings on compact disc. In 1991, on her first album for a couple of years, she is almost totally reliant on Rigo Star for composition, arrangement and instrumentals. *Désolé* is a deeply unsatisfying album – uneven, over-produced and only really working when Mbilia's voice starts to dominate the sound. This was then followed by the bizarre *Exploration* – a soukous/rap experiment featuring the combined talents of Bel, Star, Madilu and Trouble Funk.

1986	GEN 120	Beyanga
	C 2021	Bel, Ley & Tess: Nadina
1987	GEN 122	Bel & Ley: Contre Ma Volonté
1988	MCB 001	Phénomène
1991	66887-1	Désolé
1991	KIP 184	Exploration (US release)

Bantous de la Capitale. Formed in Brazzaville in 1959, the Bantous, like OK Jazz, have proved to be one of the most exciting and durable outfits on the continent. Once again, Volume 1 provides the full story for this amazing university of rumba. Graduates include Nino Malapet and Essous (two of the most gifted horn players on the continent), Kosmos, Tchico, Pamelo Mounka on vocals and the great guitarists Papa Noel and Master Mwana Congo. The older material is rarely seen but should comprise the bed-rock of any rumba collection. Buy on sight.

The band made an excellent return to the studio with the ambiguous LP of 1989, *Monument*, featuring the combined talents of Edo, Essous, Pamelo Mounka and newcomer Mick Jeager. Others playing regularly with Les Bantous in the late 1980s included Nino Malapet, Kosmos, Pandy and Celestin, under the overall guidance of the Chef D'Orchestre, Pamelo.

1989	TTB 003	Monument
	BSM 997	Ave Marie Limbisa
1990	R 0001	Jo San

Essous, Jean-Serge. Veteran sax player and long-time Bantous frontman returned to the top with his 1989 solo effort.

| 1989 | 46010-1 | Trois S |

Papa Noel. Master guitarist with numerous outfits, including Bantous and OK Jazz.

| 1989 | REM 790 | Za Moke |

Kosmos. Long-time Bantous vocalist. Brother of Pierre Moutouari.

1983	SAS 40	Ba Camarades
1984	SAS 44	Naleli Congo
1988	BM 005	Etat Civil

Mounka, Pamelo. Singer and composer and probably the finest singer on the Congo side of the River Zaïre. Volume 1 outlines early career and discography.

| 1987 | VME 001 | L'Amour et la Danse (Bantous) |
| 1990 | AH 90157 | The Come Back (Pamelomania) |

Bokelo, Johnny. Veteran guitarist and superstar of the 1960s now in his 50s. Little was heard from him for a decade but he bounced back in the early 1980s and has remained at or near the top ever since.

1983	JBI 001	Liwa Ya Ndika Somo
	SHA 27	A.S. Biliman
1989	BOX 009	Tout Ça C'est La Vie
1990	ESPERA26989/94	Anti-Balle

Massa, Bumba. Veteran vocalist from the Zaïre scene who appeared to peak in the early 1980s with a series of lovely albums, only to bounce back in 1990 with *Baromètre* – a hit from Washington DC to Lusaka. Seldom heard in the West, Mr Massa has released dozens of albums throughout Central and East Africa and is rightly regarded as a major star.

| 1990 | MB 50564 | Baromètre |

Verckys et L'Orchestre Veve. By the 1980s Verckys had completely retired from live shows to concentrate on his music empire – nightclub, equipment agency, studios, pressing plant, etc. If even half the stories are true, then Verckys, former sax player in OK Jazz, boss of Veve and 'enfant terrible' of the Zaïrean music scene, deserves a volume to himself. The 1987 release, a rare event these days, features Lukoki ably supported by Assi Kapela, Djo Mpoyi and Dizzi (the last two from OK Jazz). The Veve studio, with its own identifiable sound, continued up until 1991, producing dozens of LPs which found their way through licensing agreements to Zambia, Kenya and Tanzania. Rumours from early 1991 suggest that Verckys had left Zaïre altogether.

1987	EVVI 3	Diatho Lukoki et Veve Int.

Mangwana, Sam. Perennial favourite throughout the continent for his light and lilting vocal touch, his pan-African sentiments, his constant touring and his reputation for only working with the best musicians. His albums are in constant demand and there is no sign that his skills are waning. A favourite of both Franco and Tabu Ley, Sam is a legend in his own life-time. Once again, those items listed below are in addition to the longer discography in Volume 1. His last five albums all proved to be best-sellers, with *Alhadji* going furthest in its search for a truly tropical sound. Most recently, he has been reported in the US working with Brazilian musicians.

1968	360166	Sam & Les Maquisards
1979	DO 002	Suzana Coulibaly (I. Coast)
1981	ALS 079	Sam & African All Stars Vol. 1
	ALS 086	Sam & African All Stars Vol. 2
1982	BIR 008	Consommez Local
	SER 104	Nsimba Eli (Also CEL 6639)
1984	ALP 2	Les Champions (Also CEL 6730)
	PAM 05	Canta Moçambique (Also SAM 04)
1988	SYL 8336	Alhadji
1989	38775	+ Franco: For Ever
	RMU 850	+ Franco: Lukoli
1990	SYL 83101	Megamix
	0020	Fatimata/Capita General

Tiers Monde. An occasional vehicle for the talents of Sam, Ndombe Opetum and the late sax maestro Empopo Loway Deyesse.

1980		Nouvelle Formula
1985	REM 590	Ndombe Opetum: Djefano

	DI9 55L	Ndombe Opetum: Hortense
1987	EDISURYA 003	Empopo Loway: Kibola-bola
1989	IAD 5003	Tiers Monde
1990	SIC 002	Mobomano

The School of Zaïko

Thu-Zahina, Orchestre. Often quoted as the strongest influence on early Zaïko. Unobtainable.

1977	CO 6415981	Orchestre Thu-Zahina

Zaïko Langa Langa (formed Zaïre, 1969). Volume 1 provided a concise history of the band which has now come to challenge OK Jazz and Tabu Ley as the standard bearers of the modern Zaïrois sound. Prolific, inventive, high powered, resilient and above all immensely popular in Zaïre, Zaïko could well be the best band in the country. However, success overseas has proved much more elusive through a combination of poor management, internal division and an incomprehensible reluctance by promoters and companies to back the group. Zaïko's music reflects the real difference between, on the one hand, western pop and African music and, on the other, between Kinshasa-based bands and Paris productions.
Free, relaxed, innovative and handled by master musicians, Zaïko's music opens up new areas of adventure and appreciation. Over the years their rise to prominence has been stately and unhurried; Kinshasa providing a better barometer than Paris. Zaïko have now been a major force in African music for over two decades. This volume acknowledges their crucial contribution by presenting an essay by Martin Sinnock on the history of the band and by combining an earlier discography with their most recent efforts to present (we hope) the definitive discography to date. Readers should, however, be aware that very few of the albums listed below are still available. We advise you to search out and subsequently treasure any album you can lay your hands on. One word of caution: like most Zaïrean bands, the lead track is often the first on side B. This can lead to a certain confusion over the actual title of the record. I have followed the practice of using company titles where possible.

From village headman (Nkolo Mboka) to family of God (Familia Dei)

Throughout the 1950s and 1960s, Congo/Zaïre music was dominated by the classic Zaïrean rumba of Kalle's African Jazz, Franco's OK Jazz, Tabu Ley's African Fiesta (later Afrisa) and a host of similar outfits. Comprising a line-up of guitar, brass and rhythm section fronted by four or more vocalists, this format flourishes today in both Zaïre and neighbouring countries like Kenya, Tanzania and Zambia. Indeed, a parallel could well be drawn between the classic rumba orchestres and the big band format of the American jazz/swing era. But to the youth in Kinshasa the sound had become staid and predictable, more associated with their parents than with the street-wise, post-independence generation to which they belonged. Like the youth of the world in the late 1960s, they wanted the opportunity to express their own opinions, develop their own style and listen to their own sound. The break came in 1969 when a group of middle-class students led by percussionist D.V. Moanda formed a new group called Zaïko Langa Langa from the ashes of Orchestre Belguid, a Kinshasa-based band which had taken its name when one of its members returned home after studying in Belgium. The new group dropped all European references by calling themselves Zaïko – a combination of Zaïre–Congo. The original band comprised Moanda, Nyoko Longo on vocals and Pepe Manuaku on guitar, expanding quickly as new members were recruited, including Matima on lead guitar, Zamanguana and Teddy Sukami on rhythm guitars, Oncle Bapius on bass, Mitshio on drums and another percussionist, Ephraim. Finally, there was a young, talented, former choirboy by the name of Jules Wembadia who joined as front-line vocalist, now better known as Papa Wemba.

The band recorded their first singles in 1971 (sadly no longer available), featuring Wemba's distinctive vocals backed by the hard, rough-edged guitar sound – unusually for the times they used no horns. In time, this raunchy guitar sound, combined with a tight snare drum played to almost militaristic precision, became the 'Zaïko sound'. During these early years many talented young singers (who were eventually destined to become stars in their own right) joined the band, including Gina 'La Poète' Efonge, Evoloko Jocker, Bimi Ombale and Mavuelo Somo. However, the organisation's ability to recruit such outstanding talent always tended to work against itself as Zaïko was never able to hold on to its precocious and charismatic young stars, who were constantly leaving to establish new outfits. Inevitably they took other musicians with them who would immediately be replaced by a new group of 'trainees'. This process, repeated time and time again over the next two decades, produced a host of top quality bands reading like a veritable 'Who's Who' of contemporary rumba. Papa Wemba was one of the first to move (in 1974), forming first Isife Lokole, then Yoka

Lokole, before settling down with Viva La Musica in 1976. But the same divisive forces were then set loose in Viva themselves and over the years the band, successful in their own right, produced their own crop of stars, including Kofi Olomide, Emeneya Emerite and Victoria Eleison, Fafa de Molokai and Strervos Niarchos. Pepe Manuaku, the original Zaïko guitarist, lasted a decade until he too moved on in 1980 to create Grand Zaïko Wa-Wa, another outfit which would in turn spawn a new generation of stars including singers Bozi Boziana, Evoloko Jocker and guitarist Roxy Tshimpaka, who in 1981 left Grand Zaïko with bassist Djo Mali and singers Esperant, Djuna Djumana and Dindo Yogo to form Langa Langa Stars. Bozi had been an early 1970s recruit to Zaïko but soon found himself involved with Minzota Wella Wella, Wemba's Isife Lokole and Yoko Lokole with Pepe Manuaku. In 1977 he returned to Zaïko for another four-year spell prior to the formation of Langa Langa Stars in 1981. From there he moved on to yet another 'School of Zaïko' outfit called Choc Stars, formed in 1984 by singer Ben Nyambo. Bozi stayed two years before moving on again to form his own Anti-Choc, who, by the late 1980s, had become one of the hottest outfits on the Kinshasa scene.

In addition to these many off-shoot bands, the individual members of Zaïko were also incredibly prolific in the recording studios of Brazza, Kinshasa, Paris and Brussels with excellent solo albums from stars like Likinga Redo, Gina Efonge, Lengi Lenga, Bimi Ombale, J.P. Buse and Dindo Yogo. There were also many collaborative efforts by Nyoko Longo, Wemba and Ombale and a host of other projects involving members of the band. However, despite all this factionalism and proliferation, a small core of musicians remained loyal to the original Zaïko Langa Langa. Led by Nyoko Longo, this core group comprising Matima (guitar), Bapius (drums), Zamanguana (rhythm guitar) and Meridjo (drums) have somehow managed to stay together and, now operating with the sub-title Nkolo Mboka (Village Headman), they can justifiably claim to be the true Zaïko.

The biggest split came in 1988 when another core group of veteran members, led by drummer Ilo Pablo and vocalist Bimi Ombale, went on the road using the name Zaïko Langa Langa. Bimi had composed much of Zaïko's best material, including songs like 'Liposa', 'Ima', 'La Blonde', 'Elina Ngando', 'Sandra Lina' and 'Nibe', and they are no longer available to Nyoko Longo's band. The latest in a long line of defectors, the new group dubbed themselves Zaïko Langa Langa Familia Dei (Family of God) and immediately set about building a new unit which could match the the old. Bimi and Pablo took with them several other stars from Zaïko, including three of the best guitarists, Petit Poisson Avedila, Beniko Popolipo and Jimmy Yaba. Bimi and Pablo also took two of the best singers in the persons of J.P. Buse and Lengi Lenga. From the rhythm side they took conga player Manzeka plus a couple of animateurs, Marius and Bebe. Finally, they absconded with the keyboard star (a comparatively recent addition to the Zaïko line-up), Jose Piano-Piano. New recruits were brought in to complete the line-up including Djo Mali (of Langa Langa Stars and Choc Stars) Petit Cachet (Langa Langa Stars) and Vonvon Kabamba and Djo Moplat (both from Orchestre Oka). At first it seemed as if the Nyoko Longo's original line-up had been decimated but he retained sufficient strength in depth to rebuild effectively. For a start, the guitarist Matima has stayed, becoming a key member not only as 'Chef D'Orchestre' but also as sound engineer. Others, like Zamunagana, Bapius and Meridjo, provided a solid experienced back-up and within a short time the band was back on the road as a 26-piece outfit with the new recruits adopting a high profile as the more established musicians dropped into the background. New guitarists arrived including Muanda Shire (Minzota Wella Wella) and Baroza (Grand Zaïko) and a new drummer, Patcho Star (Victoria Eleison), who either doubled up with Meridjo or, when the stage was too small, alternated with him. Other recruits came from Orchestre Oka and Langa Langa Stars. Finally, they brought in synth player Lolaba Alpha from Orchestre Best to give a new layer and texture to the overall sound.

Dindo Yogo is arguably the most distinctive vocalist to have worked with Zaïko. He had started his career with Orchestre Macchi alongside guitarist Nseka Huit Kilos, who later found fame in Victoria Eleison and Tabu Ley's Afrisa. Yogo himself lent his voice to the particular 'feeling' which Zaïko generated. From his 1969 hit 'Lolo Muana', he was able to carry this 'feeling' through his own band Etumba Na Nguaka and on to Viva La Musica and Langa Langa Stars before (seven or eight albums later) joining Zaïko in 1983. He quickly became established as one of the brightest stars in the Zaïko galaxy with his 'voix cassée', or broken voice, becoming one of the most instantly recognisable elements in the band's repertoire. Indeed, it was his exquisite harmonisation with Longo, Bimi, Lengi Lenga and Buse which carried the Nkolo Mboka line-up into and beyond the dramatic schism of 1988. Nyoko Longo, for his part, spends less time on stage than in the past, allowing Yogo to pass on the 'feeling' to the other new singers.

Both branches of Zaïko flourished towards the end of the 1980s. Familia Dei tended to follow the classical Zaïko style which had served so well for so long while Nkolo Mboka were drawn to the equally exciting style of Dindo Yogo's band, Etumba Na Nguaka. In 1989 Dindo released several Zaïko-supported solo albums while Nkolo Mboka released the magnificent *Jetez L'Eponge*, one of their finest moments on vinyl. That same year Longo brought the band to London for the first time (although they were frequent visitors to Paris and Brussels), playing a hastily arranged, one-off show at Hammersmith Palais. Under normal circumstances the band play a five-hour, late-night set but on this occasion they were unceremoniously curtailed after a short but satisfying two-hour set. For British audi-

ences, it was the first opportunity to experience the real magic of the extended, Zaïko-style, seben (i.e. the faster, middle section of contemporary rumba/souk-ous). By the beginning of the 1990s, Nkolo Mboka were attaining new heights of excellence and popularity. They strengthened the guitar section by recruiting Gege and the star vocalist Malage de Lugendo, both from OK Jazz.

Zaïko have always been known as much for their dance moves as for their music, introducing such new dances as the Cavacha and the Volant in the 1970s, Zekete Zekete and Sundiama in the 1980s and more recently the Mayebo. The last-mentioned had been scheduled for an Easter 1990 release on the LP *Ici Ça Va . . . Fungola Motema*, but when the project was delayed, almost every other band in Kinshasa picked up on the new dance before Zaïko (Nkolo Mboka) had even officially introduced it. 'Mayebo' had been developed by Nkolo Mboka's animateur, Nono, throughout 1990 while over on the Familia Dei side Bimi Ombale had also been trying to develop a solo career, eventually parting company with Ilo Pablo early in 1990 to cut his own outstanding album *Balle De Match*, poaching Nono to introduce the Mayebo. Bimi's last contribution to Familia Dei was on the outstanding *L'Oiseau Rare*.

In 1991 both branches of the Zaïko family played in the UK to enormous critical acclaim, although the slightly longer tour by Nkolo Mboka was marred by poor publicity, transport problems, cancelled shows and the absence of Dindo Yogo, the only member unwilling to sign a tour contract forbidding session recordings with other bands, known in Zaïre as 'Nzong-Nzing'. Yet the tours served notice that what was effectively the best-kept secret in African music was about to be broken. For the first time, the Zaïko sound was unveiled in the UK to positive press and public acclaim. The prospects of considerable international success for Zaïko are now higher than at any time in the last two decades.

Zaïko Langa Langa (Nkolo Mboka)

1970s	360 092	L'Afrique Danse
	MGL 003	Oldies and Goodies (1985)
	360 117	+ Viva La Musica: L'Afrique Dance
1975	2C06215751	Non-Stop
1976	INLS 6116	Plaisir De L'Ouest Afrique
1978	SAF 50076	Editions Veve Vol.6
1981	GIP 001	Mobembo
	FCZ 001	Sarah Djenni/Volant

	GIP 002	Amour Suicide
1982	FCZ 002	La Toute Neige
	4649	Bambatuye
1983	IADS 007	Tout Choc-Anti Choc/ Muvaro-Etape (Also REM 20)
	FCZ 004	Milles Sourires
	PZL 3368	Zekete Zekete 2ème
	MGL 001	Zekete Zekete 3ème
1984	EVVI 03	Crois-Moi
	PZL 84001	On Gagne Le Procès
	19757	Espoir Na Ngai
	REM 100	Mère Tity
	CM 635	Wina
	EQ 4001	De Paris à Brazzaville
Mid-1980s	DS 8011	Nkolo Mboka Vol. 1
	DS 8012	Nkolo Mboka Vol. 2
1985	KKM 001	En Europe
	MPL 003	Beniko Popolipo
	PZL 85002	Ziko Eyi Nkisi
	PZL 85003	Tala Modela Echanger
	PZL 8586	Pusa Kuna
	MGL 003	Ndonge: Oldies and Goodies
1986	REM 450	Kay Kay
	PZL 199	Eh Ngoss Eh Ngoss
	MA	Thy Thy Na
1987	ESP 8440	Bongama Kamata Position
	ESP 8444	Nippon Banzai (Also PZL 86/87)
	ESP 8445	Subissez Les Conséquences
1988	ASLP 1028	Direct From Abidjan
	BNM 5004	Bimi Ombale & Zaïko
	8687/208	Papa Omar (Also NGOSS 86/87)
	SIC 001	Les Atalaku du Zaïko Langa Langa (Cass.)

	VDA 4001	Nkana
1989	ASLP 1037	Zaïko Eyi Nkisi – Mokili Echanger
	BNM 5006	Mbelengo Zouk & Inongo
	CA 681	Jetez L'Eponge
1990	ANC 11220	Creuser L'Ecart
	KBK 901	20ème Anniversaire
	PZL 8284	Ici Ça Va . . . Fungola Motem (Also MOTO 1, 1991)

Familia Dei/Zaïko. The other major half of the Zaïko split. Core members include Popolipo on guitar, Ilo Pablo on drums and Mandjeku on congas.

1989	ESPERA 289124	L'Oiseau Rare
1990	ESP 8472	Présente Ilo Pablo
1991	SF 005	Cessez Le Feu
	MS 004	Simon Delacroix & Zaïko Langa Langa
	LP 29121	Au Revoir Prince Bong
?1991	ESPERA 9063	Sans Frontières

Yogo, Dindo (b. Djangi Dindo Yogo). One of the most familiar voices of the last decade. Known in Zaïre as 'La Voix Cassée'.

1985	19765	Prix Nobel de la Paix
1986		Y Pas de Sot Métier
1987	453 041	De Tokyo–Paris– Kinshasa
1989	MAF 004	Ngai Naye & Klay Mawungu
	MA 4009	C'est La Vie
	MA 4015	Dindo Yogo
1990	MA 4041	Ami Ya Bomwana
	REM 820	Piscos
	4041	La Vie Est Heureuse

Wemba, Papa, and Viva La Musica (b. Shungu Jules Wembadia, Kasai, Zaïre, 1953). Papa Wemba first came to public notice as a youthful front-line vocalist with Zaïko Langa Langa. He left in 1974 and set up his own band, Isife Lokole, and then, in 1976, established the better-known Viva La Musica. Check the Sonodisc album for late 1970s sounds. Despite his eccentric/SAPEUR appearance (see p. 133), he remains one of the strongest guardians of Zaïrean folklore, willing to work outside a basic rumba framework when the material demands. By the 1980s his reputation was secure both as a solo star and as leader and part-time member of Viva. In 1984 he participated in an all-too short-lived 'School of Zaïko' supergroup called Les Guerres de Stars, along with equally gifted friends Bozi Boziana, Lita Bembo and the rising vocal star, Esperant. However, Wemba's career went into overdrive in the second half of the decade, signing with Stern's for two UK releases, starring in cult movie *La Vie Est Belle* (with a minor role for Pepe Kalle), establishing the concept of SAPEURISM and releasing a series of varied, accomplished and very collectable LPs. In 1988 he worked with the controversial French producer Martin Messonier and came in for criticism for 'westernising' his music. Wemba, in *Folk Roots* (July 1989), shrugged off the comments. 'Yes, I do like it. There have been Zaïrois who have complained that it's not real Zaïrean rumba, but they just can't accept anything a bit out of the ordinary.' TV documentaries and international tours followed as Wemba became the most visible of the Zaïrean stars. His insistence on juxtaposing high fashion with a conscious research of Zaïrean folklore makes his act not only stylish but musically satisfying. He has a proven track record of success, and with the experience to deal with the western media on his own terms, Wemba looks set for an even bigger impact in the 1990s.

1970s	360 117	L'Afrique Danse
	IDD 2536	+ Viva
1983	IADS 006	+ Viva: Mwana Molokai
1984	REM 140	Firenze
1985	TCHIKA 07	Les Guerre de Stars
	EQ 3193	+ Viva: 8ème Anniversaire
1986	AR 082	Mavuela
	BMP 001	Siku Ya Mungu
	REM 10	Mwana Molokai
	REM 110	+ Viva: Alangando
	REM 560	Ma Bijoux
1987	AM 87001	+ Strervos Niarchos: Dernier Coup
	TIP 001	+ Viva: Prendre à César
	ESP 8438	+ Viva: Love Kilawu

	PASS 01	+ Les Djamuskets
1988	ST 1026	Papa Wemba
	ST 1028	La Vie Est Belle
	ESP 8449	Destin Ya Moto
	ESP 8450	Au Japon
1989	ESP 8459	+ Viva: Nouvelle Génération à Paris
	ESP 8466	+ Viva: Modobo Gina + France Frère
1990	GKP 2855	+ Viva: Sango Pamba
	NM 46302	+ Viva: Biloko Ya Moto

Viva La Musica. More than a backing band, now officially known as the School of Viva, one of the centre-piece bands of the 1980s. Prolific and more mainstream than Wemba's solo outings.

1988	MA 4031	Salakeba
1989	MA 4032	+ Stino: Femme Sans Bijoux
1990	GKP 2855	13ème Anniversaire
	NDK 8807001	+ Wemba: Le Roi Pouvic Shouna
1991	DSK IM	+ Wemba: Mokili Ngele
	AL 001	Ba Mbila
	MA 4046	Reddy Amisa + Viva + Wemba
	CD 53902	Maréchal Rive-Kone et Ayatollah
		Pachamac de Viva La Musica

Olomide, Kofi. Rising star of soukous who, by 1990, had become one of the top attractions throughout Central Africa. He started his musical career as a guitarist before joining Papa Wemba and Viva La Musica as backing singer. By the mid-1980s his solo (and more adventurous) career was established, laying the ground-work for the critical successes of the early 1990s. Largely Paris-based, he has not hesitated to make maximum use of studio expertise from both the Paris soukous school and the Cameroonian contingent. In 1990 his Tcha Tcho beat outlined a possible future direction for a largely sterile studio sound, a slightly slower-paced momentum building into a quality rumba finale.

1986	YK 87001	Olomide & Yakini Kiesse
	ADM 1341	Olomide et Fafa de Molokoi
1987	T 1510	Kiki Ewing
	MA 4006	Ngobila
1988	KL 07	Henriquet
1989	KL 031	Elle et Moi
	TCHATCHO 1301	Petit Frère Ya Jesus
1990	ST 1031	Tcha Tcho (Also MCKL 031)
	ESP 8480	Les Prisonniers Dorment
1991	KIV 001	Alive (Video)

Clan Langa Langa. Another loose Langa formation. Look out for material by Gina Wa Gina/Gina La Poète Efonge.

1986	REM 120	Ami Mondzo
1987	ABD 2001	Le Trio Julema/Yenga Yenga Jnr du Clan Langa Langa: Bongo Bouger
	ABD 2002	Le Trio Julema/Yenga Yenga Jnr du Clan Langa Langa: Mon Marie
1988	BNM 5003	J.P. Buse du Clan Langa Langa: Idia
1989	NM 46301	Les Surdoues du Clan Langa Langa: Cauchemar
	SIC 004	Dona Mobeti du Clan Langa Langa
1991	CDBT 12912	Aimedo du Clan Langa Langa: Georgia (+ Shimita, Luciana, Lokassa)
	BIEMA 001	Gina Wa Gina & Clan Langa Langa: Lorenzo

Victoria Eleison. School of Zaïko led by the inimitable Emeneya and formed in 1985. Toured Europe in 1987. Emeneya graduated through the ranks of Viva La Musica before forming Victoria in 1985. Occasionally known as Victoria Principal, the band in fact has two teams, one Kinshasa-based and the other Paris-based. Emeneya (a.k.a. Joe Kester) scored heavily in 1989 with *Nzinzi*. In 1991 they played a short European tour with a stripped-down

12-piece band which proved perfectly capable of delivering the goods.

1985	REM 270	Sans Préavis
1986	REM 370	Commission
	REM 500	Explosion
1988	KL 02	Deux Temps
	REM 600	Kimpiatu
	REM 610	Jamaika
	EVVI 120	Mokosa
1989	KL 04	Nzinzi
1990	TCP 001	J.P. Swiss & Victoria Eleison
1991	LP 53314	Boulhos Loupino & Emeneya: Kassika Manda

Historia. Off-shoot from Victoria formed in 1984 and led by vocalist Cartouche. They have since disappeared from view.

1985	REM 530	Faux Parisien

Ombale, Bimi (b. Kinshasa, 1952). Started his career with Zaïko in 1969 before briefly joining Tabu National. A gifted singer/composer, he has composed over 50 Zaïko hits, including 'Zena', 'Joliba' and 'Sandra Lina'. Led the breakaway Familia Dei faction in the late 1980s.

1988	BNM 5004	
1989	BNM 5006	Mbelengo Zouk et Inongo
1990	LD 01	Balle de Match
	ANC 11220	La Poule Aux Oeufs D'Or

Langa Langa Stars. See Volume 1 for early discography. Formed in 1981 by Evoloko, Bozi and Roxy.

1986	REM 480	K.O. Debout
1987	REM 620	La Belle de Bangui
1988	REM 720	Gateau Ya Anniversaire
	REM 730	Papa Lokotro
1989	REM 770	Tostao
1991	RMU 990	Kinshasa Brazza Boyoka

Jocker, Evoloko. Outstanding vocalist and an early recruit to Zaïko, believed to have developed the 'cavacha' style. However, he left the band in 1974 to continue his studies in Europe. He teamed up briefly with Bozi but eventually returned home to establish Langa Langa Stars after another brief spell with Wemba. Langa Langa Stars released over a dozen albums in the early 1980s (see Volume 1) but Evoloko stood out as the star and towards the end of the decade adopted a higher profile as a solo (SAPEUR) star. His 1991 album *Mingelina B52* was an enormous critical success.

1984	EVVI 47	La Carte Qui Gagne & Langa Langa Stars
	EVVI 71	Done Bis & Langa Langa Stars
1987	IZD 10101	Mbengue & Langa Langa Stars
1989	RMU 990	Lisala Ngomba & Langa Langa Stars
1991	FDB 100058	+ Langa Langa Stars & Papa Wemba
	FDB 01	Mingelina B52

Grand Zaïko Wa-Wa. Formed by original Zaïko guitarist Manuaka Waka in 1980. Reputed to have the hardest guitar arm in Zaïre with sublime sebens stretching out for 30–40 minutes.

1984	REM 280	Zeke Ya Pamba
1985	REM 400	Mwasi Ya Solo
1986	REM 510	Santamaria
	KJ 001	Ba Pensées
1988	REM 670	+ Empire Bakuba
1989	425 003	Shimita et Grand Zaïko: Muntu Ku

Minzota Wella Wella. Early School of Zaïko outfit formed in 1972.

		Danse Caneton à L'Aisement
1986	EQ 3191	En Colère
1988	REM 540	Deuxième Bureau
1989	SNLP 008	Abiba
1990	K 4219	Nana Lubutu

Niarchos, Strervos. Front-line vocalist of some repute, plays with all and sundry. Often over-dressed and nicknamed 'Le Ngantshie', he has accompanied stars like Wemba, Rigo, Bozi and Evoloko.

1987		Dernier Coup de Sifflet
1989	LP 39503	+ Evoloko
	KL 015	La Religion Ya Kitende

Choc Stars. Formed by Ben Nyambo in 1984 as a rival orchestra to Zaïko Langa Langa. They are known and respected as much for their group albums as as a collective of talented backing musicians for other home-grown stars such as Defao and Carlito. Now known as the kings of 'romantic rumba' but perfectly able to belt out a surprising seben.

1983	REM 40	Jardin de Mon Coeur
1984	REM 160	Nono
	REM 170	Jaminata
	REM 180	Amour Infini
	REM 190	Mwana Suka
1985	REM 310	+ Langa Langa Stars: Tshala
	REM 460	Monza (45 r.p.m.)
	REM 470	Bozenga Ya Bateke (45 r.p.m.)
	CHOC 055	A Paris
	REM 580	Koreine
1986	ORB 009	Choc = Shock = Choc
	REM 680	Mauvais Souvenir
	REM 690	Nalandaka Te
	ORB 010	Awa et Ben
1987	REM 740	Sandra La Blonde (A Paris Vol. 2)
	MA 4007	Defao & Choc Stars
	ESPERA 618	Oko Ndizo Mbongwena Emonani
1988	BNM 5007	Pêche de la Femme
	KL 013	Chagrin-Dimone
	KL 018	Carnaval Choc Stars (Medley)
	ESPERA 289122	Munduki Elelo

	MA 4016	Debaba
1989	KM 3091	Carlito/Debaba/Choc Stars
	BDC 001	Bel Ami De Wolo
	ESPERA 698924	Choc Stars & Ben Nyambo (Double)
	ESPERA 623	Kelemani
	38773-1	Ibrahim Bula
	REM 780	Choc Stars & Carlito
	MA 4030	Debaba
1990	DO 889L	Premier Amour
	NGAPY 1188	A Paris
	BNM 5007	Au Grand Complet
	KM 3091	Carlito et Debaba du Choc Stars
	ESPERA 29043	Oka Polisson Chaufe
	0908 DF	Defao et Son Groupe

Anti-Choc. Breakaway faction led by influential Bozi Boziana. Now considered to have the edge over Choc Stars. In 1990 the loose formation known as Anti-Choc headlined two impressive shows in London, opening the doors for other 'School of Zaïko' bands. The 1991 outing, *Realité*, omits Bozi but does include Wally Ngonda on guitar and the up-and-coming talents of Deesse, a striking front-line female singing sensation, and Skola, the second of the female front-line.

1984	JPM 30384	Bozi & Pablo
1988	ST 1022	Anti-Choc
	SIC 003	Bozi & Jolie Detta: Tshala
	REM 640	Kokoti
1989	AMG 101	Zongela
	MA 4029	Bon Anniversaire Nelson Mandela
	MA 4038	Bozi & Choc Stars
	NGAPY 1089	Bozi Boziana
1990	SDM 001	Bozi & Pepe Kalle: Santa
	SIC 003	Bozi, Anti-Choc & Jolie Detta
	MA 4013	Sans Frontières
	EVVI 85	Mon Mari Est Gabonais
	JIT 015	Au Bout du Fil
1991	GKP 2759	Realité
	MA 4040	Dansez Nza Wissa

The 'School of Zaïko' continues to provide the real cutting edge of contemporary African music with its unique combination of style, skill and unlimited musical imagination. This is music with spirit, far from the sterile studio formulae of rival outfits, and fully equipped to explore contemporary African music to the very frontiers of cultural imagination.

The soukous mainstream

Kalle, Pepe and Empire Bakuba (b. Kabasele Yampanya, Kinshasa, 1951; band formed 1972). Of all the Zaïrean stars to make a breakthrough in the 1980s, Pepe Kalle and Bakuba are perhaps the biggest in terms of popularity, recordings and sales (and in the case of Pepe Kalle, in size). Known affectionately as 'The Elephant of Zaïre', 'Le Bombe Atomique' and 'The Giant of Africa', Kalle entered the 1990s with almost two decades of experience behind him and a rough-and-ready rumba sound which had thrilled audiences throughout Central Africa. Indeed, if a poll were to be taken today as to who should fill Franco's shoes then Pepe Kalle would win hands down. Yet, like many others, Kalle had to work his way up from humble beginnings. He made his début in 1968 in the exalted company of Kalle and African Jazz before moving on to establish African Choc in 1970 with Papy-Tex and Dilu. Working in the same wave of youth music which produced Zaïko, Pepe Kalle responded to the Authenticité campaign by changing the name of the band to the better-known Empire Bakuba. Over the next two decades the band moved from strength to strength on the basis of tight studio productions and entertaining live performances. Above all, they kept up a steady stream of innovative dances, including the Essombi, Oh Nager and Kwassa Kwassa. By the early 1990s they were much in demand outside Zaïre and complied with tours of Europe, USA, Japan and the Antilles as well as Africa. Strictly Kinshasa-based, they are now one of the top bands on the continent.

1980s	EVVI 45	Cherie Ondi
	REM 220	Zabolo
	REM 260	Amour Propre
	8730	Obosini Kisonde
1985	PF 77013	Bonana 85
	REM 360	La Belle Etoile
	REM 410	Trop C'est Trop
	REM 490	Muana Bangui
	K 4222	Tête Africaine
1986	DK 006	Adieu Dr Nico

	SYL 8324	Pepe Kalle + Nyboma
	REM 550	Allah
	DV 001	Livre D'Or
1987	ACMP 1001	Makassi Calcule
	SYL 8334	Kwassa Kwassa
	SYL 8338	Bakuba Show
	LS 47	Joe Dikando
	211083	Dadou Folklore
1988	SYL 8358	+ Nyboma: Moyibi
	REPRO 01	Nzoto Ya Chance (Also LN 1)
	31001	L'Argent Ne Fait Pas Le Bonheur
	REM 670	Bakuba + Grand Zaïko Wa-Wa
	SIC 002	Ya Moseka de L'Empire Bakuba
1989	91080	Chante le Poète Simarro
	REPRO 1	Kwassa Kwassa
	MA 4034	Show Times
	BB 002	Atinze Mwana Popi
	AR 1007	Pom Moun Paka Bouge
	AR 1012	Ce Chak Carnaval
	NS 49908LP	Le Tube de Vos Vacances
1990	ORB 062	Gigant-Afrique
	AR 1012	Ce Chale Carnival
	MDL 301	Mavuela Somo + Pepe Kalle

Blaise, Theo (b. Theo Blaise Kounkou, Congo). Talented vocalist with regional success in the early 1980s.

1980	EFA 010	L'Eden
1981	EFE 024	Gemile (Also TBK 006)
1983	79394	Zenaba
	79396	Belle Amicha
	79397	Celia
1984	ALP 2	
	ASLP 941	Bella Amicha

Moutouari, Pierre. Congolese-born vocalist with several top albums from the mid-1980s.

1984	LP 8101	Le Retour
1985	PM 001	Tout Bouge
	PM 100	Aissa
1986	LP 8101	Missengue
1989	46004	+ Michel et Michaelle: Mbolo
1990	9596	Tumba

Moutouari, Michel. Brother of Pierre and a gifted singer in his own right. His 1990 effort featured the guitar pyrotechnics of up-and-coming soloist Nene Tchekou.

1987	TLS 97	Les Vacances au Paris
1990	ACP CG 003	Mon Ami et Ma Femme
1991	ACP CG 009	Maître Sokete

Tchico (b. Pambou Tchicaya Tchico). Prolific and talented singer known as 'La Voix D'Or du Congo'. His early career was with the Bantous before moving to Nigeria with the Waka Waka Band. Early solo albums from 1971–2 included *Feu Rouge* and *L'Amour Maternal*. In 1979 he teamed up with Lolo Lolita to record one of Africa's all-time classics – the unforgettable *Jeannot*, which is still widely available. In 1983 he moved to Paris ahead of the crowd and helped establish one of the first Congolese supergroups, Les Officiers of African Music, with guitarist Denis La Cloche and fellow vocalist Passi-Jo. In 1985 they released their first British album on the Globestyle label, *Full Steam Ahead*. By 1990 he had released over forty albums (see Volume 1 for earlier work), and although his star is currently on the wane, the irrepressible Tchico will surely return to front-line action in the future. Tchico fans will want to check a new version of *Jeannot* on BM008. With the demise of Les Officiers, Tchico established a new working band called Kilimandjaro.

1988		20 Ans de Carrière
	KRL 001	+ Kilimandjaro: Soukous Machine
1989	BM 008	+ Kilimandjaro: L'Ambiance à Paris
1990	ACPCG 004	Special 90

La Cloche, Denis (b. Denis Loubassou). Paris-based master guitarist who first came to wider public notice with Les Officiers. The 1989 solo album also features Geo. Bilong.

1986	19764	Saka Saka Show
1988	DLL 003	La Sema Sema
1989	CIL 8735	Souks'man du Congo
1990	AR 1015	Amour Protégé

Puati, Lumingu (b. Matadi, 1941). Started his professional career as a bass player with Orchestre Rock-En-Jazz in 1960. Between 1962 and 1965 he was a member of Orchestre Mickey Mickey before joining Dr Nico in African Fiesta in 1965, with whom he toured most of Africa. He cut a few singles and two albums in the early 1970s but nothing more was heard until the disappointing return in 1987.

| 1987 | ESP 7523 | Zorro |

Mabiala, Prince Youlou, and L'Orchestre Kamikazi Loningisa. Ex-OK Jazz vocalist and former partner of Fan Fan, who, during the early 1980s, became one of the most popular singers in Congo/Zaïre with over a dozen albums to his credit. Orchestre Kamikaze were also an extremely gifted outfit who could work from a slow ballad to Zaïko-type sebens in a three-gear change. Early work is highly recommended.

1985	REM 30	Judoka
1988	NK 5114	+ Virmiche/Angelou Chevauchet
	REM 390	Karibu
		Mon Avocat a Voyage
1989		Amina Coulibaly (With Kamikaze)

Somo Somo. Brainchild of Mose Se Sengo, a.k.a. Fan Fan, Somo Somo have enjoyed several incarnations. See Volume 1 for full story. More recently, Fan Fan has been strangely silent, still based in London and recording a few sessions, prior to re-launching Somo Somo in 1991.

| 1986 | TESP 8432 | Kizolele |
| | ST 1014 | Paris |

Bembo, Lita, and the Stukas. Stalwarts of the Kinshasa scene, the Stukas enjoyed enormous local success in the late 1970s but largely failed to make the transition into the 1980s. Lita Bembo, band leader

and vocalist, inventor of the popular 'saccade' rhythm, continued on his own to become an impressive solo star.

| 1987 | ESP 8437 | A Tout Coeur |
| 1989 | ESPERA 26989/100 | La Renaissance d'un Legend |

Master Mwana Congo. Sublime guitarist of long standing who graces any studio session. Extremely active in Paris towards the end of the 1980s, he continued with a series of solo albums including the 1990 hit *C'est du Tao Tao*.

1982	79403 Ma	Parole
1983	79412	Brigitte
1984	79423	New Style
1988	ANC 1187	Les 2 'A's & Freddy De Majunga
1990	1837	C'est du Tao Tao

Muana, Tshala. By the mid-1980s Tshala had established a solid reputation in Zaïre, Europe and West Africa for her languid dance rhythm – the mutuashi. Until the mid-1980s she doubted her own ability – a female singer with a non-rumba rhythm – but a return to Kinshasa in 1986 from her Paris base convinced her. By 1990 Tshala was clearly in the top half dozen of younger Zaïrean stars with several No. 1 albums in the UK African charts and a reputation stretching from Senegal to Zambia. She remains ambitious for even wider exposure but, unlike so many of her contemporaries, sees no need to change the music which has brought her so far. As she says: 'African music is so rich, there is no need to change it. I represent West Africa with my music and besides if I let go of my roots, the African public would drop me and I would have nothing.' By the late 1980s her albums were increasingly appreciated and she appeared on several early Zaïrean videos. She is a singer now approaching the peak of her powers.

1981	ARCS 3690	Amina
1984	TM 058	Kami
1985	SAS 051	Mbanda Matiere
1986	SAS 057	M'Pokolo
1987	ESP 1304	Antidote (45 r.p.m.)
1988	SYL 8376	Munanga
1989	66873	Biduaya

1990	ESPERA 620	Nasi Nabali
	ESPERA 621	La Divine
	SR 781	Space Original (Cass.)
1991	SHAN	Soukous Siren
	KL 056CD	Tshala Muana

Love, M'Pongo. See Volume 1 for career and discography. M'Pongo died suddenly and tragically in 1989. An irreplaceable loss. Her final album shows her at near best – a Bopol-assisted Syllart Paris production.

| 1982 | | Nzenze |
| 1988 | SYL 8386 | Partager |

Abeti. A highly respected female singer who is now in the forefront of Zaïrean female vocalists. Her career started in the early 1970s and she has released a great deal of material on vinyl. See Volume 1 for early discography. Her 1991 release was highly rated, featuring Lokassa on guitar in a zouk–soukous hybrid. Characterised by tight harmonies and a kick-start approach, Abeti remains one of the few African musicians to have played in China, touring in 1989 and headlining a show in pre-Tiananmen Square Peking.

	AM 33	Je Suis Fâché
1985	ANS 8406	Tourda Nini
1990	ACDC 27749	Best of Abeti
1991	JIP 024	Bebe Matoko
	FDF 300057	La Reine du Soukous (CD)

Elali. New female singer.

| 1991 | 82087 | Ayaye |

Isa, Lady. Up-and-coming female singer ably assisted on 1989 album by Bopol, Syran and drummer Boffi. Her first LP was released in Kenya and subsequently re-released in 1990 on the Espera label. Proved to be a bigger hit in Kenya than Europe.

| 1989 | KARI 007 | Malimbo |
| 1990 | ESPERA 29063 | Ale Mama |

Tape, Miga. Female vocalist assisted by Rigo and Sammy Massamba.

| 1990 | KL 010 | Golozi |
| 1991 | JIP 027 | Ayele |

Coco, Ammy. Rising female singer now based in Côte D'Ivoire. Her first LP featured the talents of Lokassa, Shimita, Ballou and Eddy Gustave.

| 1990 | S 1834 | Djagura |

Kinshasa–Paris

Leading Zaïrean musicians had been drawn to Paris and Brussels since the early 1950s, mainly for better recording opportunities and occasional shows to resident Zaïreans. But by the early 1980s this trickle had become a flood as dozens of musicians and several complete bands settled in Paris. The reasons for this exodus are not difficult to find and start with the lack of decent recording studios in Zaïre and the control exercised over recording and performing facilities by the hegemony of established acts like OK Jazz, Afrisa and above all Verckys. The other side of the coin related to better facilities in Europe and the possibility of earning a reasonable living from the booming interest in and acceptance of African music.

Between 1985 and 1990 this core group of 50–100 musicians churned out an enormous amount of vinyl. Some would say too much since the basic soukous sound was seldom altered as top personnel simply moved from one soukous session to the next. A few groups became firm favourites (Soukous Stars, Quatre Etoiles, Loketo and others) but the basic formula was for an ambitious singer to put together a studio band and take it from there. Several key musicians thereby appeared on literally dozens of albums, with Rigo Star, Pablo, Diblo, Dally Kimoko, Lokassa, Ballou Canta, Aurlus Mabele and Armando appearing to be most in demand.

During the same period the Zaïrean stars came into increasing and regular musical contact with other Francophone musicians based in Paris. For this reason, we often find Zaïreans working with the Cameroonian Paris contingent and, to greater effect, with Antillean zouk musicians. By the late 1980s Paris had become the source of exciting new tropical music cocktails comprising a wide range of styles and influences, from soukous and makossa to zouk, soca and lambada, to rock, reggae and raga.

Finally, and usually quite distinctively, there was another group of musicians coming to Paris but not as residents. They were all associated with the Zaïko/Choc/Viva La Musica school of modern music, who continued to use Paris for recording facilities. These sessions could last for several months, and since the bands were in temporary residence France and the rest of Western Europe was regularly treated to stunning live sets. The following section of this chapter concentrates on those musicians who now use Paris as a base.

Kanda Bongo Man (b. Kanda Bongo, Inongo, Zaïre, 1955). Along with Papa Wemba, Kanda proved to be the soukous sensation of the 1980s and is also an impressive businessman who manages to keep ahead of the game by running his own label and managing his own affairs. His reputation, spread by constant touring, striking videos and local licensing contracts, now encompasses most of Africa. Yet despite his enormous artistic success and close attention to business he still finds some problems irresolvable. In 1990 he toured Australia and commented, 'When you see a turn out like that you have to ask yourself why can't we sell more records? I will never know what the record companies are doing. With such a number of people and they can't sell 3,000 records. Crazy.' In 1989 he toured Japan commenting, 'They buy more African records, treat us with more respect than those we've had a relationship going hundreds of years with.' Musically, Kanda has developed a high-speed soukous style enriched with current dance styles – from the Kwassa Kwassa to the Mayebo – although his style remains instantly recognisable. He also has firm views about the current state of African music: 'Zaïrean music has to move; the problem is that Senegalese, Malian and Gambian music are seen as roots music and as such they are promoted with that paternalistic bias, whilst popular African music, like ours, is seen as dropping all things African from it. They do not have an idea of what African music is' (*World Beat*, June 1991). Strong stuff, but given the incontrovertible fact that soukous is the only truly pan-African style yet sells in tiny quantities outside the continent, it is hard not to agree with Kanda. The Bongo Man's star has been rising steadily over the last decade and he is now one of the most acclaimed musicians in Africa. Most of his output is widely available on the Hannibal label (now part of Rykodisc), who regularly re-package albums for the European market.

1981	AR 00181	Iyole
1982	AR 00981	Djessy
1984	BM 0055	Amour Fou
1985	ORB 005	Non-Stop Non-Stop
1986	BM 0056	Malinga
1987	BM 0057	Lela Lela
	HNBL 1337	Amour Fou/Crazy Love
1988	BM 0058	Sai Liza
1989	HNBL 1343	Kwassa Kwassa
1990	BM 0059	Isambe
1991	HNBL 1366	Zing-Zong

Quatre Etoiles. Mid-1980s supergroup of incredible pedigree formed by Bopol, Nyboma, Syran and Wuta May. See Volume 1 for early career and

discography. Although the group still exists, the individual musicians have mostly moved on to other things, occasionally regrouping (in 1988 and 1990) for splendid dance-floor recordings.

1986	SYL 8376	6 Tubes
1988	FS 401	Four Stars (Live)
1991	66895	Souffrance

Bopol. Talented bass and guitar player. More than ever in demand as a session man. Paris-based and able to pursue an impressive solo career.

1988	PG 87101	Sambela (With Syran)
1989	BM 05	Innovation
	82426	Dada Micha
1990	SYL 8397	Belinda

Nyboma. Velvet-voiced singer and all-time classic rumba vocalist. Again, an impressive solo career tucked in-between sessions.

1988	CEL 8724	+ Bakuba
	INLPRX 008	+ Bovi: Innovation Vol. 8
1989	SYL 8358	+ Pepe Kalle: Moyibi
1990	82804	+ Madilu: Stop Feu Rouge

Syran. Since the semi-demise of Quatre Etoiles he seemed to keep a low profile towards the end of the decade but bounced back with the 1990 hit *The Best of Paris* – and for once this is no exaggeration on an album where Syran calls in his debts and gets the proper response from Nyboma, Bopol, Wuta May, Kimoko, Diblo and Lokassa.

| 1990 | HYSA 1185 | The Best of Paris |

Kass Kass. Short-lived Paris based 'supergroup' led by Passi-Jo.

1988	ST 1018	Kass Kass
1989	82443	Passi-Jo & Kass Kass
	82417	Kass Tout
	38744	Danger & J.P. Ramazoni

Passi-Jo (b. Kinshasa, 1949). A fine singer with many studio sessions to his credit, Passi-Jo was born into a family of travelling troubadors. His first major engagement was with Orchestre Veve, then under the direction of Verckys. Strongly influenced by Bakongo rhythms, he was one of the founder-members of Les Officiers. On his 1987 solo outing he was assisted by the guitar skills of Syran.

In 1989 he appeared amongst a remarkable line-up of stars for an LP which strangely failed to register. Stars included M. Clay. Petit Poisson, Michel Moutouari, Master Mwana and Andre Pamomiel.

1987	JND 5104	Mi Nawe Yele
1989	8512	Bana Congo
1990	82443	Kass Kass Connection (Cass.)
1991	115545	Kass Kass Tout

Pablo. Pablo Lubadika Porthos. See Volume 1 for discography and career of a true star. Towards the end of the 1980s he seemed to concentrate on a session career for his immaculate guitar and bass skills. The most recent release is the 1986 LP listed below.

| 1986 | BIZ 013 | Pablo & Tutu: Safula |

Star, Rigo (a.k.a. Ringo Star). Top-drawer guitarist and producer enormously influential in his high-speed soukous style who, between 1985 and 1990, was the most sought-after session musician, appearing on over 50 LPs. By 1990 he was working almost exclusively with Mbilia Bel.

1984	79429	Tour à Abidjan
1986	MA 4005	Ringo Star
1989	MA 4017	Ai Ai Ai & Kofi Olomide

Loketo. Late 1980s supergroup formed in Paris by a core of six stars – Aurlus Mabele, Mav Cacharel and Jean Baron on vocals, Diblo and Mimi Kazidoni on guitars and Mack Macaire on drums. By 1989 they were established as the hottest guitar band in Paris with several very successful albums and a brisk touring schedule. In 1990 they struck gold with *Extra-Ball*.

1986		Amoreaux Etranger
1988	410011	Super K
1989	410081	Mondo Ry
	JP 006	Trouble
1990	JIP 017	Extra-Ball

Dibala, Diblo (b. Kisingani, 1954). Often described as the fastest of all Zaïrean guitarists, Diblo amply represents the post-Nico guitar tradition. His early years were spent in Kisingani on the bend of the Zaïre River before the family moved to Kinshasa in 1960. He modelled his style on Dr Nico and found his first job with the celebrated Orchestre Bella Bella.

In 1975 he moved to Paris with his friend Kanda and together they scraped a living. In 1983 they both tasted the limelight for the first time with the release of Kanda's *Iyole* – an album which exposed a wider public to Diblo's guitar virtuosity. Their success was due in no small part to their unorthodox approach to rumba. As Diblo explained (*World Beat*, June 1991), 'We found that people liked the instrumental part best . . . so why lose time with slow singing parts when people do not understand the words anyway.' Following his success with Kanda, Diblo moved on to form a new supergroup with singer Aurlus Mabele – the famous Loketo (meaning 'hips' in Lingala). Now firmly based in Paris, Diblo found himself in high demand as a session musician on the busy scene there. The band changed personnel quite often but still spins on the Mabele–Diblo axis. They toured the US in 1989 and 1990 to thunderous acclaim.

Mabele, Aurlus. One of the first session singers to make an impact with streamlined Paris soukous. His first couple of albums from the mid-1980s set the standard for dance-floor soukous. Now based in Paris, he gets through an enormous amount of session work and still finds time to tour extensively (USA, Antilles, Canada, Guyana). In 1989 he established his working musicians under the name L'Orchestre N'Dimbala Lokole de Brazzaville. Founder-member of supergroup Loketo, whose 1990 *Remix* re-introduced many of Aurlus' hottest songs to a new public – including 'Femme Ivorienne', 'Cameroon OK' and the ever-popular 'Loketo'.

1987	JP 001	Africa Moussos
1988	JP 011	Soukous La Terreur
1989	CPSC 345	La Femme Ivorienne (With Loketo)
1990	P 01	Laissez à Tomber
	JP 004	+ Loketo: Remix
1991	JIP 021	Embargo & Loketo

Baron, Jean. Gifted singer, made his big breakthrough in 1991 with the Loketo-assisted LP.

| 1987 | TLS 100 | Problème Sentimentale |
| 1991 | JIP 026 | Comme Un |

Soukous Stars. The latest Paris-based supergroup, comprising, initially, Lokassa (rhythm guitar and founder); Ballou Canta (vocalist and founder); Dally Kimoko (lead guitar and founder); Shimita (vocalist); Zitany Nell (vocalist) and Ngouma Lokito (bass). After several impressive collective albums, including the major soukous hit of 1990 (*Megamix Vol. 1*), the musicians took turns in fronting the band for a series of highly acclaimed dance-floor albums.

1990	38779	Megamix Vol. 1 (a.k.a. Lagos Nights)
1991	AT 091	Lokito & Soukous Stars
	KBK 908	Kimoko & Soukous Stars: Tobina
	381002	Yondo Syster & Soukous Stars: Bazo

Canta, Ballou. Veteran singer from the late 1970s graduating through spells with Tele Music, Ray Lema, Pamelo Mounka, Zao and Abeti before helping found the Soukous Stars in 1989. The LP *Bolingo Sonia* was the DJs' delight of 1990.

1985	79420	Sambala
	5401	Maryline
1989	LP 31846	Dama-Diallo
1990	1829	Bolingo Sonia & Soukous Stars

Lokassa, Ya Mbongo. Outstanding guitarist very much in demand throughout the 1980s. He started his career in Rochereau's Afrisa before helping Sam Mangwana to organise the African All Stars in Abidjan in the early 1980s. By 1983 he was based in Paris, playing on dozens of albums before forming Soukous Stars in 1989 with Kimoko, Shimita and Ballou Canta. Amongst his solo efforts look out for *Marie Jose*.

		Marie Jose
1986	IVALP 008	Adiza
1990	38779	+ Soukous Stars: Megamix Vol. 1 (a.k.a. Lagos Nights)

Shimita. Vocalist/animateur and founding member of Soukous Stars. Made his first solo album in 1988. His 1990 outing involved Pablo, Kimoko and Rigo. He had earlier graduated from Grand Zaïko Wa-Wa

| 1988 | 425 003 | Mabili |
| 1990 | SYL 8377 | Amidjo |

Kimoko, Dally (b. Ndala Kimoko). Solo guitarist. Played with Orchestre Kamale before joining Sam and the boys in the African All Stars, eventually

becoming a member of Soukous Stars and much-requested session star.

| 1989 | 05102 | Titina |
| 1990 | KBK 908 | Dally Kimoko & Soukous Stars |

Nolo, Djo, and Choc Musica. Rising star of the late 1980s with a sudden and prolific output. Led by Djo on drums and vocals, Choc Musica are a loose coalition of musicians with no steady line-up.

1988	REM 750	Voiture
1989	ESP 8465	Malryhama
	MOL 007	Bineta Bis
	MA 4023	Jolie Medina & Cartouche
	MA 4035	Play-Boy
1990	KL 021	Fatima-Benita

Zizi, Fidele. Mid-1980s superstar, ranking along with Aurlus Mabele as pioneer of Paris studio soukous. His early career included spells with Orchestre Mando Negra and the seminal Los Nickelos – a Brussels-based student band.

| 1983 | ASLP 979 | Au Revoir Cherie |
| 1988 | ESP 8425 | Mobali Sans Avenir |

Lema, Ray (b. in a train station, 1946). As a child, Ray studied organ in the church for five years, admiring Hendrix and starting to drift into music. His first public show was Beethoven's *Moonlight Sonata*. He then entered university but was already playing in Kinshasa clubs adding keyboard expertise to various stars such as Kalle, Abeti, M'pongo Love and Tabu Ley. In the early 1970s he became involved with the Ballet du Zaïre and between 1974 and 1978 toured Zaïre studying folklore. In 1978 he won the coveted 'Maraccas D'Or' for his work with Group Ya Tupos and the following year won a Rockefeller grant to study in the US. By this time, Lema had more than proved his talent in a number of areas from choreography and folklore to the more familiar rhythms of Zaïrean soukous. During the 1980s Lema has emerged as one of Africa's most acclaimed musicians with a clutch of LPs, numerous TV appearances and a reputation as a musician who refuses to be typecast into the soukous mould. In the early 1980s he worked out of Paris, including a spell with the Bwana Zoulou Gang, a short-lived band featuring Manu Dibango. Today, having signed with Mango, Lema is on the verge of massive international acclaim as a talented musician and shrewd observer of the global music scene. Apart from his solo work, he remains much in demand for his technical skills, programming instruments and lending a keen ear to session work.

1979	CEL 6631	Koteja-Koluto
1980s	34001	Tosangala (With Bwana Zoulou Gang)
1985	CEL 6658	Paris–Kinshasa–Washington DC
1986	CEL 6756	Médecine
1988	MLPS 1000	Nangadeef
1990	MLPS 1055	Gaia
1991	083 142	Ray Lema Live (Video)
	083 148	Various (Lema/Kanda/Tabu Ley): Zaïre Groove (Video)

Dens, Bibi. Top vocalist who served a long apprenticeship in Abidjan producing the early 1980s classic *The Best Ambiance*. Struck back in 1990 with *J'Aime Ça*, a massive hit in France but failing to register elsewhere.

1985	ROUNDER	The Best Ambiance
1987	TAN 7001	Sensible
1990	GHBM 0002	J'Aime Ça (With Les Marymbas) (Also CEL 66874)

Cacharel, Mav., et Son Groupe Kebo (b. Poto-Poto, Congo). Powerful vocalist with several hit albums in the late 1980s, he made his first professional appearance at the age of 13 and proceeded through a number of youth bands before winning the annual RFI prize for up-and-coming talent in 1983. On the strength of the prize he moved to Paris and took up residence as a session singer. 'Kebo', the name of his band, is a popular street sound in Brazza and Kinshasa as well as an attitude. Now based in Paris, he appeared briefly as a core-member of Loketo.

1988	KL 036	Pour Toi
1991	08351	Louzolo

Fimbo, Jarrys (b. Fimbo Mongalenge, a.k.a. Jarrys, Zaïre, 1956). A talented vocalist, Jarrys played with several youth bands before his career took off in 1979. He then joined the Stukas, with whom he released two singles in 1981 and two more in 1983 before moving to Paris in 1986. His first LP was released in 1987 and the highly acclaimed *Ambiance*

Non-Stop followed in 1990. Along the way he has had spells with Choc Stars, Victoria Principal, Victoria Eleison and a brief spell with Zaïko in 1984.

1987		
1990	MA 4033	Ambiance Non-Stop

Majunga, Freddy de. Enormously influential synth player and producer. Played with virtually everybody in Paris towards the end of the 1980s and released several top-quality albums. Majunga, however, was born in Madagascar so please refer there for biography.

Nell, Zitany. Lead singer who scored twice towards the end of the decade with dance-floor hits. Supported by the cream of the session men – Bolingo, Kimoko, Pablo, Shimita, Diblo and Lawu, Nell had cut his teeth in Ivory Coast with his own band, Generation 86, before moving to Paris and continuing the good work with Soukous Stars.

1985	ASLP 990	Sulia Tantine (With Suzy Kasseya)
1989	KL 044	L'Embarras du Choix
	38762	Marcory Gasoil

Zao. Congolese humorist who can still turn out excellent dance tracks. His stage name is derived from Zero-Admis-Omnipresent (Nothing-Admittance-Success).

1985	BAE 4011	Ancien Combattant
1986	BM 003	Corbillard
1989	82463	Patron
1990	82418	Moustique

The best of the rest

Adeley, Olomide. Coincidence – or an example of musical name stealing (see Kofi Olomide above)? Olomide is still a fine singer whose 1990 LP was remarkable in that Rigo Star played everything there was to play.

1990	MM 20	L'Amerlook

Bipoli (b. Bipoli Tshande). One-time singer with Victoria, made his solo début in 1991 accompanied by both Deesse and Jolie Detta and with guitar solos by Nene Tchekou.

1991	BS 4854	Engambe

Boxingo, Jean

| 1989 | WS 47601 | Donkale (With Loketo) |

Katalas, Mascot de. Congolese-born singer. Burst on scene with 1988 hit.

| 1988 | | Amour Academique |
| 1989 | 0910 MC | Mbula Malsanga |

Kassanda et L'Orchestre Malaika Int. Recorded at Veve in Kinshasa by Mimi Ley, this poor-quality pressing is more than balanced by the classic rumba sound.

| 1988 | AFRLP 008 | Nzoto Ya Depence 'Mace' |

Lawu, Fede (b. Nzau-Kabviku). Singer/animateur calling on Majunga, Bolingo and others for his non-stop soukous medley.

| 1989 | IDS 890 514 | Soukous Non-Stop |

Moya, Ringo. Fine drummer with vast session experience.

| 1987 | TAN 7011 | Dansez Zaïre |
| 1989 | RM 121 | Village Wassa |

Poati, Prosper. Vocalist who enjoyed reasonable success with first solo album.

| 1990 | AC 425 | Muana Sukh |

Rega, Privat. New singer assisted by Mabele, Canta and assorted Antilleans for a delightful zouk–soukous mélange.

| 1990 | JP 0010 | Demele |

Tontons, Les. For once, a new group rather than a solo singer. Led by Buffalo Kawongolo Kibwanga, they were formed in 1989 as a studio band, featuring the combined talents of Master Mwana, Salsero and Pablo on bass. Buffalo also doubles on horns.

| 1990 | AFMS 012 | Tour D'Afrique |

Tutu (b. Tumba Tutu-de-Mukose). Vocalist supported by Pablo.

| 1990 | BR 012 | Solitude |

Ty-Jan et Les L.P.P. Plus Canta and Kimoko. Ty-Jan offers vocals, synths and drums on mediocre studio work-out.

| 1990 | JP 008 | Sort Les Gazes |

X-Or Zobena et Les Professionels. Veve recording for the Kenyan market.

| 1989 | SNLP 007 | Atipo |

Zaïstars. Short-lived supergroup mixing soukous and zouk.

| 1989 | ERI 45001 | Nellyana |

Zeza, Tadi. Vocalist helped along by Master Mwana and Sammy Massamba.

| 1988 | 72439 | Banatha |
| 1990 | TDZ 113 | Soleil des Iles |

The rest. Hundreds of albums are released in Zaïre, Congo and Europe every year. The overall quality is extremely high and I have tried to indicate those albums which are a cut above the rest. Those listed below can be considered interesting but not crucial to an understanding of Zaïrean music over the last five years. Inevitably, by the time we come to write Volume 3, many of these musicians will have entered the top league, making it important to start listing their achievements now.

1987	T 5001	Lezard Trompeur: Papy Ndoumbe
	ESPERA 617	Klody: Commandez Sans Problèmes
	LS 91	Moro Beya Maduma: Mamema
	LS 92	Molengo Show: Asso-E
1988	T 881	Ikwai: Celina
	MIRAT 001	Le Couple Tsholo Nkese: Nalukanga
	MA 4018	Sakis et Orchestre: Le Mandina
	FM 1395	Fafa de Molokai: Le Grand Maestro
	HP 002	Sheiro: Y'En à Marie
	ESP 8457	Sambadio et Les Vivacité Melodia

	OBA 183	Edo Bruno et Pepe Dutronc
	TCM 1	Charlston Marquis
1989	LP 1419	Mazgel: Mokili
	AND 33887	Tala Samquita: Qui Saurait
	ESP 8458	Maika Munan: N'sea
	AT 079	Yoka Lokita
	LB 236	Djo Cassidy et Les Zombi de Brazza
	K 2001	Oliveira: New Song
	BNM 5005	La Zaïkomania: Olasi
1990	1999	Petit Poisson Avedila: Kabibi
	KD 001	Djo Poster: Mal De Toi
	AR 1013	Geo. Bilongo: Locomotive Arrive
	KL 035	L'Orchestre de La Jeunesse
	SSL 1425	Les 5 Venus: Metal 5
	SSL 1426	Sammy Massamba: Beni Soit Ton Nom
	SPE 101	Likinga Redo: Maliya

Compilations. Since the 1960s a great deal of material has appeared on compilation albums, principally those in the following series: L'Afrique Danse; Les Merveilles du Passé; Bridge Over the Congo. There are also a number of good Nigerian-made compilations in the following series – SOP, SPOT and PLPS.

1986	CDORB 907	Compact D'Afrique (Mabele, Choc Stars, Bongo Man, etc. – excellent)
	OMA 102	The Sound of Kinshasa (Original Hits from the 1950s and 1960s)
1987	EVW 3	Heartbeat Soukous
1989	ACDC 27748	The Best of Zaïre Music (Anti-Choc, Abeti, etc.)
1991	CD 36501	Les Merveilles du Passé 1957–75 (Highly recommended)

Into the 1990s

SAPEUR. Meaning the Society of Ambianceurs and Persons of Elegance, the SAPEUR phenomenon of high-class fashion consciousness cannot really be separated from the Paris–Kinshasa music scene. Inspired by Papa Wemba, the craze for designer clothes and footwear spread like wildfire from Kinshasa throughout Francophone West Africa. On occasions, it seemed as if the dress was of more importance than the music – posing more enjoyable than dancing.

Suede Suede. Vocals, percussion and harmonica are all that Suede Suede need to set up a new sound from Zaïre more akin to Nigerian fuji than rumba. Lack of instruments underlines the driving power of Suede Suede. By 1990 record companies were anxiously scouting around for material, although the original group had long since split, spawning several competing outfits by the same name. Plenty available in Kinshasa on cassette. Crammed Disc, from Belgium, released the first LP internationally.

1991	CRAWM 1LP	Toleki Bango

Taz Bolingo. All-female rumba band formed in 1989 and by 1991 starting to make an impact in the region and beyond. With songs composed by Hitachi and sung by Sarah Medina, the band cut their first vinyl in 1990, helped in the studio by Manuaku Waku from Grand Zaïko.

1990	SR 751	Souci Ya Age Na Ngai Te (Cass.)
	ASLP 460	Souci Ya Age (Kenyan pressing)
1991		Loi Talion

Wenge Musica. Led by J.P. Mpiana, the band appeared on British TV and immediately became highly sought after.

1991	MBS 001	Kin E Bouge (CD)

Asiatiques, Les. Another new guitar band to keep an eye on.

1990		Calamité

20 Gabon

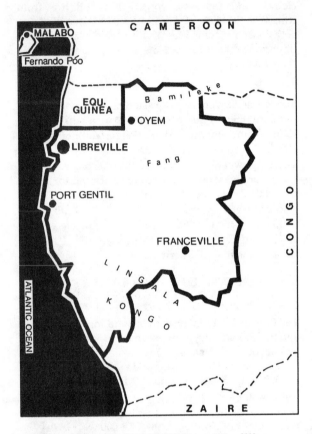

CAMEROON
MALABO
Fernando Póo
EQU. GUINEA
Bamileke
OYEM
LIBREVILLE
Fang
PORT GENTIL
FRANCEVILLE
CONGO
LINGALA
KONGO
ATLANTIC OCEAN
ZAIRE

(ECONOMY AND SOCIETY. Pop.: 1.2 million.
Area: 267,000 sq. km. Capital: Libreville.
Independence: 1960. Currency: CFA franc.)

The early history of Gabon remains something of a mystery, although it is now accepted that the first inhabitants were pygmy hunters, followed, in the sixteenth century by the Galoa, the Nkoni and the Fang from neighbouring Cameroon, and in the eighteenth century by the Urungu. By the sixteenth century the Portuguese, French and British were all trading in slaves, ivory and tropical woods. In 1849 Libreville was founded as a settlement for freed slaves and from this coastal power base the French steadily colonised the rest of Gabon. In 1888 Libreville became the capital of the entire French Congo and in 1910 Gabon became a separate colony in French Equatorial Africa, finally attaining independence in 1960. Two years later Leon

M'ba was elected president until his early death in 1967 allowed Albert Bongo to assume control. Bongo moved swiftly to establish his personal power using family members and friends in key positions. The one-party state was officially established in 1973 and since then Bongo has regularly been re-elected in a series of fraudulent elections. However, Gabon has enjoyed several decades of political stability and is today the second wealthiest country in Africa, with an economy based on vast oil reserves, migrant labour and the employment of thousands of French technicians. The French also maintain a military capability in Gabon which has frequently been used to enforce French policy in Gabon and other parts of Africa.

During the early 1980s Bongo faced and survived several coup attempts, arresting and occasionally executing opponents. But by the early 1990s the regime was under more intense pressure as the wind of change blew through Africa, and in 1990 a wave of government repression sparked off major riots in Port Gentil.

TRADITIONAL MUSIC

Please consult Volume 1 for background information on Gabonese traditional music and for a seven-record introductory discography.

MODERN MUSIC

Akendengue, Pierre (b. L'Ile d'Aouta, 1944). Poet and singer and one of the most imaginative and accomplished musicians in Africa. Volume 1 outlined his early career and provided a discography up until 1986. Thereafter, he displayed his true versatility, turning his hand to dance music and scoring heavily with the excellent album *Nandipo*. In 1987 he released *Pirogier* and provided the soundtrack for the film *Sarraounia*. On his 1989 outing he added soukous, zouk and latin beats to his standard incisive lyrics. The 1990 album marked a welcome return from Pierre, whose reputation grows with every release.

1987   AKN 13005   Piroguer

                                 Epuguzu

                                 Sarraounia

1989	ENC 141	Espoir à Soweto
1990	66882	Silence

Diablotins, Les. Please see Volume 1 for biography and discography of top rumba outfit. Sadly, nothing new since 1987.

Missema. Large pro-Bongo female band formed in 1977 and much in demand for formal state occasions.

1985	MI 2001	Mi Yendi Missema
	MI 2002	Avec Missema en Vacances
1986	MI 2003	Missema au Centenaire
	MI 2004	Missema Stars
1987	MI 2005	10 Ans Chant Omar Bongo 20 Ans
1988	MI 2006	11 Ans

Madama, Etienne

1985	EM 001	Jonas
1986	ESP 17903	Soweto

Nguema, Hilarion. Nguema is now one of Gabon's biggest stars with two big-selling LPs in 1987, followed up with the classic *Crise Economique*, drawing support from such Paris luminaries as Star, Alhadji Touré, Bilong and backing vocals from Charlotte Dada. During the early 1980s he fronted Orchestre Afro-Success, steadily refining his technique until he emerged in the mid-1980s as a master guitarist perfectly equipped to synthesise two extremely powerful neighbouring styles – makossa from Cameroon and soukous from Zaïre. In 1989 he collaborated with Dina Bell and Ben Decca for the excellent LP *Turbo Hits 89*.

1983	SAF 50103	L'Amour N'est Pas Force
1987	SAF 55101	Espoir
	MH 102	Le Retour de La Vétéran
	MH 103	Quand L'Homme Est Content
1988	MH 104	Gabon Pays de Joie
	MH 107	Crise Economique
1989	MH 112	+ Decca & Bell: Turbo Hits 89
1990	MH 118	La Détente

Assele, Angele. Talented female singer with several albums to her credit and numerous session appearances.

1985	MD 1767	Esperança
1986	MD 1773	Amour Sans Frontières
	MD 1775	Du Balai

Revignet, Angele. Another Gabonese Angele, like Assele, with several LPs and many session appearances.

1987	AR 100	Taximan

Essessang, Orchestre. Large soukous band with an impressive five-piece vocal front-line. Led by Leon Metogo, they can produce a variety of rhythms and styles.

1990	13561	Milang Mi Si

Mi'Kouagna de Mounana. Big band led by solo guitarist Dhovys Bakuandja.

1990	MKA 102	Rabi Kounga

N'Goss Brothers. One of Gabon's newest 'School of Zaïko' guitar bands. Financed and supported by Gustave Bongo (N'Goss), nephew to the President. Fine vocals and guitar work-outs.

1989	GB 1001	Okula Biri Ngossanga
	GB 1002	Dance Oke-Oke

Grande Teke Teke Ambah, Le. Solo artiste supported on this occasion by his own band, Les Aves Stars, and Soukous Stars. In 1990 their latest album received considerable airplay in the UK from John Peel, doyen of the alternative airways. A high-paced soukous selection with Lokassa very much in evidence.

1988	GA 002	
1990	GA 49625	Belokilo

Inanga, Aziz. Known as 'La Tigresse de Gabon', Aziz served up a number of traditional dance tracks on her 1991 recording.

1991	KIV 002	Aziz'Inanga

Gance, Zacharie. Turning to Cameroon for support in the form of Kamga, Penda and Seba.

1987	NZ 708	Le Mouvement

N'Gomateke, Emy Laskin. Veteran Gabonese vocalist and guitarist who had several regional hits in the mid-1980s before forming the group Wanzama with Vivick and Placidy. On the first Wanzama album they enlist the help of Pablo. On the 1987 recording he turned to his musical brothers for assistance.

1985	1258	Mes Meilleurs
1987	005	Ngomateke et Orchestre Canon Star: Jessia La Banguissoise
1991	LP 53035	Wanzama: Parasite de Nuit

N'Goma, Oliver

| 1991 | 53171 | Bane |

Ondo-Mobale, Pierre Marie. A new singer on the Gabon scene supported on his first release by Angele Assele. Recorded in Studio Nkoussu, Libreville.

| 1988 | S 118194 | Donguila |

Madingo, Makaya. Widely regarded as being in the top three along with Nguema and Akendengue. Totally unknown in the west.

Bongo, Madame. Ex-wife of President Bongo and leading vocalist with Kunabeli de Masuku. In 1985 the president made it illegal to record cassettes from albums – the rumour was that this was only done to boost sales of his wife's record. The stores responded by pulling all her albums from the shelf. Shortly afterwards Madame Bongo left the President for another musician. A truly unbelievable story.

Sambat, Alex. Classically trained composer who has worked with M'Mah Syllah as well as putting down several albums of his own.

| 1986 | SAMBG 682 | Le Transgabonais |
| 1987 | IV 004 | Guadeloupe |

Batassouagha, Ma Philo. One of the leading female vocalists in Gabon.

| 1986 | MPHB 1244 | Phi Pepe |

Zing, Pierre Claver

1985	DPX 816	Eya Moan
	DPX 825	Essap
1986	SAS 045	Opwa
1987	BB 03	Ekang Ye

Others

1986	ESP 17903	Madama
1987	1344	Maman Dede Avec Les Anges
	MD 1777	Eferol Eboa: Arrêtez

21   Angola

(ECONOMY AND SOCIETY. Pop.: 9 million. Area: 1,247,000 sq. km. Capital: Luanda. Independence: 1975. Currency: Kwanza.)

Angola, comprising over a hundred different ethnic groups, suffered under a particularly brutal and backward form of Portuguese colonialism for almost four hundred years. The Portuguese had no interest in anything other than slaves and it was only after the abolition of the trade in the mid-nineteenth century that they set about establishing some kind of administration in the areas beyond the coast. Resistance to colonial rule continued throughout these centuries and it was not until 1922 that Portugal finally claimed to have 'pacified' the entire country. Much of the initial Portuguese settlement was by convicts, and white settlers did not appear in any great number until after the Second World War. But their brutal exploitation of African labour and the extreme racism of the ruling class sparked off the liberation war in 1961, building on the earlier resistance of the post-war cultural revival. In 1961 two groups launched the armed struggle – the MPLA and a Bakongo-based group which later became the FNLA. As the struggle developed the FNLA, backed by Zaïre and the western powers, made the destruction of the MPLA, rather than of the Portuguese, their major objective. Meanwhile, in the south, Jonas Savimbi had launched a third group,

called UNITA, which also sought accommodation with the west and eventually formed an open alliance with South Africa.

With the collapse of fascism in Portugal in 1974, the way was clear for the independence of all the African colonies and Angola was to achieve this the following year under the leadership of Agostino Neto and the MPLA. Both UNITA and FNLA, with heavy western and South African support, stepped up their war on the Marxist MPLA, who responded by inviting thousands of Cuban troops to come and help their beleaguered army. In the ensuing civil war (1975–91) it is estimated that over a half a million people were killed, more than two million became refugees and most of the fragile infrastructure of the country was destroyed, principally by the South African-backed forces of Savimbi.

In 1979 the poet/intellectual President Neto died suddenly from cancer and was replaced by Eduardo Dos Santos, who continued the struggle against UNITA. During the 1980s the Angolan people suffered terribly at the hands of South Africa and UNITA as schools and clinics were destroyed and a large proportion of the budget was consumed by the Army. Various efforts were made to end the conflict but with the USSR and Cuba supporting the MPLA and the US and South Africa supporting UNITA, it proved impossible in the prevailing Cold War atmosphere. The turning point came in 1986 when Angolan and Cuban forces defeated a South African-backed UNITA army at the decisive battle of Cuito Cunene. The South Africans then realised that they could not defeat Angola militarily, but such had been the cost of the war on one of Africa's potentially richest nations that by 1990 the Angolan Government accepted a US peace proposal and UNITA was officially recognised as a political party with elections promised.

Four centuries of colonial rule and three decades of civil war have left Angola an impoverished and divided nation. Yet Angolan art in all its forms has somehow been able to survive. The 1991 settlement will present tremendous opportunities to reconstruct the economy and start the task of nation-building.

TRADITIONAL MUSIC

1960s   LLST 7311   Music of the Tshokwe People of the Angolan Border

LLST 7313	Sanza and Guitar. Music of the Bena Luluwa (Angola/Zaïre)

SONGS OF THE REVOLUTION

1970	VPA 8321	Canti dell'Escercito i Liberazione MPLA
1975	SDL AS8	Angola Chiama: Guerra Di Popolo MPLA (Italian)
	NKA	Angola Beurijdt (Dutch)
	FW 5442	Angolan Freedom Songs
	6803 044	Humbi-Handa-Angola
	6810 955	A Victoria e Certa

MODERN MUSIC

From independence in 1975 and until the introduction of multiparty democracy in 1991, Angolan culture reflected the political and ideological views of the ruling MPLA along the lines of 'National Culture develops from progressive traditional values, and at the same time deepens its revolutionary spirit and takes on a scientific character.' Within this philosophical approach, the Angolan Government played an extremely interventionist role in the development of popular culture, establishing unions of writers, schools of sculpture and a national union of artists and composers. The Government also sponsored dozens of provincial choirs, over 600 folkloric groups and a number of urban pop groups. Yet this should not be taken to mean that Angolan music is in good shape. War-induced poverty has meant that little money was available to upgrade recording facilities and it is estimated that while there is a good live scene, Angola has produced fewer than fifty albums in the last twenty years.

Modern Angolan music offers a variety of patterns and styles which reveal deep traditional roots as well as Caribbean and Latin (most noticeably Brazilian) influences. For example, the 'semba' rhythm of the Kimbundu region (known in Brazil as the 'samba') is both a traditional sound and the spirit of modern Angolan music. Other popular styles defy an easy distinction between traditional and modern, as in the case of the 'n'gola' folklore which derives from a mix of traditions in the not-too-distant past. Another popular style is the 'fado' tradition – a melancholy ballad style drawn from Portuguese music. More recently, tours by Cuban bands and the Kassav bandwagon have added to the broad spectrum of sounds and influences in Angola.

During the 1970s and 1980s all musical activity in Angola occurred through INALD, the state cultural agency, along with its commercial wing – ENDIPU. The only studio in the country also belonged to the state in the form of the radio station's 8-track facility. All recordings appear initially on the INALD label, although the agency has been prepared to license material to other companies, most notably IEFE in Lisbon. In such a situation, bands pay to record then try to interest foreign companies in the product with the state manufacturing discs for local consumption (possibly through a Cuban pressing deal). In effect, this means that there are very few full professional bands in the country and these include state-sponsored outfits like the Army and Air Force Bands – a situation similar to that existing in Ghana and Mali during the heady days of socialist state sponsorship. Under these circumstances, singers tend to move around, playing with different bands and thus establishing individual rather than group reputations. There are no official cassettes available but bootlegging is common practice with tracks lifted from imported Zaïrean, Cape Verdean and Brazilian albums. Local music is actively promoted on the radio and TV with the result that the country has been able to resist the invasion of western pop music. However, as the country retreats from MPLA militancy this situation is likely to change, and while a greater openness may see more Angolan music reaching the rest of the world, it also carries the clear danger that local culture will be at risk from imported music. Already by 1991 there were signs that the situation was changing with a Swedish-funded pressing plant coming on line (surely a mistake when the rest of Africa is moving inexorably towards cassettes) and various private sector proposals to establish recording studios.

Kafala Brothers. Moises and Jose Kafala, guitarists and singers, perform in Kimbundu, Umbundu and Portuguese. Theirs is one of the first Angolan records to go out on international release. Sponsored by Anti-Apartheid Enterprises, they toured the UK in 1988 and 1990 to solid public acclaim. Their lyrics are alternatively sad and hopeful, reflecting the reality of the Angolan situation.

1989	AAER 001	Ngola

AKA, Trio. Comprising Abanga, Abunda and Kandundanga, the Trio AKA play an up-tempo, light guitar style in true Lusophone fashion. The 1989 recording was made at the National Radio Studios in Luanda, sponsored by AA Enterprises and distributed by Stern's.

1989	AAER 002	Mama Cristina

Bastos, Waldemar. Singer/songwriter based in Lisbon with a sophisticated blend of styles drawn from the entire Lusophone world (although he occasionally slips into soukous). On *Angola Minha Namorada* he is supported by Brazilian bassman Jorge Degas (released on the Valentim de Carvalho label).

1983	ODEON 42125821	Estamos Juntos
1990	EMI 7939251	Angola Minha Namorada

Bonga (b. Dande, 1942). Initially an athlete and footballer who made his name with the famous Portuguese club Benfica. On his earlier albums Bonga modernises Angolan folklore. On *Kandandu* he draws on musicians and ideas from all over Lusophone Africa, while his late 1980s albums feature music and poems from Angola, Cape Verde and Brazil. His music retains a distinct Zaïrean feel but in a more relaxed afro-latin mood. Bonga remains incredibly popular inside Angola, although when he tried to open a club in Luanda he ran into stiff opposition from a government who felt him to be pro-UNITA. He is now based in Lisbon.

1972	NR 893001	Angola 72
	NRPS 601	Racines
	NRPS 606	Kualaka Kuetu
	6810619	Raizes
	LDX 74720	Kandandu
	PS 609	Marika
1987	14230028	Massomba '87
1990	CD 5052	Paz Em Angola

Os Jovens Do Prenda, Orchestre. Formed in 1965 in the Luanda ghetto of Prenda, hence the name – The Youth From Prenda. One of the first electric bands to utilise traditional rhythms, they became identified with the liberation movement. They remain one of the top bands in the country. The first international release (PIR 40-1) is taken from a live recording in Germany, 1990. They also feature, along with several bands from Mozambique and other front-line states, on the 1991 compilation *2 Beat! Apartheid* (PIR 29-1).

1980s	IEFE 042	Musica de Angola
1991	PIR 40-1	Berlin Festa

Lando, Teta. Popular singer.

1986		Semba Rythmee
1990	NALP 6000	Independencia
1991	CHRISROD	Menina de Angola

Dimba Dya Ngola. Led by Boano Da Silva, Dimba are a 12-strong dance band drawing on various other musical styles, including soukous and Cuban idioms.

	IEFE 059	Luanda Cidade Linda

Silva, Mario Ray. Very popular singer now based in Paris.

1982	CCD 123	Sungaly

Others

	EST 830924	Rui Duna: Memorias
1981	CCD 115	Orquestre Caravela: Amour Sans Frontières
1983	ASLP 982	Bobongo Stars: Divorce
	MAN 001	Bobongo Stars: Marguerida
	IEFE 056	Sensacional Maringa: Lelu'ezeda

22   São Tomé and Príncipe

(ECONOMY AND SOCIETY. Pop.: 120,000, Area: 964 sq. km. Capital: São Tomé. Independence: 1975. Currency: Dobra.)

These two tiny Atlantic Ocean islands contain six identifiable groups of people: mestizo descendants of African slaves; the Angolares – fishermen reputedly descended from shipwrecked Angolan sailors; the Forros – post-emancipation children of slaves; the Servicais – migrant labourers from other parts of Lusophone Africa; the Tongas – children of Servicais born on the islands; and finally a 4,000-strong European population. The nearest part of mainland Africa is Equatorial Guinea.

The islands were first settled by the Portuguese between 1469 and 1472 and for the next five centuries acted as a major staging post in the shipment of slaves from Kongo to the Americas. The domestic economy was also slave-based, centred on massive cocoa and coffee plantations. Eventually slavery was abolished, only to be replaced by a contract labour system which differed little from what had gone before, although it did bring contract labourers from Angola, Mozambique and Cape Verde who added to the islands' cultural diversity. Slave revolts were commonplace and were brutally suppressed by the Portuguese colonialists until the mass-mobilisation in 1974 finally forced them to quit. Independence was declared in 1975 under the leadership of Manuel Pinto Da Costa.

Da Costa faced early problems from both the left and the right and in 1978 both Angola and Cuba sent troops to São Tomé to prop up his regime. Since then, the island has established a non-aligned foreign policy and pragmatic economic policies, including a vibrant private sector and close economic ties with Portugal and the West.

MODERN MUSIC

Modern music from the islands reflects influences from larger mainland neighbours, and although the Portuguese discouraged the development of a modern urban sound and attempted to control all cultural development, a few recordings did emerge after independence through the Lisbon-based company IEFE.

Africa Negra. Top guitar band on São Tomé during the 1980s.

1983	IEFE 043	Africa Negra 83
	IEFE 046	Angelica
	IEFE 052	Alice

Umbelina, Gilberto Gil (b. San Antonio, Príncipe, 1948). Started with harmonica at the age of 11, absorbing a number of influences including music from Angola, Benin and, of course, Portugal. At the same time, he was listening to local 'matacumbi' and 'decha' rhythms. In 1967 he picked up the guitar and formed his first band – Os Diablos do Ritmo – with the intention of revitalising local traditions. In 1970 he moved to Lisbon and finally arrived in Paris in 1978, having realised just how few musicians were able to make a living from music. By the early 1980s he was playing again, recording one album and combining local dance styles with Brazilian touches.

1980s	CEL 6762	Voa, Papagaio, Voa!

23 Central African Republic

(ECONOMY AND SOCIETY. Pop.: 3 million. Area: 622,984 sq. km. Capital: Bangui. Independence: 1960. Currency: CFA franc.) For map, see p. 90.

The CAR is a landlocked, mountainous state in Central Africa peopled by the Baya and the Banda, who together comprise more than half of the population. Other major ethnic groups include the Baka and the Zande. However, like most of Central Africa, the country was severely depopulated during the three centuries of slave-trading, with CAR possibly suffering more than most by virtue of being a frontier zone between two competing slave systems – the trans-Atlantic and the trans-Saharan. When both trades disappeared in the mid-nineteenth century, the various peoples of CAR started to regroup, before the French imposed a hasty and cruel form of colonialism following a brief tussle with the Belgians. Colonialism meant the quest for rubber concessions and within two generations of the abolition of slavery the population was suffering under a particularly cruel form of forced labour. The colony was finally and fully conquered between 1909 and 1912 with the 1930s and 1940s being characterised by widespread famine and repression.

Finally, after a decade of political organisation led by MESAN, CAR gained independence in 1960 under the conservative leadership of David Dacko. But his pro-French policies failed to stimulate the economy and in 1966 he was overthrown by Jean-Bedel Bokassa, an ambitious veteran of another colonial war, in Vietnam, who had been put in charge of the army in 1962. For the next 11 years, Bokassa ran down the economy (with strong western backing) and embarked on one of the great tragi-comedies of the modern African period. In 1976 he turned CAR into the Central African Empire and, modelling himself on Napoleon, made the country into the laughing stock of Africa. His rule was entirely arbitrary and by the late 1970s the country was bankrupt. Bokassa was finally overthrown in 1979 and Dacko returned to take charge until he too was overthrown by General Kolingba in a coup in 1981. Political parties were banned once again and the rest of the decade was characterised by the politics of managing a slide into bankruptcy. Bokassa inexplicably returned home in 1986 expecting a hero's welcome. He was promptly arrested and sentenced to life imprisonment.

TRADITIONAL MUSIC

Thanks largely to the ethnomusicological research of Simha Arom the traditional music of CAR is better researched than the modern music. (See the papers of the 1967 Berlin Conference.) F. Bebey and Gerhard Kubik have also contributed to a better understanding of the region's traditions. More detailed work has also been done on the harp tradition amongst the Azande, the horn ensembles of the Banda–Linda, the sanza traditions of the Gbaya, the ritual music of the Ngbaka Mabo and the satires of the Nzakara, the last-mentioned being recorded in 1987 for a limited edition cassette.

1970s	OCR 11	République Centrafriquaine
	OCR 13	Musique Centrafricaine
	OCR 43	Musique Centrafricaine Vol. 2
	BM 3012310	Central African Republic
	Harmonia Mundi	Chants et Dances de la République Centrafricaine

MODERN MUSIC

1984	AP 029	Jude Bondeze: Tene Sango
1985	ZIG 1257	Kokomba Stars: Lungu Aye
1986	ZEM 022	Sultan Zemblatt: Mea Culpa
1990	KG 44701	Kangala: Je Reviendrai Mama

24 Equatorial Guinea

(ECONOMY AND SOCIETY. Pop.: 421,000. Area: 28,051 sq. km. Capital: Malabo. Independence: 1968. Currency: CFA franc.)

Comprising the large island of Bioko (formerly Fernando Po), a number of smaller islands and the mainland area of Rio Muni, sandwiched between Cameroon and Gabon, Equatorial Guinea remains one of the most obscure corners of Africa. Inevitably, the islands and the mainland enjoyed separate histories until they were united by the Spanish in a single colony at the start of the twentieth century.

The earliest European contact came in 1470 when the Portuguese settled on the islands, and for the next four centuries Fernando Po was used by several European nations as a base for the slave trade. However, during the nineteenth century the Spanish began to dominate the islands, while other European powers established bases on the mainland. The new borders of the colony were only finally established in 1900 and in many respects the Spanish continued to pay more attention to Fernando Po than the mainland. With the onset of fascism in Spain, both parts of the colony came under a particularly backward type of colonialism which supressed nationalist sentiment and retarded political progress amongst the African population. Eventually, however, political parties did emerge and through a slow process of political advance independence was finally secured in 1968 under President Macias Nguema.

Nguema moved quickly to assert both his anti-Spanish feelings and his Fang nationalism. Relations with Spain deteriorated sharply (the country had been left bankrupt at the time of independence), and in a poisoned atmosphere Nguema cracked down hard on all opposition and democracy came to an end. The resulting dictatorship proved to be one of the most brutal in Africa, with widespread allegations of torture and mass murder. Relations with Spain were eventually broken and little is known of what happened in the country over the next decade. From an economic perspective, the country was effectively run into the ground until the 1979 takeover by Teodoro Nguema opened up the country and economy to the wider world. In 1982 Nguema devalued the currency, clearing the way for incorporation into the Franc zone in 1985, indicating a major shift away from Spain and towards France. Recent events have served to confirm the fragility of political freedom in Equatorial Guinea. It remains a scarcely known, isolated country with little to recommend it to either visitors or inhabitants.

MUSIC IN EQUATORIAL GUINEA

Numbering 80 per cent of the population, the Fang dominate political and cultural life. Other, smaller groups include the Kombe, Balengue and Bujeba. On Bioko island, society is composed of the Bubi (20 per cent) and the Fernandinos, descendants of freed slaves, as well as a substantial Fang population, originally brought to the island under the Spanish system of forced labour. Very few recordings have ever been made in Equatorial Guinea but the mass in Fang may occasionally be available. With next to nothing in the way of domestic recording facilities, the population rely on traditional music and imported Zaïrean music for their pleasure and relaxation.

Bessoso. Le Grand Bessoso.

| 1985 | 001 B | Kawuima |
| 1986 | SAS 053 | Y'On Sofa |

Efamba

| 1986 | 001 E | Mame Ane Mot Duma |

Maele

| 1985 | M 5656 | Madjing Mawoc |
| 1990 | AT 092 | Saturnino |

25 Rwanda

(ECONOMY AND SOCIETY. Pop.: 7.2 million.
Area: 26,338 sq. km. Capital: Kigali. Independence:
1962. Currency: Rwanda franc.)

A mountainous, landlocked state with three ethnic
groups – the Hutu majority (90 per cent), the Tutsi and
a few Twa pygmies. The Twa were the first inhabitants
and were joined around AD 1000 by the Bantu Hutu,
and subsequently the Hamitic, cattle-herding Tutsi in
the fifteenth century. The Tutsi soon became the
master-class ruling the Hutu in a near feudal relationship. However, over-crowding and environmental
degradation created social and economic tensions
between the two groups. Tutsi supremacy was
reinforced by German colonialism (1890–1916) and
then by Belgian colonialism (1916–62) with Tutsi
dominating education. In 1959 Hutu resentment boiled
over into widespread violence and the Belgians
decided to pull out, leaving the UN to supervise
elections, which were won by the majority Hutu party
led by Gregoire Kayibanda. In 1963–4 communal
violence erupted again with Hutu reprisals forcing
thousands of Tutsi into exile in neighbouring Uganda
and Burundi. Another burst of anti-Tutsi sentiment
finally led the Army to seize power in 1973 under
General Habyarimana. Elections in 1978 gave some
legitimacy to the Army-controlled MRND, although
civilians took over most ministries. The economy,
however, remained in desperate condition, with
ecological damage and massive over-farming in a
country with the highest population density in Africa.
In 1984 the Government was forced to introduce a
severe austerity programme backed by the World Bank
and other international donors.

TRADITIONAL MUSIC

Very little music from Rwanda has ever been recorded
and even less has appeared on the international
market. There is a state-sponsored national orchestra
which maintains local musical traditions and they can
be heard on the excellent double album *Bantu*.

	BM 30L2302	Music From Rwanda
	OCR 19	Rwanda-Rwacu (National Anthem)
1986	CIC 8401.2	Various: Bantu

MODERN MUSIC

Even less is known about contemporary Rwandan
music, although travellers report the enormous popularity of rumba. We can only suppose that what music
there is comes on cassette.

Impala de Kigali: Vol. 4

Impala de Kigali: Vol. 5

Andre Sebanani & Impala

26   Burundi

(ECONOMY AND SOCIETY. Pop.: 5.5 million. Area: 27,834 sq. km. Capital: Bujumbura. Independence: 1962. Currency: Burundi franc.)

Like neighbouring Rwanda, Burundi is a tiny, land-locked state dominated by the Hutu (80 per cent) although political power has traditionally been held by the Tutsi (15 per cent). Less than 1 per cent of the population are Twa pygmies. As in Rwanda, the Tutsi formed the feudal ruling class, although they failed to create a centralised state. Again, as in Rwanda, the country first came under German rule and then Belgian rule, with both varieties of colonialism serving to reinforce the power of the Tutsi, who acceded to power in 1962 when the Belgians departed. The early years of independence were characterised by growing political instability, culminating in the 1965 Hutu uprising, which was followed by a brutal purge of Hutus in the Army and bureaucracy. In 1967 Colonel Micombero seized power, surviving until he too was overthrown in 1976. But communal tension had not disappeared and in 1972, following another outbreak of anti-Tutsi violence, the Tutsi embarked on a sustained policy of 'selective genocide', systematically killing all educated Hutu. Total deaths were estimated to exceed 200,000. Colonel Bagaza took over in the 1976 coup but could do little to remove underlying tensions and he went the way of his predecessor in another coup in 1987. The new head of state, Major Buyoya, continued to rely on minority Tutsi support and in 1988 the Hutu rose again in another series of violent incidents. Over-populated, incredibly poor and with several centuries of communal violence, it is hard to see any way forward for Burundi until the Hutu majority achieve some degree of political representation.

TRADITIONAL MUSIC

The best place to start remains the Ocora collection, originally put together in 1967 and regularly repackaged. This album contains a wide variety of traditional styles including sanza, single-string bows, flutes, zither and a variety of vocal techniques. There is also an early recording of the Master Drummers, formerly the ensemble of the Tutsi royal court. Internationally famous, they have toured widely and provided an early reference point for people interested in African music. Twenty-five strong and displaying enormous power and energy, the Drummers should on no account be missed when they next go on tour. The group have suffered from sporadic record deals with several companies. Hopefully their music will be more readily available with the 1991 Real World recording.

1982	OCR 40	Burundi – Musiques Traditionelles
	ARN 33682	Les Maîtres Tambours du Burundi
	VPA 8137	Musica del Burundi
1991/2	RWLP	(A mini-LP on cassette and CD – no further details available.)

PART V

East Africa

27 Kenya

(ECONOMY AND SOCIETY. Pop.: 25 million.
Area: 582,644 sq. km. Capital: Nairobi.
Independence: 1963. Currency: Kenyan shilling.)

Pre-colonial Kenya was inhabited by groups of pastoralists and agriculturalists with the Masai as the principal military power. The coastal area had been known to the outside world for centuries and by the early nineteenth century was under the control of the Sultan of Zanzibar. By the mid-nineteenth century Britain was already encroaching on the Zanzibari trading empire and by the end of the century had broken their economic power and started moving inland. In 1893 Britain declared the area a protectorate, with full colonisation of the settler variety starting in 1920. British colonialism in Kenya thereafter worked consistently for the white settler interests, with racial segregation having been formalised by the 1915 Lands Ordinance, which was to become the focus of early Kenyan resistance to colonial rule.

By the end of the Second World War all the various contradictions in the Kenyan colonial system were coming to the fore, culminating in the violent revolt known as Mau Mau. Between 1952 and 1956, the British adopted many questionable tactics in attempting to suppress the revolt, including classic counter-insurgency measures during which almost 15,000 Kenyans died, and although Mau Mau was defeated militarily, it triumphed politically as KANU, under Jomo Kenyatta, swept to power in 1963 and settler society collapsed. Kenyatta immediately adopted a pro-western, pro-market policy and proceeded to consolidate KANU's power in what was now a one-party state. Opponents were killed or exiled and by the time Kenyatta passed on in 1978 all political opposition had been crushed. The new President, Arap Moi, briefly flirted with reform before continuing the political and economic policies of his predecessor. But the economic situation proved precarious, dependent as it was on the export of tea and coffee. Tourism offered a third source of revenue and by the late 1980s, despite growing debt, a rapidly rising population and increasing political tension, Kenya had somehow established a glowing reputation with western tourists and businessmen. By the early 1990s pressure on Moi to democratise the system was growing but the President proved to be a stubborn man and it remains to be seen whether the wind of change will blow through Kenya.

TRADITIONAL MUSIC

The traditional music of Kenya has been particularly well researched by Kenyan musicologists, and readers are referred to the books of Senoga-Zake (1981 and 1986). For a summary of trends, developments and an introductory discography please refer to Volume 1.

1990   Nonesuch 972066   Kenya & Tanzania:
                           Witchcraft and Ritual
                           Music

MODERN MUSIC

Volume 1 contained a detailed account of the post-war development of urban popular music, drawing on the published research of Low, Roberts and Kubik (see Bibliography). Since then a great deal more research has been conducted by Harrev (1989), filling out the picture without altering the basic analysis. Secondly, between 1985 and 1991 a great deal more Kenyan music reached the international market as part of the 'World Music' phenomenon.

The work of Harrev deserves special mention for its thoroughness and close attention to the business side of affairs. Harrev also develops an interpretative framework for the early twentieth-century development of music in East Africa which neatly complements the post-war analysis offered in Volume 1.

The story really starts in the early twentieth century when white society introduced the first wind-up gramophones, importing western popular music exclusively for the white market. However, German ethnomusicologists were also active in Tanzania and in 1902 cut the very first field recording in Africa. As colonial society developed, new middle classes emerged (both African and Indian) for whom ownership of a gramophone was a real possibility. The Indian community, largely concentrated in the commerical sector, used music from gramophones to attract customers to their shops. By the 1920s a considerable number of Black American, European and Indian records were being imported. As demand for records increased, HMV decided to send the Zanzibari singer Siti Binti Saad to record in their Bombay studios, and by 1930 this channel was responsible for the dissemination of taraab music up and down the Swahili coast. HMV were soon joined by Columbia and between them they released over 500 78 r.p.m.s. Odeon, later part of EMI, also started recording traditional music in Uganda in 1931 but already the twin bind of colonialism was serving to restrict the development of a specifically African sound. On the one hand, colonialism encouraged a sense of inferiority to white culture, while on the other, the European companies were trying to sell this 'inferior' music back to the African population. By 1939, with EMI now enjoying a virtual monopoly, annual sales were in the region of 200,000 copies, of which 80,000 were in a local language – the rest, presumably, being a mixture of European, Indian and Arabic music.

The development of the business inevitably slowed down during the War but in 1947 a new, independent company was established to challenge the dominance of the multinationals. Called the East African Sound Studios and releasing material on the Jambo label, it was based in Nairobi but also recorded (usually in cinemas) in both Dar Es Salaam and Kampala. By 1952 they had developed a substantial catalogue including music from the Kings African Rifles, dance music from the Coast Social Orchestra, numerous taraab releases (Maulidi, Musa Maruf, Siti Ganduri, etc.), as well as a comedy collection by Ustad Omar. Most music, however, was in the popular 'dansi' style featuring guitar – a universal favourite – as well as accordions and strings. Songs were by this time being composed and sung in all the major local languages, including Swahili, Kikuyu, Luo, Luhya and Luganda. Early stars of the 1940s and 1950s included Ally Sykes, Funfi Konde, Peter Bernard and Obondo Mugati.

By 1951 Jambo had released over 200 items, recording locally and sending the masters to the UK for pressing by Decca – EMI's great rival. Yet the system was cumbersome and unreliable and in 1952, now renamed East African Records, the company decided to invest in their own pressing plant. In that year they were able to press the first ever records in East Africa. By 1953 they were pressing 12,000 discs a month exclusively for the African market, mainly back-catalogue until they started recording again in 1955.

One of the first artistes to start recording was the guitarist Fadhili Williams, who eventually became assistant to the Danish manager, Larsen. Fadhili helped with A & R and over the next few years they recorded hundreds of musicians, mainly guitar players who turned up every Tuesday for auditions. Williams and Larsen also continued recording in Uganda and Tanzania, scoring heavily with 'Safari Ya Kilimanjaro' by Tanzanian flautist John Ondolo (50,000 copies) and Williams' own version of 'Malaika'. In an interview with Harrev in 1987, Larsen explained how the studio operated: 'There was nothing like contracts or anything like that. It was all arranged by mouth. When we had agreed on a recording (two titles) they were paid shs 300 per record. . . . When the recording was made, the tape was sent to British Homophone in London. They made the matrices which then came down by air-freight.'

During the mid-1950s business dipped considerably as cheap radios appeared on the market for the first time. Furthermore, the fragile shellac discs constantly required new needles if sound quality was to be maintained. However, despite these problems, other labels began to appear alongside Jambo and HMV. These included the Indian-owned Mzuri label in 1949, AGS, Rubina, Rafiki and, in 1952, a subsidiary of the South African company Gallo. By 1957 there were almost fifty different labels available in Kenya with local companies accounting for forty of them. These included ASL, who, in the late 1950s, were the first to release Zaïrean music (Kalle and African Jazz) on the East African market. By 1960, with monthly sales in the region of 20,000, the company turned to juke boxes to promote the music and were soon running over sixty machines in and around Nairobi. Gradually, over the years, some talented individuals began to stand out from the host of gifted amateurs who wanted to record. The opening of new clubs around the city also made it possible for semi-professional musicians to survive. At the same time the various curfews and restrictions introduced during Mau Mau served to slow down the development of an African social music scene, despite the fact that many European companies encouraged African music as part of the developing consumer society. In 1958 one of the first truly professional groups appeared when the Jambo Boys were formed under the leadership of Fadhili Williams to act as a studio band for East African Records.

Other stars of the late 1950s included the two 'dry' guitarists from southern Zaïre, Edouard Masengo and

Jean Bosco Mwenda, as well as Isabella Muthiga, Daniel Katuga, John Mwale and Stephen B. Ngumao. Many of these musicians hosted their own radio shows on the new East African Broadcasting Company established in 1959. During the early 1960s several new studios were established as companies tried to meet the new quality demands of 45 r.p.m.s. Harrev has estimated the number of 78 r.p.m. records issued in East Africa in the post-war years to be in the region of between 3,000 and 4,000, with total annual sales in the region of 150,000. These vernacular records laid the groundwork for the eventual emergence in the 1960s and 1970s of a star system and of a strong and vibrant urban pop music scene led by such local stars as Atori Susu and the Bunyore Band, George Mukabi (pioneer of 'omutibo' and 'sukuti' guitar styles), John Mwale, Isaya Mwinamo, John Nzenze and David Amunga. Volume 1 picks up the story from the 1960s onwards, looking at the emergence of modern pop styles rather than the development of the music business.

1980	SSLP 001	Safari Souvenirs (Mostly guitar/Fanta bottle style, includes Fadhili Williams, Nasil Kazembe, Daudi Kabaka, etc.)
1981	SSLP 002	Safari Souvenirs Vol. 2 (includes John Ondolo, Them Mushrooms, etc.)
1982	AGSLP 2008	John Mwale & Reuben Shimbiro: Rekodi Zilizopendwa
1985	AGSLP 2010	Various: Marashi Ya River Road

Abana ba Nasery. Led by Shem Tube (b. Mwilonje, Western Kenya, 1939). Tube moved around a great deal as a child, hence his schooling was limited to only five years. But by this time he was already taking an interest in music and in the 1950s he formed a band with friends, including Enos Okola (on Fanta bottle!). In the early 1960s they were joined by Justo Osala, also on guitar, and played at local dances throughout Western Kenya. They made their first recordings in 1968, reproducing their two-guitar acoustic sound known locally as 'omutibo', an older recreational style originally played on a local seven-stringed lyre. Abana then recorded on a regular basis until Tube changed the name to Mwilonje Jazz Band in 1973. Later recordings involved electric guitars and bass. Basically part-timers, Tube and his group remain farmers in the Western region, only travelling to Nairobi to record. Amazingly, since the band own neither electric nor acoustic instruments, songs are composed and rehearsed in the head prior to the trip

to Nairobi. In 1989 Globestyle released a selection of recordings on acoustic guitar with bottle accompaniment. Other material is unlikely to be available. The Globestyle album includes excellent sleeve notes by Werner Graebner. The group toured the UK in 1991.

| 1989 | ORB 052 | Classic Acoustic Recordings |

Kabaka, Daudi (b. Bulukhoba, Kakamega District, Kenya, 1939). Early life spent as a chorister and student at Clavers College, Nairobi. His career in music started at the age of 14, making his first recording a year later. By the 1960s he was a highly respected virtuoso guitarist, known in Kenya as 'The Revealer of Secrets'. He recorded his first LP in 1976.

1976	PS 33003	Kenyafrica
1977	DKO 2	Mtoboa Siri Says
1980s		Hits
		Golden Hits
1984	POLP 554	+ Maroon Commandos: Pesa Maradhi

Benga

Benga, an indigenous Kenyan style combining the use of local languages and drawing on local dances, emerged during the 1970s in Western Kenya. Characterised by up-tempo rhythms, thumping bass and a unique guitar style, the Benga boom picked up force throughout the 1970s, peaking in the mid-1980s as a major musical force, although it remains a popular and exciting style. Shirati Jazz led the commercial charge, although by the mid-1980s Sega Matata were enjoying considerable success. Other groups to look out for include Victoria Kings and Kilimambogo Brothers.

Misiani, D.O., and Shirati Jazz (b. Nyamagongo, Tarime District, Tanzania). Early influences included religious music and his elder brother, Raphael Oro, who had acquired a guitar while serving with the Kings African Rifles. But while his brother basically strummed the guitar, Daniel was more enamoured with the faster, local finger-picking style known as 'Ubele'. Other early influences included the 78 r.p.m. recordings of Bosco, Losta Abelo, John Mwale and Ben Blastus O'Bulawayo. The young Daniel faced two obstacles in his efforts to become a musician – he needed to acquire an instrument and he needed to overcome his father's resistance to his choice of career. When his father broke his first guitar he had to start over again and eventually left home and found his way to Nairobi and then Mombasa. In 1964 he formed his first band, the Victoria Boys, and in May 1965 made his first recordings for the Kassanga label. These were acoustic but with the money he earned from them he was able to buy an electric guitar, whereupon he changed the name of the band to the Shirati Luo Voice – a strong ethnic identification in what was an era of strident nationalism and nation-building. The name was then changed again to Orchestra D.O. 7 Shirati Jazz. Since then, the band and its leader have been one of Kenya's favourites.

The 1970s proved to be enormously successful in terms of single sales but by the 1980s local bootlegging had largely destroyed the vinyl market. None the less, Shirati Jazz remained a full-time working band playing hotel and club residencies, making short tours of Kenya and often being called upon to perform at state and ceremonial functions. In 1987 they embarked on their first European tour and recorded an album for Arts Worldwide of London on the World Circuit label. Their star continued to rise in the 'World Music' firmament and towards the end of the decade they were much in demand with albums appearing on both Globestyle and Earthworks plus a steady local release of new material.

1975	JCLP 001	The East African Hit Parade
1976	PS 33034	D.O.7 Shirati Luo Voice Jazz Band
1978	DO7 3102	I Am Still the King of History
	PL 40526	Sheroline
	MEA 708	Shirati Jazz
		Kenya I Love You
1987	WCB 003	Benga Beat
1988	AFRI 004	My Life and Loves
1989	ORB 064	Piny Ose Mer: The World Upside Down
	CDEWV 13	Benga Blast
1990	ATILP 001	Mungu Ibariki Kenya
	JCLP 022	Long Life to Mary
	POLP 580	Rose Atieno

Kapere Jazz Band. Formed in 1986 by William Owidi Jakapere and Polycap Otieno Ofuo, both from South Nyanza and born in the early 1960s. Both are professional men for whom music is an inspiring sideline. Now a part-time, five-piece, neo-traditional outfit, they are heard to excellent effect on the *Luo*

Roots compilation. Other Luo bands featured include Orchestra Nyanza Success led by Paddy Onono, who also accompanies the veteran Ogwang L. Okoth on a couple of tracks.

| 1990 | ORBD 061 | Luo Roots |

Swahili

Swahili music evolved during the immediate post-war era in the bars and clubs of the rapidly expanding urban centres. Initially it drew on indigenous 'ngoma' traditions but was subsequently enriched by both Cuban and Congolese influences. In time, Tanzanian musicians came to dominate the market for Swahili pop through influential bands like Simba Wanyika and Super Volcano, led by the late lamented Mbaraka Mwinshehe.

Simba Wanyika. Formed in May 1971 by brothers Wilson Peter and George Peter Kinyonga (b. Kigoma, Tanzania, 1950s). The brothers grew up in Tanga on the coast where as teenagers they learned to play guitar. They began performing as Happy Jazz but turned professional in 1966 when they joined Jamhuri Jazz Band, one of the most popular Tanzanian outfits. The brothers stayed with Jamhuri Jazz for the next four years until moving to Arusha in 1970, where they received sponsorship in the form of equipment from Kilimanjaro Textiles to form Arusha Jazz. It was then that a third brother, William Peter, joined as percussionist. The group then decided to move to Kenya, eventually settling in Mombasa, where they were based for the next four years. In 1972 their gamble paid off when they received a recording contract from Polygram. They quickly returned to Tanzania to recruit more musicians, including Omar Shabini on rhythm guitar. They also changed their name to Simba Wanyika – Lions of the Wilderness. It was an opportune time to purvey their brand of Swahili pop since Benga (an indigenous Kenyan style) was becoming increasingly popular and the new Simba Wanyika were largely unrivalled in their specific market. Musically, Wanyika were moving away from rumba copyists, developing their own harder style by incorporating trap drums and the characteristic rim shots. Their dominant position was further reinforced by the closure of the border with Tanzania in 1975, leaving them unchallenged inside Kenya. Characterised by smooth harmonies from brothers Wilson and George, the band went from strength to strength with a massive national following, releasing over 70 singles during the 1970s.

Sadly, however, discord was growing in the band and some members, led by Omar Shabini, decided to quit, forming a rival outfit, confusingly known as Les Wanyika. Simba regrouped, bringing in new musicians from both Morogoro Jazz and Super Volcano. In 1979 they demonstrated the power of the new outfit with the hit *Sikujua Utabadilika*. However, the problems leading to the original split had not disappeared and early in 1980 George led all the musicians away from Wilson to create Orchestra Jobiso, who, like Les Wanyika, immediately became another rival to Simba. Wilson and William struggled on for a few years but George eventually changed his mind and rejoined Simba Wanyika, occasionally working with Jobiso on personal projects.

Meanwhile, there were also problems in Les Wanyika, with vocalist Issa Juma leaving to establish Super Wanyika, adding to the confusion of names. Indeed, this confusion has spread to record companies, who have occasionally been found guilty of not knowing exactly who they were recording. In an effort to demystify the situation, Simba Wanyika added the word Original to their title, striking back with the top seller of 1984 *Shillingi*. By the mid-1980s Simba Wanyika Original were the top band in Kenya, with a string of hits to their credit. But by then cassette piracy was robbing musicians of royalties and in 1988 Simba Wanyika decided to stop working with Polygram (although they later returned) and instead switched to the Washington-based label The African Music Gallery. In 1989 they toured Europe to tremendous acclaim and are now on the verge of international recognition.

	POLP 506	Jiburudisheni Na Simba Wanyika
	POLP 510	Vol. 2
1984	POLP 540	Shillingi
1985	POLP 552	Halleluya
1988	POLP 565	Dunia Haina Wema
	AMG 003	Baba Asiya
	POLP 572	Mapenzi Ni Damua
	POLP 574	Maisha Si Nguvu
1989		Live In Europe

Wanyika, Les. This group grew out of Simba Wanyika, taking the majority of the original band with them. This division of Wanyika was led by Professor Omari Shabani. Big hits include 'Pauline' and *Sina Makossa*. They initially included Issa Juma until he too opted out, forming Super Wanyika Stars with the remnants of Orchestra Jobiso. The new band proved to be an enormous success and lasted throughout the 1980s until Shabini fell out with guitarist Ngereza in 1990 and moved over for a spell to the Everest Kings.

1980	MEA 716	Sina Makossa
1984	POLP 513	Pamela
1988	POLP 582	Nilipi La Ajabu
1989	POLP 598	Nimaru
1990	POLP 606	Les Les Non Stop

Super Wanyika Stars. Led by Issa Juma. Band formed in 1981 from the fall-out of the original Simba Wanyika. In 1989 DisqueAfrique licensed the earlier classic *Sigalame* via Serengeti for a UK release. Like the other two Wanyikas, the Stars enjoyed a successful decade in the 1980s, until Issa Juma suffered a stroke in 1988 and dropped out of the business.

1981		New Dance Les Les
1983	POLELP 001	Metatizo Nimeyazoea
	NYIKALP 01	Mpita Njia
1984	NYIKALP 02	Pole Pole
	ANAC 15	Sigalame
1985	NYIKALP 03	Bwana Musa
1986	NYIKALP 04	Sigalame II
	ANAC 19	Mwana Wa Ifwe
	ANAC 18	Safari
1989	AFRILP 008	Sigalame
	SER 131	Issa Juma and Super Wanyika

Jobiso, Orchestra. Another off-shoot from Simba Wanyika which George Peter occasionally uses to record with.

1985	POLP 549	Dunia Kigeu-geu
1988	POLP 574	Maisha Si Nguvu
1989	POLP 577	Natafuta Mwali

Maroon Commandos. Military band from the 7th Battalion of the Kenyan Army, led by Habel Kifoto. Formed in 1970, they made their breakthrough the following year with the hit single 'Emily'. Sadly, during a 1972 Kenyan tour, their bus crashed, killing several musicians. The band was demoralised and dropped out of music until 1977 when they returned with another hit entitled 'Charenyi Ni Waso'. They remain one of the country's top attractions.

1984	POLP 514	Kusema Na Kufanya
	POLP 518	Riziki Haivatu
	POLP 532	Dawa Nimuone Hani

	LZE 68	Usiniambie Unaenda
1986	POLP 554	+ Daudi Kabaka
	POLP 555	Hasira Na Hasara
1990	POLP 600	Mwakaribishwa Na Maroon
1991	POLP 608	Bonya Kuche

Pressmen Band. New outfit emerging from hotel circuit background. Popular with younger audiences for sophisticated blend of local and international sounds.

1990	CBSN 034	Dash Dash

Kabaselleh, Ochieng Wuod Ogollah. Singer and guitarist with two late 1980s hit albums. Leader of the Automatic Lunna Kidi Band.

1985	JILP 010	Afrika Man
1990	ATILP 002	Sikul Agulu
	ATILP 006	Come Back to Africa

Mavalo Kings. Seven-piece Benga band led by vocalist Fresh Ley Lucas Mwamburi. Known as 'the cousins' of Wanyika.

1988	POLP 581	Heshima Kidogo
1989	POLP 599	Tembea Kijana

Omar, Prof. Junior Abbu. Leader and lead guitarist of twelve-piece outfit, The Orchestra Mas System.

1989	POLP 590	Mawazo
1990	POLP 602	Sumu Ya Mapenzi

Them Mushrooms. Popular reggae–Benga band.

1985	POLP 548	New Horizon
1989	POLP 573	Going Places

Kikuyu

Kamaru, Joseph. Moderniser of Kikuyu traditional music who also sings in Swahili and occasionally ventures into the Benga style. Renowned for his social commentary and controversial lyrics, which have landed him in trouble in the past and again most recently in 1990 when all copies of his current cassette were impounded in a fit of government paranoia. He first recorded in 1966 and although popular has never become rich, bemoaning the high cost of equipment – something he believes holds back the development of Kenyan bands at the expense of Zaïrean and Tanzanian outfits. Currently leading the Kamaru Superstars.

1986	CSKSS 164	Kamaru's 14 Hits
1988	LP 102	The Best Of
1990		Prayers for the Country

Kamau, Daniel (a.k.a. Councillor D.K.)

	SGL 123	Ningwite Nawe

If in Kenya check out rising Kikuyu bands like Mbiri Stars and Kiru Stars – both with several hits to their credit.

Kamba music

Kilimambogo Brothers. Formed by three brothers (b. 1950, 1952, 1954). The band was formed in 1973 and success followed two years later with the hit single 'Ktala Kyakwa Na Meli'. Sadly, the leader of the band, Kakai Kilonzo, died recently, and will be sorely missed. Look for recent recordings by off-shoot group called the OKB Stars.

	LESC 103	Call It A Day
	LESC 107	Shangilia Christmas
		Greatest Hits
	KLBLPS 001	Maisha Ya Town
1987	PAM 03	Simba Africa

Other important Kamba musicians to watch out for include Peter Muambi and the Kyanganga Boys, the Ngoleni Brothers. The Kalambya Sisters still perform and are often remembered for their early 1980s hit song 'Djalenga'. They were recently joined by the Kalambya Boys.

Zaïrean bands

Super Mazembe. Zaïre/Kenyan band originally formed by the mysterious Zambian Nashil Pinchen Kazembe in 1973. (See Zambia.)

1970s	AITLP NP2	African Super Star Vol. 2
1983	205340320	Kaivaska
1984	EMALP 0550	Wabe-Aba
1990	AFRILP 007	Maloba D'Amor (Re-release of early hits – also DSCAF 007)

Mangalepa, Les. One of Kenya's most successful Zairumba bands led for over a decade by Bwamy Walumona, guitarist and composer. The band was formed in 1975 and for over a decade regularly topped the charts before being forced to return to Zaïre following a 1985 government crackdown on foreign nationals in the music business. They later returned and remain one of the country's top attractions.

1970s		Amua! Chafua!
1978	SAF 50096	Pambana-Pambana
	ASLP 913	1st Anniversary
	ASLP 919	Action All The Way
	ASLP 921	Live on Tour
	ASLP 928	Lisapo
1983	ASLP 988	Safari Ya Mangalepa
	JJLP 005	Greatest Hits
1985	ASLP 413	Madina

Walumona, Bwamy (b. Bukavu, Kivu, Zaïre). Guitarist and composer, Bwamy grew up in Lubumbashi, where he was recruited by Baba Gaston into the Baba National Band, which brought him to Kenya in 1975. Bwamy stayed with the band for less than a year before leading a revolt of musicians and forming his own group known as Les Mangalepa. For the next fifteen years Bwamy led the band to great success throughout East Africa. Then in 1990 he suddenly quit the pop music business and joined the Chrisco Fellowship Church, condemning his years of drinking and womanising and turning his considerable talents to gospel music.

Gaston, Baba, and L'Orchestre Baba National (b. Ilunga Wa Ilunga, Lubumbashi, Zaïre). Joined his first band in 1970, moving to Kenya in 1975 with Baba National, where he eventually settled. He has made a number of hit singles and recorded half a dozen albums of classic rumba during the 1980s.

1983	ASLP 1004	Revival
1985	ASLP 1006	Safari
	POLP 900	20th Anniversary
	POLP 901	Greatest Hits Vol. 1
	POLP 933	Greatest Hits Vol. 2

Lovy, Orchestre Super. Rumba veterans with several LPs to their credit in the late 1970s and 1980s.

1980s	LVLP 01	
	LVLP 02	
1982	LVLP 03	Nelly
	LOVY 04	Ye Ye Ye
	LOVY 07	Keba Yo

Virunga, Orchestre Band. Formed in 1980 and since led by Samba Mapangala (b. early 1950s, Matadi, Zaïre). Raised an orphan, Samba's early musical influences included church music, rumba, rock and blues. By the 1970s he was a regular performer in the Kinshasa clubs and in 1975 formed his own band, Les Kinois. The same year he moved to Uganda and stayed for two years before settling in the safer environs of Nairobi. In 1980 he disbanded Les Kinois and formed Orchestre Virunga (Volcano). The band quickly established a reputation with their light and spacey guitar work and solid dance rhythms. In 1984 they became one of the first East African bands to score an international success, with a UK release on the Earthworks label. In 1989 Mapangala returned to the international scene with a Paris-recorded LP helped by countrymen Quatre Etoiles. The album was released only in Kenya on CBS. Later that year he returned to record a tribute to Franco, again only for the Kenyan market. Stars of the band include Samba himself as lead vocalist and the shimmering lead guitar work of Lawi Somani. By early 1991 the band was back in Europe with several shows in the UK and a new record looking for a good home.

The band is now truly international, incorporating Zaïrean, Kenyan and Tanzanian musicians with vocals in both Lingala and Kiswahili. Almost inevitably, the multinational line-up wrought changes in the overall sound, something Samba accepts gladly, although his own roots remain in the Franco–Sam Mangawana school of music. The 1989 Paris album, supported by Passi Jo, Wuta May, Bopol and Syran, marked a change of emphasis towards hi-tech, Paris, seamless soukous. The real sound of the band is best heard live or on domestic Kenyan material. In 1991 the band signed to London-based Stern's for a one-off studio recording. Highly recommended.

1984	ERT 2006	Malako Disco (Also AR 0986)
1988	ASLP 454	Gina Monganza et Monga Monga Stars & Samba Mapangala
	ASLP 927	Disco Time
	JLP 0069	Greatest Hits
		Safari

1989	IVALP 071	Virunga & Quatre Etoiles as 'Vunja Mifupa' (CBS Kenya)
1990	CDEWV 16	Virunga Volcano (Malako Disco [remastered])
1991	ST 1036	Feet on Fire

Vundumuna. Formed in 1984 by Zaïrois Frantal and others (Frantal, b. Kisingani, Zaïre, late 1940s). Frantal was introduced to music whilst still at school, learning guitar and singing in a church choir. In the late 1960s he took up music full time, becoming the Director of Orchestre Succes Le Peuple. In 1972 he moved on to form Orchestre Boma Liwanzo with former members of Orchestre Révolution. By the mid-1970s the band were frequent vistors to other parts of East and Central Africa, releasing a number of singles and several albums along the way. By the 1980s the band was based in Nairobi, touring the Indian Ocean Islands and Malagasy. In 1981 he dissolved Orchestre Boma and for the next two years starred with Orchestre ShikaShika, until he helped form his current band, Vundumuna, in 1984. Drawing on up-tempo soukous rhythms and the folklore of Central Africa, Frantal now sings almost exclusively in Swahili. On his most recent outing he featured the gifted Zaïrean singer Lessa Lassan, who had sung with Dr Nico and African Fiesta in the 1960s and 1970s.

1989	AMG 005	Sala Molende

Others. While these bands dominate the Kenyan rumba scene, others to watch out for include Orchestre Popolipo, led by veteran vocalist Lessa Lassan, and Orchestre Zaiken. Moving beyond rumba, although today most bands play a Benga–Swahili–rumba mix, Kenya enjoys one of the liveliest club scenes in Africa with dozens of other bands performing regularly to enthusiastic audiences. They cannot all be listed here but for those fortunate enough to visit, the following are to be recommended: Ibeba System; African Jambo Band, led by Sammy Kasule; Professor Naaman and the Nine Stars Band; Safari Sound; and the Forest People.

1987	POLP 560	Ibeba System: System in the City
1988	POLP 584	Ibeba System: Ibeba New Wave
1989	POLP 585	Nine Stars Band: Amani
	POLP 594	Everest Kings: Mama Kei

1990	POLP 601	George Watailor & Kahumbu Success
	POLP 603	Sammy Mwambi & Mwanyeka
	POLP 605	Aziz Abdi & Orchestre Benga Africa
1991	POLP 609	Nairobi Matata Original
	POLP 610	Ulinzi Orchestra: Sina Uwezo
	POLP 611	Prof. M.B. Naaman and the Nine Stars Band: Mama Wa Kambo

Compilations

1980s	POLP 316	Tribal Songs of Kenya (Pop music)
	SWAH 001	Djalenga (UK mini-album)
1984	ASLP 406	The Best Songs of 1984
1989	ROUND 5030	Various: The Nairobi Beat (Shirati Mbiri Young Stars, Kilimambogo, Maroon Commandos, Kalambaya Sisters, etc.)
1990	CDEWV 21	Various: Guitar Paradise of East Africa (D. Kamau, Super Mazembe, etc.)
	ORBD 061	Various: Luo Roots (Kapere Jazz, Nyanza Success, etc.)
1991	CDEWV 24	Various: Kenya Dance Mania

Kenya overseas

Tam Tamu. Meaning 'Sweet – Very Sweet', Tam Tamu are a London-based Benga band formed by guitarist Zak Sikobe in the late 1980s. Zak, a gifted guitarist, had cut his musical teeth back in Kenya before arriving in London in the mid-1980s. He soon carved out a name for himself in London's African circuit with seminal bands Somo Somo and Taxi Pata Pata. In Tam Tamu he is joined by ex-Gloria Africana stars Boni Wanda and Aziz Salim. Their first UK album was released in 1991 and demonstrated a wide mastery of styles including a reworking of 'Malaika'. Other sources the band draw on include mitibo, shikuti, Benga, the 'dry' acoustic style and taraab.

1991   BABLP 1   Pendo

Christian tradition

Despite Islamic influences along the coast, Kenya remains basically a Christian country with a substantial corpus of recorded choral music. See Volume 1 for discography.

1988   POLP 525   Kwaya Ya Uinjilisti Ya Vijana: Kila Mtu Na Mzigo Wake

Kenyan pop

1991   848 6171   Chicco: Papa Stop The War

      848 6181   Chimora: Mayibuye Iafrika

Various

1989   KAYALP 004   Muungano National Choir: Safari

      K 002   Mzee Jomo Kenyatta: In Memoriam (Speeches, national anthem and other patriotic songs)

Taraab

The word itself derives from the Arabic verb tariba, which means 'to be moved or agitated', and is linked to the concept of profane trance in performance as well as to the music itself; adopted into KiSwahili it has come to mean a group of musicians getting together to entertain themselves and others. It describes the event as well as the music performed as in 'are you going to the taraab tonight?'. (Graebner, 1989: Sleeve notes for CD ORB066 *Zein Musical Party: The Style of Mombasa*)

Over the centuries, African and Arab traditions have enriched each other to the extent that it is almost impossible to disentangle the cultural and musical roots of modern coastal Swahili music. Even today, specifically Arabic instruments are found along the coast from Somalia to Mozambique, while African drums and lyres can be found throughout the Arabian peninsula.

Taraab, as a distinct musical style, was first introduced to Zanzibar in 1870 by Sultan Barghash, who had invited a troupe of Egyptian musicians to play at his court. He was sufficiently impressed with their work to send a Zanzibari called Muhammed Ibrahim to Cairo to learn how to play. On his return, he trained a few friends and started up the first Zanzibar Taraab Orchestra. In 1905 a second orchestra was formed, consisting mainly of Arabs and named the Akhwan-Safa. They played regularly at the Darajani Club in Stone Town, Zanzibar. A third group apeared in 1908, formed by Comorians based in Malindi and called Naadi Shub. All these early orchestras sang in Arabic. But by the 1920s the first African orchestras singing in Swahili were being formed, indicating that what had begun as upper-class, palace music, had become popular music. It was probably during this period that the Arab court taraab fused with older African, specifically Swahili, traditions – Swahili epic poetry, ngoma (drum) music and the 'gungu' dance – to produce the taraab of today. Werner Graebner, in the informative sleeve-notes to the Globestyle four-volume series, states that the roots of this modern taraab stretch back to the 1930s when Egyptian films started appearing, featuring large film orchestras. These orchestras were in turn copied by the youth of coastal East Africa, reviving and revitalising the older clubs and orchestras of the early twentieth century.

In musical terms, taraab, while sounding old and timeless, is in fact extraordinarily open to the incorporation of new instruments, rhythms and styles. John Storm Roberts, on the sleeve notes of OMA 103, expresses this vitality particularly well: 'But Tarabu, like so many complex and living things, refuses to be thrust into neat bags. It's an extremely lively art form sprung from a classical culture, still immensely popular, drawing all the time from old and new sources, a major part of the social life of the Swahili people.' During the 1930s instrumental influences were mainly Arabic, including the lute (ud), pottery drums (darbuk), a guitar-like instrument (gambuz) and the Middle Eastern zither (ghanun or ganoon). During the 1940s and 1950s new instruments like the violin, guitar, accordion and tabla were successfully incorporated as the music moved from acoustic to electric. Stylistically, new genres were also introduced, including latin rumba (via Zaïre). However, the main turning point in the story of taraab came with the 1964 revolution in Zanzibar, when the Arab presence and tradition were de-emphasised. Names were changed, records destroyed, as the Afro-Shirazi party sought to de-Arabise the island.

Kenya

The specifically Mombasa version of taraab has been traced to the turn of the century, when the blind singer and musician Mbaraku was active, and seems to owe more to Indian influences on Swahili popular culture than the Arab-influenced taraab of Zanzibar.

Maulidi, Juma (b. Mida, Malindi, 1941). With the early death of his father, Juma never had the chance to attend school and grew up in the company of taraab musicians. In 1960 he formed his own group – The Young Musical Club. However, things did not work out and Maulidi abandoned music for several years, only returning in 1971 when he joined Zein Musical Party in Mombasa. In 1972, together with keyboard player Mohammed Adio Shigoo, he formed Maulidi and Party. Playing a mix of styles to suit either formal weddings or less formal occasions, the group first recorded in 1973 and have made over 35 cassettes of their music in the years since. The 1990 Globestyle album features eight musicians, playing organ, accordion, guitar, bass, assorted percussion and tablas, and, of course, Maulidi himself on vocals.

| 1984 | OMA 103 | Various: Songs the Swahili Sing |
| 1990 | ORBD 58 | Mombasa Wedding Special |

The 1984 compilation was the first taraab/tarabu album widely available outside East Africa. Featuring a variety of early 1980s taraab, it includes tracks with clear Indian film influence, classic Arabic taraab, Lebanese-sounding violin pieces, electric Mombasa and even a taraab cha cha cha.

Zanzibar

Saad, Siti Binti (b. Kisauni, Zanzibar, 1880–1950). A legend in her own lifetime not only in Zanzibar but along the entire Swahili coast. Discovered as an amateur vocal accompanist, she moved into Zanzibar town and became a professional singer able to make a very good income from her career. She could sing in three languages (Swahili, Arabic and Hindustani) and was appreciated by all classes of people. With a substantial Indian population already buying records in East Africa, it was not as strange as it may appear for Binti to record for HMV in Bombay. She was the first East African artiste to make commercial recordings, and as her reputation grew so her records found their way to the Belgian Congo, the Comoros, Somalia and Southern Arabia. Her success between 1928 and 1939 was such that local agents for HMV and Columbia in Zanzibar were encouraged to establish studios on the island, with records being pressed in the UK. It is estimated that during the 1930s and 1940s Binti made somewhere in the region of 150 78 r.p.m.s for HMV, Columbia and Odeon. These records are now impossible to find but cassettes of her music still circulate in Zanzibar.

Ikhwani Safaa (Malindi Musical Club). One of the very first taraab orchestras, the club was first formed in 1905 but was forced to change its name in the wake of the 1964 revolution. (They have since changed back.) With a revolving membership down the decades, the club has performed in East Africa and the Gulf states, while several of its current membership visited the UK in 1985 as part of the National Taraab Orchestra. They can be heard to good effect on ORBD 033.

| 1988 | ORBD 033 | Ikhwani Safaa Musical Club: The Music of Zanzibar Vol. 2 |

Culture Musical Club. Founded in 1958 under the name 'Shime Kuokoana' – a call to preserve something which is about to be lost. In 1964, after the revolution, they changed their name to the more neutral Culture Musical Club. Today, the club has about 200 members, of which about 35 are active musicians, although not fully professional. They combine the twin purposes of playing for enjoyment and to keep Swahili culture alive, performing at weddings, state functions and religious events as well as socially. Their music can be heard on ORBD 041.

| 1989 | ORBD 041 | Culture Musical Club: The Music of Zanzibar Vol. 4 |

Ahmed, Abdullah Mussa (b. Zanzibar, 1943). Reckoned to be the best ganoon player on the island. Joined the Ikhwani Safaa in 1962, played with several orchestras in Dar-Es-Salaam and rejoined the Malindi Club in 1980. Parted company in 1985 and now plays freelance for many orchestras, particularly the Women's Clubs, who do not always have their own orchestras. (See ORBD 032)

Saleh, Seif Salim (b. Zanzibar, 1942). Multi-instrumentalist who started on mandolin before learning flute and violin. Also an accomplished vocalist. Joined Ikhwani Safaa as a teenager before continuing academic studies in Dar and London. He is currently Director of Culture and member of the National Taraab Orchestra. He can be heard playing with Abdullah Mussa on ORBD 032.

| 1988 | ORBD 032 | Seif Salim Saleh & Abdullah Mussa Ahmed: The Music of Zanzibar Vol. 1 |

| 1989 | ORBD 040 | Music Clubs: The Music of Zanzibar Vol. 3 |
| 1990 | ORBD 044 | Black Star & Lucky Star Musical Clubs: Nyota |

Tanzania

Although the taraab of Zanzibar and the Kenyan coast remains the best known and most recorded, taraab also flourishes on the Tanzanian mainland. The mainland bands appear to be much less organised and do not record. Their role remains social, with amateur performers and long, 15–20 minute songs. The leading outfit is the Egyptian Musical Club in Dar-Es-Salaam, established in the 1920s. Cassettes of taraab are widely available in both Kenya and Zanzibar, including well-worn copies of classic taraab from the 1940s onwards. Names and clubs to look out for include the following.

	CSABA 7	Black Star Music Club
1971	CSABA 12	Egyptian Musical Club Vol. 1
	CSABA 13	Egyptian Musical Club Vol. 2

Matona, Issa. Born in Zanzibar and not really playing in the taraab style. Recorded two mid-1980s albums for the Tanzania Film Company.

| 1985 | TFCLP 003 | Kimasomaso |
| | TFCLP 004 | Uliyenae Umzuie |

28   Tanzania

(ECONOMY AND SOCIETY. Pop.: 26.3 million. Area: 945,087 sq. km. Capital: Dar-Es-Salaam. Independence: 1961. Currency: Tanzanian shilling.)

Pre-colonial Tanzania was an area of huge social diversity with over 120 different peoples and languages. The nineteenth century was generally a period of state-building and economic development before several disastrous epidemics and the onset of colonial rule put an end to local progress. At the 1884 Berlin Conference Tanzania became a German colony, and when resistance came to a head in 1905 in the famous 'Maji Maji' rising, the Germans brutally suppressed it with a vicious scorched earth policy. However, in the aftermath of the First World War, the colony was handed over to the British, who ruled until independence came under Julius Nyerere in 1961. Tanzania (a merger of Tanganyika and Zanzibar) became a one-party state with a definite socialist bias in 1964 and by the 1970s had become the standard bearer of Third World socialism, having espoused the ideology of self-reliance first enunciated in the famous Arusha Declaration of 1967. Yet despite favourable loans and other aid from more progressive western countries and an impressive commitment to pan-Africanism, Tanzania failed to progress economically and steadily slid

into debt and poverty. The 1979 invasion of Uganda to help overthrow Idi Amin further added to the financial squeeze. In 1985 Julius Nyerere stood down as President and was replaced by Ali Mwinyi as the representative of the sole political party – the CCM (Chama Cha Mapinduzi – Party of the Revolution). Mwinyi came from Zanzibar and his accession to power did much to reassure Zanzibaris after earlier anti-Arab feeling from the mainland party. From 1985 onwards, Tanzania moved rapidly in the direction of economic liberalisation and by the early 1990s was debating the best way to democratise the political system. By then, Nyerere, as a symbol of anti-imperialist protest, had almost been forgotten as the Tanzanian socialist experiment ground to a halt.

TRADITIONAL MUSIC

Considering the wealth and diversity of Tanzanian traditional music, it is surprising that none is available on record in the country. Today, and indeed for most of the twentieth century, Tanzanians refer to traditional music as 'ngoma', a Swahili word meaning both music and dance and which is now used generically to describe the music, the dance and the occasion at which they are performed. Almost inevitably, Hugh Tracey made some of the earliest surviving recordings (1954); available at the time on the Gallo label but hard to find these days.

1955   GALP 1320   Tanganyika Vol. 1 No. 25
(featuring Gogo, Hehe,
Sukuma, Zinza, Zaramo,
Meru, Chaga and
Nyamwezi)

In an effort to preserve the traditional cultural heritage, various government bodies and state organisations formed 'ngoma' troupes with membership drawn from various ethnic groups. Lyrically, these troupes address the issues of the day and praise political leaders, urging people to support the Government. They perform a well-rehearsed set of material, reflecting the ethnic composition of the group, but to a seated rather than participatory audience – in other words, the very opposite of traditional ngoma. Readers interested in ngoma and the 'beni' brass band tradition should consult T. Ranger, *Dance and Society in East Africa*. One ngoma track which is occasionally available is the medley by the National Dance troupe appearing on *Musik Fran Tanzania*.

| 1989 | CAP 1089 | Musik Fran Tanzania (Part of Swedish-funded adult education project, Karibu) |

Bagamoya College of Arts. The Bagamoya College of Arts, to the north of Dar-Es-Salaam, has become a stronghold of Tanzanian musical traditions. When the musicians visited London in 1984 they were recorded, thus becoming the first release on the impressive Triple Earth label. Led by Hukwe Zawose, the album features a broad spectrum of traditional music and instruments – a top-quality recording.

| 1984 | TERRA 101 | Tanzania Yetu |

Master Musicians of Tanzania. Comprising Hukwe Zawose, Lubeleje Chiute and Dickson Mkwama on zithers/fiddle, marimba and bells respectively. Top-quality London recording eloquently described by one reviewer as 'Raw and wracked, a chorus of exquisite harmonies. Wilder than all rock and most rap, silkier than all soul, drawn from traditions even older than Cliff Richard. Songs of the war against poverty and hunger.'

| 1987 | TERRA 104 | Mateso |
| | VID 25011 | The Art of Hukwe Zawose (On the JVC Ethnic Sound Series, 36) |

MODERN MUSIC

The period between the late 1940s and the 1970s can be regarded as the era of the dance bands. As in many other countries in the 1940s, Cuban music proved extremely popular, with recordings by such bands as the Sexteto Habanero and the Trio Matamoros available on the acclaimed GV series. In time, cha cha cha arrived in Tanzania, with both styles having a profound influence on the evolving local scene. One of the first big bands was La Paloma, formed in 1948 and based just outside Dar in Morogoro. They later changed their name to the Cuban Marimba Band, bringing in an electric guitar in 1954. The lead singer was Salim Abdullah, who became the country's favourite star until his untimely death in a car accident in 1965. Two of their recordings can be found on the early compilation album *The Tanzania Sound*, released

in 1987 and providing an excellent introduction to the top bands of the 1960s and 1970s.

| 1987 | OMA 106 | The Tanzania Sound |

Mwinshehe, Mbaraka. Known as 'The Franco of East Africa', Mwinshehe was born in Morogoro and started playing music as a kid with a kwela outfit known as Cuban Branch Jazz. In 1964 he moved on to the Morogoro Jazz Band, staying for the next eleven years and laying the foundation for his now legendary reputation. (His biography was published in Swahili in 1982.) In 1975 he moved on to form Super Volcano, taking seven musicians with him from Morogoro Jazz. Over the next four years Mwinshehe recorded several albums and a host of singles, now occasionally available on Polygram Kenya. In 1979 Mwinshehe was tragically killed in a road accident on the Mombasa–Malindi highway. See Volume 1 (Kenya) for discography.

Morogoro Jazz Band. Active from the 1960s, they survived the loss of Mwinshehe and recorded a couple of fine LPs in the mid-1980s.

| 1984 | POLP 500 | Morogoro |
| | POLP 502 | Mfululrowa Wa Musiki |

Assosa & Legho Stars Orchestre. New band led by singer Tshimanga Assosa, a founding-member of Orchestre Maquis (see below) who left in the 1970s to return to Kinshasa. He returned in the early 1980s to join Orchestre Makassy, for whom he co-wrote their big hit 'Mambo Bado', which is featured on the Virgin 1982 release *Agwaya* (see below).

Bantu Group Band. Led by Kasimbagu Kaabhuka.

Nuta Jazz Band. Formed in 1964 and one of the longest-lived of the local bands. They have also acted as a training school for musicians, many of whom moved on to other bands like Mlimani Park and Orchestre Safari Sound. In 1977 they changed their name to Juwata Jazz band. They are currently led by guitarist Saidi Mabera, who joined in 1973. Arrangements are by Joseph Lusungu and M'nenge Ramadhani, veterans from the mid-1960s.

| 1987 | POLP 557 | Zilizopendwa (Old is Gold) |

Jamhuri Jazz

| 1988 | POLP 1013 | Hits (Cass.) |

159

Maneno, Ally. Born in Tanzania, Ally has made his career in Kenya. As a child he was influenced by the music of Bob Marley and Mbaraka Mwinshehe and joined Orchestre Dar International on leaving school. He then moved on to Les Mwenge before crossing the border into Kenya. Next, he formed Isse Isse Stars, mixing soukous with reggae, with the support of a local businessman who owned the equipment. They recorded a reasonably successful album for Polygram but the backer lost patience and seized the equipment. Ally tried to put together another band but was obliged to turn to session work and touring with other bands including a spell with Joseph Kamaru's band.

1980s	POLP	Ndugu Tuelewane

Victoria Jazz Band

1971	RCA 741 104	Victoria Jazz Band 71
1977	741 104	1977
	ZC0648233	Victoria Kings

Washirika Tanzania Stars Band. Led by guitarist Nurdin Athumani.

Various

1977	AIT 502	Tanzania Police Band: The United Republic of Tanzania
1988	AHDLP 6005	Tanzania Hit Parade 88 (Vijana, Maquis, Safari, etc.)

Zaïrean bands

Zaïrean musicians based in Tanzania face a different set of problems from those their countrymen encounter in Kenya. For although Dar-Es-Salaam provides a more vibrant setting for their skills and more appreciative audiences, the country as a whole is much poorer. Their problems are therefore largely the same as many Tanzanian bands and include the absence of recording facilities, cassette piracy and the cost of new equipment. The Government, for its part, neither helps nor hinders their work. Indeed, the Zaïrean sound is so popular in Dar that it is now probably the best place to hear classic rumba outside Kinshasa. Local recording opportunities are largely non-existent and in the past bands used to travel to Nairobi to record. However, over the last few years, this has become too expensive and they now send poor-quality tapes to the TEAL factory in Zambia to be pressed into records which are then sold at shows. Leading Zaïrean bands active during the late 1980s include Orchestre Safari Sound, Orchestre Makassy, Orchestre Maquis, the Dar International Orchestre and, of course, Remmy Ongala and his merry men. Top venues include Milimani Park, Stereo Bar, Silent Inn and Safari Resort.

Makassy, Orchestre. Led by Kitenzogu 'Mzee' Makassy, the band remain one of the few Tanzania-based outfits to establish a name outside the country, principally on the strength of their 1982 release on the UK Virgin label. Makassy himself is from Kivu in Eastern Zaïre. Graduates include Remmy Ongala and Fan Fan. In fact, several tracks on Remmy's *Songs for the Poor Man* (see below) are reworkings of Makassy material from the late 1970s.

1982	V 2236	Agwaya
1984	ZEMKC 1	Muziki Orchestre Makassy

Mlimani Park, Orchestre. Formed in 1978 when a dozen musicians, many of them graduates of Dar International, came together under the management of Tanzania Transport and Taxi Drivers' Association. In 1982 they won the national music contest and established their reputation with a string of hits including 'Kassim' and 'Neema', which was voted song of the year in 1985 and 1986! The core of the group, including singers Ilassani Bitchuka and Muhiddin Maalim and guitarist Abel Balthazar, had served with Nuta Jazz before forming Dar International in 1978. Bandleader, arranger, guitarist, sax player and driving force is Michael Enoch, a veteran of the local scene, having joined the Dar Jazz Band as early as 1960. He no longer performs with the band due to illness. In 1983 the band moved from the Taxi Drivers' Association to the Dar Development Corporation, hence the full name 'DDC Mlimani Park'. They have released several albums with Polygram and Ahadi in Kenya, some of them under the pseudonym 'The Black Warriors'. Finally, nine tracks have been released in Germany on the Monsun label. In 1985 the group suffered a blow when six members were lured away by a local building contractor/music entrepreneur to form International Orchestre Safari Sound. For a few years Safari Sound gave Mlimani Park a run for their money but when Bitchuka returned to Mlimani, they resumed top spot.

1983	POLP 523	Taxi Driver
1980s		Bubu Ataka Kusema (Black Warriors)
		Nalala Kwa Taabu (Black Warriors)

1986	AHDLP 6002	The Best of DDC Mlimani Park
1988	AHDLP 6006	The Best of Vol. 2
	POLP 579	Maisha Ni Kuona Mbele
1989	POLP 589	Dua La Kuku
1990	MSCD 900902	Sikinde Vol. 1 1980–7 (CD)

Safari Sound, Orchestre. Not to be confused with International Orchestre Safari Sound, led by Ndala Kasheba and comprising principally Zaïreans. Kasheba plays a twelve-string guitar and comes from Shaba province, arriving in Tanzania in 1969 and joining Safari Sound in 1979. When the owner of the equipment failed to renew his contract with the band in 1985, Kasheba went solo but the band fell apart.

| 1984 | TFCLP 001 | Dunia Msongamano (Recorded at Tanzania Film Company) |

Maquis Original du Zaïre, Orchestre. The story starts in 1966 in the town of Kamina in Zaïre's Shaba province when some young local musicians launched a band called Orchestre Super Gabby. By 1972 the band had renamed itself Orchestre Maquis du Zaïre and had moved to Tanzania. The group proved enormously popular and decided to stay. Today, with a total membership approaching 40 musicians, Orchestre Maquis continue to thrill Dar audiences and are one of the most popular fixtures in the Tanzanian scene. Like most bands in Tanzania, their recorded output fails to do justice to their durability and popularity. (I saw them play to a packed hotel in Dar late in 1990 and can personally testify to their rumba power and grace.) It will not be easy to track down copies from their limited vinyl output, but visitors to Tanzania can at least select from a number of locally produced casettes. In 1985 founding-member and leader Chinyama Chianza passed away with leadership falling to guitarist Nguza Mbangu (a.k.a. Viking). He led the band until 1987 when he struck out on his own with Dekula Kahanga (a.k.a. Vumbi) taking charge in his place. A lead guitarist with a new sharp sound, Vumbi revitalised the band and put them back on top with their late 1980s hit 'Ngalula' – a track which appears on *Tanzania Dance Bands Vol. 2*.

1980s		Malelisa
1986	AHDLP 6001	Karubandika
1987	AHDMC 005	Angelu (Cass.)
	AHDMC 007	Clara (Cass.)

| 1988 | AHDMC 011 | Ngalula (Cass.) |
| 1991 | MSCD | Tanzania Dance Bands Vol. 2 |

Ongala, Remmy, and Super Matimila (b. Ramathan Mtoro Ongala, Kindu, Zaïre, 1947). Remmy was introduced to music at an early age through his father, who was a singer, sanza player and dancer. However, at the age of nine, Remmy lost both parents and life became hard. He dropped out of school and by the age of 17 was in his first band, a youth group known as Bantu Success. At this stage Remmy performed as a drummer and a singer but his family were not happy with his career and in 1966 he left the group and returned home. By this time he had switched to guitar and, in 1968, could not resist returning to the music business and joined Success Mwachame. In 1969 he moved on to Mickey Jazz and scored heavily with two hit songs entitled 'Siska' and 'Sukuma' before moving to Toro in Uganda for a season at the Mountain of the Moon Hotel with Grand Mika Jazz led by Rachid King. From there he moved on to Kenya where he joined ex-OK Jazz guitarist Fan Fan in the much-loved Orchestre Makassy. However, disputes arose and in 1980 Remmy moved on to form the first version of Matimila.

By 1984 the band had assumed its current line-up of three guitars, bass, sax, trumpet and drums. Now based in Dar-Es-Salaam, they continue to play Zaïrean rumba and Remmy admits to Franco being one of his earliest influences, along with the Tanzanian star guitarist Slim Abdullah. In 1988 the band toured Europe and North America, releasing their first international album for WOMAD. The band feels comfortable in a number of Zaïrean styles and has been known to break loose on occasion, à la Zaïko. Being based in Tanzania (which has no vinyl production facility) has limited the band's recorded output and they remain essentially a live band, working out occasionally at Radio Tanzania. Remmy Ongala remains the best-known musician based in Tanzania and despite growing international exposure has not changed his rootsy African style. He is highly critical of other musicians such as Bopol, Salif Keïta and Youssou N'Dour, whom he claims have compromised African music. A charismatic and compelling performer, Remmy returned to the UK in 1990 and recorded *Songs for the Poor Man* at Peter Gabriel's prestigious Bath studio. A household name throughout East Africa with a growing international audience, Remmy lives in suburban Dar with his wife and three children.

1987	MC 507	Kifo
1988	WOMAD010	Nalilia Mwana
	AHDLP 6007	On Stage With

1989	RWLP 6	Songs for the Poor Man

Vijana Jazz. Formed in 1971 and composed of Tanzanians playing in East African rumba style.

1980s	MSK 509	Mundinde (Cass.)
1986	AHDLP 6004	Mary Maria

Reports from Klaus Frederking (1988) and my own assessment (1990) agree that the scene in Tanzania is looking up, with several new bands appearing towards the end of the decade, a development significantly helped by changes in foreign exchange and import regulations making it easier to import equipment. Names to watch out for include Legho Stars, Tancut Alimasi and Bima Lee. Finally, I would like to thank Klaus Frederking (and indirectly Werner Graebner) for some of the material appearing in this chapter.

29   Uganda

(ECONOMY AND SOCIETY. Pop.: 17.5 million. Area: 236,860 sq. km. Capital: Kampala. Independence: 1962. Currency: Ugandan shilling.)

Uganda, as an extremely fertile area, has a history of inward migration, including Bantu groups from the west, Nilotic peoples from the north and Hamitic peoples from the north-east. Between the tenth and the nineteenth centuries a number of powerful kingdoms emerged based on sophisticated agricultural production. Bunyoro grew to be the most powerful, but by the time of the arrival of the first Europeans in the mid-nineteenth century, Buganda had emerged as the strongest kingdom. The British, the French and the Germans all competed for power but by the end of the century it was the British who had secured a number of protectorates over this strategic area. Yet by ceding a great deal of power to the kingdoms through a system of indirect rule, the British hindered the development of a unitary state – something which was to have disastrous consequences for the country in the second half of the twentieth century.

The area was run by the British as an agricultural colony, producing cotton and coffee for export. Some effort was made to develop an educational system but political developments lagged behind neighbouring colonies. Indeed, it was only in 1958 that Milton Obote

was able to establish the UNC to press for independence, which duly arrived in 1962. Obote tried to promote progressive policies but the country remained split between the modern nationalism of the UNC and the neo-feudalism of the various kingdoms. Meanwhile Idi Amin, as head of the Army, was playing an increasing role in events and when Obote left the country in 1971 for an international conference Amin seized power in a coup welcomed and possibly even encouraged by the British. From then on it was downhill all the way as Amin systematically looted the country, brutally suppressing all opponents in what came to be one of the greatest tragedies in modern Africa. In the first few years alone, more than 100,000 people were killed and the economy collapsed. British interests were nationalised, the Asian population expelled, the Israelis raided Entebbe airport and Amin threatened both Kenya and Tanzania. Meanwhile the atrocities continued with an estimated 100,000 more citizens losing their lives between 1974 and 1977. Finally, it became clear that this brutal rule could not continue and in 1978 Tanzania invaded the country with the express purpose of getting rid of Amin. The next few years witnessed several changes of government as subsequent regimes tried to rebuild the shattered country, culminating in the return of Obote to power in 1981. In 1986 Museveni took power after a protracted guerilla war and was able to bring some stability and sanity to what had been one of Africa's richest countries. Yet by the late 1980s a new scourge had appeared in the form of AIDS, known locally as 'Slims'. Few countries have suffered as much as Uganda since independence. We can only hope that the good start made by Museveni will bear fruit and that he will receive the international assistance necessary to rebuild the economy.

TRADITIONAL MUSIC

Please see Volume 1 for a brief introduction to the traditional music of Uganda. The recording of traditional Ugandan music began in 1929 with the British Odeon label and by the 1950s there were several labels operating in the country, recording a variety of traditional music for release on 78 r.p.m.s such as The Young Baganda Singers' Party, Kibirige and Budo Party, Nanyoga and Party, and a number of school and cathedral choirs. In 1956 a German-owned pressing plant started up in Kampala but had collapsed by the end of the decade. Thereafter, recordings and manufacture took place mainly in Kenya.

1960s	GALP 1319	Music of Uganda
	KMA 10	Uganda 1
	ETH 4503	Africa – South of the Sahara
1988	KCF 1001	Various Traditional Songs, Dances, Hymns and Carols from Kitabi, Uganda. (Cass. only, Scottish)
1991	SHAN 65003	Samite: Dance my Children, Dance (Multi-instrumentalist and singer, equally at home on African or European instruments. Now based in USA)

MODERN MUSIC

The collapse of the economy and the barbarism of the Amin–Obote years has meant that very little Ugandan music has been recorded. During the 1960s Kampala rocked to imported Zaïrean rumba and rumba has since remained the main influence on Ugandan music. For some idea of what was popular during the 1960s check out the excellent sampler from Original Music. Stars of the 1960s included Charles Soglo, Fred Sonko, Bily Mbowa, Kawaliwa, Moses Katazza, Eli Wamala, Fred Masagazi, Freddie Kigozi, Orchestre Melo Success, the Kampala Six and the Equator Sound.

| 1988 | OMA 109 | The Kampala Sound |

Mutebi, Peterson Tusubira (b. Minyonyo, Uganda, 1950). Born into a family of teachers and musicians, Peterson received his early music training in the church choir. Growing up in the comparatively peaceful 1960s, he listened to, and was influenced by, foreign stars like the Beatles, Jim Reeves, Tom Jones, Cliff Richard (after whom he named his son) and, from closer to home, Tabu Ley and Franco. Popular local bands included the Kanyike Band and Womala, although they were studio rather than live groups. The Cranes were also influential and indeed continued in the more troubled 1970s as the country's top band. Throughout the 1960s all top Ugandan musicians were obliged to travel to Nairobi

to record or to try to make the best use they could of the government radio studios.

By this time Idi Amin had taken over from Obote, and although he enjoyed music and was a great socialiser, his policies were so destructive and, on occasions, barbaric that it was obvious that Uganda was regressing. Yet despite the difficulties, Peterson persevered with his chosen career and in 1972 went into the government radio studios and recorded eight songs, which were subsequently released on four singles. The following year he travelled to Nairobi to record his first album, claiming to be the first Ugandan to record an album in Kenya. By this time Peterson had developed his own Kadonkam style (a mixture of indigenous and C & W). The LP was released on the Associated Sound Productions label.

Live shows featured dozens of different styles performed by a 16-piece outfit supported by a dance troupe. They played both traditional and guitar dance band music. A second LP followed in 1976 with several more in the 1980s. In-between, Peterson was releasing numerous singles with impressive top sales of over 20,000.

Backed by his band, the Tames, Peterson Mutebi has long been one of Uganda's major stars, no mean achievement in a country with such a troubled recent past. His most popular songs include 'Regesie', 'Tezaali Mbiro', 'Nyongera Ku Love' and 'Rose Sembera'. He sings in a number of languages, including Toro, Swahili and Luganda, and tends to deal with a wide range of issues in his lyrics, from love and education to politics and elections. He admits that in the past times have been extremely hard with the general sense of insecurity, night-time curfews and little money all contributing to the problems of musicians. He remains active in the Uganda Federation of Theatre Arts and hopes that a positive attitude by the Museveni Government to the music industry, and their support for the Uganda Performing Copyright Association, will bear fruit in the form of increased royalty payments.

In 1990 he visited London in an effort to promote his music overseas and was well received by a number of companies. We can only hope that enthusiasm can be translated into a concrete record deal so that we can all enjoy his professional approach to music-making.

1973	KG 100	Love Enzigumivu
1976	TMLP1001	La Bimuli
1979	TMLP1002	Ekirabokyo
1983	TMLP1003	La Voyage au Rwanda
1985	TMLP1004	Bon Ame

Oryema, Geoffrey (b. Uganda, early 1950s). Geoffrey Oryema burst upon an unsuspecting public in the summer of 1990 with a number of highly acclaimed performances on the UK festival circuit and a hauntingly beautiful LP released on Peter Gabriel's Real World label. Oryema grew up surrounded by music; his father played the nanga, a seven-stringed harp, while his mother was director of the Heart Beat of Africa, Uganda's national dance troupe. His grandfather and uncles were also storytellers and musicians. While still in his teens, Geoffrey learned to play the nanga, guitar and thumb piano, and, later, the flute. By this time he was also composing his own material, with no shortage of suitable subjects in a country slowly being pulled apart by ethnic tension and political mismanagement. His happy childhood came to a tragic end when his father, a minister in Obote's government, was kidnapped and killed on the orders of Amin. As the politics of repression plumbed new depths, it was clear that the whole family was now at risk and in due course Geoffrey was smuggled out of the country in the boot of a car.

From Kenya he moved on to Paris, perfecting his musical skills along the way, particularly on guitar and lukeme. Exile also provided the theme for many of his songs, such as 'Makambo', 'Solitude' and 'Exile'. As an accomplished musician he was able to combine all the folklore of his youth while, by singing in Swahili as well as Acoli, his audience grew to encompass Kenyans and Tanzanians as well as Ugandans.

He arrived in the UK in the late 1980s and found a big fan in Peter Gabriel. On his first LP, appropriately entitled *Exile*, he was joined by Brian Eno (who also produced), Gabriel and others from Gabriel's band. While not destined for massive sales, it was a critical success and surely points to major creative achievements in the future. Since then, in 1991, Oryema has contributed 'Suzanne' to the double LP of Leonard Cohen cover versions, *I'm Your Fan*.

For an appreciation of how he now views the relationship between music and his own biography we can do no better than quote Oryema himself: 'Music accompanies everything in my culture. There is music for digging in your garden; to accompany the dead to their final resting place; if there is a visit by a Head of State it will be sung about. This music is not dead; it will never die. It is constantly changing, renewing itself.'

1990   CDRW 14   Exile

Afrigo. Probably the top pop band of the late 1980s and early 1990s. An eleven-piece guitar band, they are led by guitarist Moses Malovu. They play an easy paced, classic rumba with the usual fine guitar work and trenchant brass associated with the style. In 1990 they linked up with David Essex, the erstwhile UK pop star, then working as the travelling ambassador for VSO – a British-based volunteer recruitment agency. A few tracks were recorded, later to appear on a 1991 VSO fund-raising LP by Essex. In 1991 Afrigo arrived in the UK for a series of highly acclaimed shows. The only LP currently available, and obviously the latest in a long series, provides an excellent example of what Ugandan musicians can do.

1989   TAB 008   Music Parade Vol. 8

Lutaaya, Philly Bongoley (d. 1989). Described as the Bruce Springsteen of Uganda, Philly died in 1989 from AIDS, having spent the last years of his life trying to educate fellow-Ugandans to the dangers of the disease. A US documentary entitled 'Frontline: Born in Africa' was made of the last few months of his life.

Kanyike, Freddy, and the Rwenzoris. Popular dance outfit.

Katumba, Jimmy, and the Ebonies. Top-class guitar band who survived the 1980s to make an impact overseas with UK tours in 1989 and 1990.

Queen of Love

30   Ethiopia

(ECONOMY AND SOCIETY. Pop.: 50 million.
Area: 1,221,900 sq. km. Capital: Addis Ababa.
Independence: Never colonised. Currency:
Ethiopian birr.)

Ethiopia has played a central role in African history for
over two millennia, since it emerged from the ashes of
the Axum kingdom in 500 BC. Christianity arrived in
the fourth century AD but for the next thousand years
the country was isolated from other Christian areas by
the rise of Islam in north-east Africa. Early European
contact came through the Portuguese, but when they
were expelled the country's feudal system almost
self-destructed through a series of long and bitter civil
wars. However, by the mid-nineteenth century, during
an era of growing European involvement in Africa, the
two emperors, Tewodoros and Menelik, were able to
resist European encroachment and establish an expanded, highly centralised empire in the Horn of
Africa. Haile Selassie, the last in the imperial line,
assumed the throne in 1930 and set about modernising
the empire. Yet time was against him, and when the
Italians under Mussolini looked to Africa for a new
Roman empire their covetous eyes fell on feudal
Ethiopia. The conquest, in 1936, was a one-sided affair
and the Italians ruled the area until they were ejected
by the British in a major campaign in the Second World
War. The British re-instated Haile Selassie, but despite

his glowing international reputation the Emperor
failed to modernise the country and by the 1960s
pressures and divisions were growing along class as
well as religious and ethnic lines. By the early 1970s all
these pressures, as well as several civil wars and
catastrophic famines, were coming to a head, erupting
in the Marxist-oriented revolution of 1974 which
brought Colonel Mengistu to power.

Efforts were made to drag the country into the
twentieth century but the brutality of the regime
proved incapable of either stopping the Eritrean and
Tigrean national struggles or preventing the massive
droughts and famines of the 1980s. Furthermore, with
an avowedly Marxist regime in power, Ethiopia
became embroiled in other Cold War struggles in the
region, most notably over the Ogaden region of
Somalia. By the late 1980s the combination of military
defeat and economic collapse had brought the junta to
its knees and in a dramatic upheaval in early 1991 the
regime collapsed with Mengistu escaping to Zimbabwe. It is too early to predict what direction the new
men in power will take, and how they will resolve the
various contradictions in Ethiopian society, but there
can be no doubt that the last two decades have
witnessed some of the most difficult times in all of
Ethiopia's troubled history.

MUSIC IN ETHIOPIA

I must thank Nick Dean of Natari Records for much of
what follows.

The music of Ethiopia is enormously varied and
ranges from original tunes played on a single
traditional instrument through to modern electric pop
bands. Most music can be traced back to the Christian
Church, adapting to changing circumstances but still
comprising the basis of today's modern sounds. The
highlands of central/south-eastern Ethiopia are home
to most of the current popular styles, with Tigrean and
Eritrean music coming from the north and east of the
country. The most recognisable style is known as
'achinoy', with its unmistakable melancholy feel, while
the most popular styles, at least to western ears, are the
'chichika' and the 'ambassel', which together make up
most of the modern output. 'Iskista' is a rather startling
style of dance music in which the head, chest and arms
move in various directions in a series of jerks.

While most bands utilise guitar, sax, drums and

keyboards, it is worth mentioning other, more traditional instruments still in common use. These include the 'wishint', a type of flute; the 'kebaro', a medium-sized drum beaten by hand or with short, thick drumsticks; the 'krar', a form of lyre; and the 'masenqo', a type of lute played with a bow. Traditional music is still widely played but cannot really compete with modern pop sounds.

Although the rest of the world does not see or hear much Ethiopian music there is a lively and vibrant scene inside the country with no shortage of talent. Unfortunately, this is where most of it stays. Virtually all music is released on cassette, with only a couple of stars enjoying a wider exposure with material available on vinyl. The reasons behind this situation are not hard to find and include the absence of any copyright control, the prevalence of piracy (although the Ethiopian Music Association is attempting to correct this) and the absence of any reasonable studios. In such a situation, the industry is organised on the basis of hundreds of small and fiercely independent shops who issue their own recordings, made on the spot in small back-room studios. The lack of modern recording facilities and sub-standard duplicating equipment inevitably produces poor-quality finished cassettes. It is now estimated that hundreds of new titles arrive on the market every year. During the 1950s and 1960s new material came out on vinyl (with Philips operating a branch in Addis until the mid-1970s), but by the end of the 1970s the market was entirely cassette-oriented. The only decent studio is the government-owned TV studio, but with the collapse of the revolution in 1991 there are now high hopes that the private sector will become involved.

Trying to catalogue cassette-only releases is an almost impossible task since, in the absence of any copyright system, local manufacturers do not use code numbers but simply print the name of their shop on the back of the cassette, with the artiste's name and track-listings on the front. A further difficulty is the fact that over 90 per cent of cassettes are printed in Amharic. Occasionally a date will be included but since Ethiopia uses both the Gregorian and the Julian calendar more confusion arises. The cassettes listed here are or have been available outside the country but will take a great deal of effort to track down. One useful starting point for would-be enthusiasts must be Natari Records, exclusive importers for an impressive range of hard-to-find African material. Before proceeding to cassette listings, it may be useful to indicate Ethiopian music which has appeared on vinyl.

TRADITIONAL MUSIC

Comprising over 75 different peoples and cultures, Ethiopia presents a mosaic of traditional sounds, drawing on both secular and sacred traditions. The sacred tradition, related to the fourth-century Christian Church, utilises a variety of instruments, including drums, rattles, trumpets, plus vocals, and can produce a deep hypnotic groove.

1970s	TGN 102	Various: Music of Desert Nomads
	LLST 7244	Ethiopian Urban and Tribal Music
	GEMA 011228	Ethiopian Wedding Songs
	OCR 75	Various: Musiques Ethiopiennes
1980s	WRS 100	Various: Ethiopian Collection

MODERN MUSIC

The modern pop scene really started in the 1920s, growing out of the military bands and encompassing outfits like the Imperial Bodyguard Band. The Italian invasion of 1936 brought in a range of new influences, including Italian dance band music, but it was really during the 1950s that Ethiopia underwent its own 'musical revolution'. External influences on the emerging indigenous style included rock and roll, with Elvis as the principal model. Dozens of new, cosmopolitan clubs sprang up and Ethiopian pop music became considerably more westernised. By the time of the revolution in 1974, music was undergoing several important changes. For a start the Church assumed a much lower profile while the Military Government became more involved in the cultural development of music as a tool of national unity. Other pop bands came under government control, with musicians as salaried government employees. The Government also established state-funded theatre-troupes producing a new form of contemporary folk-theatre. On the other hand, with over 50 per cent of the national budget going to the Army, the Government argued that they had higher priorities than music. We now await the consequences of the collapse of the Mengistu regime on the development of music in Ethiopia.

Aweke, Aster (b. Begemdr, near Gondar, late 1950s). Her family moved to Addis when she was one, and she started singing professionally in 1977, releasing several local cassettes before moving to Washington DC in 1979. Her career then picked up considerably, playing first to a large resident Ethiopian community and scoring with hits like 'Hode' and 'Teyim'. Over the next decade she consolidated her reputation with half a dozen more cassette releases, playing the Washington restaurant scene with occasional out-of-town shows. Then, in 1989, she signed up with the London-based Triple Earth label, who brought her talent to a much wider audience. Aster suddenly found herself with an international reputation for her utterly extraordinary voice and a wider appreciation for her charismatic stage shows. That same year she played Ronnie Scott's in London to ecstatic reviews and even succeeded in punching a hole in the increasingly complacent approach of mainstream pop journalism. In 1991 she entered the studio again with Triple Earth for her second international release. Aster has done more than any other Ethiopian artiste to open up western ears to the music of Ethiopia and can be considered a truly international star.

| 1989 | TERRA 107 | Aster |
| 1991 | TERRACD 110 | Kabu |

Roha Band. Premier Ethiopian band who back other solo singers on various recordings. Led by Giovanni Rico and formed after the 1974 revolution. Still going strong today. Their only vinyl release is from the Belgian Crammed Disc label where they support Mahmud Ahmed.

| 1980s | CRAM 047 | Ere Mela Mela |

Debebe, Neway. One of the leading popular singers, who usually records and plays with the famous Roha band. He has issued many splendid recordings, often with fellow singers Tsegaye Eshetu and Areghagn Werash as the Three Flowers. His music is basically guitar, drums and plenty of sax played in a fast jazz/blues style with Neway's distinctive Hindi-style vocals. Like most artistes in Ethiopia, he writes all his own material.

1985		Vol. 1 (Kaifa recording with the Roha Band)
1986		Vol. 2 (Kaifa recording)
1988		Vol. 3 (Kaifa recording)
1990		The Three Flowers (Original Samson recording)

Mellese, Netsanet. Started out a choir-girl before becoming a sweet-voiced vocalist with several recordings to her credit. She produces a softer and more melodic sound than many of her contemporaries. Several cassettes from Electra and Original Samson are likely to be available.

Ahmed, Mahmud. Probably the top-selling artiste in the country. He is famous for his powerful vocals, sung in a slower and more melodic style than Neway. He usually records with the Roha Band but has also worked with Ibex, Dahlack, Venus and the Imperial Bodyguard Band. He started life as a

shoe-shine boy in Addis and has since come a long way, now owning his own music shop. His material is available on the Supersonic, Original Sound and Mahmoud Music Shop labels plus the Crammed Disc LP noted above.

Ahmed, Mahamad (a.k.a. Towil). More westernised style than Mahmud, with the keyboards making the running accompanied by Mahamad's plaintive vocals.

| | + Ajobe Keyefu Band (Kaifa recording) |

Gaddisa, Getachew. Modern guitar, keyboard, drum line-up in the style of Neway, but lacking his vocal range.

| 1982 | Getachew Gaddisa (Kaifa recording) |

Ashagari, Martha. Similar in style and sound to Aster's early Ethiopian-only cassettes.

| 1982 | Martha Ashagari (Tango) |

Hailu, Maretha. Modern pop singer with a superbly plaintive voice. Material available on Legehar Music Shop label.

Kebede, Aster. Sweet-voiced singer in a bluesy style.

| | Vol. 1 (Tango) |

Eshetu, Tsegaye. Young pop singer with a powerful melodic voice.

| 1983 | Tsegaye Eshetu (Soul Kuku Music Shop) |

Mengesha, Kenedy. Top-selling artiste with several albums to his credit. His high-pitched voice has recently been put to good effect, duetting with several up-and-coming female stars.

	+ Roha Band (Alem Music Shop)
	+ Yeshemeget Dubale (Negarit)
1991	+ Birtukan Dubale (Negarit)

Abate, Amelmal. Silky-voiced female star with several good albums of sensual, bluesy music to her credit.

Amelmal Abate (Kaifa recording)

Tamru, Ephraim. Popular young singer who has released several albums of middle-of-the-road material.

Ephraim Tamru (Electra Music Shop)

1989 + Roha Band (Ethio Music Shop)

Belew, Semahegn. Young singer sounding like Neway Debebe. Material available from Tango Video and Music.

Awel, Mohammed. 'Gurage' music, in which Awel is a leading star. Up-tempo traditional dance music. Available on Original Lula.

Abdrehman, Wabi. Another gurage star with a more modern musical line-up.

1990 Wabi Abdrehman (Ethio Music Shop)

Alemayehu, Kiross. Hailing from Tigre and purveying a neo-traditional style, Kiross is a major star in Ethiopia. The basic rhythmic beat is provided by hand-clapping backed by the 'krar' and 'masenqo'.

Wedajo, Zerihun. Basic Tigrean music wherein the traditional instruments and hand-clapping are replaced by keyboards and drums.

1990 Zerihun Wedajo (Yered Music Shop)

Kenge, Bahiru. Traditional singer accompanied on 'masenqo'.

Wareq, Asnakech. Female singer backed by 'krar'.

1989 Bahiru & Asnakech (Ambassel)

There are dozens more artistes and bands (as well as shops) who have not been mentioned above. Their material may be available through Natari, otherwise check them out when next in Addis. Stars to look out for include the various army and bodyguard bands, the Four Stars Singers, the Walias Band and the Dahlak Band.

31 Sudan

(ECONOMY AND SOCIETY. Pop.: 24.3 million. Area: 2,505,813 sq. km. Capital: Khartoum. Independence: 1956. Currency: Sudanese pound.) For map, see p. 166.

Sudan is the largest country in Africa and comprises a low-lying plain split by the River Nile. Ethnically, it moves from an Arab north to an African south, reflecting climatic changes from dry desert in the north to lush tropical rain forest in the south. With a glorious and varied past, most of Sudan came under Muslim influence in the centuries following the death of Mohammed in AD 632. During the Middle Ages Sudan was a prosperous area, sitting astride the Saharan trade, controlling the Nile and on the route to Mecca. By the nineteenth century both the Egyptians and increasingly the British sought control over the area. The Islamisation of Sudan had been a slow process, but, in 1881, as Egypt tried to tighten its economic exploitation of Sudan to help pay the cost of the Suez Canal, and itself came under British colonial control, the Sudan rose up against the non-Islamic oppressors in the famous Mahdist Uprising which saw the death of General Gordon. The resulting Mahdiya state was short-lived and was attacked by several neighbours as well as by a variety of western powers. Finally, in 1898, Lord Kitchener defeated the Mahdists at Omdurman and established British colonial power over what was officially known as the Anglo-Egyptian Condominium. For the next 50 years the British ruled Sudan along typically colonial lines, developing whatever infrastructure was appropriate to the export of raw materials. However, this limited development also helped produce both an influential bourgeoisie with roots in the nineteenth-century Mahdist movement and a new industrial working class. Then, in 1952, in the wake of the Egyptian revolution, pressures for independence increased and the British moved quickly to accommodate these wishes. However, they rejected southern demands for secession or some kind of federalism and when the African/Christian south exploded into violence in 1955 the British brutally put down the revolt after virtually isolating the region from the rest of the country. When independence came the following year, Sudan was already in the throes of civil war.

Throughout the 1960s, as conditions for an already vulnerable economy worsened, Sudan witnessed a range of regimes until Colonel Nimeiri emerged as the army strong-man in 1969. Nimeiri initially looked to the left, legitimising the communist party and establishing links with the Soviet Union, but after an abortive coup attempt in 1972 he moved steadily to the right and became increasingly drawn into the capitalist orbit. The country embarked on several large development projects, but with the price of cotton dropping and continuing civil war in the south, it teetered on the brink of collapse. One response was an early experiment in privatisation, benefiting mainly Saudi and Kuwaiti capitalists, and in 1980 there was talk of Sudan becoming 'The bread basket of the Arab world'. This was not to be and from then onwards Sudan faced a growing number of problems, culminating in the catastrophic drought and famine of 1985. This is not the best place to explore the reasons underlying the famine and readers are advised to look elsewhere to remind themselves of that particular tragedy – one which, along with the Ethiopian famine of 1984, did more to put Africa in the headlines than anything since the Biafran War of 1967–70.

Since the 1985 famine Sudan has staggered from one human crisis to the next while all the time the civil war rages in the south, draining away any possibility of recovery. In 1983 Nimeiri attempted to impose Sharia (Islamic) law on the country, thereby intensifying southern fears, and when he flew to the US to seek aid in 1985 he was replaced in a bloodless coup by General Abdul Rahman Swaredahab. Rahman lasted until 1989 when he too was overthrown by the Army, having failed to end the war, improve the economy or alleviate the degradation of the environment. Brigadier El-Bashir then took control of a country increasingly characterised by famine, drought and death.

TRADITIONAL MUSIC

In 1969 the celebrated ethnomusicologist David Fanshawe toured Sudan and made a number of fine field recordings deposited at the BBC Sound Archive. The early 1960s also witnessed several field recording tours undertaken by ethnomusicologists commissioned by the BBC.

	MC 9	Musik der Nubier
	MC 10	Dikr und Madih
1976	FE 4301	Dinka War Songs and Hymns

170

FE 4302	Dinka Women's Dance Songs	
FE 4303	Music of the Sudan Vol. 3: Burial Hymns and War Songs	
STLP 500	Music and Songs of Abdul Karim	
VDE 30294	Soudan: Pays des Nouba	

MODERN MUSIC

1940s–1960s

al-Kashif, Ibrahim. Perhaps the most famous Sudanese 'pop' singer of his day. With either traditional accompaniment or with a full Egyptian orchestra, Ibrahim's music was appreciated throughout Sudan and beyond. Like most of his contemporaries, he usually recorded in Cairo. He hit his peak of popularity in the years immediately after the Second World War and prior to independence in 1956.

al-Fallatia, Aisha. Famous Sudanese singer, recorded in Cairo.

al-Mustafa, Ahmad. Moderniser of folk songs, popular in the early 1950s. Perhaps best known as the composer of 'Ristair Sudan' – a widely-played song of hope for the country composed during the Nimeiri regime.

abd-al-Mu'in, Ismail. Singer working in modern Sudan/western idioms. Usually supported by full Egyptian traditional orchestra.

Sulemein, Hasan. Another popular post-war singer, recorded in Cairo.

1970s–1980s

There is no real record industry in Sudan, nor any legislation governing performing or copyright. Musicians make a living on a busy live circuit but in the absence of any protection bootlegging is rife. Yet the musicians and people of Sudan remain generous in their talent and money. In 1985, in the aftermath of the highly publicised famine, Sudanese musicians became involved in a massive project called Sudan Call to raise funds for the victims. Although it received minimal publicity (against the massive media exposure of Live Aid), Sudan Call was climaxed with an all-day open-air concert with musicians using the media to encourage other Sudanese to give what they could. Over two million Sudanese pounds was raised – the poor sacrificing for the poor in a way the west could scarcely contemplate.

Salim, Abdel Gadir. Oud player and vocalist. Accompanied by accordion and tabla. In 1987 he recorded in London for a highly acclaimed Globestyle album.

1987	ORB 039	Stars at Night
	WCB 002	Sounds of Sudan Vol. 1
1991	WCD 024	The Merdoum Kings Play Songs of Love (CD)

Gubara, Mohamed. Tambour player and vocalist.

1986	AW 61273	Noora
1988	WCB 005	Sounds of Sudan Vol. 2

Mubarak, Abdel Aziz El. Sudan's leading contemporary vocalist with a ten-piece accordion-led backing band. Mubarak is not only from a musical family but from a whole village of musicians.

1987	ORB 023	Abdel Aziz El Mubarak
1989	WCB 010	Straight from the Heart

Others

	STA 273	Ibrahim Hussein: Concert
	EMISDS 78	Kamal Killa
	SPMC 005	Various: 12 Sudanese Hits
1988	1784	Mohammed Wardi
		Hamza El Din: Eclipse
		Various: Sudan Select

32   Somalia

(ECONOMY AND SOCIETY. Pop.: 6.3 million. Area: 637,657 sq. km. Capital: Mogadishu. Independence: 1960. Currency: Somali shilling.) For map, see p. 166.

Known as the 'Black Berbers' to early Greek and Arab writers, the Somalis have an ancient history which archaeologists and linguists are only now beginning to decode. For several millennia the Somalis have enjoyed trading links with the Arab world, India and the East African coast, although the majority of the population remained pastoral and scattered. Islam arrived in the eighth century but the next few centuries were characterised by feuding principalities interspersed with periods of peaceful commerce. However, from the sixteenth century onwards raids from neighbouring Ethiopia grew in frequency and intensity while first the Arabs and subsequently the Ottoman Turks took control of the coastal ports. By the time of the 'Scramble for Africa' several European powers as well as Ethiopia were in a position to partition the area between them. Eventually, after decades of 'pacification', Italy in the south and Britain in the north emerged as the respective colonial powers. But ultimate authority proved elusive, and after the Italian occupation of 1940–2 Somalia came under a number of different administrative systems, including British colonialism, Ethiopian imperialism and a return of Italian colonialism in 1949. Finally, in 1960, the Italian and British colonies were united and the country moved quickly to independence. But given the recent confused political past, the new government proved both inefficient and inept and was overthrown by Siad Barre in 1969.

Between 1970 and 1977 Barre adopted a left-leaning programme and was heavily supported by the Soviet Union. However, Barre also pulled Somalia into the Arab League, and when the 1974 revolution in Ethiopia installed a Marxist regime, relations with the USSR deteriorated as Somali–Ethiopian tension erupted in the first Ogaden crisis. In 1978, in a cold and calculating switch, Barre opened up relations with the US as Cold War politics came to dominate events in the Horn of Africa. In 1979 he declared a state of emergency and brought the country under direct military rule. For the next ten years Barre's rule became increasingly autocratic and idiosyncratic. In 1990 he was overthrown and we must now wait to see what the future holds for this impoverished and troubled country.

Today, most of Somalia is thinly populated by nomadic pastoralists with population only concentrated in the towns and along the banks of the two main rivers. Sunni Muslims comprise 99 per cent of the population. The Government runs two radio stations – Radio Mogadishu and Radio Hergeisa – in the north of the country.

CULTURE AND SOCIETY

The Somali language has a great tradition of oral poetry, often accompanied by a music most closely related to Arabic forms. Drums, tablas, ouds, flutes and violins are all used in contemporary Somali music. (See Volume 1 for further details.) There is no record market in Somalia, with cassettes dominating the scene and featuring music recorded live at shows. There is also a more urban popular style known as 'metallic', which includes modern electric instruments. Very, very little Somali music is available outside the country, although the Somali service of the BBC holds a huge archive of taped music. Taraab is also popular. The Original Music sampler is the best place to start any investigation of modern Somali music. More modern musicians to search for include Abdullahi Haji Sulfa, Ahmed Naasi, Dur Dur, Haussein Shiekh and the Radio Singers, Mayamed Sulayman, Sahara Mohammed, Shamuuri and Wiil Iyo Walid.

| 1971 | F 8504 | Sheikh Haussein: Baijun Ballads |
| 1986 | OMA 107 | Various: Jamiila (Songs from a Somali City) |

33 Djibouti

(ECONOMY AND SOCIETY. Pop.: 530,000. Area: 21,783 sq. km. Capital: Djibouti. Independence: 1977. Currency: Djibouti franc.) For map, see p. 166.

A small but strategically important country, contemporary Djibouti is inhabited by a surprisingly diverse mixture of Afars, Issas, Somalis, Arabs and Europeans. Prior to French colonisation, the Afars and Issas were nomadic peoples with ties to Ethiopia and Somalia respectively. But strategic and political criteria broke up traditional boundaries in the Horn of Africa and by the time the French arrived in 1862 traditional society was already under threat. During the next thirty years the French undertook the construction of a railway to Ethiopia, thereby establishing Djibouti as a key port and entrepôt for Ethiopian trade.

Little other development occurred during colonial rule and by the 1940s opposition to French rule was mounting, expressed most strongly by Somali nationalists keen to establish a Greater Somalia. The Somalis in Djibouti were initially supported by the southward-looking Issas, but the French supported the Afars as a way of undermining the Somali population. Meanwhile, Haile Selassie in Ethiopia was still claiming the territory as part of a Greater Ethiopia. During the 1960s the French tried hard to suppress the Somali party in Djibouti and thousands of Somalis went into exile. Reluctant to grant independence to such a strategic possession, the French increased their military presence during the 1970s, installing barbed wire fences around the capital. Pressure on the French to leave mounted with a number of violent demonstrations and plenty of support from the Organisation of African Unity and the Arab League. But while independence did come in 1977, it was severely circumscribed by agreements to maintain a French presence.

Today, Djibouti is an impoverished country with an extremely hostile climate. The Issas, for the most part, have settled in the capital, while the Afars retain a nomadic life-style in the interior.

CULTURE AND SOCIETY

Djibouti is largely a Muslim country with Arabic as the official language. French is also widely used with national broadcasting being mainly in this language.

ACCT 38212   Musique de Djibouti (Songs in Somali, Afar and Arabic)

34 Madagascar

(ECONOMY AND SOCIETY. Pop.: 12 million. Area: 587,041 sq. km. Capital: Antananarivo. Independence: 1960. Currency: Malagasy franc.)

Madagascar, the fourth largest island in the world, remained unpopulated until the fifth century AD when Malayo-Polynesian and African settlers arrived. Over the next thousand years the island developed in almost complete isolation with a marginal Arab influence. The Portuguese were the first Europeans to arrive, followed briefly by the British, before France finally colonised the island in the late nineteenth century. By this time France had helped the Merino kingdom establish suzerainty over the entire island and so a unitary state existed through which the French could govern. Yet the colonial period was marked by frequent outbreaks of resistance followed by massive retribution, such as that which followed the Rising of the Red Shawls at the end of the nineteenth century, and the urban unrest of 1947–8. In 1960 the French were able to manipulate the independence process to ensure a continuity of influence, maintaining a number of military bases under the pro-South African, fiercely anti-communist rule of President Tsiranana. However, his neo-colonialist government proved unable to deliver economic prosperity and in 1972, following

student riots and strikes, he handed over power to General Ramanantsoa, whose government severed ties with Israel and South Africa, closed French bases and established diplomatic links with China. But political unrest continued and in 1975 two quick changes in government left the radical Ratsikira in power.

Ratsikira quickly moved to adopt more socialist policies through a gradual decentralisation of power within the context of a one-party state. In 1981 he was able to suppress a coup attempt but unrest continued over educational and employment issues. By 1985 the Malagasy economy was in such poor shape that Ratsikira was forced to accept the terms of an IMF structural adjustment programme and introduce market-oriented reforms.

In 1986 the infamous 'Kung Fu' riots erupted when members of the 10,000-strong Kung Fu society went on the rampage, leaving over fifty dead. The remainder of the decade was characterised by continuing unrest and economic crises. Finally, in 1990, Ratsikira bowed to the inevitable and, although fighting a strong rear-guard action, accepted the principle of a return to multiparty politics.

TRADITIONAL MUSIC

Until the mid-1980s, there was virtually no overseas interest in either the traditional or the modern music of Madagascar. Then, in the space of three years, two British journalists (Shinner and Anderson) and a record company team (Globestyle) made a series of visits which resulted in several serious articles (Shinner – *Folk Roots*, October 1988; Anderson – *Folk Roots*, May 1991) and a number of impressive recordings. Much of what follows is drawn from their work.

The 'valiha' is perhaps the most impressive of all the traditional Malagasy instruments. A 16–21-stringed zither, it is probably of South-East Asian origin, and can be found in various forms across the islands from the bamboo prototype to the 'marovany' design found in the south to the 'valiha vato' made from corrugated iron. The most famous valiha player was Rakotozafy, who enjoyed truly national appeal due both to his immense talent and the exposure provided by radio. The valiha is associated with several religious ceremonies including the 'Tromba' or spirit possession, much as the mbira is used in Zimbabwe. Until 1972 the valiha remained a forbidden instrument to the descendants of slaves. Thereafter, when the restrictions were lifted, it became the focus of a back-to-the-roots movement and was incorporated into many acoustic/electric guitar bands.

A second important instrument is the 'sodina' – the Malagasy flute. This is easily made and was used to provide light entertainment by children minding cattle. Its leading exponent for over five decades is the veteran performer Rakotofra. Other important traditional instruments include the 'jejy voatavo' (a stringed instrument with a calabash resonator) and the 'lokang bara' (a three-stringed fiddle).

While some instruments have been incorporated into popular urban music, as throughout Africa, Malagasy music also incorporated non-traditional instruments introduced by the French. Out of this mix came, for example, the 'Hira Gasy' of the central highlands. Taking the form of all-day competitive playing, 'Hira Gasy' combines French military drums with trumpets, flutes, clarinets and violins. The subject matter of the vocals is always contemporary while the entire performance is accompanied by dancers and a great deal of audience participation.

Madagascar, befitting such a cosmopolitan country, offers a tremendous diversity of traditional culture, drawing from African, Indonesian, Islamic and European roots. The recent opening up of the economy will certainly put some of these traditions at risk.

For either the traditional or the modern music of Madagascar it is difficult to see beyond the excellent albums released by Globestyle. The three Ocora albums are also excellent introductions to Malagasy traditional music. Recorded in 1963, they feature various traditional instruments including flutes, drums and xylophones, and, a more recent introduction, the accordion. In 1989 a team of German ethnomusicologists visited the island, releasing two fine CD collections in 1990. Volume 2 deals with the music of the south in a generous 64-minute collection covering a variety of traditional and neo-traditional styles.

Rakotozafy. Performed in a family band featuring his wife on vocals and percussion and his son as a dancer. He died in prison for inadvertently killing his son. One of Madagascar's leading valiha players.

| 1988 | ORBD 028 | Famous Valiha Vol. 4 |

Sana, Mama. Seventy-year-old female valiha star who has never recorded.

Randafison. Virtuoso valiha player, formerly leader of Ny Anstaly – a traditional ensemble. Visited UK in the late 1980s.

| 1990 | PS 65046 | Samuel Randafison and Others: Madagascar: Le Valiha |

Rakotofra. He learned to play the sodina-flute as a child but after his parents died when he was ten he moved to Antananarivo where he worked as a baker during the night while playing for pleasure during the day. In 1947 he played for the French President, Charles de Gaulle, and his star was clearly on the ascendant. In 1967 he played in Algiers and over the next few years also performed in such places as France, Germany, Nigeria and the neighbouring Indian Ocean Islands. In 1986 he visited the UK as part of the group Kalaza.

| 1980s | VID 25012 | The Art of Rakotofra |
| 1988 | ORBD 027 | Flute Master Vol. 3 |

Others

	CLVLX 436	Folklore de Madagascar
1984	OCR 24	Musique Malagache
	OCR 18	Various: Vahalila
	OCR	Various: Airs à Danser
1986	ORBD 012	Madagasikara Vol. 1
1991	FUEC 706	Madagaskar 2: Music of the South (CD)

MODERN MUSIC

Modern Malagasy music grew from several roots, including tradition, imported French styles and instruments and a wide variety of pan-African influences such as kwela and rumba. Popular, indigenous styles include the 'watsa watsa', the 'basesa' and the 'salegy'. In common with other Indian Ocean Islands, the 'sega' is also widely enjoyed. During the 1970s a lot of Malagasy music was recorded (mainly on 7" singles) at the country's two 8-track studios – one of them government-owned. However, by the late 1980s original music had largely disappeared from the market as the bootleg cassette took over. Very, very little local music was legitimately available as the Malagasy youth turned to western pop music, now readily accessible following the opening up of the economy in 1988. The best introductions to the modern music of Madagascar are the 1986 Globestyle compilation and the 1990 German compilation featuring Sammy, Jean Emilien, Kalaza, Rossy and an example of 'Hira Gasy'.

1986	ORBD 013	Current Popular Music
1990	FUEC 704	Madagascar Vol. 1: Music in Antananarivo (CD)
	MA 90 006	Various: Megamix

Malagasy. Afro-jazz fusion band who made a considerable impact in the 1970s. The line-up comprised Sylvain Marc – multi-instrumentalist; Ramolison – drums; Del Rabenja – sax and valiha; Ange Japhet – bass; Gerard Rakotoarivonyy – bass; and Jel Gilson – ondioline. Based in Paris in the early 1970s.

1971	LD 33908	Malagasy
1973	PALM 5	At Newport-Paris
	PALM 4	Madagascar Now
	PAL 056	Frank Ramolison: Fiesta in Drums (Drummer with Malagasy, playing here with C. Vandor – jazz drummer)

Mahaleo. Major stars of the 1970s playing both American styles and, later, roots Malagasy incorporating traditional instruments. Founded by Dama Zafimahaleo, they were at one stage known as the Beatles of Madagascar. Big hits included 'Voasary' and 'Lendrema'. Now in semi-retirement, the 1991 recording was made in Germany during the 1980s.

1977	LPP 187	Mahaleo
1990	SF 90 001	Henri Ratsimbazafy/ Mahaleo
1991	WDR 39914	En Concert

Mandour. New group of the late 1980s experimenting with an electric valiha.

Emilien, Jean. Kabosy player who made a conscious effort to rediscover his roots and to blend traditional songs with popular dance music. He travelled widely around the island learning new material and disappeared for so long that people thought him dead. He resurfaced in 1988 to sign a deal with a French company but nothing was heard from them again and he is still waiting for the big chance. He offers us three songs on FUEC 704.

Rossy (b. Paul Bert Rahasimanana, Antananarivo). Singer and founder of the group of the same name and one of the most popular 'kabosy' groups on the island. As a youth he enjoyed the new-found freedom of the post-1972 revolution, participating in street corner 'soava' sessions – a new combination of traditional instruments and highly politicised lyrics. In 1975 he decided to form his own band, adding drums to the basic 'soava' style of hand-clapping and singing. However, he was against the way in which French military drums had 'colonised' Malagasy music (see the 'Hira Gasy') and looked instead to African percussion. In time, he himself picked up the accordion and, along with Mahaleo, introduced the 'kabosy' or Malagasy guitar to a modern electric line-up. He is now well known around the island with a growing reputation overseas following tours of West and East Germany. The band own their own equipment and have released a number of records, including three from Germany.

1983	PL 528	Nehmt Die Kabossy
1990	MA 89 001	Mitapolaka
1991	CEL 66856	Double Duree

Jaojoby, Eusabe. Popular 'salegy' pop band with enormous potential but nowhere to go.

Ratsimbafasy, Henri

| 1979 | LPP 196 | Madagaskar: Le Lamba Blanc |

Tarika Sammy. City-based trio in folk tradition, playing all the main traditional instruments. Enjoyed some publicity on British radio and featured on two compilation albums. They argue that it is extremely difficult to make a living from traditional music and are now looking to augment their sound with more modern equipment.

Majunga, Freddy de. A gifted musician whose inclusion here may surprise those who considered him to be either Zaïrean or Antillean. Freddy's star rose rapidly in the late 1980s as he emerged as a studio musician of the highest order. By 1989 he had cut his first solo album but it was the 1990 recording which brought him to a wider dance-floor public. Now Paris-based.

| 1988 | | Les Deux 'A's (With Master Congo) |
| 1989 | JIP 018 | I Kembe |

| 1990 | | Soudiaba |
| 1991 | LP 51287 | La Fête au Village |

Religious

| 1980 | MAV 3041 | Ankalazo Ny Tompo: Religiöse Lieder Aus Madagaskar |

Various

1970s	PALM 1	A Madagascar
1990	MA 90 001	Ejema: No Problemes
	MA 90003	Ramoroson Wilson: Chansons Eternelles Vol. 2
	MA 90 004	Feon'ala: Batrelaka
	MA 90 005	Poopy: Andao Handihy

THE COMOROS

(ECONOMY AND SOCIETY. Pop.: 470,000. Area: 2,236 sq. km. Capital: Moroni. Independence: UDI from France 1975. Currency: Comoros franc.)

Comprising four small islands approximately 300 km east of Mozambique, the Federal Islamic Republic of the Comoros, as it is now officially known, was settled by Malayo-Polynesian sailors in the fifth century AD. Over the next ten centuries the islands were steadily settled by Africans and Arabs, becoming a centre of the Indian Ocean slave and spice trade. Between the tenth and fifteenth centuries they became a refuge for Shirazi settlers from the Persian Gulf area, and although they were able to establish a number of rather precarious sultanates, their internal divisions and rivalry made French conquest a simple task in the mid-nineteenth century. By then, the islands had been Islamic for over ten centuries, although culturally they had more in common with the East African Swahili coast; even today the lingua franca is a local variant of Kiswahili.

The French ruled the islands from Madagascar and Reunion with an extremely stern form of colonial absolutism: local opposition was suppressed, newspapers banned and politics made illegal. By the 1960s the Comoros had become one of the most isolated countries in the world. Then in 1968 the islands were rocked by a series of riots and strikes, and although ruthlessly suppressed, the French eventually conceded the right to form political parties. Dozens of parties then appeared, divided evenly between those in favour of independence and those in favour of retaining close ties with France. The early 1970s were marked by more political unrest, and when a referendum was held on the issue of independence, over 95 per cent voted in favour. In 1975 the Comoros declared unilateral independence under President Abdallah, but in one of the shortest political reigns in Africa he was overthrown within a month by right-wing, pro-French forces. In 1976 a second coup, led by Ali Soilih, resulted in the withdrawal of French aid, and as the economic crisis deepened, the new regime nationalised French property and expelled all French settlers. And so the Comoros revolution was launched, liberating women from the neo-feudal grip of Islam, and, in an era now known as 'Le Période Noire', dismissing all civil servants and burning all government files. The chaos was not helped by the sudden return of 20,000 Comorians from Madagascar, where an outbreak of communal violence had left over a thousand dead. As revolution turned to repression, opposition to the rule of Soilih increased and in 1978 a group of mercenaries led by Bob Denard overthrew Soilih and invited Abdallah to return.

Once again political parties were banned. Relations with France were patched up and Denard and his men assumed the role of presidential guard. Faced with this de facto mercenary state, the opposition tried to unite and launched an unsuccessful coup in 1985. However, it was to be Denard himself who made the next move, seizing power in a highly publicised 1989 coup. This forced the French Army to intervene. Denard left quietly and in relatively free elections President Gohar assumed power. Economically, the Comoros remain precariously balanced between poverty and collapse. Over 60 per cent of the land is held by French settlers, who also dominate the business sector. Comorians rely on subsistence agriculture with copra providing the only export. Per capita income is less than $100 per annum and the Comoros remain one of the poorest countries in the world.

Music from the Comoros

1975	FE 4243	Music of the Comoro Islands
1984	CMD 102	Ali Affandi: Safari Manga
1989	1987	Tropic Island: Wana Zidjana

MAURITIUS

(ECONOMY AND SOCIETY. Pop.: 1.12 million. Area: 2,040 sq. km. Capital: Port Louis. Independence: 1968. Currency: Mauritian rupee.)

Mauritius is located about 500 km east of Madagascar and is made up of one main island and three tiny islands. By the end of the fifteenth century, Arab and Malay sailors had made contact but it was the Dutch who first settled the island in the sixteenth century, importing slaves and exporting ebony. In 1715 the French arrived and massively increased the importation of slaves from Africa and Madagascar. In 1767 the islands came under direct French control until the British conquest in 1810. When slavery was finally abolished the British turned to Indian indentured labour, and by 1860 two-thirds of the population was of Indian descent.

By the twentieth century Mauritius had one of the most diverse populations in the world, reflected in two official languages – French and English, with Creole as lingua franca and 20 per cent of the population speaking Hindi. There is also a large Chinese commercial class, although real economic power remains in the hands of the Franco-Mauritian plutocracy.

The first efforts towards political emancipation appeared from the Indian working class, who, by the 1930s, were organising strikes and demonstrations. Thereafter, the British followed classic colonial policy by suppressing working-class movements and moving towards independence through gradual constitutional change. Independence finally came in 1968 under Dr Ramgoolam, who held power for the next 14 years through a judicious use of coalition politics. Yet the islands remained extremely poor, relying on the export of sugar to France and subject to ferocious Indian Ocean cyclones. Tourism is now the third biggest earner of foreign exchange with over a quarter of a million arrivals by the late 1980s. In 1982 Jugnauth took over from Ramgoolam but by the late 1980s his government had been racked by a number of drug scandals.

Culture in Mauritius

With such a complex ethnic make-up it is not surprising that Mauritian culture displays a similar diversity with annual Muslim, Hindu, Chinese, Tamil and Catholic festivals. In creole society (an Afro-Malagasy mix) the 'sega' continues to hold sway and is thought to have originated in Africa as both a dance and a general word for tunes and melodies. The actual origin is unclear, however, and although there are definite African roots in the music, it appears that the style itself is native to Mauritius, from where it spread to neighbouring islands in the Indian Ocean. The original instrumentation was fairly basic, comprising the 'ravanne' (a drum), the 'triang' (triangle), the 'bobre' (a two-stringed lute), the 'catia-catiac' (shaker) and the 'maravanne' (a box shaker). In time, as creole emerged as the lingua franca of the slaves, lyrics, often of a saucy and provocative nature, were sung exclusively in the language. And as creole spread, so too was sega carried to neighbouring islands, becoming 'the soul and beating heart' of the western Indian Ocean.

By the nineteenth century, sega was widely enjoyed, although it did not stand still and by the end of the century a number of varieties had developed, including 'sega typique', the classical version, 'sega salon', which was danced at home and 'sega hotel', which is self-explanatory. More recently exponents have at-tempted to blend sega with reggae to produce 'seggae', as well with jazz to produce 'sejaz'. But there were also differences between the islands, with Rodrigues, a more isolated island, developing 'sega barre' or 'sega coupe', a more vigorous and Africanised form of 'sega typique'. In Reunion, on the other hand, the sega became more commercialised and cosmopolitan and is only slightly reminiscent of 'sega typique'. In the Seychelles 'sega' is a slower and more restrained dance, apart from the tourist version which retains some of the vibrancy of the original.

Today sega is widely enjoyed as a national style, although it was not always so and the Catholic Church did its best to stamp it out entirely for its suggestive movements and rebellious lyrics. Another obstacle lay in the growing size of the Indian population, who initially opposed sega because of its African origins. However, by the 1950s and 1960s sega was universally acceptable with growing popularity to rival rock and roll. More recently 'segatiers' have introduced the full range of modern, electric instrumentation, although the acoustic, percussive traditions continue to flourish on more informal occasions.

By the 1970s sega was in full flight, encouraged by nationalist sentiment and the onset of the tourist boom. The songs have become shorter and local recordings more sophisticated as segatiers try to crack the international market, almost inevitably through the French connection. Early pioneers in Paris included Gaetan de Rosnay, Maria Sega and Gillas Sala, although it was only during the 1980s, as more French people became aware of Mauritius and overall interest in African music increased, that sega has been able to establish its own cultural space in the French musical universe. Local stars who succeeded in France include Clarel Betsy, Gaetan Valentin, Alain Permal, Cyril Labonne and Johnny Sheridan. Betsy, for example, has released over 20 albums and a dozen cassettes. More usually, however, material is recorded in Mauritius, pressed up in France and re-exported to the islands with impressive local sales of up to 20,000 copies for a popular hit. Little known in Britain, despite the efforts of domiciled Mauritians, sega remains a clearly identifiable and enjoyable African style which does not stand still. Perhaps the future holds the promise of a wider international success.

Frère, P'tit (b. Alphonse Ravaton, late nineteenth century). Widely regarded as the 'father of sega typique', Frère first came to the attention of the wider public in the 1950s with a series of self-composed hits like 'Roseda', 'Anita' and 'Papitou'. But it was not enough to make a living and he worked at many other jobs to support his career as a 'segatier'. Royalties were almost unknown and he made very little from his most famous composition, 'Tamasa'. However, his work was widely respected. He was awarded an MBE from the UK Government and as late as 1975 was still recording for Ocora. As a singer, dancer and

179

master of the accordion, Frère will always be identified as the key figure in the development of sega.

1975	OCR 558601	Sega Ravanne et Sega Tambour

Lebrasse, Serge (b. 1930). 'The Crown Prince of Sega', Lebrasse learned sega styles from Frère, his neighbour. In the early 1950s he started performing on his own, composing several well-known hits such as 'Mamo Mo Le Marnier'. Yet, like Frère, without copyright protection, he found it difficult to make a living professionally until his third commercial recordings broke through. By the early 1960s, however, his music was seriously rivalling imported western pop. Since then he has toured widely, both around the islands and to Europe. In 1969 he was awarded the MBE for services to Mauritian culture, with his children following him into the business.

Claudio. A relative newcomer to the scene, Claudio scored first in 1980 with 'Bhai Aboo'. But his career really took off when he was appointed tourist adviser with overseas tours and gained a reputation for turning anything into a sega. He still plays 'sega hotel' to enthusiastic audiences, but is best known as the exponent of 'sega moderne'.

Babale. Singer/composer who doubles up as a fisherman. His breakthrough came in the 1980s with 'Dife Bengal', which was followed by wider media exposure and the start of a recording career.

Jean-Claude. Son of a segatier, Jean-Claude is currently one of the leading musicians on the islands.

1987	P 5088	Pile Pile
	P 5133	Belle Mer
1989	P 5125	Segas from Mauritius
1990	CDP 5128	Les Meilleurs Segas
1991	P 5147	Pat Pa Toua

Others

1986	P 5104	Meli Melo: Reste Encore
1987	P 5097	Fiesta Mauricienne
1989	P 5124	Mario Armel: Segas from Mauritius
	P 5130	Various: Segas de L'Ile Mauritius
	MCP 5133	Roger Clancy: La Case Andrea (Cass. only)

1990	P 5141	Johnny Sheridan: Bethleem
1991	CDP 5153 (CD)	Payet Marco: Lie de Passion
	P 5153	Marcelino: Dialsa Mauricien

REUNION

(ECONOMY AND SOCIETY. Pop.: 600,000. Area: 2,510 sq. km. Capital: Saint Denis. Independence: Still an Overseas Département of France. Currency: French franc.)

A small, volcanic island 650 km east of Madagascar, Reunion was known to Arab geographers for centuries but was only settled in the seventeenth century by French settlers and African and Malagasy slaves. In 1715 the French introduced coffee as the main cash crop, stepped up the importation of African slaves and turned Reunion into a classic slave society. The English briefly took control (1750–64 and 1810–14), but French power prevailed and in the nineteenth century they turned the island into a sugar colony, looking to India for indentured labour when the supply of slaves from Africa dried up. Always a poor country linked to the ups and downs of the sugar business, Reunion today totters on the brink of permanent impoverishment. Over 70 per cent of the land remains in French hands and with 25 per cent adult unemployment it is no surprise that over 6,000 Reunionnaise migrate annually to France. Facing only sporadic (and low-key) demands for independence, France remains in charge – an embarrassing anachronism in the late twentieth century.

Culture in Reunion

Reunion's population is principally composed of Afro-French creoles with substantial Indian and Chinese minorities. Culture reflects this mix with the ubiquitous 'sega' appearing in many different varieties. In Reunion the sega is danced as a shuffling, shaking polka while the slower and more melancholy 'maloya' developed from nineteenth-century slave traditions. Local instruments include the 'houler' drum and the 'caiamb' – a type of maraca. During the twentieth century accordions and guitars were added to the basic sega sound. The island has always enjoyed a lively music scene with many cassettes and albums available – the latter produced in France.

The most impressive exponents of sega and maloya are Gerard Pillant and Le Groupe Creolie and the 25-strong Entincelles Pannonaise. Other folklore traditions are maintained by groups like Pangar, Lev La Tet and Jeunesse Komela. By the late 1980s Reunion was responding enthusiastically to another brand of Afro-French creole music – zouk from the Antilles, particularly Kassav and Zouk Machine. The music of Reunion is seldom found outside France but a great deal is usually available on various French labels like Piros.

1983	ESP 8411	Marie-Josee et Roger Clancy
1984	DPX 805	Various: Les Tropics de Paris
1985	TP 5087	Various: Dansez Avec
1986	P 1514	J.L. Deny: Marie-Reunion
	CMV 1201	Mimi: Maloreve
1987	P 1515	Harold Nelson: Facteur
	P 8601	Ile de la Reunion: Radio D'Amour
	P 8503	To-Fock: Reunion Maloya
1988	P 1526	Patrick Thirel: Elle est Jolie
	P 1529	Stephanie et Groupe Folklorique
	P 1530	Various: Segas
	P 1531	Michele Admette: The Prince of Sega
1989	P 1532	Guibert Lebon: Cafrine
	P 1534	Max Luaret: Mon Vieux Papa
	P 1537	Harry Payet: Gramoun
	P 1538	Jean Claude Gaspard: Li Bon
	P 1539	Narmine Ducap: Craze Salle Verte
	OS 55004	Ravan: Gramoune
	OS 55005	Les Cuivres de la Reunion
	DS 389407	Joseph Gereone: Made in Reunion
1990	CDP 5123	Various: Compil Créole (CD)
	CDP 5135	Max Lauret: Mon Vieux Papa (CD)
	CDP 5136	Michele Admette: Les Meilleurs Segas (CD)

	P 1546	Guibert Lebon: Boulki-Boulka
1991	CDP 5150	Ziskakan: Bato Fou
	OS 55006	Jozzi: Douleur Mafate
	P 1552	Nadege: United Musics of the South
	OS 70002	Rivages Créoles: Sélection
	P 1554	Various: Compil Tropical
	OS 70003	Ousa Nousava: Ote La Line (CD)

SEYCHELLES

(ECONOMY AND SOCIETY. Pop.: 71,000. Area: 376 sq. km. Capital: Victoria. Independence: 1976. Currency: Seychelles rupee.)

The Seychelles, a scattered group of 92 tiny islands, is situated approximately 1,000 km north of Madagascar. The majority creole population provides the lingua franca although French and English remain the official languages. The islands were first discovered in 1502 but it was not until 1742 that the French started to settle the previously uninhabited territory. In 1810 Britain took control of the islands and for the rest of the nineteenth century they were administered from Mauritius, finally becoming a separate crown colony in 1903. Political development was generally a slow and conservative process, dominated for the first half of the century by the planter class. However, by the 1960s the two key personalities in the island's recent history, Albert Rene of the radical SPUP and James Mancham of the conservative SDP, had arrived on the scene, with independence coming in 1976. Mancham lasted only one year as prime minister until he was replaced in a mini-coup with Rene assuming power. This meant a fundamental change in economic and foreign policy as the Seychelles moved away from the open-door, market economy of Mancham towards a much more radical approach involving a diversification of the economy away from dependence on tourism. Rene also introduced a number of progressive social reforms, although, given over two centuries of colonial rule and a tiny resource base, the islands remain highly dependent on the rest of the world. Then, in 1981, the island's image as a tourist paradise was shattered by a mercenary plot, hatched in South Africa, to overthrow the socialist government of Rene. The attempted invasion was repelled but Rene felt the need to tighten up security and in 1979 he established a one-party state. At the same time, Mancham has not abandoned his plans for a return and as late as 1990 was still lobbying the British parliament for assistance in re-introducing party politics to the Seychelles.

Culture in the Seychelles

The main cultural survivals are the 'sega' and 'moutia' dances. The Seychellois sega is very similar to its Mauritian cousin, while the moutia is an altogether more sombre affair drawing on work chants and prayers. During the 1980s the left-leaning government of Rene decided to give more support to local culture and established a National School of Music and a National Cultural Troupe to promote creole culture and identity. To begin with, overt jingoism marred this otherwise progressive development but by the late 1980s both institutions were throwing up an impressive crop of young singers and composers. At the moment, the most popular star is Patrick Victor, whose records and cassettes sell well on the local market. Other rising stars to watch out for include David Philoe, Raymond Lebon, Camille Jones and Dorothé Hudson. The island also boasts an older tradition kept alive by travelling 'Camtole' bands featuring fiddle, banjo, accordion and drums.

| 1975 | OCR 558554 | Musiques Oubliées des Iles |
| | OCR 558534 | Kamtole des Iles |

PART VI

Southern Africa

36   South Africa by Trevor Herman

A SWAZILAND   B LESOTHO

(ECONOMY AND SOCIETY. Pop.: 36 million. Area: 1,211,037 sq. km. Capital: Pretoria. Independence: White minority rule. Currency: Rand.)

The period opened in September 1984 with yet another round of massive government repression, and the declaration of a state of emergency the following year. Clearly, the efforts of the ANC and the UDF to keep the government under constant pressure were starting to bear fruit. Yet, despite a number of cosmetic changes to the apartheid state, South Africa continued to pursue its policy of destabilising neighbouring states with raids in Lesotho, Botswana and Zambia and covert assistance to UNITA in Angola and RENAMO in Mozambique.

Inside the country the white regime pursued a dual policy of political liberalisation to appease international opinion whilst cracking down hard on internal opposition and introducing a covert policy of dividing the black majority population. Under this policy, support was given to the Inkatha Movement to undermine the support of the ANC, producing a rapid escalation in township violence. At the same time the ruling Nationalist Party, suffering reverses abroad and under pressure from international sanctions, started to dismantle many of the superficial aspects of the apartheid state, a process which led directly to the release of Nelson Mandela in February 1990 and the

unbanning of the ANC. However, while some progress had clearly been made, it became increasingly obvious that not only would it be difficult to dismantle apartheid entirely but that there were many powerful forces who did not want to see it go at all.

At the time of writing, the situation in South Africa remains grim, with over 11,000 dead in the last six years. The ANC has borne the brunt of this orchestrated violence, and although progress has been made, it is by no means an irreversible process. The year 1992 sees the majority black population still without the vote, black education and health care still seriously underfunded and the white population still holding nearly 90 per cent of the land. We can only hope that the progress towards a free, united and democratic South Africa will not be undermined by an all too easy abandonment of international sanctions and the determination of the right wing to sabotage a peaceful settlement.

MODERN MUSIC

During the 1980s African music increased steadily in popularity, establishing a permanent niche in the international scene. And it would be no exaggeration to suggest that contemporary South African music played a central role in this process through the excellent Earthworks compilations, Paul Simon's *Graceland* album and tour with Ladysmith Black Mambazo, the album releases and frequent touring of Mahlathini and the Mahotella Queens, the rise to stardom of Johnny Clegg and Savuka and, more recently, tours by top artists the Soul Brothers and rising star Mzwakhe Mbuli. Finally, reggae star Lucky Dube has struck gold several times, both with wider African audiences and further afield in the USA, Japan and France.

Volume 1 dealt at some length with the early history of South African township music and readers are accordingly referred to that volume for background reading. This volume takes up the story again in 1986 and hopes to highlight some of the central political and musical developments of the last five years.

The unfolding political drama in South Africa provides a violent and uncertain backcloth to recent musical developments. On the one hand, since 1990 musicians have been able to sing freely about liberation without being detained or their albums banned. Many famous exiles have returned home, including Miriam Makeba and Hugh Masekela, while several home-grown stars have become international household names. Yet, despite a few positive political changes which, if they lead to economic improvements, will benefit the black music industry, the overall situation of musicians in South Africa is characterised by many of the problems we have encountered in other African countries. There is a serious lack of suitable venues, whilst limited live shows and time to rehearse undoubtedly hold back the full development of one of the most vibrant and powerful traditions in Africa.

On the other hand, several local stars have triumphed musically despite the problems and we shall look at their stories in the following pages. South Africa enjoys a lively and cosmopolitan music scene with international pop, soul, reggae and rap as popular as local styles. Yet the local styles still flourish and it is these styles and stylists to which we now turn.

This chapter adopts slightly different criteria from the rest of the book when we deal with discography and the issue of availability. The author has, for example, produced a recommended rather than a comprehensive discography. The reasons are simple and arise from the sheer quantity of African music released in South Africa. Secondly, since its stately rise to prominence over the last decade, the modern music of South Africa is now available on a growing list of international labels with good material increasingly licensed to a number of global concerns. This chapter therefore combines a selected listing of recommended albums with a more detailed approach to the labels on which they appear. It is also more strictly concerned with developments since 1986 and, consequently, less attention has been paid to the past than with other countries. For background context and early developments readers are urged to consult Volume 1 as well as several impressive accounts of early musical history. In particular, we recommend the work of Blacking, Coplan, Kerkhoff, Kivnick and Tracey (see Bibliography).

Mahlathini and the Mahotella Queens. During the 1960s, along with their backing musicians, the Makgona Tsohle Band, this group was often referred to as the 'Beatles of South Africa' because of their use of modern instruments and superb harmonies. Their 'mbaqanga' style drew on various roots, including traditional music, American jazz, kwela, marabi and pop, to produce what is today a myriad of styles and idioms. Late 1960s and early 1970s material by the Mahotella Queens, with and without Mahlathini, is featured on the Earthworks release *The Kings and Queens of Township Jive*. During the 1970s Mahlathini split from the Queens and recorded fierce mbaqanga music with his band, Ndlondlo Bashise (a.k.a. The Mahlathini Guitar Band). Some of the finest tracks of that period are to be found on *The Lion of Soweto*, with more classic cuts on the way from Earthworks.

The modern sound of Mahlathini and the Queens was first introduced to the international public on the now-famous 'Indestructible Beat of Soweto' series of LPs. During 1983–5 the group reformed and recorded as a studio band only. But in 1987 they returned to live performances, culminating in extensive overseas tours as well as recording two of their greatest albums, *Thokozile* and *Paris-Soweto*. Both should be considered essential purchases, with their latest offering, *Mbaqanga*, also a worthy contender.

By the early 1990s the group had probably played more international gigs than any other African artistes, although the touring happened almost by accident when they were asked to fill in at short notice for Ladysmith Black Mambazo, who had a prior commitment to Paul Simon. The show took place at Angoulême in France and the band were an immediate hit. From there, further bookings were made and the band started serious touring. Between 1988 and 1991 they played over two dozen shows in the UK, countless dates in France and the rest of Europe, with massive tours of the USA, Japan and Australia. The LP *Thokozile* proved to be the big breakthough, coinciding with early tours and establishing a new benchmark for mbaqanga. Celluloid (France) helped finance the *Paris-Soweto* recording and provided crucial support in establishing a French base for the band. Sympathetic management has also been an important factor in the band's success.

Today, Mahlathini's spectacular deep, rasping vocals and the awesome, sweeping harmonies of the Queens are amongst the most instantly recognisable sounds to have come from Africa. The raw power of his voice has become one of the wonders of the musical world, with his extraordinary ability suddenly to switch on some secret, inner volume control and increase his already loud singing into something approaching a friendly sonic boom. This vocal master is then accompanied by sudden flurries of intense traditionally-inspired dancing, with the Mahotella Queens (Hilda, Nobesuthu and Mildred) dipping and jiving at his side, their unsurpassed harmonies sending shivers down your back and filling any hall with a warm glow. Meanwhile, sparks are flying from Marks Mankwane's guitar, bass runs popping from the hands of Joseph Makwela alongside the drums of Philomon Hamole – and that's without considering the added power and punch of sax and keyboards (see *Indestructible Beat of Soweto*, vols 1–3).

1987   CDEWV 4   Mahlathini: The Lion of Soweto (Earthworks)

1988	CDEWV 6	Mahlathini and the Mahotella Queens: Thokozile (Earthworks)
1988	66829-2	Mahlathini and the Mahotella Queens: Paris-Soweto (Celluloid – France, Polygram – USA)
1990	CDEWV 20	Various: The Kings and Queens of Township Jive (Earthworks)
1991	KA2	Mahlathini and the Mahotella Queens: Mbaqanga (Celluloid – France, KAZ – UK, Polygram – USA)

Soul Brothers. It is not difficult to work out why the Soul Brothers have been the most popular band in South Africa over the last 16 years, both in terms of live shows and record sales. The group is led by David Masondo (lead vocals) and Moses Ngwenya (keyboards). They have developed a distinctive 'mbaqanga' style with swirling Hammond organ through Leslie speakers, riveting, biting guitar by Maxwell Mngadi, deep solid bass, velvet yet forceful vocals by a team of singer-dancers, unstoppable rhythms and the best horn section in modern times, featuring sax-jive maestro Thomas Phale. Superior choreography and the stunning quality of the music combine to produce the devastating grandeur of their live shows, surprising audiences outside South Africa, including those in the UK and on a very successful tour of Australia. The group are currently planning a major international assault for 1992.

Their most important release to date is *Jive Explosion*, featuring many of their most dynamic songs from the mid-1980s, including 'Akabongi', 'Phuma Layikhaya', 'Inhlalayenza' and 'Uthando'. Earlier, spectacular hits are included on the compilation LP *The Kings and Queens of Township Jive*. New, powerful material will be highlighted on the forthcoming *Indestructible Beat of Soweto Vol. 4*. The Soul Brothers are one of the very few bands who run their own record company. The 1990–1 international tour merely whetted the appetite of their numerous fans. Future tours and album releases should confirm their status as one of Africa's great groups. Modern and sophisticated, but still packing a mighty, rootsy punch, they are not to be missed under any circumstances.

1987		Xola (Soul Brothers Records)
1988	CDEWV 8	Jive Explosion (Earthworks)
		Usibali (Soul Brothers Records)
1989		Impimpi (Soul Brothers Records)
		Hluphekile (Soul Brothers Records)

Ladysmith Black Mambazo. Quite simply the best gospel and traditionally-inspired 'a cappella' group in South Africa. They were introduced to a wider world on Paul Simon's *Graceland* tour and album, achieving considerable success with their call-and-response routines and peerless harmonies under the leadership of Joseph Shabalala. Ten-strong, and famous at home for nearly two decades, they toured the world in the wake of *Graceland* and have recently released an excellent series of recordings. Live shows are characterised by moving and dancing in unison, often as a response to a few choice dance-steps or soulful lines from the leader. Essential albums are *Shaka Zulu* and *Inala*. In 1990 Penguin USA published a full account of their story in Helen Kivnick's *Where is the Way?: Song and Struggle in South Africa*.

1986	66819	Inala (Shanachie – USA)
		Phansi Emgodini (Shanachie – USA)
1987	WX 94 925582-2	Shaka Zulu (Warner Brothers)
1990	7599-26125-2	Two Worlds, One Heart (Warner Brothers)

Other notable gospel choirs well worth checking out include Holy Cross Choir, Amadodana Nineveh, Amadodana Ase Wesile and Abarorisi Ba Morena, as well as those titles listed below.

| 1985 | | Izikhova Ezimnqini: Ivangeli Lakudala (Gallo – SA) |
| 1986 | | Holy Spirits Choir: Okholwa Kujesu (Teal – SA) |

Holy Spirits Choir: Kabelo
Ya Ka Entle
(Teal – SA)

Izikhova Ezimnqini:
Khaya Elihle
(Gallo – SA)

1991   King Star Brothers:
Izidumo Zase Ncome
(Tusk – SA)

Dube, Lucky. Lucky began his career as a mbaqanga-pop artist, later changing to reggae, which has now brought him undreamt of fame and fortune in South Africa and beyond. Although he was strongly influenced by the music of Peter Tosh, Bob Marley and Jimmy Cliff, he later developed his own style, adding township musical elements and dance-steps to create something fresh and exciting. He is now the top-selling singer in South Africa and is particularly popular in the USA, France and Japan. He has also won approval for his sound in Jamaica, the home of reggae, playing Reggae Sunsplash in 1991. His main messages remain those of peace and togetherness. There can be no doubting his pan-African appeal and he has now replaced Alpha Blondy at the cutting edge of modern African reggae.

1989	66834	Slave (Celluloid – France, Shanachie – USA)
1990	66872	Prisoner (Celluloid – France, Shanachie – USA)
	LUCKY D6	Captured Live (Double LP, Gallo – SA)

Others

1991   Various (including Dube and his former band, The Slaves): Reggae Strong For Peace (Gallo – SA)

The Slaves: Kneel Down (Gallo – SA)

O'Yaba: Tomorrow Nation (Gallo – SA)

Johnny Clegg and Savuka. Renowned for his traditional dancing and afro-pop music, Johnny Clegg's groups, first Juluka and now Savuka, have played an important role in breaking down racial barriers and helping local black music appeal to a wider audience. In 1988 Clegg's first international release, *Third World Child*, was a runaway success, selling over a million copies and leading to a sold-out tour of France, including nine consecutive nights at the prestigious Zenith in Paris. The album also sold well in the USA and Canada, where audiences were won over by the powerful live shows, and Johnny became one of the first African stars to appear on the Johnny Carson Show. Other countries, including the UK, also enjoyed the live shows but album sales proved disappointing. Subsequent releases showed a smaller township music content and many believe that this led to reduced sales. Johnny Clegg and Savuka still command a loyal following and remain a force to be reckoned with. A return to live shows and a strong new album are promised for 1992.

1987	CD-EMC 3526	Third World Child (EMI)
1988	CD-EMC 3547	Shadow Man (EMI)
1989	CD-EMC 3569	Cruel Crazy Beautiful World (EMI)

Mango Groove. This group is fronted by a female pop vocalist and their light dance music relies on an excellent township-style horn section. Besides pop, the main influences are kwela and marabi (see Volume 1). They recently took their show on a massive national tour, playing stadiums and other large venues, and in 1991 their first LP caused a frisson of excitement outside South Africa.

1989	174356-2	Hellfire (Stern's)
1991		Hometalk (Warner Brothers – USA)

Mbuli, Mzwakhe. Charismatic 'People's Poet', Mzwakhe Mbuli and his intensely swinging township jive band are the newest musical sensation on the South African scene. In 1990–1 he made several highly acclaimed tours to the USA, Canada, Western Europe, Scandinavia and the UK, establishing his name internationally. Back home, Mzwakhe and his band fill stadiums, with his strong commitment to freedom and justice allied with uncompromising lyrics and irresistible music guaranteeing a gripping live performance and frenzied support from audiences. He has captured the hearts and minds of both urban and rural audiences at home and now seems set for much wider international exposure.

His career began almost by chance in 1981 when he recited two of his poems at the funeral of an activist to lift the spirits of his comrades. From then on, many people came to hear his words at political and cultural events. Severely harassed, attacked and frequently detained by the authorities, living underground for two years, Mzwakhe still managed to record two albums for Shifty Records, his voice and lyrics set to rough and ready music. The compositions were powerful but the recording itself was ragged, using a variety of session musicians. *Change is Pain* is the better of the two, although *Unbroken Spirit* also contains important messages. Eventually Mzwakhe quit Shifty to take full control over his future musical direction.

Then, in 1989, Mzwakhe decided to a create a new, permanent band to integrate fully his singing, chanting and recital with driving dance music. Also, with his own band, he could now rehearse them to the required standard of performance. The power and quality of the new, full-time band marks a quantum leap forward and bears little resemblance to what came before. The new sound is a unique blend of South African music, heavily influenced by marabi, jazz, kwela and mbaqanga. In 1990, Rick Glanvill of the *Guardian* described his show in the following terms: 'Seeing him perform is like momentarily tapping into the national grid, although the shock is a purely cultural and pleasurable one.'

Nearly seven feet tall, Mzwakhe dominates live shows with his sheer presence and smoky, atmospheric vocals. Supported by his female back-up vocalist, he unleashes the finest traditionally-inspired dancing ever witnessed. The energy, intensity and style simply has to be seen to be believed. The band is driven by stunning guitar, non-stop chords, riffs and volcanic eruptions, with keyboard washes and tight three-part harmonies. The rhythm section includes explosive but subtle drumming and deep, solid bass with added spice in the sax parts. Performances build to a massive climax as the group moves to full overdrive, described by Mzwakhe as 'total fireworks'.

In June 1991 this magic was captured on tape during Mzwakhe's first big-budget recording. The latest album, *Resistance is Defence*, appeared on the Earthworks label in early 1992. Lyrically, the new material is as controversial as ever, with songs tackling real problems in contemporary South Africa. 'Uyeyeni' (how long must you people suffer before you join the struggle for justice), 'Tshipfinga' (remember those who gave their lives for freedom) and, crucially, 'Land Deal' all deal directly with present and future issues. The entire album is powerful, relevant and musically stunning.

1988	ROUND 4024	Change is Pain (Pirhana – Germany, Rounder – USA)

1989		Unbroken Spirit (Shifty – SA)
1992	CDEWV 25	Resistance is Defence (Earthworks)

Fassie, Brenda. Brenda is currently the top female star in South Africa. Her shows pack a real punch, with the music varying from dynamic, soulful, township disco to rather less appealing bubblegum froth. Songs like 'Good Black Woman', 'Promise', 'Too Late For Mama' and 'Black President' will satisfy most audiences. Her 1990 mini-international tour dispelled any doubts about her ability to deliver on stage what she delivers on record. Her biggest rival remains Yvonne Chaka Chaka, who has also enjoyed considerable success, touring throughout Central, Southern and West Africa. Check out her song 'I Cry for Freedom'.

1989		Brenda Fassie: Too Late For Mama (CCP/EMI)
1990		Brenda Fassie: Black President (CCP/EMI)
		Yvonne Chaka Chaka: I Cry for Freedom (Dephon/Teal)

African Jazz Pioneers. Led by veteran marabi star Ntemi Piliso on sax, the band started in the 1980s to recreate the sounds and live fun of 1950s and 1960s South African jazz. With a great horn section, warm riffing and a modern, forceful rhythm, the group is comprised of musicians drawn from the classic marabi era as well as new converts to the style. A favourite club band who always swing hard.

1990	KAZ 14	African Jazz Pioneers (KAZ – UK, Celluloid – France)

Modern-traditional

In recent years fewer traditional albums have been released, and the tendency for introducing synthesisers to traditional music can often spoil a fine, rootsy recording. The following artistes are well worth further investigation.

Elimhlophe, Ihashi. Spine-tingling vocals, heavy stomping beat, electrifying zulu-guitar music. Also featured on *The Indestructible Beat of Soweto Vol. 4.*

1986		Intandane (Soul Brothers Records)

1989   Uqanduqandu (Soul
                               Brothers Records)

Khanyile, Noise. Noise's gigs guarantee a good
time. Noise is renowned for his traditional violin
playing but he can also turn out a powerful
zulu-guitar sound. Performances include the usual
line-up of instruments plus female support singers
and dancers.

| 1988 | CDORB 045 | Art of Noise (Globestyle – UK) |
| 1989 | | Itwasa Lika Puzushukela Namagugu Akwazulu (Tusk – SA) |

Other recommended traditional Zulu musicians include Uthwalofu, Moses Mchunu and Sipho Mchunu.
Obed Ngobeni is one of the foremost Shangaan disco
artists, with gruff vocals, special guitar tunings and a
crashing beat. Also listen to the great song 'Madyisa
Mbitsi' by J.J. Chauke and the Tiyimeleni Young Sisters
on the *Freedom Fire* compilation. Modern Sotho
traditional music remains very basic with rough,
raw-voiced vocals, a plodding beat and piano accordion highlighting this attractive sound. The best group
probably remain Tau Ea Linare. Recommended recordings are listed below with a more comprehensive
introduction and discography in Volume 1.

1988		Inkunzi Emdaka: Buya Mama (Teal – SA)
1989	SH 64003	Oben Ngobeni: My Wife Bought A Taxi (Shanachie – USA)
	QBH 1084	Thomas Chauke & The Shinyori Sisters: Shimatsatsa No. 9/ Humelele No. 2 (Tusk – SA)
1990		Sipho Mchunu: Umhlaba Uzoboya (Tusk/Third Ear Music)

Classic sounds

Gallo's excellent African Classic series is increasingly
allowing people to hear, once again, some of the most
interesting sounds from the 1950s and 1960s, long since
deleted but now available again. For your delectation
and delight, we can recommend The Jazz Epistles,
South Africa's first jazz band, including Kippie

Moeketsi (sax), Hugh Masekela (trumpet), Jonas
Gwanga (trombone), Dollar Brand (piano), Johnny
Gertze (bass) and Makaya Ntshako (drums). The
album was first released in 1962. Barney Rachabane
plays a pivotal role on the album *Tribute to Zacks Nkosi*,
one of the early stars to bridge the gap between marabi
jazz and sax jive music. The two volumes of *Township
Swing Jazz* from the 1950s include such artistes as the
Skylarks (featuring Miriam Makeba), the Father
Huddleston Band (with Hugh Masekela), the Jazz
Dazzlers (with Kippie Moeketsi), the Elite Swingsters
and many other groups. The thrilling pennywhistle
sounds of Spokes Mashiyane can be found on the
excellent *King Kwela* album.

Trojan, the reggae label, have recently started
re-releasing sets of 1960s and 1970s sax and accordion
jive. It is probably best to start with *Township* which has
the widest selection of music. The *Drum* album also
contains a great selection of cuts.

1990	66892-2	The Jazz Epistles: Jazz Epistle Verse 1 (Celluloid – France)
		Various: A Tribute to Zacks Nkosi (Celluloid – France)
	66893	Various: Township Swing Jazz Vol. 1 (Celluloid – France)
	66894	Various: Township Swing Jazz Vol. 2 (Celluloid – France)
	66891-2	Spokes Mashiyane: King Kwela (Celluloid – France)
	66890-24	Various: King Kong, the Musical
	TWLP 002	Various: Bringing It Down (Trojan)
	TWLP 003	Various: Transkei Special (Trojan)
	TWLP 004	Various: Township (Trojan)
		Various: Drum – South African Jazz Jive (1954–60), (Monsun/Line – Germany)

Mbaqanga-fusion

Steve, Kekana. A singer's singer, Steve is one of the country's favourite vocalists.

1990	Izifungo (CCP/EMI)

Sello 'Chicco' Twala. A top producer as well as township-disco star. His live shows often feature up to twenty on stage.

1990	Papa Stop The War (Dephon/Teal)
1991	Nomari (Dephon/Teal)

Ngema, Mbongeni. One of South Africa's top playwrights as well as a gifted musician. His musicals include *Asinamali* and *Sarafina*. His smash hit 'Stimela Sase Zola' appears on *The Indestructible Beat of Soweto Vol. 4*.

1985		Stimela Sase Zola
		Sarafina (Mango)
1988	CCD 9811	Time To Unite (Mango)

Philip Tabane and Malombo. Veteran star featured on two Earthworks samplers as well as several solo outings.

1988	BIG 002	Malombo (Kijima)
1989	979 225-2	UNH (Nonesuch)

Tananas. Club favourites with their weird and wonderful sound – amplified acoustic guitar, bass and explosive drumming. A powerful fusion trio mixing jive and jazz.

	Tananas (Celluloid – France)
66880	Spiral (Celluloid – France)

Mabuse, Sipho. Late 1980s star, famous for his hits 'Jive Soweto' and 'Ti Nyanga'.

1987	CDV 2425	Sipho Mabuse (Virgin)
1988	V 2582	Chant of the Marching (Virgin)

Stimela. A popular funk-type group formerly led by singer/guitarist Ray Phiri. Ray has recently been working on his own material, with a new album due for release in 1992. In the meantime, he is probably best known as a key-collaborator on *Graceland*.

1991	Siyaya (Gallo)

Amadodana Ahlangene. The album recommended features the last recorded vocals of Sipho Madondo, former lead singer with Amaswazi Emvelo and also rhythm guitarist with the Makgona Tsohle Band. He died from an asthma attack in 1990.

1990	Khulumani Khulumani (Gallo)

Sakhile. Fusion band which includes top session stars like Sipho Gumede (bass) and Khaya Mahlangu (sax).

1991	Africa Echoes: Phambili (Kaz)

Big Voice Jack (b. Aaron Lerole). This is a new recording from one of the top 1960s 'groaners'.

1991	Groovin (Umkhonto/RPM)

Khumalo, Bakithi. Bass player from the *Graceland* sessions.

1988	Step on the Bass Line (CCP/EMI)

Others

1987	ROUND 11549	Various: Homeland (Rounder – USA)
1988	SH 43051	Various: The Heartbeat of Soweto (Shanachie – USA)
1990	66847-2	Various: Zulu Hits (Celluloid – France)
	66867-2	Various: Soweto Megamix (Celluloid – France)
		Prophets of the City: Our World (Ku-Shu-Shu/Teal)
	BIG 007	Various: Hi-Jivin (Kijima)

Local jazz and the return of the exiles

The welcome return to South Africa in 1990 of Hugh Masekela, Miriam Makeba and Abdullah Ibrahim (Dollar Brand) should certainly help enliven the local jazz and jazz-influenced scene; yet another piece of the political and musical jigsaw slowly fitting into place. Top local musicians include Barney Rachabane, Winston Mankunku Ngozi, Basil 'Mannenberg' Coetzee, Ezra Ngcukana, McCoy Mrubata, Duke Makasi, Robbie Jansen, Victor Ntoni and Ratau Mike Makhalemele.

Ibrahim, Abdullah (a.k.a. Dollar Brand). His 1988 *Mindif* album was used as the soundtrack for the French film *Chocolat*. *African River* followed in 1989 and his latest work, *Mantra Mode*, was recorded and released in South Africa in 1991. Kaz Records in the UK has also re-released a superb series of earlier material on budget-priced CD, vinyl and cassette. They are an excellent place to open a Dollar account. Abdullah feels intensely about his music, still experimenting and trying different combinations of musicians on his recordings. He now hopes to establish a music foundation to assist young musicians.

1988	ENJA 5073-50	Mindif (Enja)
	KAZ 102	African Sun (Kaz)
	KAZ 103	Tintinyana
	KAZ 104	Blues For a Hip King (Kaz)
	KAZ 108	African Horns (Kaz)
	KAZ 101	Voice of Africa (Kaz)
1989	ENJA 6018-2	African River (Enja)
1991		Mantra Mode (African Echoes/Sun)

Masekela, Hugh. In 1991 Hugh toured South Africa for the first time in thirty years. A brilliant instrumentalist, his last two albums were *Tomorrow* and *Uptownship*. His music has always defied easy categorisation as he mixes jazz, marabi, mbaqanga, pop and a variety of other African styles with his own idiosyncratic sound. He became a powerful part of the *Graceland* extravaganza, and, more recently, has played week-long sessions of hard-blowing music in London's clubland. In 1988 he took part in the Wembley concert to celebrate Mandela's birthday, joining Miriam Makeba on stage. Both have recently returned home to South Africa. Hugh Masekela remains one of Africa's true mega-stars, yet, by changing labels so often, his back-catalogue is notoriously difficult to track down.

1985	RCAL 6015	Makeba & Belafonte: Songs for Africa (RCA – US)
1987	254573-2	Hugh Masekela: Tomorrow (WEA)
1988	925673	Miriam Makeba: Sangoma (Warner)
1990	PD 83070	Hugh Masekela: Uptownship (WEA)
1991	849 313	Miriam Makeba: Eyes on Tomorrow (Polygram – Italy)

Others

1986		Winston Mankunku: Jika (Avan-Guard – Australia)
1987	J 673	Basil Coetzee: Sabenza (Nonesuch)
1989		Barney Rachabane: Barney's Way (Jive – SA)
		Ezra Ngcukana (Jive – SA)
		Robbie Jansen: Vastrap Island (Sea/Tusk – USA)
1990		Ratau Mike Makhalemele: Thabang (WEA – USA, Tusk – SA)

Unfortunately, Dudu Pukwana, Chris Macgregor and Johnny Dyani, stalwarts of the exiled South African London jazz scene during the 1960s, 1970s and 1980s, did not live to return to a freer South Africa. May they rest in peace.

Conclusion

The most important musical events abroad in support of a free South Africa were organised by Artists Against Apartheid. Wembley Stadium in London was the setting for two massive internationally-televised concerts. First, in 1988, dozens of concerned musicians donated their performances to celebrate Mandela's 70th birthday while he still languished in prison. The show was also able to draw attention to the horrors of apartheid. Then, in 1990, after 27 years in prison, Mandela was released to massive international acclaim and was able to be a guest at a second Wembley show to celebrate his release, while once again bringing the situation in South Africa to the world's attention. Jerry Dammers and Little Steven were thus finally able to perform in front of the man whose cause they had championed for so long.

Despite serious difficulties and setbacks, the political situation in South Africa still looks towards a much brighter future. Continuing international support for further progress towards full democracy remains vital. The international success of so many talented South African musicians is one important way of keeping South Africa in the forefront of the global conscience.

Newcomers to the wonderful variety and vitality of modern South African music can sometimes be bewildered by the profusion of styles and stars. Amongst the top stars, Makeba, Masekela, Ibrahaim and Mahlathini and the Queens are already top-drawer international attractions, capable of filling concert halls anywhere in the world. More recently they have been joined by Johnny Clegg, Soul Brothers and Lucky Dube. Many more stars are ready to join this élite list and, as we argued in Volume 1, the ultimate and complete arrival of South Arica on the global music stage will depend on the resolution of one of the most difficult yet straightforward problems in Africa. We can recommend most highly the records listed below for a solid and exciting introduction to the best South African music of the last decade.

1987	CDEWV 1	Various: Thunder Before Dawn, Indestructible Beat of Soweto Vol. 2 (Earthworks)
1989	CDEWV 14	Various: The Indestructible Beat of Soweto (Earthworks – world, except Shanachie – USA)
1990	CDEWV 17	Various: Freedom Fire, Indestructible Beat of Soweto Vol. 3 (Earthworks)

37 Zimbabwe

(ECONOMY AND SOCIETY. Pop.: 10 million. Area: 389,700 sq. km. Capital: Harare. Independence: 1980. Currency: Zimbabwean dollar.)

Zimbabwe, a landlocked high plateau in Southern Africa, is peopled by various Shona groups (80 per cent) and the Ndebele (19 per cent) as well as a minority white population and various migrants from neighbouring countries. The Shona first moved into the area in the ninth and tenth centuries, quickly overcoming various indigenous groups and establishing the foundations of the Mwene Mutapa and Rozwi kingdoms, which were to survive until the nineteenth century. However, Portuguese slave traders were active in the area from the seventeenth century and seriously weakened the power of these kingdoms. The Ndebele, for their part, moved into the area in the early nineteenth century as part of the great Zulu 'Mfecane' or disruption.

Towards the end of the nineteenth century, British mining companies began to move in from the south and in 1890 an armed column invaded the area and established a new capital at Salisbury (now Harare). In 1893 the Ndebele were crushed by British forces, but when they rose up again in 1896 in the first war of liberation (Chimurenga) they allied with the Shona,

only to be brutally suppressed once again. The white community swelled rapidly and in 1923 was able to establish a self-governing colony with the British supposedly looking after African interests. This, however, was not to be the case, and after seizing all the best land the white community proceeded to run the country for their own interests with scarcely a word of rebuke from Britain, the ostensible colonial power. In 1953 the white regime established the Central African Federation against African wishes, and when the Federation collapsed in 1964 (and with both Zambia and Malawi moving rapidly to black majority rule) Southern Rhodesia unilaterally decided to declare independence, setting the scene for neo-apartheid policies, international isolation and a bitter civil war between black and white. The black nationalists split into two parties – ZAPU, led by Joshua Nkomo, and ZANU, led by Robert Mugabe. The war intensified towards the end of the 1970s, and after the failure of the white regime to establish Bishop Muzorewa as a puppet ruler, all parties came together at the Lancaster House talks in London, arranged a ceasefire and set a date for black majority rule and legal independence.

Independence, under Robert Mugabe, was duly proclaimed in April 1980 and the new government set about trying to heal the bitterness of a century of exploitation and ten years of armed conflict. The economy, already one of the most highly developed in Africa, underwent an immediate recovery as Mugabe tempered his Marxist rhetoric with pragmatic policies and cashed in on the boom in mineral prices. A programme of land reform was also launched, while, by the end of the decade, Zimbabwe was flirting with privatisation, a reduction in state controls and increased direct foreign investment. In political terms, Mugabe achieved a great deal in unifying the country, reassuring the white community while dealing fairly harshly with dissident Ndebele factions. By 1990, as the rest of Africa moved towards multi-partyism, Mugabe was declaring his intention to establish a one-party state.

TRADITIONAL MUSIC

The traditional music of Zimbabwe is almost always associated with the mbira. Once called the 'Soul of the Shona', this instrument comprises metal keys, numbering from eight to well over fifty, mounted on a wooden frame with an accompanying resonator. However, while the mbira is central to the Shona, other traditional instruments continue to meet both the recreational and ritual demands of modern society. These would include the 'hosho' – a rattle equivalent to the western maracas; the marimba (a xylophone); the 'nyanga', or horn; the 'chipendani', or one-string fiddle; the 'madare', or ankle bells; and of course the 'ngoma', or drums. Although the use of these instruments was discouraged during the years of settler government, by the 1980s they had all found modern exponents and were commonplace in urban pop music. Very little traditional music is available on LP either inside or outside Zimbabwe, although several mbira recordings can occasionally be tracked down. However, the traditions have not disappeared but have instead been incorporated into modern dance music in a conscious effort to revive the Zimbabwean past and retain continuity with pre-colonial life. Of course, they also maintain an independent existence in the rural areas, where they remain central to cultural life.

Chiweshe, Stella (a.k.a. Rambisai, Shona). Stella has been a major innovator in the mbira tradition for well over a decade. As a child she challenged men's traditional dominance in this tradition, overcame their hostility and by the time of independence in 1980 was performing at both public functions and private occasions. She is an established star both at home and in Europe, where she toured on several occasions in the 1980s. In a sense Stella has been able to avoid many of the problems facing women in the Zimbabwe music business by settling in Germany with her husband. For despite her talent and success there are still traditional ceremonies from which she is excluded.

In 1989 Stella appeared on the highly acclaimed TV series 'Under African Skies' and had an unlikely club hit with 'Ndizvozvo'. Backed by her band, the Earthquake, Stella began to make a major international impact towards the end of the decade. Stella is also a spirit medium, working through the mbira to evoke the spirits of the ancestors. This can involve playing for several days to facilitate spirit possession. The mbira is a sacred instrument to the Shona and in the decade since independence the mbira tradition has re-emerged as a powerful musical force in Zimbabwe – either directly through the performances of stars like Stella or as a stylistic influence on 'jit'-style guitar playing. As one reviewer of *Ambuya* exclaimed, 'If this tradition got any more alive, it would probably explode!' Early in 1991 Stella released yet another roots rocker on the unsuspecting public in the form of *Chisa*. Combining her own mbira skills with thumping rhythms and some cute marimba, the album provides an excellent showcase of Stella's exhilarating vocals. Nicknamed 'Rambisai', Stella enjoyed widespread radio coverage in 1989 and appeared on the CSA female compilation album of 1989.

1988	ORB 029	Ambuya
1989	FEZ 003	Ndizvozvo (45 r.p.m. mini-LP)
	CSLP 5003	Women of Africa Vol. 1
1991	PIR 27	Chisi

Maraive, Dumi Abraham. Mbira player accompanied by wife and daughter. He has developed a new mbira style called Nyunga Nyunga Mbira.

| 1985 | ZML 1027 | Tichazomuona |

Mpidzi, Torera. Gifted mbira player featured on the soundtrack of the Biko movie *Cry Freedom*.

Mujuru, Ephat. Zimbabwe mbira star who led the post-independence mbira revival with his backing group, Spirit of the People. In 1989 he re-released his classic LP *Mbira Music* while in 1991 Lyrichord dug into their extensive vaults to re-issue his *Rhythms of Life* on compact disc.

1982	ZML 1003	Mbira Music
1984	ZML 1013	Mbavaira
1986	ZML 1033	Mutumukuru
1991	LYRCD 7407	Rhythms of Life

MODERN MUSIC

During the late 1980s the popular music of Zimbabwe enjoyed an extremely high profile in the west. From a slow start, Mapfumo made the early running, introducing his own brand of 'Chimurenga' to European and American audiences. By the middle of the decade the Bhundu Boys were everybody's favourite live band while The Real Sounds, John Chibadura, Four Brothers, Marxist Brothers and Stella Chiweshe consolidated the international appeal with excellent albums and regular touring.

Zimbabwean music combined a number of appealing features. These included political militancy, which appealed to white liberal sentiment everywhere; dance-floor acceptability, which made even the most unlikely traditional musicians into disco stars; an easy linguistic accessibility for the pop press; imaginative and sympathetic western record companies; but, above all, hard work, and an accessible guitar and vocal style now known as jit-jive. The Bhundu Boys remain the world's best known exponents of 'jit-jive', initially brought to Zimbabwe by soldiers returning home from exile in Tanzania. 'It was faster, more urgent – a kind of East African rumba which kept people dancing all night long because of its infectious beat.' In time it was combined with traditional mbira melodies to provide its distinctive sound.

Earthworks, CSA and, almost inevitably, Serengeti pioneered the western commercial response to the high quality music flooding out of the newly independent country, aided and abetted by UK radio DJs (Gillet, Kershaw and Peel) who went overboard in their praise for the jit-jive style of the Bhundu Boys, Four Brothers and the Marxist Brothers. Influential John Peel eventually described Zimbabwe as the source of the most sublime music in the world.

Press and TV coverage followed with Zimbabwe musicians featuring in several acclaimed TV documentaries as journalists flocked to Harare praising bands, beers and business. By the early 1990s Zimbabwean music was firmly established as one of the most commercial sounds in Africa. Of course, this should not give the impression that commercial success depends on western support, but there can be no doubt that in the late 1980s western press and media threw their not inconsiderable weight behind the music of Zimbabwe.

In Volume 1 of Stern's Guide the contemporary music of Zimbabwe received a fairly perfunctory treatment. This was because Fred Zindi had just published the excellent *Roots Rocking in Zimbabwe* (Mambo Press, Harare, 1985 – new edition 1990) and there was no need to duplicate the information contained therein. This is still the case and anyone interested in the Zimbabwe pop scene should consult Zindi's book – a model for research into contemporary African music. However, given the widespread popularity of Zimbabwean music, it would be a grave injustice to the many marvellous performers in Zimbabwe not to include a longer chapter on that country.

If Volume 1 provided a summary of the development of modern Zimbabwean music and Zindi's book provides a more detailed story (both should be referred to), a more recent account comes from Caleb Dube and fills in a few of the gaps from the first half of this century. Dube first discusses the development of 'township music' between the 1920s and 1960s as a combination of indigenous African and western popular music and a continuation of pre-colonial oral traditions. The music grew through struggle. 'While whites entertained themselves playing golf and dancing, blacks were enjoying their township music.' Other influences included the wider exposure to western pop music and the dissemination of music by the Central African Broadcasting Services based in Lusaka, Zambia. Specifically African styles which all enjoyed periods of popularity included marabi, tsabatsaba, kwela, jazz and rumba. Out of this kaleidoscope, fuelled by a desire to create a specifically Zimbabwean musical idiom, eventually came the sounds we now identify as Zimbabwean. A good account of the 1940s to the 1960s comes from Cecilia Makwenda (forthcoming), who argues persuasively that the recent popular music of Zimbabwe is best regarded as belonging to a 'recent tradition'.

Many musicians contributed to the evolution of the modern sound, including August Musarurwa (composer of *Skokiaan*), George Sibanda (a Bulawayo-based C & W star) and other guitarists like John White, Manyanyatha, Sabelo Mathe and Josiah Madebe. During the 1930s and 1940s these stars performed at various social functions, occasionally playing for money but mainly fulfilling the role of entertainer. Others active in the 1940s and 1950s were the Bantu Actors, led by Kenneth Mattaka, the Epworth Theatrical Strutters, Ali Vintuale, Dorothy Masuka, De Black Evening Follies, the Hilltones, the Crazy Kids, Pinetops Band, the Broadway Boogies, Milton Brothers, Golden Rhythm Crooners, the Cool Four, Faith Dauti, City Slickers, Amon Josamu, City Quads, Arthur Nxahe and the Harare Mambos. Influenced by various other African styles but above all by black American music, these early stars were forced to perfect vocal harmonies while performing on sub-standard equipment. Very little of this generation of music has survived on disc.

Mattaka, Kenneth, and the Bantu Actors. Magician, actor, singer, who performed with his family as a black music pioneer. The Bantu Actors helped train many other later stars including De Black Evening Follies who later toured Northern Rhodesia.

Dauti, Faith (a.k.a. 'Short-Gun-Boogie'). Pioneering female star who was extremely popular with the song 'Hama Nevabereki Huyayi' and who proved that a woman could perform on stage and still be a good mother – a breakthrough against the widespread sentiment that women should not go on the stage. Other important early female stars were Vic Chingati, a nurse turned music entrepreneur, Sylvia Sondo, Linna Mattaka, Mabel Mbingwa, Margaret Pazarangu, Tabeth Kapuya and Joyce Ndoro.

Sibanda, George. Popular guitarist of the 1940s in the 'ukuvamba' style. Sibanda is also credited with introducing the steel guitar sound. Along with Josaya Hadebe (subject of a University of Zimbabwe publication), George died penniless, having sold composer's rights for a flat fee.

Masuka, Dorothy. One of the few women artistes to emerge from the Zimbabwe music scene, Dorothy has been around for several decades. Although born in Bulawayo, Dotty cut her teeth further south, moving to South Africa in the 1950s where she sang with the likes of Makeba, Masekela and Letta Mbula. In 1989 she performed several shows with the Golden Rhythm Crooners in Harare and arrived in the UK to record with Fred Zindi and Clifford Mataya, two excellent musicians who double up as author, producer and A & R man respectively. Dorothy Masuka, the 'Queen of Zimbabwe Blues and Jazz', was reckoned to be even more popular than local stars during the 1940s in Sophiatown, South Africa.

1988	STARPLATE 001	Ingalo
1989	CSLP 5003	Women of Africa Vol. 1
1991	MLPS 1074	Pata Pata (CD)

Harare Mambos. Formed by Green Jangano (b. 1930s). Veterans of the Zimbabwe music scene, the Harare Mambos have survived the ups and downs of the music business through good copyright repertoire, the occasional original hit and advertising work for leading companies. At the height of their fame in the 1960s, the Mambos were running three bands; although still active they have now shrunk back to one unit run as a family business. Today their music is seldom available either inside or outside the country.

| 1985 | | Ngatigarei |

Mapfumo, Thomas. By the early 1990s Thomas's reputation as a major African star was secure – he had struggled and suffered against injustice and corruption, he had influenced an entire generation of Zimbabwean musicians and had introduced thousands of non-Africans to the world of African music. Volume 1 provides a fairly comprehensive background biography which more recent information has not significantly challenged. The discography presented below attempts to be comprehensive, although cataloguing singles is unfortunately beyond its scope.

Since 1986 Mapfumo has been able to consolidate his international career without sacrificing his local reputation and popularity. He has not been influenced by western styles, critics or technical developments but has concentrated on his roots approach to both musical development and the social and political issues of the day. As he explained in a 1990 interview,

> I am a roots man and I think that it is my attitude that leads these youngsters and makes them do the right thing, follow the right directions. They really got to understand this type of music, not to make a fusion out of it, but make it danceable. Then, although the music is militant, it will make the people happy.

Mapfumo's music has not, however, always won such easy acceptance. During the 1970s he challenged both the minority white settler regime and the prevailing taste of his own people, at that time biased towards imported western pop and Zaïrean rumba. Mapfumo therefore had to overcome hostility from both the racist government and his own people to his innovative use of mbira rhythms on electric guitar. His

re-Africanisation of Zimbabwe pop music ranks as one of his greatest achievements. Yet with his commitment to equality and the elimination of poverty, Thomas was in no position to rest on his laurels, given growing evidence of corruption in the new government of Robert Mugabe. Thomas absolves Mugabe from any direct blame but singled out his close supporters for biting criticism in the 1990 hit single and album *Corruption*. On the subsequent release, *Chamunorwa*, Mapfumo was again on the attack, but to a deeper, more traditional style called 'ngororombe'. Originally a shebeen penny-whistle style, Mapfumo consciously picked 'ngororombe' for its enormous folk memories, resonant with more contemporary reggae inflexions. In 1989 he toured the US and Europe to enormous acclaim as his new material and older, repackaged, material became available in increasing quantities. There are those who worry about Mapfumo's continuing attacks on government and fear that the one-party state may at some stage exact retribution. I believe these worries to be unfounded and that Thomas will continue to compose and oppose, perform and reform for many years to come.

1976	ASLP 5000	Hokoya
1980	ELP 2004	Chimurenga Singles (1976–80)
1983	ELP 2005	Ndangariro
1984	ERT 1007	Mabasa (Work)
1985	ROUGH 91 ERT 1008	Chimurenga for Justice Mr Music
1986	EMW 5506	Gwindingwi Rine Shumba (1980–6)
1987	ASLP 5001	Greatest Hits
1988	TML 100	Zimbabwe-Mozambique
1989	AFROPOPWW	Live at SOB New York
	MLPS 1019	Corruption
1990	CDEWV 22	Shumba (1975–84)
	MLPS 1075	Chamunorwa

Sithole, Jonah (b. Zvishavane, 1952). Started his musical career in 1969 as a bass guitarist following his brother into the Jairos Jiri Kwela Kings. Then, in 1970, he moved on to join the Limpopo Jazz Band as lead guitarist, playing for three years as resident band at a Harare hotel. In 1974 he briefly joined the Great Sounds before moving out of Harare to join the Pepsi Combo in Mutare. Once again he stayed for three years, picking up many different styles before a chance meeting with Thomas Mapfumo in 1978 brought the two stars together in a new band called the Black Spirits. They did not last long, split and then reunited in the Blacks Unlimited, utilising the core of Jonah's band. This time round it proved to be a fruitful relationship, combining Jonah's guitar skills with Thomas's songwriting and vocal talents. Today, the two are inseparable.

Areketa, Tobias (d. 1990). Musician who had played with Mapfumo and the Blacks Unlimited in the mid-1980s. Set out on a solo career in 1986 when he recorded *Mavambo* – a massive hit in Zimbabwe. He died suddenly in 1990.

1987		Mavambo

Bhundu Boys. Since their meteoric rise to fame in 1986, the Bhundu Boys have seen both good and hard times in pursuit of a major record deal. Volume 1 outlines the early years and we now pick up the story in 1987 when the Boys finally found a major deal with American giant WEA. In many respects it was a disaster. The Boys were in the big league and although *True Jit* enjoyed sales many others would be envious of it was a critical failure with the cry going out that the Bhundu Boys had compromised their music for commercial success and that something had been lost. The year 1988 was busy, with a trip to Japan (shows cancelled due to Hirohito's funeral), gigs in Germany supporting soca ace David Rudder and a disappointing return trip to Zimbabwe, where, according to local sources, 'they bombed'. Something was clearly going wrong for a band which had been described by one enthusiastic Los Angeles critic as 'The greatest live act since Springsteen.'

WEA encouraged the band to record their next LP in Zimbabwe in an effort to try to recover the sound and feeling which underwrote their first albums. *Pamberi* duly presented a rootsier sound reinforced with mbira and other traditional instruments. But sales were still not good enough for WEA and in 1990, amidst a great deal of mutual recrimination, band and label parted company. The band accused WEA of not promoting the band and the albums adequately (a familiar complaint given the experience of Sunny Ade) and there can be no doubt that more resources could and should have been allocated. For their part, the label felt that the Bhundu Boys were losing appeal and, in any case, they were perhaps not the best band in Zimbabwe after all. With all this behind them, the Boys returned to what they knew best, stunning live shows and a sympathetic, if somewhat smaller, record label. By the start of the new decade, and despite the departure of front man Biggie Tembo, the band appeared to be in fine form again with solid shows in Europe and the UK.

Yet the whole experience from 1987 to 1990 somehow leaves a sour taste in the mouth. They were not and will not be the last African band who fail to find success with major record labels.

1983	RUG 100	Chekudya Chose
1986	AFRILP 02	Shabini
1987	AFRILP 03	Tsimbodzemoto
1988	WEA	True Jit
1989	WEA	Pamberi
1990	AFRILP 007	Absolute Jit: Live at King Tut's Wah Wah Hut, Glasgow
1990		Bye Bye Stembi (Import 12")

Real Sounds. Please refer to Volume 1 for background details of a band who have become one of the most respected and popular bands to have emerged from Africa during the 1980s 'World Music' boom. The band enjoyed considerable success towards the end of the 1980s. In 1987 they were the focus of the prestigious British TV Arts programme 'The South Bank Show' and continued to play regularly in both UK and Zimbabwe. *Wende Zako*, their first British release, confirmed the band's quality and in 1989 they recorded a follow-up in a Harare studio, produced by Norman Cook, formerly of the Housemartins, a successful British pop band. They had previously worked together on the Real Sounds' single 'Oye Oye' and the band reciprocated by playing on Cook's solo album.

1984	ZML 1015	Harare
1986	12ZIM 400	Non-Aligned Movement (12")
	2ZIM 350	Murume Wango (12")
1987	COOK 004	Wende Zako
1989	BIG 1LP	7 Miles High
1990	CHERRY RED	Get Real

Success, OK. One of the earliest Zaïrean rumba bands to make an impact on Zimbabwean musical consciousness, they arrived in 1970 and within a few months were down to two musicians, Andrew Ngoyi and Joseph Kishala. Over the next few years they set about recruiting leading Zimbabwean musicians, including James Chimombe (b. 1951, d. 1990), a top vocalist and guitarist. By the mid-1970s OK Success was one of the foremost bands in the country, charting with hits like 'Baba va Boyi' and 'Amai'. Their albums are seldom seen outside Zimbabwe.

Mutukudzi, Oliver (b. 1952). By 1990 'Tuku' had become almost as popular as Mapfumo in Zimbabwe. Like so many others, he began his musical career in a church choir. But it was not all singing and Oliver also acquired a 'Teach Yourself Guitar' manual. In 1975 he made his first radio shows and in the same year joined the Wagon Wheels alongside Thomas Mapfumo. Together they reached No. 1 with 'Dzandimomotera'. In time, however, Thomas moved on. The band, who had rechristened themselves the Black Spirits before Mapfumo's departure, were to release their first LP, *Ndipewo Zano*, under that name in 1978.

During these years of apprenticeship, Oliver's style was heavily derivative of current Congolese rumba, but, having worked with Mapfumo and by developing his songwriting talents, more specifically Shona rhythms and arrangements began to appear. From that time onwards there was no looking back. Mtukudzi went on to exploit the lifting of the curfew in 1979 by putting his band on the road, performing his hit songs live and boosting LP sales. He toured widely in the region, visiting Zambia, Botswana and Malawi, and set up his own Tuku label. By 1990 he had amassed a stupendous 36 gold discs performing alongside such international stars as Chapman, Springsteen and Gabriel at the Amnesty Concert (1988) and had established a growing reputation outside Zimbabwe with several highly acclaimed UK releases. Playing a style he calls JiJaS (Jit-Afro-Jazz), Oliver tends to dominate the studio recordings, using his eight-piece band mainly for live performances. His voice has been described as being more soulful than rootsy but this does not really mean much in terms of the overall sound, which is melodic, varied and well produced. In a mid-1980s interview with Fred Zindi, Oliver replied to those critics questioning his chosen style:

I describe my music as tradition, based invariably on the local sound which began in Zimbabwe before I was born. There are several versions of this traditional beat, depending on the region. There is Mbakumba, Nhxuzu, Katekwe and Jerusalema, all of which stem from different parts of the country. These are the rhythms I have listened to and somewhere along those lines lies my own beat. I have tried to combine all these beats which are true, free expressions of Zimbabweans from each region . . . to make a national rhythm.

Oliver has also moved on lyrically, writing in Ndebele as well as Shona to put across his views on the major social issues of the day – poverty and suffering. Disciplined, serious and modest, his live act belies the professionalism which he applies to music and the message he puts across. His music is now regularly available outside Zimbabwe through a licensing arrangement with the British label CSA. His earlier material is more difficult to find, with Zindi listing ten albums between 1978 and 1985.

1978		Ndipewo Zano

1980	BL 241	Africa
1981	BL 304	Pfambi
1982	ZC 214	Wawona
1983	BL 450	Greatest Hits
1984	BL 479	Hwema Handirase
1985	BL 502	Mhaka
	TEL 2015	Africa
1987	ZIL 214	Wawona
1988	TKLP 1	Strange Isn't It?
	TKLP 2	Nyanga Yenzou
	ZIL 299	Zvauya Sei?
1989	TKLP 3	Grandpa Story
	ZIL 220	Sugar Pie
	CSLP 5001	Sugar Pie (UK release)
1990	CSLP 5005	Psss Psss Hello (UK release)

Malax, Ndux, and the Stone Sounds. Sotho band.

	JAB 510	Njelele

Madzikatire, Elijah, and the Boro Band

	JAB 508	Imba Hainzarwo
1987	JLP 1008	Torofika (Brass courtesy of Real Sounds)

Mapfumo, Susan (b. Harare, 1947). Susan enjoyed a fairly orthodox childhood before a traumatic divorce in 1969 led first to depression and subsequently a determination to make it as a singer. She started out in 1972 singing alongside Thomas Mapfumo before moving on to gain more experience with bands such as the Pied Pipers and OK Success. Over the years she has learned to struggle against manipulation, exploitation and outright sexism. She now has her own band, including two brothers, and with considerable commercial success (four gold discs) she is able to resist the double discrimination of being a musician and a woman. She remains committed to performing in rural Zimbabwe and has eschewed overseas work.

Devera Ngwena. Led by Jonah Moyo. Masters of Zim-Rumba equally at home with traditional styles and rhythms. Formed in 1979 with the backing of the Mashaba Mine Company, Devera Ngwena are one of the most commercially successful bands in Zimbabwe. They started out covering Zaïrean hits but over the years have developed their own material and style. Immensely popular with the Zimbabwean working class, Devera Ngwena's appeal lies in their straightforward musical approach and the day-to-day topics discussed in their lyrics. They have toured Botswana, Mozambique and, in 1988, the UK to excellent audience and press response. They also spread the word through radio, doing a number of live radio sessions.

1982	ZML 1001	Devera Ngwena
	ZML 1004	Vol. 2
	ZML 1006	Vol. 3 (Also SUH 1005)
1984	ZML 1009	Vol. 4 (Also SUH 1013)
	ZML 1011	Vol. 5 (Also SUH 1021)
	SUH 1028	Vol. 7: Debbie
1985	ZML 1024	Vol. 8
	SUH 1033	Greatest Hits
	SUH 1040	Ndatambura Newe
	SUH 1046	Vol. 10
1986	ZML 1026	Masvingo Ne Carpet
1987	SUH 1050	Vol. 11
1988	KK 01	Taxi Driver
1989	OH 1 LP	Follow the Crocodile

Chibadura, John (b. Mazowe, Zimbabwe, 1957). Grew up in time-honoured fashion tending his father's goats after school and during vacations. When he left school he looked for a more rewarding vocation and became first a lorry hand, then a driver. In 1980, the year of independence, he moved to Harare and was soon impressed with singer Tinei Chikupo, who performed at John's local bar, the Mverechena Night Club. He also observed the rise and rise of Oliver Mutukudzi and decided to try to develop his own nascent musical skills. In 1981 he formed his band and scored first time round with début LP and hit single *Upenyu Hwandinetsa*. In 1982 he followed up with the second LP and in 1985, 1986 and 1987 was awarded gold discs. In 1988 he exceeded all past success with *Zuva Rekuva Kwangu*, a veritable mega-hit. Towards the end of the decade he visited UK on two occasions with his six-piece Tembo Brothers Band, four musicians and two dancers. He released two popular albums in the UK in 1989 and 1990 and toured the UK successfully in the wake of other Zimbabwe bands who had captured the public imagination. John has clearly made it into the big league, although, a shy and retiring man, he has clearly seen hard times in the past. In *Folk Roots* (October 1988) he had this to say about music:

What I want is music. I will listen to any musician in the world. . . . I have a family of three children. They eat by music, they are clothed by music. My car, my house, they come from music. So I respect my music. It is my industry. [But] Some musicians . . . have gone all the way and taken all they can of European styles. You must do that or not imitate at all. We won't be staying here. We will come for maybe a month and then go. That way your people are still excited with our music and we do not lose our roots. It keep us on our toes to come here but mostly we have both feet on the ground back home.

1981		Upenyu Hwandinetsa
1982	ZIL 212	Kugarika Tange Nhamo
1985	ZIL 221	Mudzimo Wangu
1986	ZIL 216	$5000 Roora
1987	ZIL 208	Sara Ugarike
1988		Zuva Rekuva Kwangu
1989	CSLP 5002	The Essential John Chibadura
1990	CSLP 5004	More of the Essential John Chibadura

Four Brothers. A four-piece guitar band formed in 1978. Initially comprising Never Mutare (bass), Frank Simanda (lead), Alick Chipaika (rhythm) and Marshall Ticharwa Munhumumwe (drums and vocals), in 1987 Simanda was replaced by Edward Matigasi. To begin with, the band was little more than a breakaway faction of The Great Sounds, but they enjoyed immediate success with a 1980 gold record for *Makorokoto* and also for the follow-up LP *Umbayi*. By the late 1980s they were firmly ensconced as one of the country's top attractions, working out of a base at Harare's Saratoga Bar. In 1989 they achieved a further commercial breakthrough when they featured on the UK label Stylus compilation double which brought them to the attention of high-street record buyers. The UK based Cooking Vinyl albums came via Serengeti.

1986	KSALP 111	Rugare
1987	KSALP 119	Ndakatambura Newe
1988	BAKE 004	Makorokoto (Re-release)
	COOK 023	Bros
1989	SFPS 070	The Peel Sessions (Rugare)
1989	FRY 005	Uchandifunga Dance Remix (12")

| 1990 | KSALP 104 | Tonosangana Ikeko (Featuring Patrick Mkwamba) |
| | KSALP 124 | Rudo Chete |

Majaivana, Lovemore (b. Lovemore Tshuma, Gweru, 1952). As a child Lovemore started singing in a church choir where his father was minister. He joined his first band, aged 15, in 1967 as a drummer, becoming enormously popular in the Bulawayo district. He then switched to singing, covering Tom Jones and Elvis numbers and performing on the hotel and nightclub circuit. In 1974 he returned to Bulawayo and spent four years singing with the Marisha Band. In 1978 he returned again to Harare forming Jobs Combination as a vehicle for his talents. Musically, the repertoire was varied, covering a variety of popular styles. In 1980, after several successful singles, they recorded their first LP, *Isitimela*, which shot to the top of the charts. The band then split and, following a couple of months singing with the Real Sounds, Lovemore joined the Zulus, a Victoria Falls outfit which already included two of his brothers. This group provided the security Lovemore had been looking for and in 1984 they released *Salanini Zinini*, a more traditional album featuring folk songs taught by his mother. Today, Lovemore's material is totally Zimbabwean and he has rejected the early foreign influences. If talent and ambition are enough to guarantee success, then we will surely hear more of Mr Majaivana. In 1990 he toured the UK and released his first international album.

1980	MUSI 2000	Isitimela
1984	MUSI 5000	Salanini Zinini
1987	TRALP 2004	Jiri
1990	ZIM 003	Amandala

Jairos Jiri Band. Led by the blind Paul Matavire, JJB, highly rated by Zimbabweans, are little known outside the country, despite releasing six LPs to date and touring Germany in 1988. They act as representatives of Jairos Jiri, the Disabled Musicians' Society.

| 1986 | KSALP 112 | JJB Style |

Ilanga. By the late 1980s Ilanga, playing up-tempo music with bass and organ emphasised, were being described as the hottest band in Harare – no mean achievement in a city of so many stars. The album *Visions Untold* remained top of the Zimbabwean charts for an unprecedented 25 weeks. The band split up in 1988 when Comrade Chinx left to pursue a solo career with the Barrel of Peace. Chinx

(b. C. Chingaira) had another smash hit in 1988 with 'Zvikomborero Kasimba'. A live version is included on his 1988 solo outing. Female singer Busi Ncube also contributed material to Ilanga and can be heard with the band on the *Women in Africa* compilation. Despite the loss of the charismatic Chinx, Ilanga have continued to progress, touring the UK in 1991.

1988	ILGLP 2	Visions Untold
	CHINX 1	Crde Chinx: Ngorimba
1989	CSLP 5003	Women of Africa: Busi Ncube
1990	CXLP 1	Crde Chinx: Early Hits

Marxist Brothers. Also known as the Orchestra Dendera Kings, led by Simon Chimbetu. An eight-piece guitar band.

1983	MUSI 300	Mwara We Dangwe (Goodbye Sandra)
1985	MUSI 800	Kunjere Kunjere
1986	MUSI 900	Dendera Resango
1987	MUSI 902	Afrika
1988	DALP 100	Kuipa Chete
1989	DALP 200	Marxist Brothers

New Black Montana. Popular jit-jive guitar band.

| 1988 | KSALP 100 | New Black Montana |

Manatsa, Zexie, and the Green Arrows. The band was formed in 1975 in Bora and was initially led by Sam Luke Mahufe playing copyright music. In 1977 they came to the attention of a South African producer who advised them to turn to tradition, and, although they were afraid of losing their fans, they agreed and cut their first album, *Chipo Chirorwa*. The album sold over 25,000 in the first month and the band reformed as the Green Arrows. They then moved to Harare and cut a number of best-selling singles, touring widely. They are currently led by Zexie Manatsa on vocals and Stanley Manatsa on lead guitar. The 1981 album was produced by West Nkosi.

1975		Chipo Chirorwa
1977		Hama Huyayi
1981	BL 277	Mutzimi Ndiringo
1983	KSALP 101	Antonyo
1988	JLP 1011	Soccer Stars

Nyami Nyami Sounds. Six-piece guitar band formed in the early 1980s in Kariba, a lakeside town in Northern Zimbabwe. They started as a rural youth band, recording several singles in the late 1970s as the Angoni Family before switching to Nyami Nyami. Like many others they started out as a band performing rumba covers, but by the time of their first album in 1984 they were starting to incorporate distinctly local idioms into their sound.

1984	ZML 1014	The Sounds of Nyami Nyami
1985	ZML 1019	Fundo Inokosha
1986	ZML 1030	Kwira Mudenga

Robson, Banda, and the New Black Eagles

1983	KSALP 102	Sidudhla
1987	KSALP 121	Ngoma Ngairere
1988	KSALP 113	Soweto

RUNN Family. The 1988 LP includes a moving tribute to the late Samora Machel, President of Mozambique.

| 1988 | KSA 410 | Hatichina Wekutamba Nayo |

Frontline Kids. A youth band aged between 15 and 18 playing a new and exciting blend of mbira and jit-jive. Formed in the late 1980s, they toured the UK in 1991 to widespread acclaim.

| 1990 | ZINLP 005 | Hipenyu |

Chanjerai, Daisy. Female session singer. Her work can be heard on the second *Women of Africa* compilation.

| 1991 | CSA | Women of Africa Vol. 2 |

Ncube, Doreen. One of Zimbabwe's leading night-club performers and sister to Busi of Ilanga fame. She rose to prominence as the vocalist with the famed Pied Pipers (see Volume 1) but little has been put on vinyl apart from the outstanding 'Mahlalela' on the 1989 compilation.

| 1989 | CSLP 5003 | Women of Africa Vol. 1 |

Mabokela, Sarah. Sadly died in 1988, by which time she was a well-respected gospel singer. She contributed two titles to the CSA 1989 compilation.

| 1989 | CSLP 5003 | Women of Africa Vol. 1 |

Simba Brothers. Guitar band led by 'Mkoma' Ketai.

| 1987 | MUSI 404 | Rukodzo |

Chimombe, James, and the Ocean City Band. Singer-guitarist, graduate of OK Success, who died tragically in 1990.

| 1987 | ZIL 218 | Munakandafa |

Sungura Boys. Zimbabwean jit/rumba stars.

| 1987 | JLP 1009 | Tasarira Nhamo |

Talking Drum. African rhythms, English lyrics and synths make this 1987 recording sound more South African than Zimbabwean.

| 1987 | TDLL 100 | The Song – The Dancer |

Two Stars and Kasongo Band

| 1987 | MUSI 403 | Kudzidza Hakuperi |

Black, Umfolosi. Vocal group who have been singing together since childhood. They have a wide repertoire, with each member composing material. They are rising stars in a busy local vocal scene and in June 1990 toured the UK to accompany the release of their first LP. The album demonstrated their personal approach to close harmony, singing in the Zulu 'a cappella' style of Ladysmith Black Mambazo. Digitally recorded in London, *Unity* serves as a showcase for Ndebele music and features the soulful lead voice of Sotsha Moyo.

| 1991 | WCB 020 | Unity |

Zhimozhi

| 1988 | JLP 0101 | Munepamoromo |

Zimbabwe Cha Cha Cha Kings

| 1988 | ZML 1041 | Umbiso |

Zindi, Fred. Musician, writer, promoter and producer.

| 1975 | ZIM 01 | Zimbabwe on Fire |

Zvishavane Sounds

| 1987 | ZML 1032 | Mutongi |

Others

1985	BL 513	Johnson Mkhalal: Sunshine Boots (Accordion jive)
1989	KSLP 101	Kasongo: Pambasa (Zimbabwean rumba)
1990	JFLP 1001	Jordan Chataika & His Sisters
	RTCP 7	Tusanang Sounds: Inzwsa

Compilations. Zimbabwe has been exceptionally well served by companies willing to compile representative albums of the country's top musicians. Sometimes, given the bewildering quantity and variety of African music now reaching the western market-place, it is difficult to know where to start. Compilation albums represent perhaps the best way forward.

1988	CSLP 5000	Various: African Sunset
	EWV 9	Various: Zimbabwe Frontline (Mutukudzi, Four Bros, Banda Devera Ngwena, Mapfumo, Moyo, Nyami Nyami, etc.)
1989	EWV 18	Various: Spirit of the Eagle (Mapfumo, Banda, Four Bros)
	MUWZ 100	Various: Music of Zimbabwe Vol. 1 (Blues Revolution, Outsiders, Bright Stars Function, Exodus Sound Blast, Hurungwe Sounds, United Brothers, Speed Limit, Shirinhema Jazz – an excellent, authentic Zimbabwe compilation of ZimJive stars)

| 1990 | AFRILP 006 | Various: Advance Kusugar (RUNN Family, Sea Cottage Sisters, Master Chivera, etc.) |

Zimbabwe gospel

Manyureke, Machanic, and the Puritans
(b. Bulawayo, 1950s). Became a Christian as a teenager, picking up guitar along the way. In the early 1970s he formed a Salvation Army band called the Gospel Singers. Work was never in short supply, including a visit to Soweto, where he fully realised the power of music to communicate. In the early 1980s he disbanded the Singers and formed a smaller, more flexible outfit which he named the Puritans. This meant that he could now play for any church or denomination rather than strictly reflecting the Army outlook. Despite the usual problems besetting Zimbabwean musicians – expensive equipment, poor transport and poor recording facilities – Machanic soldiers on and has not been averse to changing his style and sound to suit his audience. He toured the UK in 1990, returning the following year to widespread acclaim. A preacher and an evangelist, Machanic is seldom short of work. In 1990, he was the subject of an hour-long video filmed in the UK.

1988	NDLP 17	Zakewu
1989	NDLP 25	Ndeyeiko Nyaya Iyo
	COOK 25	Machanic Manyureke
1991	GBV 007	Live At The River (Video)

Kunenyathi, Knowledge

| 1990 | KSLP 102 | Knowledge Kunenyathi & Kassongo |

38　Zambia

(ECONOMY AND SOCIETY. Pop.: 8.2 million. Area: 752,614 sq. km. Capital: Lusaka. Independence: 1964. Currency: Kwacha.)

For several millennia the area of modern Zambia has stood at the crossroads of Africa with important trade routes passing through from east to west and north to south. As various ethnic groups travelled these routes, many settled in Zambia, thus producing a heterogeneity of culture and language almost unequalled in Africa. Today, a single village can thus contain Cewa, Yao, Swahili, Lamba and Tonga influences in terms of both language and culture. In terms of social organisation, pre-colonial Zambia contained various formations, from the stateless Tonga to the kingdom of the Lozi. By controlling the trade routes, various Zambian societies had become quite powerful by the time British imperial expansion drew the region into its orbit in the late nineteenth century. Cecil Rhodes spearheaded the northward thrust of British capital in search of cheap labour for the South African mines, and when copper was discovered in 1906, the British South Africa Co. made substantial investments in the mines – extracting over £80 million worth of copper and spending only £5 million on local development. By 1924 the area was under Colonial Office control, and,

with a substantial white settler population employed in the mines or as farmers, inter-war politics were closely linked to plans for a federation with the neighbouring settler colony – Southern Rhodesia. Federation was widely regarded by Zambians as a means of perpetuating white control, hence early nationalist agitation condemned moves towards this goal.

In political terms the ANC, led by Harry Nkumbula, made the early running, but when he agreed to participate in Federal elections a more radical wing split from the ANC and emerged as the United National Independence Party, led by Kenneth Kaunda. When elections were held under universal suffrage for the first time, Kaunda and UNIP swept to power, leading the country to independence in 1964 and a dissolution of the Central African Federation (which had also included Nyasaland – now Malawi). In 1972 Zambia became a one-party state and Kaunda moved quickly to establish his and the party's supremacy over most aspects of Zambia's economic and political life. Unfortunately, the mid-1970s also witnessed a catastrophic decline in the export value of copper and by the end of the decade the economy was in deep trouble – a situation not helped by Kaunda's creditable financial and political commitment to various liberation movements, including the ANC, SWAPO and ZAPU. Sadly, Kaunda did not always play the right cards and ended up supporting the anti-Mugabe forces in the Zimbabwean war and UNITA in its struggle against the MPLA in Angola. As debt mounted and state-run enterprises proved inefficient (as well as corrupt), internal opposition increased, culminating in the pro-democracy movement of the early 1990s. Finally, on 1 November 1991, Kaunda and the UNIP were toppled in the country's multiparty elections by Frederick Chiluba and the Movement for Multi-Party Democracy. Sadly, there are no easy economic solutions on the horizon, and although the liberation wars are largely over, a new internal enemy, in the form of the AIDS virus, has now appeared, with potentially catastrophic consequences for the country.

TRADITIONAL MUSIC

Volume 1 provided a sketchy introduction to Zambian traditional music, introducing the various instruments, discussing social significance and identifying several dances. The richness and diversity of this tradition continues to be investigated by musicologists, while contemporary musicians in the Kalindula style continue to exploit the rich vein of rhythm and melody. Unfortunately, very little traditional Zambian music appears on disc or cassette. Enthusiasts should begin research with various recordings made by Hugh Tracey in the 1940s and 1950s for the International Library of African Music. During these two decades he made field recordings of the Lala, Aushi, Bemba, Luvale, Chokwe, Ngoni, Lozi, Tumbuka, Henga and Yao. Unfortunately, these recordings are extremely hard to locate – they could never be considered really commercial, although several companies, including Folktracks in the UK and Kaleidophone in the US, have licensed parts of the catalogue.

1960s	GALP 1327	Guitars Vol.1
	GALP 1503	Guitars Vol.2
1970s	ER 12013	Inyimbo: Songs of the Bemba
	FE 4201	Music of the Petauke Vol. 1
	FE 4202	Music of the Petauke Vol. 2
1982	ARN 33605	La Voix des Masques de Zambe (Troupe Nationale de Danse)

MUSIC AND THE MINING INDUSTRY

It is not often that we find recorded music directly reflecting the reality of industrial life, for the obvious reason that, apart from the mining enclaves of Southern Africa, the vast majority of Africans lived and worked outside industrial culture. The exceptions to this generalisation inevitably include Zambia, whose recent history cannot be separated from the history of copper mining. The copper industry, based around Ndola/Kitwe, began in the 1920s and for the next 70 years shaped the economic and cultural destiny of the country. To start with, the mines made enormous demands on Zambian labour, drawing men from traditional society and introducing them to the cash economy. Traditional ethnic ties were weakened (although they did not disappear) while new social relationships sprang up. Culturally, this transition involved the coming together of various traditions, the appearance of new instruments (principally the acoustic guitar) and the composition of new songs commenting on changes in society. As in South Africa, miners' songs can also be interpreted as a form of

cultural resistance to the domination of white capital. The collection of Zambian miners' songs appearing on OMA 112, *Songs from the Copperbelt*, also draws attention to the close pre-colonial and post-colonial links between Northern Zambia (the Ndola–Kitwe area) and Southern Zaïre (the Shaba province). For the purpose of comparison we include the excellent cassette featuring the Katanga acoustic guitar style of Southern Zaïre, recorded around the same time. Readers who wish to pursue this 'Copperbelt' acoustic tradition should consult John Low's informative and entertaining *Shaba Diary*. *Songs from the Copperbelt*, recorded by Hugh Tracey in 1957, reveals a variety of styles and influences, ranging from the semi-professional performances of Stephen Kasumali to the utilisation of South African, Zaïrean and American country rhythms. This is an important musical document illustrating the transition from traditional to modern society and demonstrating the wide range of influences on contemporary Zambian music.

1950s	Cass. only	Katanga Guitar
1960s	TR 23	Town Dances with Guitar (Bemba)
1989	OMA 012	Songs from the Copperbelt . . . Zambian Miners' Songs (Featuring Stephen Kasumuli, William Siwale, John Lushi, William Mapulanga, The Four Pals, Mbasela Kunda, etc.)

MODERN MUSIC

Volume 1 provided a very short introduction to the modern music of Zambia – very little was available outside the country and, apart from the work of Wolfgang Bender and Francis Nwanza, very little had been written about the contemporary music scene. When I was offered two months' work in Zambia in late 1990 I was more than happy to accept and was able to combine my other duties with many interviews with musicians, engineers and record company owners. Special thanks go to Graham Skinner of DB Studios, Mr Khusayo of Zambia Music Parlour, Stewart Lamb of Teal Records, Herman Striedl and David Nkhata. With their help I was able to piece together a more coherent account of the development of popular music in Zambia over the last forty years.

The story of the first four decades of this century remains unclear. Little music, if any, was recorded, and although African society was rich in music and culture, it remained largely localised and performed in traditional settings. As far as is known, the first field recordings were made in the 1940s and 1950s by South African musicologists Hugh Tracey and Harry Franklin. But music from much further afield was beginning to appear through the imported records of the white mining community, through the influences of the churches and, finally and most significantly, through the broadcasting of music by the Central African Broadcasting Service (CABS) from the late 1940s onwards. The radio helped shape taste, with country and western music proving to be immensely popular for its straightforward story lines and clear diction. Between 1948 and 1954 the radio station also developed a commercial wing and every year despatched staff around the country to record traditional music. These music safaris lasted for up to a month and involved loading a Presto recording machine onto the back of a Chevy pick-up and venturing forth. Itineraries were broadcast beforehand on the radio, with up to fifty people congregating at town halls and schools to record their music. The engineers travelled with a box of coins, paying 2/6 per recording. If the engineer felt the recording was suitable, the acetate would be sent back to Lusaka for broadcast. (More recently, the Swedish Government has funded an archival retrieval project whereby what is left of these early recording efforts is transferred on to new master tapes deposited in the National Archives.)

Almost everything around was recorded, from the mass in Bemba to traditional drum ensembles, but little was ever kept. Back in Lusaka, Federal Broadcasting played the discs every Saturday morning with local musicians casually dropping in to add the occasional live recording. Alick Nkhata was one of the first engineers and toured widely, picking up different local melodies and rhythms. This imaginative approach to local culture was able to reach the majority of the population, who tuned in on local 'sauce-pan' radios, and despite the preponderance of imported music, these musical safaris enabled thousands of local musicians to record at least once and thus helped revitalise Zambian music and encourage musicians.

By the 1960s singles were beginning to appear from a small pressing plant on the Copperbelt, but it was the 1962 visit by Louis Armstrong which proved to be the decisive event in modern Zambian musical consciousness. He was the first musician of international stature to perform in the country – and he was black. Alick Nkhata was, of course, the most prominent indigenous musician and by the early 1960s Nashil Pinchen was starting to develop an electric Zambian sound. During this period Zambia consisted of two distinctive societies – the white (Mazunga) society, relaxing in expensive hotels and exclusive clubs and listening to 'mazungu' music, whether imported or performed by Zambian musicians; and the black society, congregating in urban beer halls run by city and town councils. There were not many black dance halls or clubs and urban entertainment revolved around Saturday evening village dances featuring local instruments and a

few acoustic guitars. Many musicians were popular in their own areas, but without the means to acquire instruments and with few venues to play at, the whole development of a modern urban African sound lagged behind that of the rest of Black Africa. A few Zambian musicians found work playing mazungu music in Lusaka hotels, with bands like the Big Gold Six, the Lusaka Radio Band and the Broadway Quintet proving to be the most popular. During these years, western pop bands like the Beatles wielded enormous influence, later to be replaced by heavier rock bands, although country and western retained its mass appeal.

In 1962 the Central African Federation (Zambia, Zimbabwe and Malawi) collapsed and then in 1965 Rhodesia declared unilateral independence. Sanctions were imposed and the hitherto close relationship between Northern and Southern Rhodesia was shattered. Prior to this date, the kwela and simanje-manje music of South Africa had been gaining in popularity, but when the border was closed and the source cut off, Zambians started looking north to the music of Zaïre. Since then, the biggest threat to the development of Zambian music has come from rumba, with luminaries such as Dr Nico, Franco and Tabu Ley developing fanatical followings in the major urban centres. A few local stars emerged but copyright was the rule of the day and in this respect Zambia seemed to have lost a generation of musicians somewhere between the pioneering work of Alick Nkhata and the Federal Broadcasting Corporation and the emergence of a distinctly Zambian sound from the mid-1970s onwards.

However, in 1972 another seminal event occurred when afro-rock superstars Osibisa arrived in Zambia. In a series of shows they were able to demonstrate not only the commercial appeal of their music but the simple fact that African styles could compete on equal terms with imported rock, country and western and, latterly, reggae and rumba. Osibisa proved to be an enormous influence on many musicians and by the mid-1970s the Zamrock phenomenon was in full swing with Smokey Haangala, the Witch, the Black Power band and many others developing an indigenous rock style drawing on both western styles and a conscious search into the Zambian past. James Brown had also made an enormous impact (playing in Lusaka in 1967) so the three key performances of Armstrong, Osibisa and Brown go a long way in defining the shape and sound Zambian music was to adopt in the 1960s and 1970s.

Over the next few years a consensus began to develop amongst musicians, politicians and producers that something really should be done to develop a Zambian style which could compete with both neighbouring and overseas traditions. The turning point came in 1976 with Kaunda's important 'Watershed Speech', when the President decreed that 90 per cent of music played on the radio be of Zambian origin. Of course this was a tall order given the underdevelopment of the Zambian music business, but the intention was clear and musicians responded, although not quite in the way Kaunda had hoped. For although some like Paul Ngozi, Mike Nyoti and Nashil Pinchen Kazembe continued their creative exploitation of the Zambian musical past, many more simply switched from 'mazungu' music to Zaïrean rumba. With guaranteed airplay, bands were virtually created out of nothing as dubious entrepreneurs and promoters cashed in on the business of Zambianisation.

Of course there were many respectable companies and producers around and, once the boom was over, they proved responsible for many fine recordings. The market was still dominated by 45 r.p.m.s but as the 1970s progressed an increasing number of well-conceived albums appeared alongside imported pop, rock and reggae. During these years, the vast majority of recordings were made at Lusaka's DB studios run by Graham Skinner, a veteran of the old broadcasting musical safaris. The other major company was Teal Records in Ndola who had started life as a subsidiary of the South African company Teal, who also maintained other subsidiaries in Zimbabwe and Malawi. In Zambia, DB was responsible for recordings while Teal handled production. The biggest star of the period remained Pinchen Kazembe, whose albums were by then topping sales of 50,000.

But by the late 1970s the Zambian economy was running into trouble and the market for records started to dry up. People could no longer afford record players, while foreign exchange problems made it increasingly difficult to import instruments and equipment. Even today, DB Studios still use recording equipment originally installed in the 1950s – an 8-track Brenell.

Yet despite the problems, the music business continued to move forward. Lonhro took over Teal and the new company started promoting Zambian bands in a more serious way. Mr Khuswayo also started to promote Zambian bands through his Music Parlour empire, while the Government continued to provide moral support, even if material support proved to be beyond them. In strictly musical terms, the shortage of equipment, the new consciousness of Zambians and the support of sympathetic companies all combined to encourage a more serious search for truly indigenous sounds. Traditional instruments, for example, took on a new significance in the absence of electric equipment. By the mid-1980s the fruits of these various efforts were beginning to appear in the form of new Kalindula bands like Amayenge, Serenje and Masasu. An all-too brief break in the economic crisis supported this cultural renaissance as beer gardens sprang up in the suburbs, providing new venues and appreciative audiences. By 1985 the Big Five had emerged – Amayenge, Serenje, Masasu, Shalawambe and Julizya – occasionally supported by outstanding solo vocalists Akeem Simukonda and P.K. Chisala. At the same time interest in African music was booming in the west and in 1988–9 all the top bands were able to

tour the UK with the help of influential DJ Charlie Gillet, the WOMAD organisation and even the British Council. With the Zambian companies keen to make licensing deals (almost bending over backwards to get their product overseas), by the late 1980s half a dozen excellent Zambian albums were jostling for attention in the overcrowded 'World Music' shelves of western record shops.

Back home, Kalindula was booming with newer, rougher groups springing up to challenge the reputations of the Big Five. It almost seemed as if the Zambian sound would take over from rumba entirely until the late 1980s kwassa kwassa craze swept dance fans back into the Zaïrean fold. Inspiration for the new Kalindula bands came from both the urban centres and the rural villages as street-wise kids drew from Zambian slang, football slogans and motoring metaphors to create a new street culture with Kalindula as its musical expression. Despite political unrest, three-figure inflation and a collapsing economy, the beer somehow flowed and Kalindula took off amid scenes reminiscent of the mid-1970s music revolution. By 1990 Zambian music was beginning to make an impact overseas – in Kenya and in Zimbabwe and Namibia as well as the west. However, we should always be careful not to exaggerate western interest in any African style, and although the conscious efforts of the 1980s paid off with a higher international profile for Zambian music, this progress was subsequently put at risk by the collapse of Mondeca Records early in 1991 in the wake of the British economic recession.

Nkhata, Alick (b. Kasama, 1922). Alick was born into a mixed marriage of a Tonga father and a Bemba mother, thereby inheriting characteristics of both ethnic groups, particularly the Bemba, who possessed a long poetic and musical tradition. He was trained as a schoolteacher but was barely out of his teens when he was caught up in the Second World War and sent to Burma as a sergeant in the East African Division. In 1946 he started working with Hugh Tracey, recording African music in Zambia and neighbouring countries, before he joined the Central African Broadcasting Service as an announcer/translator. It was only then that he admitted to playing the guitar 'and singing a bit'. His earliest song and still one of his most popular was 'Salapo', but through the rest of his repertoire he seemed able to combine traditional and contemporary idioms, urban and rural influences, past and present. His main work remained as an announcer but in time he formed his own Quartet, with whom he made many recordings at the Radio Station studio. With an active and fertile mind, Alick was able to compose songs on many contemporary topics, including local issues like bride-price and witchdoctors and political issues like vaccination and promoting government policies. Between 1962 and 1964 he turned his attention more fully towards politics, writing several campaigning songs for

Kaunda and UNIP. However, after independence his music took a back seat to other government work when he was appointed Director of Broadcasting and Cultural Services. In 1974 Alick retired to his farm at Mkushi, singing and composing in his spare time. His farm was adjacent to a ZAPU camp of Zimbabwean guerillas which in October 1978 was attacked in a 'Hot Pursuit' raid by white soldiers from over the border. Alick was caught in the cross-fire and killed instantly.

In 1991 RetroAfric re-issued a selection of Alick's most popular material on compact disc. As the sleeve notes conclude: 'If his murderers destroyed him, they were unable to destroy his art, which lives on in these recordings.' We now estimate that Alick composed upwards of 100 popular songs, of which about half have survived the ravages of time. His first recordings took place in 1949 when he accompanied Hugh Tracey to the Gallo Studios in South Africa. Unfortunately, we do not have copies of the political songs Alick composed in the early 1960s when, during the 'Cha Cha Cha' troubles, he helped make the colonialists dance to an African tune.

| 1964 | | Independence |
| 1991 | RETRO 4CD | Salapo |

Shitumba, James (b. Ndola, 1929). Started performing in 1943 with a local choir and on completion of secondary school moved to Lusaka to take up a career in medicine. During the early 1950s he performed with the Medical Swing Stars Choir and continued singing while moving from one profession to the next. By this time he was broadcasting part-time with the Federal Broadcasting Corporation, where he met Alick Nkhata. Nkhata warmed to Shitumba's warm melodic voice and invited him to join him in the Alick Nkhata Quartet. Alick taught him to play guitar and during the late 1950s and early 1960s they recorded together regularly. In 1963 Shitumba returned to radio broadcasting, staking his claim to fame by translating the national anthem from English to Bemba.

Lusaka Radio Band. The band existed as two different entities in two distinct periods. During the 1950s the band were composed of members of the Northern Rhodesian Police Band and as such often provided backing to Alick Nkhata. The second Lusaka Radio Band emerged from the UNIP Party Band, which had played between 1962 and 1964 in the run-up to independence. The band were led by Alick Nkhata and together they produced a number of political and campaigning songs for the party. For this precise reason, the Radio Station refused to play them and consequently they were never recorded – a vital piece of recent Zambian history gone forever.

The second version of the band included musicians who later reformed as the Broadway Quintet and subsequently as the Big Gold Six. Other members, in government service, were kept together under Nkhata to try to popularise a unique Zambian sound. These musicians, themselves often drawn from other groups like the AfroCubans and the Tiger Swingsters, included Bestin Mwanza, Agrippa Kalele and George Mlongoti.

Broadway Quintet. Five-piece outfit formed in 1962 as a party band for the UNIP. Original members were drawn from an earlier generation of Lusaka hotel bands such as the Rhokana Melodies, the Crooners, De Black Evening Follies and the City Quads. They played what was referred to at the time as 'mazungu', or white, music, covering western pop hits for hotel audiences. Led by keyboard player Tonny Maonde, they continued into the 1980s, winning the country's best band award in 1981.

| 1976 | ZTZ 4 | Amalume |

Big Gold Six. Initially sponsored by BAT Tobacco (hence the Big Gold Six), the band were the sole survivors of early attempts to establish a Zambian dance sound. They continued playing throughout the 1970s, recording several albums and representing Zambia at FESTAC in 1977.

Tembo, Lazarus (b. Eastern province, 1945). The young Lazarus went blind at the age of eight. He was then in mission school and the staff encouraged him to turn to music. He started composing and learning how to play various instruments, eventually passing the Cambridge Music exams. On becoming a minister in Kaunda's government, his musical career had to take a back seat.

| 1976 | | Kola |

Kaunda, Kenneth. President of Zambia from independence in 1964 until his electoral defeat in 1991. Dubbed 'The White Handkerchief Man' by Franco during a 1987 Zambian tour, Kaunda developed the concept and theory of African Humanism. His career is well documented elsewhere but it is often forgotten that Kaunda is an enthusiastic amateur musician who carried a guitar on his back as he toured Zambia in the early 1960s leading the nationalist struggle against white minority rule. He has always taken a keen interest in culture and in 1989 finally recorded his exhortation to hard work and discipline, 'Tiende Pamodzi' – an acoustic guitar tune which was subsequently and somewhat bizarrely remixed in London as Kaunda's Club Mix.

| 1990 | Red Records | Tiende Pamodzi (12") |

Kazembe, Nashil Pinchen (b. 1932). Veteran Zambian star whose life is shrouded in mystery; many believe him to be a Kenyan or a Zaïrean, although he was actually born in Zambia's Luapula province, home to so much good music. He started his adult life as a policeman in what was then Northern Rhodesia, lasting a year before joining the annual trek of migrant labourers to the South African mines. And it was in South Africa that Pinchen put together his first band – the Bantu Melodies. They lasted for just over a year before Pinchen moved to Zaïre, where his father had recently died. In 1953 Pinchen returned to music, re-establishing the Bantu Melodies in Kolwezi, with whom he toured the country. Yet his restlessness was reasserting itself and in 1957 he settled in Uganda before moving on to Kenya in 1959. There he met Peter Tsotsi Juma, with whom he formed the Congo Kids based in Mombasa. They lasted until 1962 when Pinchen moved on to Nairobi, creating the Congo River Boys, who were renamed the Equator Sound Boys when they became the studio band of Equator Studios. The band stayed together until 1970, backing many up-and-coming Kenyan stars on studio sessions and also releasing material under their own name, including massive regional hits like 'Malaika' and 'Kufiki Nairobi'.

This was to be one of the most stable and productive periods in Pinchen's life, and when the band collapsed in 1970 he immediately reformed the African Eagles Lupopo with long-time colleague Peter Juma, recording another batch of East African classics, including 'Comrade Kaunda', 'Sweet Na Musokwe' and 'Lunch Time'. During these years in Kenya, Pinchen proved to be one of the pioneers of rumba with a regional reputation stretching from Zaïre to Zanzibar. In 1972 he returned home for some shows in Zambia but a serious brawl at one of them jeopardised the entire tour. Between 1972 and 1975, Pinchen was back in Kenya, working behind the scenes as a moving force behind the celebrated Orchestre Super Mazembe, already two years old and destined to become one of the great East African rumba outfits. By the late 1970s Pinchen was back in Zambia, spurning official recognition of his achievements while recording several more hits including 'Vamahala Vinata' and 'Ilyo Nali Na Ba Willie'. Finally, between 1983 and 1986 Pinchen found employment at home as an engineer for Teal Records in Ndola. But his health was beginning to fade and in 1988 he entered the studio for what was to be the last time, laying down the tracks for his late 1980s hit album *4 x 4 Wheel Drive*.

Pinchen finally passed away in 1991, leaving a wife and six children. Throughout his career he had played and recorded in six countries, working with and influencing an entire generation of East and Central African rumba stylists. Yet, with so many hits to his credit, Pinchen remained a most elusive and private person. At his peak, his albums sold in excess of 50,000 copies with singles often approaching the 100,000 mark. A quiet, private family man, his career exemplified the no-frills, no-hype approach to music making in Africa. He will be sorely missed.

1979	PSL 2000	Top Luapula Hits
1980	EMA 0520	Mazembe
	EMA 0530	10th Anniversary
1981	LPKZ 10	The Best Of Vol. 1
1982	EMA 0540	Double Gold
1983	V 2263	Kaivaska
	NPS 001	Nashili Malenda
1984	THH 005	Hot Hits (Also UAMLP 1010)
1988	NPK 101	4 x 4 Wheel Drive
1990	NPK 2	African Super Star Vol. 2

Mulemena, Emmanuel. Leader of top pop band Mulemena and the Sound Inspectors, Emmanuel died tragically in 1982 – rumoured to have been one of the first AIDS victims in a country and a business which have been decimated by the virus. Emmanuel sang and composed in Kaonde, Bemba and Nyanja, guaranteeing national appeal for his guitar-based dance style. Curiously, Mulemena was one of the first African musicians to work with a drum machine and even after his death the band continued to operate without a drummer. On his death the band continued for several years as the Mulemena Boys in respect for his memory, but when several of them also died the band collapsed. The name was revived by a different set of musicians who now perform as the Junior Mulemena Boys, playing in a more rootsy, Kalindula style. The *Tribute* LP remains one of the country's best-sellers with music fans in Zimbabwe also starting to pick up interest. Mulemena was responsible for developing the 'machancha' beat, drawn from Kaonde tradition. This remains his key musical legacy.

1973	ZMLP 2	Shuka Shuka
1974	ZMLP 3	Zimbabwe Must Be Free
1982	ZMLP70	Tribute to Late Emmanuel Mulemena
1984	ZMLP 72	Special Dedication to Fallen Heroes
1988	ZMLP 79	Junior Mulemena Boys: Nya Ngale

Chambeshi Lifers. Formed in 1965 by Hamilton Simpungwe and Webster Lamba, both born in Chambesi. Playing a sparse form of traditional music they were 'discovered' by Khuswayo in 1975 and recorded their first album the following year.

1976	ZMLP 9	Tazara

Haangala, Smokey. One of the first musicians to feel the benefit of the 1976 music revolution, Smokey pioneered the 'Ching'ande' music of the Tonga from Southern province. Smokey soon established a following for his guitar/keyboard expertise and his willingness to comment on the social issues of the day.

1977	RAK 1	Aunka Ma Kwacha
1980	LPLP 2	Waunka Mooye

Cool Knights. Long-time hotel residency specialists. Experience and talent combine to produce note-perfect renditions of current soukous hits. They also compose original material and remain one of the most popular bands in and around Lusaka, principally for their contribution to enormously successful 'Rumba Nights' – a Zambian institution.

1976	ZMLP 13	Bana Mulenga

Fire Family. One of the most enduring of Zambian bands, formed in the mid-1970s at the urging of Nashil Pinchen Kazembe. Five-piece band strongly influenced by Kazembe and his East African style.

5 Revolutions Band. Eight-piece comedy/guitar band from Central Province playing the 'Kaonge beat', a Kalindula derivative.

1981	ZMLP 73	Kachasu Ne Ndoshi
1982	ZMLP 43	The Best of

Mwale, Anna (b. 1962). Talented vocalist who was able to get a contract with CBS Kenya – a move which catapulted her to African stardom with her albums available throughout the continent. Two hits from the early 1980s, 'Kabuku' and 'Mama Mwale', set her on her way. Now based in Germany, she performed in the UK in 1991 at a benefit for flood victims in neighbouring Malawi.

1984	ASF 3038	African Song

Zambezi. Brainchild of German musician Herman Striedl, Zambezi are a talented band who prefer the Kalindula style but can turn their hand to everything from rumba to afro-rock, covering past hits from the ex-Great Witch bassist Gideon Mulenga. Based at the Rimo Hotel, Kafue, on the Livingstone road, Zambezi have toured Germany and remain much in demand for all kinds of sporting and social functions. They have released several singles.

Traditional Justice Rockers. Roots reggae/traditional drum group based at Victoria Falls. They also feature a double marimba section and produce an ethereal, acoustic percussion sound which is popular with Zambians and tourists alike.

Airpower. Zambian air force band, extremely popular for their cover versions. They seem to have less trouble with equipment than fellow musicians. Led by Chris Tembo.

Compilations

1979	PSL 2000	Top Luapula Hits (Kazembe)
1984	IAS 001	20th Independence Anniversary (Kazembe, Evans Mulongwe, Masiye No. 1, Lima Jazz Band)
1985	IAS 002	Independence Special (Kazembe, Chisala, Herman Striedl, Rimos, Zing Zong Band, Fire Family)
1988	WOMAD 009	Shani (Amayenge, Shalawambe, Akim Simukonda, A.C. Kalusha, P.K. Chisala – a collection of recent singles)
1989	ORB 037	Zambiance (Shalawambe, Amayenge, A.K. Chisala, Kalambo, Julizya, Lubani Kalunga and Fikashala Band)
	MON 0015	Zambia (Amayenge, Shalawambe, Teddy Chilambe, Kazembe, Masasu, Chisala, Fire Family, Lima Jazz)

Zamrock

Witch, The. Zambia's pre-eminent Zamrock outfit formed in the early 1970s. Influenced equally by Eurorock stars like Led Zeppelin and afro-rock superstars Osibisa (who toured Zambia in 1972). A five-piece band featuring Chris Mbewe, Gideon Mulenga, J. Chando, J. Mvula and B. Muma. Vocals in English – instrumentals a speciality. The band split in the early 1980s and Chris Mbewe moved on to form the Afro Sunshine Band, based in neighbouring Botswana. But by the late 1980s he had lost interest in the music business, joined a church and became a gospel star.

1974	ZMLP 5	Introduction
	ZMLP 7	In The Past
1976	ZTZ 1	Lazy Bones
	ZTZ 7	Lukombo Vibes
1977	WIT 02	Janet (Kenya)

Ilonga, Ricky. Solo guitarist and singer, Ricky was a founder-member of seminal afro-rock band Musi-O-Tunya (The Smoke that Thunders – Victoria Falls). Released several hard afro-rock albums but little heard of today.

| | RILP 005 | Same Name |

Blackfoot, The. Popular Zamrock outfit.

| 1978 | ZMPL 28 | The Foot Steps |

Mlevhu, Keith (b. Chingola, 1950). Keith started his musical career at the age of sixteen, working his way through such pop and copyright bands as Dynamagic, New Orleans, the Rave Five, Macbeth and Anything. By the late 1970s Keith was ready to go solo and carved out a niche in the market for his modernisation of old Zambian melodies.

1976	KMMLP 001	Bonafumbisa
1977	KMMLP 002	Love and Freedom
1978	KMMLP 004	Touch of the Son

Ngozi, Paul. One of Zambia's favourite sons, whose early death robbed the country of one of its most gifted guitarists and producers. During his brief career with the Ngozi Family, Paul was responsible for at least half a dozen hit albums. The Ngozi Family comprised Paul on guitar and vocals, Chris Tembo on drums and Tommy Mwale on bass. The band performed in the heavy afro-rock style derived from Osibisa but owing more to Hendrix and Cream.

They scored heavily with the 1978 smash hit 'Chikokoshi'. Paul died sudenly in 1989.

1977	CL 004	45,000 Volts
1978	LAF 002	Heavy Connections
	PNL 001	Happy Trip
1979	PNL 003	The Best of (1976–9)
1980	PNL 004	Bad Character
1981	TFLP 001	Size 9

Kalindula

Kalindula is a Zambian roots music, originally from Luapula province but increasingly a generic name for most Zambian dance music. Characterised by a strong rumba bass-line and traditional drum rhythms, Kalindula emerged in the late 1970s in response to President Kaunda's plea for more indigenous music to challenge the dominance of Zaïrean rumba and western pop.

Amayenge. Formed in 1979 as the New Crossbones, the band finally emerged as Amayenge in 1985. As the Crossbones they pioneered the early development of Kalindula, being voted band of the year in both 1981 and 1982 and representing the country at the second Pan-African Youth Festival in Libya in 1983. Now a six-piece guitar band led by Chris Chali, they have continued to show the way forward with successful African tours and a 1989 tour of the UK. They have also toured the USSR and in 1989 were invited to perform at the Namibian Independence celebrations.

1988	SFPS 067	The Peel Sessions
1989	MON 003	Amayenge
1990		Kusiyana

Shalawambe. Originating in Luapula province, this five-piece band is very much a family affair, comprising three brothers, a cousin and a friend. The band were formed in 1985, although the musicians were strictly part-time, playing music in between harvests and other farming activities. Also toured the UK in 1989 and appeared in the ANC-organised Front Line Rock concert. They often perform songs by the late Alick Nkhata. In late 1990 Zambia was surprised by rumours that the band had split – thankfully these stories were vastly exaggerated and the band were simply keeping a low profile during the recording of two new LPs. Of course such rumours did not worry Shalawambe – their name means 'keep on gossiping'!

| 1989 | MON 002 | Samora Machel |

Masasu Band. Led by John Mulemena, Masasu have been one of Zambia's top professional bands for almost a decade. They introduced the 'mantyantya' style of the Kaonde from North-west province to Zambian music fans. Accepted Kalindula stylists, they toured the UK in the late 1980s, with a memorable performance in Glasgow in 1990 to celebrate the tenth anniversary of the South African Development Co-ordinating Committee (SADCC). On that occasion they were accompanied by guest vocalist P.K. Chisala.

1989	MON 004	Masasu

Julizya. Formed by guitarist Maliki Mulemi in 1986 and one of the few professional outfits in the country. A roots Kalindula band who transform traditional melodies and arrangements, further enhancing the sound and spectacle with dancers and singers drawn from the National Dance Troupe.

1988	KARI 013	Tai Yaka

Mashabe Band. Five-piece Kalindula band led by James Chisenga, playing a fine mix of traditional and modern music. (The name Mashabe means Demons.)

1985	ZMLP 71	Mashabe
1986	ZMLP 74	Mandela
1987	ZMLP 77	Mashabe Vol. 2

Makishi Band. Off-shoot from Mashabe led by Davies Chimpampie. By singing in Bemba and Nyanja, the most common languages in Zambia, this Kalindula band retains a wide national appeal. In 1990 they made a successful tour of neighbouring Zimbabwe, indicating a potential regional appeal for Kalindula.

1986	ZMLP 75	Ba Samora
1987	ZMLP 78	Vol. 2
1990	ZMLP 82	Ngomba Shaya

Majoza Band. Another fine Kalindula outfit – three guitars, drums and bass – led by composer, guitarist and vocalist C. Mubanga.

1990	ZMLP 84	Botswana Show

Kanjela Band. Six-piece guitar band from the Lusaka area. They play a mixture of styles but are mainly liked for their adaptation of Tonga beats into the Kalindula framework.

1989	ZMLP 81	Lengani Mama

Bwaluka Founders Band. Talented and popular off-shoot from the Junior Mulemena Boys.

1989	ZMLP 80	Kangube

Masiye Dancing Queens. All-female band who are prepared to tackle serious social issues. Partly for this reason, they seldom get bookings on their own and often have to operate as front-line dancers for male bands.

Serenje Kalindula Band. Formed in Serenje, Central Province, the Kitwe based outfit led by Syman Kaseba are in the forefront of the Kalindula bandwagon. Over the last few years, like all Kalindula bands, they have developed their own beat, called 'fwandafwanda'. The band was originally put together in 1976 as a four piece but soon felt the need to expand by adding two new musicians. Syman joined in 1980, giving the band some much needed leadership and direction, striking gold in 1985 with the hit single 'Chibangu Na Ba Mulemena'. This Bemba hit was soon followed by 'A Hembele', in Senga. Thereafter, as one of the most versatile of the Kalindula bands, Serenje scored time and again with hits like 'Bible Yalilanda' and 'Ibuku Lyamfwa'.

1979	ZMPL 31	Amanyamune
1988	KARI 026	Elo Yalila
1991		Abakali Bakali

Lima Jazz Band. A rural band who started up in Samfya, regional capital of Luapula province and home to Kalindula, and they perform mainly in small town halls. Currently led by Costa Chola, they are one of the most popular Kalindula outfits in the country.

1985	KARI 005	Yanga Yanga
1990		Konkotyo

Chola, Spokes, and the Mansa Radio Band

1977	ZMLP 23	Kalindula

Kalusha, Alfred Chisala Jnr. Born into a musical family, Alfred was brought up in Luapula province, home to many of Zambia's top musicians. He passed away in 1988 after a long illness. His work can be heard on the *Zambiance* compilation.

Chisala, P.K. (b. Peter Kalumba Chisala, Luapula). A gifted singer, composer and arranger, P.K. established himself in the mid-1980s and, despite being handicapped by blindness, soon won a devoted following in the country, becoming known as the Stevie Wonder of Zambia. Today, he still splits his time between music and working for the Council for the Blind and Handicapped. P.K. has recorded several singles, include his all-time classic, 'Polepole'.

Chilambe, Teddy (b. Luapula, 1948). Nicknamed 'Tandeo', he is one of the country's most gifted musicians, but, like so many others, cannot guarantee a livelihood from music and doubles up as mine-captain in Ndola. Unable to tour for obvious reasons, he started recording in 1976 and has remained at or near the top ever since. More recent material, as yet unreleased, reveals a penchant for the style of Tabu Ley.

Simukonda, Akeem. Vocalist and multi-instrumentalist.

Mwansa, John. Gifted singer who shot to the top spot in 1980 with his 'Mukamfwilwa' (Widow).

By the late 1980s the Zambian music scene was at its liveliest since the music revolution of the mid-1970s, with dozens of good bands playing at nightclubs, compounds, hotels and motels up and down the country. Bands to watch out for include Super K, Uweka Stars, Tropicals Band (jazz-blues fusion), Malimba, Oliya, the Amba 4 (female singers-dancers), Mwatashock, the Great Matakazi, Maloza, Jane Osborne (cabaret singer), Fridah Mwila (female singer), Wakasombo Kamanyora (rumba), Matakas Band (rumba), Super League (rumba), Revival (Zamrumba), Rhoda Motro (female vocalist), Super Vina, Slique and Jambo Jambo.

Reggae

As in the rest of Africa, reggae has made enormous inroads into local music over the last five years. The main impulse remains Jamaica, although Lucky Dube has a substantial local following. Few Zambian reggae bands have, as yet, recorded but the most popular performing bands include Burnin Youth, Brian Chengela and the Twelve Tribes, and Imiti Ikula Empanga, a Kitwe-based band led by Blackman Kabengele.

Choral music

1960s	TR 24	Six Separatist Hymns (Bemba)
1981	ZMPL 34	Merciful Paradise Church Choir
1989	KMB	Chitsitsimutso Choir
1990	ZMLP 85	Sweet Breeze Music Ministry: Jesus is the Lord

39   Malawi

(ECONOMY AND SOCIETY. Pop.: 8.5 million.
Area: 94,080 sq. km. Capital: Lilongwe.
Independence: 1964. Currency: Malawi kwacha.)

The earliest inhabitants of the region were the Chewa, Tumbuka and Tonga, who practised agriculture but by the seventeenth and eighteenth centuries had been caught up in the slave trade. In the nineteenth century more powerful military societies – the Ngoni and the Yao – moved in from the south and conquered the scattered groups of farmers. Later in the century David Livingstone arrived, bringing Christianity, commerce and eventually colonialism as the British declared a protectorate over the area in 1891 and named it Nyasaland. For the next seventy years, the British ran the tiny landlocked colony exclusively for the benefit of a white farming community, encouraging land alienation and producing a new class of migrant workers to the South African mines. Africans tried to resist but the 1915 Chilembwe uprising was brutally suppressed.

Then, in the late 1940s, the same issue of federation which had so antagonised the African population of Zambia inspired a somewhat belated nationalist movement – the Nyasaland African Congress. In 1958 Hastings Banda was invited home from Britain to head the movement, leading the country to independence in 1964 and remaining in power ever since. Banda moved quickly to stamp his authority on the country: opponents were exiled or imprisoned; relations were established with South Africa; and the press was heavily censored. Against this political dictatorship must be set Malawi's impressive record of economic growth, described as more a refinement of colonialism than its transformation. Large private farming was encouraged to the neglect of the peasant farmers and the country received enormous amounts of western aid. In 1977 Banda was quoted as saying that 'We do not suppress the acquisitive and possessive instinct here. Instead, we encourage it.' By 1980 this selective type of economic development had made Malawi the sixth poorest country in the world in terms of average personal income.

TRADITIONAL MUSIC

Gerhard Kubik has done an enormous amount of research into Malawian traditional music and should be consulted for further information (see Bibliography). Gerhard also worked with the Kachamba Brothers, a neo-traditional guitar and penny-whistle group whose music is occasionally available outside the country. Another pioneer of early Malawian music was Hugh Tracey, whose 'Music of Africa Series' contains many recordings of traditional music from the 1940s to 1960s. His son, Andrew Tracey, is currently working with one of the few Chopi xylophone bands left in existence, in a refugee camp in southern Malawi.

POPULAR MUSIC

Malawian music remains one of the most under exposed in the entire continent. Piracy, for once, is not a problem since so few bands have the opportunity to record. One indication of the perilous state of Malawian music is the realisation that the most popular bands in the country are still the Police Band, the Army Band and the band of the Malawi Broadcasting Corporation. In 1990 Phillip Donner of the Finnish Institute of Workers' Music (supported by the Finnish Broadcasting Corporation) worked with the radio station to transcribe all existing archival music. Otherwise, in addition to the few names mentioned in Volume 1, not much seems to have been happening in Malawi over the last five years, at least in terms of modern musical culture. Very few bands visit the country, although the Real Sounds from neighbouring Zimbabwe toured in 1990. Unfortunately the tickets were so overpriced that many citizens could not afford the entrance fee. Once admitted, the Malawian police enforced a strict no-dance policy in a bizarre effort to keep order. None the less, President Banda was said to have enjoyed the show and is rumoured to have subsidised the band's visit.

Maulidi, Maurice. Leader of a talented guitar band who have made at least one local cassette. The music is highly reminiscent of Kalindula, albeit with a slightly faster tempo and clearer guitar lines.

Makasu. Blantyre-based pop band keen to compose their own material. In the absence of recording facilities, they struggle with equipment which would be considered primitive by London bedsit standards. In 1985 they scored with a regional afro-reggae hit.

1985   Makasu Band

Zomba Hardware Band

1984   HRJVLJ 01   Bushmen Caves

Malawi Broadcasting Band and the Chichiri Queens

1974   Kokoliko Ku Malawi

Roots. Lilongwe-based band playing a mixture of reggae, rumba, pop and traditional.

Chidzanja-Nkhomo, Maria. Cabaret singer with wide repertoire drawn from afro-rock, soul and ballads. Often backed on stage by the Pamodzi Band.

Army Strings Band. Have produced several local rumba hits.

40   Mozambique

(ECONOMY AND SOCIETY. Pop.: 16 million. Area: 783,030 sq. km. Capital: Maputo. Independence: 1975. Currency: Metical.)

Inhabited by the Makua-Lomwe (approx. 40 per cent), the Thonga, the Chopi, Tongu, Shona and Makonde, Mozambique's internal development was first interrupted as early as the sixteenth century by Portuguese exploitation of slaves, ivory and gold. For the next three centuries a scattered and uneven type of colonialism further impoverished the region until in the 1930s the fascist Portuguese state decided to isolate its colonies completely. By this time the Mozambican economy was almost entirely reliant on the migration of labour to the South African mines – a system little different from the outright slavery and forced labour of the previous centuries.

In 1962 FRELIMO was created from a variety of opposition sources including intellectuals, exiles and armed militants. By 1964 it had launched the armed struggle against the Portuguese and made steady progress from then on, despite the assassination of leader Edouardo Mondlane in 1968. Thereafter, FRELIMO moved steadily to the left to become the most radical armed movement in Africa, with substantial support from sympathisers in the west. When the Portuguese Government collapsed in 1974, FRELIMO was ready for power and by the time of independence in 1975 had transformed itself from a national liberation movement into a Marxist ruling party.

Mozambique was almost immediately put under threat by Southern Rhodesia and South Africa as well as having to contend with an enormous flight of capital and skills. It was not an easy situation within which to rebuild and restructure a country with a legacy of several hundred years of exploitation. Yet progress was made in several important directions, including successful literacy and preventive health campaigns and the beginnings of economic development. But by the early 1980s Mozambique was under more sustained military pressure from the South African-backed RENAMO movement. Little more than mercenaries, RENAMO devastated the areas under their control, causing massive migration, the diversion of resources to counteract the military threat and the weakening of government control over large areas of the country.

As the economic crisis deepened, Mozambique sought a rapprochement with South Africa and attempted to liberalise the economy. RENAMO, with covert western backing, stepped up their destruction in an effort to remove FRELIMO from power. Then, in 1986, the country suffered the sudden loss of President Samora Machel in a plane crash, widely rumoured to have been caused by South Africa. He was replaced by President Chissano, but there was to be no relief from the RENAMO offensive and by the late 1980s Mozambique was on the verge of collapse. The protracted armed struggle had seriously impoverished the nation, with famine and drought now added to the mindless terrorism of RENAMO. RENAMO remain a powerful military force, secretly supported by Kenya, Malawi and South Africa. There is now every indication that a beleaguered FRELIMO will be forced to the negotiating table much as the MPLA have been forced to treat with UNITA in Angola.

The effects of the civil war were tragic, and although bare statistics cannot meaningfully illustrate the degree of human suffering, they may just indicate the scale of the disaster. Between 1980 and 1988 Mozambique suffered more than a million war-related deaths, of which more than half were children under five. Over a million people became refugees, with almost five million displaced and more than a quarter of a million children orphaned. Food was destroyed, schools and hospitals burnt down and transport routes sabotaged. No country could survive these blows alone, and although neglected by most of the world, the Scandinavian countries steadfastly supported the struggling country. By 1991 famine was again staring Mozambique in the face with 'donor fatigue' cited as the reason behind western indifference to the massive suffering. Inevitably, under such conditions, musical culture was severely disrupted.

TRADITIONAL MUSIC

As in almost every country in Southern Africa, many of the early recordings were made by Hugh Tracey and are seldom available. During the 1940s and 1950s Tracey conducted field recordings with the following ethnic groups – the Chopi, Tongu, Shangaan, Tswa, Ndau, Ronga, Sena and Nyungwe. Of pure ethnographic interest are the 1920 recordings of C. Kamba Simango, a Ndau from Mozambique.

1981	FE 4318	Music From Mozambique: Chopi Timbilia (Xylophone music)
1983	FE 4319	Music From Mozambique Vol. 3 (Chopi xylophones, chordophones and percussion)
1991	PIR 31CD	Companhia Naçional de Canto e Dança: Walawasa (Acoustic traditional music from National Company)

Durao, Eduardo, and Orchestre Durao (b. Eduardo Durao Lamussene, Gune Canda, Inhambane Province, 1952). The young Durao was taught traditional music by his father, leaving school at 17 to try to find work in Maputo. He followed various jobs until independence in 1975 enabled him to concentrate on his music. Shortly afterwards he became one of the founding-members of the Union of Mozambiquan Music and Theatre. In 1979 he joined the National Company of Dance and Song and travelled widely with the group. In 1990, assisted by a Canadian aid project, he established a timbila (wooden xylophone) school in Maputo, teaching the youth aspects of traditional Chopi culture. On his first (CD-only) release he mixes traditional acoustic music of the mbila (plural timbila) with a modern rhythm section of drums and bass. The timbila parts are overdubbed. The Chopi are highly respected for their timbila playing, although, because of the war and the disruption caused by RENAMO, many Chopi musicians have fled into Malawi, often carrying their instruments with them. For further information, readers are referred to Hugh Tracey's *Chopi Musicians: Their Music, Poetry and Instruments* (Oxford, OUP, 1948).

| 1991 | CDORB 065 | Timbila |

LIBERATION MUSIC

As in Angola, Zimbabwe and Guinea-Bissau, the armed struggle produced a vigorous tradition of freedom and liberation songs. They are rarely available today and can generally be considered to be of little more than archival interest. However, with the exception of Zimbabwe, academics have rarely concerned themselves with this impressive repository of recent oral history.

| 1980 | NGOMA 0040 | Various: Das FPLA |
| 1985 | LPP 282 | Various: Canti Rivoluzionari del Mozambico |

MODERN MUSIC

The popular music of Mozambique is only now beginning to penetrate western musical consciousness. The reasons for the underdevelopment of the Mozambican pop scene are not hard to find and include the impact of a prolonged armed struggle, a decade of RENAMO terrorism and the absolute impoverishment of the economy. The only recording studio is the government-owned facility at the national radio station, and although many bands record live for the radio station, very few have the money or the opportunity to record for vinyl or cassette. However, by the end of the 1980s several development agencies were actively investigating the possibility of establishing local recording facilities in Mozambique. Faced with the demands of fighting a civil war and trying to rebuild the economy, it would appear that initiatives of this type hold out more promise than direct government involvement.

Marrabenta Star de Moçambique, Orchestre. Maputo-based big band playing the uniquely Mozambican 'Marrabenta' style, possibly familiar to listeners from Sam Mangwana's exquisite mid-1980s LP *Canta Moçambique*. The band was formed in the mid-1960s and classic hits from that era have now been made by available by German-based Pirhana label.

1989	PIR 568 22012	Independence
1991	PIR 23LP	Piquenique
	PIR 28-1	Elisa Gomara Saia (1960s hits)

Eyuphuro. Led by Zena Bakar and Gimo Remane, Eyuphuro have from the very beginning consciously tried to preserve the traditional rhythms of their home in Nampula. But since both leaders grew up in Illa de Mozambique, one of the country's most cosmopolitan centres where Arab music meets Latin, it was inevitable that elements of both should enter the band's sound. Lyrically, the band deal with everyday matters like love and life but they also have a more pointed side where they deal with more serious social issues. In 1988 the band toured Europe and won many new fans. In 1989 they recorded in a Toronto hi-tech studio for the Real World release. The band proved to be enormously popular and they toured again in 1990 at the behest of the WOMAD organisation.

| 1980s | LPL 0131 | Parado de Sucessos |
| 1989 | RWLP 10 | Mama Mosambiki |

Salvador, Mauricio. 'Sweet' pop music from founder of Eyuphuro, known in Mozambique as 'makua' music.

| 1991 | PIR 33CD | Thamole |

Vangazy. 'Psycho beat' from Maputo.

| 1991 | PIR 32CD | Vangazy |

Awendila, Wili

| 1979 | LBM 004 | Wansati |

Tovela, Jorge

| 1978 | LMB 003 | Musica de Mozambique |

Luis, Fernando

| 1988 | ESP 8447 | Bassopa |

Compilations

| 1980 | NGOMA 0049 | Vol. 1 (Grupo Bantu/ Magide Mussa/Jose Mafer/ Os Planetas/Camal Jive) |

41 Namibia

(ECONOMY AND SOCIETY. Pop.: 1.6 million. Area: 824,292 sq. km. Capital: Windhoek. Independence: 1990. Currency: Rand.) For map, see p. 185.

Namibia, formerly South West Africa, has been one of the most troubled countries of the continent. Originally inhabited by the San, Nama and Damara, the Bantu migrations of the sixteenth and seventeenth centuries heralded the arrival of the Herero, the Ovambo and the Kavango. Life was always difficult in this largely desert area but was made doubly so from the mid-nineteenth century when the South Africans, the British and the Germans all declared an interest in the region. Eventually, the territory fell under German colonial rule with the brutal subjugation of indigenous groups and the introduction of a forced labour system. In the rising of 1908–9 it is estimated that up to 70 per cent of the Herero were killed. In 1919, when Germany was stripped of its colonies, Namibia was awarded to South Africa under a League of Nations mandate and so began seven decades of unmitigated repression. By the 1950s opposition was emerging to South African misrule – first from a small group of intellectuals, then from the contract workers. In December 1959 armed police killed over a dozen protestors (Namibia's 'Sharpeville') and all the opposition groups united under the banner of SWAPO.

Initially, SWAPO waited for UN action to end the South African occupation, but when this was not forthcoming they turned to the armed struggle, stepping up activity after 1966 when the UN finally terminated South Africa's mandate. Of course, this made no difference and South Africa continued much as before, crudely exploiting the area's mineral wealth and ignoring all appeals to relinquish power. The armed struggle lasted for the next 15 years, costing many thousands of lives and further impoverishing an already poor country. Northern Namibia was also used a base from whence South Africa could destabilise Angola, either working alone or with its UNITA allies. Meanwhile, the international arguments continued, with SWAPO recognised universally as the real government of the country. Finally, when events in Southern Africa came to a head in the late 1980s as South Africa began to feel the effects of sanctions and military defeat, the way was cleared for Namibian independence. Elections took place in November 1989 with SWAPO winning a smaller than anticipated majority. However, the margin was still large enough for it to form the first government when independence finally came in 1990.

The effects of the South African occupation between 1980 and 1988 can crudely be summarised as follows: 50,000 deaths of children under five; 67 per cent of the population below the poverty line; and massive financial losses to the country through lost investment and excessive security costs.

TRADITIONAL MUSIC

During the years of South African occupation any assertion of traditional culture was perceived as a subversive act. In rural situations, song and dance were used to inform people of the reasons underlying their oppression and even, on occasion, to disclose enemy agents. Yet, the leaders of the new Namibia are wary of completely relying on the past as the basis for modern culture. Strike Mkandla of SWAPO warned that 'Namibians need to debate very thoroughly what we define as "progressive" and "reactionary" cultural trends. . . . Change – cultural syncretism – isn't necessarily reactionary: remember that in this region it is apartheid which is the most vehement opponent of such developments. Apartheid wants to retain the reactionary, feudal and divisive tendencies which past culture can also contain' (cited in Anon., *Art from the Frontline* – see Bibliography).

Very little traditional music from Namibia has been put on vinyl and, despite the interpretation outlined above, it is to be hoped that the new government will try to record as much material as possible from what has become a completely marginalised culture.

MODERN MUSIC

The independence of Namibia in 1990 and an end to several decades of armed struggle marked an important turning point for the people of Namibia and their culture. The years of South African rule had been characterised by the all too familiar racist policy of divide and rule. The 15 major groups in the country had been deliberately segmented into specific tribal identities, each with its own radio channel and programming. As a result they were largely ignorant of the culture and music of their neighbours. Technical facilities were virtually non-existent, with the exception of the state-controlled NBC radio studio. The cost of imported instruments was, and is, prohibitive. In response to this situation, SWAPO developed one of the most coherent cultural policies on the continent, stressing the need for a departure from the past and looking to culture as the glue with which to bind society together. It remains to be seen whether the facilities can now be put in place to encourage the growth of a dynamic national culture.

Kaujeua, Jackson (b. Namibia, 1953). Jackson Kaujeua has been described as being to the Namibian liberation movement what Thomas Mapfumo was to Zimbabwe. Little is known of his early life but enough can be gathered from the fact that he left the country to go into exile in 1974. Over the next few years Jackson became the voice of the revolution with his folk songs and ballads being smuggled into Namibia, where copies of copies of copies circulated widely. He was able to compose material that made him popular with young and old alike.

In 1990, a few months after independence, Jackson returned and to his great personal embarrassment was treated as a superstar, as famous and as popular as the SWAPO political leadership. In several respects Kaujeua personifies the SWAPO cultural policy of one nation – one culture. He is able to compose and sing in all of Namibia's fifteen major languages as well as spicing up his material with rumba and mbaqanga. This eclectic style initially confused Namibians and no one could really work out if he was Herero, Damara or even Zulu. But this facility in styles and languages now stands Jackson in good stead as he strives to create a Namibian national sound. In 1990 he recorded his first LP (although he had previously recorded with Onyeka, the SWAPO Cultural Troupe) which was due for release in 1991. Fully aware of the untapped richness and diversity of Namibian culture, Jackson spent 1991 travelling the newly free country, studying and learning. We now await the results.

1991		One Step Higher

Various

1983	KZA	One Namibia One Nation: Freedom Songs
1984	IDAF 001	Onyeka: The Torch
1986	RTT 168	Robert Wyatt/SWAPO Singers: Wind of Change (12" EP)

42 Botswana

(ECONOMY AND SOCIETY. Pop.: 1.15 million. Area: 570,000 sq. km. Capital: Gaborone. Independence: 1966. Currency: Pula.) For map, see p. 185.

A large, semi-arid country, Botswana has always been unsuitable for permanent settlement, with the vast majority of the small population living around the more fertile Limpopo and Shashe rivers. The majority of the current population – Sotho-speaking Tswana – moved into the area in the early nineteenth century, subjugating indigenous groups and establishing a highly stratified and sophisticated kingdom. With an economy based on cattle, the Tswana enjoyed a period of prosperity throughout most of the nineteenth century until the area became a British protectorate in 1890. Yet, unlike their neighbours, the Twsana were able to maintain their pre-colonial social and economic organisation and it was only in the twentieth century that the area was turned into a labour reserve for the South African mines. Independence came in 1966 under the conservative Seretse Khama, who opened the doors to foreign investment, encouraged white farmers to stay and adopted a neutral stance in relation to the various liberation wars under way at the time.

The post-independence period has been characterised by political stability in one of Africa's few functioning democracies, increasing urbanisation and economic development based on cattle ranching and mining. Yet there has been a price to pay, including a white dominated mining sector, growing national debt and massive import dependency on South Africa. All this has served to hold back the development of African enterprise and social progress. When Khama died in 1980 he was succeeded by his long-time friend and supporter Dr Quett Masire. Masire retained the basic economic policies of his predecessor, although he had to contend with increasing South African aggression. Today Botswana acts as a magnet for educated Africans from across the continent.

TRADITIONAL MUSIC

The two 1990 cassettes are private field recordings available through Stern's. They were captured by John Brearley and are excellent recordings of traditional San music. The situation of the San has become increasingly difficult over the last decade – unable to maintain a traditional life-style as hunter-gatherers yet unable to find a place in modern society. Both cassettes include around 20 tracks, featuring instrumental and vocal traditions including thumb piano (dongo), mouthbow, (segorogoro), foot-bow (daketari), stringed instruments (goroshi and segaba), as well as various friction drums and percussion.

1982	PR REC	Music of the Malokos
1984	FE 4315	Kalahari San
1990	Cass.	Music of the Kalahari
	Cass.	Kalahari 2

MODERN MUSIC

The modern music scene in Botswana appears to be highly dependent on musical trends both north (in Zaïre) and south (in South Africa). Little original music comes out of Botswana and any further information would be warmly welcomed.

Mokhali, Johnny

1988	CDRL 126	Drumrock

Kgwanyape Band. Blending Tswana folk styles and traditions with Celtic mandolins, the Kgwanyape Band provide sharp and incisive social commentary on the affairs of one of Africa's few functioning democracies.

1990		Mephato Ya Maloba

first

&

foremost

Stern's Records, UK
(Distribution & Exports)
116 Whitfield Street
London W1P 5RW
U.K.
Tel. (071) 387 5550
Tel. (071) 388 5533
Fax (071) 388 2756

Stern's Music, USA
(Distribution)
598 Broadway
New York
N.Y. 10012
U.S.A.
Tel. (212) 925 1648
Fax (212) 925 1689

Appendix:
Pan-African Productions

Given the growing cosmopolitanism of many African musicians and their residence in various capitals around the world, it is hardly surprising that many of them have worked together on projects and recordings which owe less to any single tradition than to a broader pan-African sensibility. By fusing various musical styles with poetry, comedy, drama and other performing arts, such artistes have played a crucial role in developing a broader appreciation of the totality of African culture outside the continent.

African Dawn. Formed in London in 1980, this multi-media collective draws its inspiration from the popular cultures of the pan-African world. Initially they emphasised drama and poetry, but as their musical skills grew they began to add more music to their repertoire. With four albums to their credit and dozens of important events involving other stars such as Dade Krama, Toumani Diabate, Tunde Jegede, and the Last Poets, African Dawn have become, over the last decade, a powerful black cultural force on the London scene. Members are currently drawn from Ghana, Zimbabwe, Grenada, Senegal and Uruguay.

1983	AD 100	Besiege The Night
1985	AD 200	Conversation
1987	AD 300	Chimurenga
1989	AD 400	Jali

Tam Tam Pour L'Ethiope. A one-off African response to the 1985 famine in Ethiopia. The effort started with a 45 r.p.m. recorded in Paris by a variety of musicians, producers and companies, eschewing any personal profit. Those involved at this stage included Mory Kante, Ray Lema, Salif Keïta, Sousy Kasseya and Bovick. This was followed by a larger televised show from Abidjan – very much Africa's answer to Geldof's 'Live Aid', where no Africans were involved or even invited. The Abidjan line-up was impressive – Dibango, Ade, Keïta, Toure Kunda, Lema, Mory Kante, Jerry Malekani, Tony Allen, Ballou Canta, Shina Williams, Zao, M'Pongo Love, Tala, N'Dour, Pamelo Mounka and the Malapoets. Never before had such an abundance of African musical talent been assembled on one stage for one cause.

| 1985 | 880 568 | Tam Tam Pour L'Ethiopie (45 r.p.m.) |

Jericho. A true pan-African supergroup assembled for a 1986 tour to publicise the imprisonment of Fela, with musicians drawn mainly from Xalam and Ghetto Blaster, reinforced by Ray Lema and Mory Kante. No records were released.

Ghetto Blaster. Formed in Paris in 1983 from a mélange of French, Cameroonian, Beninoise and Nigerians.

| 1985 | 8 600 | People |

Select Bibliography

This bibliography, like the entire book, is directed towards the ongoing task of bringing up to date and deepening the basic information provided in Volume 1. I have tried where possible to cite only sources likely to be available, but I have also added key sources for any further research into African music. Particular mention should be made of the extremely useful new volume by John Gray (see below), for if anything in the academic world marks the 'coming of age' of a new subject, then it is the appearance of a substantial bibliographical guide.

Agovi, K.E., 'The Political Relevance of Ghanaian Highlife Songs Since 1957', *Research in African Literatures*, Vol. 20, No. 2, 1989.

Anderson, A.M., *Music in the Mix: The Story of South African Popular Music*, Ravan Press, Johannesburg, 1991.

Anderson, L.A., 'The Interrelation of African and Arab Musics: Some Preliminary Considerations', in K.P. Wachsmann (ed.), *Essays on Music and History in Africa*, Evanston, Ill., 1971.

Aning, B.A., *An Annotated Bibliography of Music and Dance in English Speaking Africa*, University of Ghana, n.d.

Anon., *Hommage à Grand Kalle*, Editions Lokole, Kinshasa, 1985.

——, *A History of Traditional Music of Kenya: Musicians and their Instruments*, Pupil's Book, Vol. 1, Jemsik Books, Nairobi, 1987.

——, *Chansons D'Afrique et Des Antilles*, Editions L'Harmattan, Paris, 1988.

——, 'Pourquoi les Ivoriens Sont-ils les Meilleurs?', *Africa International*, No. 214, 1989.

——, *Art from the Frontline: Contemporary Art from Southern Africa*, Karia Press, London, 1990.

——, 'Toure Kunda', *Africa International*, Jan, 1991.

Basden, G.T., *Niger Ibos*, London, 1938.

Bebey, F., 'Traditional Music from the Ivory Coast', *Balafon, A Quarterly Review* (in-flight magazine of Air Afrique), No. 46, Paris, 1980.

Bender, W., *Song Texts of African Popular Music*, Bayreuth African Studies Series, No. 2, Bayreuth, Germany, 1984.

——, *Sweet Mother: Afrikanische Musik*, Trickster-Verlag, Munich, 1985.

—— (ed.), *Perspectives in African Music*, Bayreuth African Studies Series, No. 9, Bayreuth, Germany, 1989.

Besingor, F., *Sons D'Afrique*, Nouvelle Edition Marabout, Paris, 1988.

Blacking, J., 'Trends in the Black Music of South Africa', in E. May (ed.), *Music of Many Cultures*, Los Angeles, 1980.

Brandel, R., *The Music of Central Africa: An Ethnomusicological Study*, Nijhoff, The Hague, 1961.

Carrington, J.F., *Talking Drums of Africa*, Kingsate Press, London, 1949.

Cathcart, J., *Hey You!: A Portrait of Youssou N'Dour*, Fine Line Books, London, 1989.

Chauvet, S., *Musique Nègre*, Soc. D'Editions Géographiques, Paris, 1926.

Chernoff, J.M., *African Rhythm and African Sensibility*, University of Chicago Press, 1979.

Chester, G., and Jegede, T., *The Silenced Voice: Hidden Music of the Kora*, Diabate Kora Arts, London, 1987.

Collins, J., 'The Concert Party in Ghana', *Musical Traditions*, No. 4, London, 1985.

Collins, J., and Cheney, T., 'Highlife & Prophecy: The Ghanaian Gospel Sound', *Reggae and African Beat*, Vol. 5, No. 2, 1986.

Collins, J. (ed.), 'My Life by Sir Victor Uwaifo', unpublished, Ghana, 1974.

——, *E.T. Mensah: King of Highlife*, Off the Record Press, London, 1986.

Coplan, D., 'The African Musician and the Development of the Johannesburg Entertainment Industry, 1900–1960', *Journal of Southern African Studies*, Vol. 5, No. 2, 1979.

——, 'The Urbanisation of African Performing Arts in South Africa', Ph.D., University of Indiana, 1980.

Cutter, C.H., 'The Politics of Music in Mali', *African Arts*, Vol. 1, No.3, 1968.

Dannen, F., *Hit Men: Power Brokers and Fast Money Inside the Music Business*, Times Books, Random House, New York, 1990.

Dargie, D., *Xhosa Music: Its Techniques and Instruments With a Collection of Songs* (accompanying cassette), David Phillip, Cape Town, 1989.

Darko, A., 'The New Musical Traditions in Ghana', Ph.D., Wesleyan University, 1974.

Dibango, M., and Rouard, D., *Trois Kilos de Café*, Lieu Common, Paris, 1990.

DjeDje, J.C. (ed.), *African Musicology: Current Trends Vol. 1*, a Festschrift presented to J.H.K. Nketia, UCLA, 1989.

Dube, C., in Anon., *Art from the Frontline: Contemporary Art from Southern Africa*, Karia Press, London, 1990.

Duran, L., 'The Mandinka Kora', *Recorded Sound*, No. 69, 1978.

——, 'The Music of the Kora', *Times Literary Supplement*, 26 February, 1982.

——, 'Kora of the Wild Featuring Malamini Jobarteh', *Tatler*, Vol. 278, No. 7, 1983.

Eshete, A., *Songs of the Ethiopian Revolution*, Addis Ababa, 1979.

Euba, A., *Essays on Music in Africa, Vol. 1*, Iwalewa House, Univ. of Bayreuth, Germany, 1988.

——, *Essays on Music in Africa, Vol. 2: International Perspectives*, Lagos and Bayreuth African Studies, Elekoto Music Centre, 1989.

——, *Yoruba Drumming: The Dundun Tradition*, Elekoto, Lagos and Bayreuth African Studies, Elekoto Music Centre, 1990.

Ewens, G., *Luambo Franco and 30 Years of OK Jazz*, Off the Record Press, London, 1986.

——, *Africa O-Ye: A Celebration of African Music*, Guinness, London, 1991.

Fiofori, T., *Bala Miller: Developing Music and Musicians in Nigeria*, Spear, Lagos, 1983.

Frith, S. (ed.), *World Music, Politics and Social Change: Papers from the International Association for the Study of Popular Music*, Manchester University Press, Manchester, 1989.

Gaskin, L.J.P., *Select Bibliography of Music in Africa*, London, 1965.

Gorer, G., *Africa Dances*, Penguin, London, 1945.

Graham, R., *Stern's Guide to Contemporary African Music*, Pluto Press, London, 1988.

——, *Da Capo Guide to Contemporary African Music*, Da Capo Press, New York, 1988.

——, 'Konimo on Broadway', *West Africa*, 22 August, 1988.

Gray, J., *African Music: A Bibliographical Guide to the Traditional, Popular, Art and Liturgical Musics of Sub-Saharan Africa*, Greenwood Press, Westport, Conn., 1991.

Hambly, W.D., *Tribal Dancing and Social Development*, Witherby, 1926.

Hanley, F., and May, T. (eds), *Rhythms of the World*, BBC Books, London, 1989.

Harrev, F., 'Jambo Records and the Promotion of Popular Music in East Africa', in W. Bender (ed.), *Perspectives in African Music*, Bayreuth African Studies Series, No. 9, Bayreuth, Germany, 1989.

Hebdige, D., *Cut'N'Mix: Culture and Identity in Caribbean Music*, Comedia, London, 1987.

Hornbostel, E.M. von, and Sachs, C., 'Classification of Musical Instruments', *Galpin Society Journal*, No. 14, 1961.

Horton, C.D., 'Indigenous Music of Sierra Leone: An Analysis of Resources and Educational Implications', Ph.D., UCLA, 1979.

Hudgens, J., and Trillo, R., *The Rough Guide to West Africa*, Harrap-Columbus, London, 1990.

Huskisson, Y., 'Record Industry in South Africa', *Progressus*, Vol. 25, No. 11, 1978.

Ismail, M., 'Traditional Music in the Sudan', *Notes on Education and Research in African Music*, No. 1, 1967.

Jones, A.M., 'African Music in Northern Rhodesia and Some Other Places', *Occasional Papers of the Rhodes Livingstone Museum*, No.4, Livingstone, 1949.

Kaba, L., 'The Cultural Revolution, Artistic Creativity and Freedom of Expression in Guinea', *Journal of Modern African Studies*, Vol. 14, No.2, 1976.

Kauffman, R., 'Shona Urban Music: A Process which Maintains Traditional Values', in W.C. Pendleton (ed.), *Urban Man in Southern Africa*, Gwelo, 1975.

Kebede, A., *Roots of Black Music: The Vocal, Instrumental and Dance Heritage of Africa and Black America*, Prentice-Hall, New Jersey, 1982.

Kerkhoff, I., 'Music in the Revolution', *Keskidee: A Journal of Black Musical Traditions*, Vol. 2, London, 1990.

Kirby, P.R., *The Musical Instruments of the Native Races of South Africa*, OUP, Oxford, 1934.

——, 'The Use of European Musical Techniques by the Non-European People of Southern Africa', *Journal of the International Folk Music Council*, Vol 11, 1959.

Kivnick, H.Q., *Where is the Way?: Song and Struggle in South Africa*, Penguin USA, New York, 1990.

Konate, Y., *Alpha Blondy: Reggae et Société en Afrique Noir*, Karthala, Paris, 1987.

Kubik, G., 'The Kachamba Brothers Band: A Study of Neo-Traditional Music in Malawi', *Zambian Papers*, No. 9, Lusaka, 1974.

——, 'Neo-Traditional Popular Music in East Africa since 1945', *Popular Music*, No. 1, Cambridge, 1981.

——, 'Malawi', in S. Sadie (ed.), *The New Grove Dictionary of Music and Musicians*, Macmillan, London, 1981.

——, 'Malawian Music: A Framework for Analysis', University of Malawi, 1987.

Latham, J., *Ashanti Ballads: Original Asante-Twi by Konimo*, Latham Services, Glasgow, 1988.

Lee, H., *Rockers D'Afrique: Stars et Légendes du Rock Mandingue*, Albin Michel, Paris, 1988.

Lonoh, M.B., *Essai de Commentaire de la Musique Congolaise Moderne*, SEI/ANC, Kinshasa, 1970.

Low, J., *Shaba Diary: A Trip to Rediscover the 'Katanga' Guitar Styles and Songs of the 1950s and 1960s*, Vienna, 1982.

Lynn, L., 'The Growth of Entertainment of Non-African Origin in Lagos from 1886–1920', MA Thesis, University of Ibadan, 1967.

Malamusi, M.A., 'The Zambian Popular Music Scene', *Jazz Research*, Vol. 16, Graz, 1984.

Manuel, P., *Popular Musics of the Non-Western World: An Introductory Survey*, OUP, Oxford, 1988.

Marre, J., and Charlton, H., *Beats of the Heart: Popular Music of the World*, Pantheon, New York, 1985.

Martin, S.H., 'Music in Urban East Africa: Five Genres in Dar Es Salaam', *Journal of African Studies*, Vol. 9, No. 3, 1982.

Mensah, A.A., *Music and Dance in Zambia*, NECZAM, Ndola, 1971.

Merriam, A.A., *African Music in Perspective*, Garland Publishing, New York, 1982.

Mhlabi, S.J., 'An African Troubador: The Music of Josaya Hadebe', Dept of African Languages and Literature, University of Zimbabwe, 1988.

Mitchell, J.C., 'The Kalela Dance', *Rhodes-Livingstone Papers*, No. 27, 1956.

Moore, C., *Fela Fela: This Bitch of a Life*, Allison and Busby, London, 1982.

Nikiprowetzky, T., 'Traditional Music in French-Speaking Africa', *Notes on Education and Research in African Music*, No. 1, 1967.

Nketia, K. (ed.), *Notes on Education and Research in African Music*, No. 2, 1975.

Okagbare, B.C., *The Songs of I.K. Dairo MBE and His Blue Spots*, Apapa, Nigeria, 1969.

Oliver, P. (ed.), *Black Music in Britain: Essays on the Afro-Asian Contribution to Popular Music*, Open University Press, Milton Keynes, 1990.

PMMK, *Cherie Samba: Le Peintre Populaire du Zaïre*, Provincial Museum Voor Moderne Kunst, Ostende, 1991.

Powne, M., *Ethiopian Music: An Introduction*, London, 1968.

Quevedo, R. (Atilla The Hun), 'Atilla's Kaiso: A Short History of Trinidad Calypso', University of the West Indies, Trinidad, 1983.

Radio France Internationale, *Musique Traditionelle de l'Afrique Noire*, Paris: No. 1, Mali, 1980; No. 2, Haute Volta, 1980; No. 4, Senegal et Gambie, 1980; No. 5, Niger, 1981; No. 6, Côte D'Ivoire, 1982; No. 7, Benin, 1984; No. 9, Cameroun, 1984; No. 14, Zaïre, 1984.

Ranger, T., *Dance and Society in East Africa*, Heinemann, East Africa, 1972.

Ricard, A., 'The Concert Party as a Genre: The Happy Stars in Lomé', in B. Lindfors (ed.), *Forms of Folklore in Africa*, Austin, Tex., 1977.

Roaring Lion, The, *Calypso from France to Trinidad: 800 Years of History*, Trinidad, n.d.

Roberts, J.S., *Black Music of Two Worlds*, Original Music, New York, 1974.

Schaeffner, A., *Le Sistre et le Hochet: Musiques, Théâtre et Danse Dans Les Sociétés Africaines*, Herman, Paris, 1990.

Seago, A., *East African Popular Music*, Heinemann, London, 1985.

Seck, E.N., and Clerfeuille, S., *Musiciens Africaines Des Années 80*, L'Harmattan, Paris, 1986.

Senoga-Zake, G., *Making Music in Kenya*, Macmillan (Kenya), Nairobi, 1981.

——, *Folk Music of Kenya*, Uzima Press, Nairobi, 1986.

Seroff, D., 'Zulu Choirs: A Brief Introduction', *Keskidee*, Vol. 1, London, 1986.

Stapleton, C., and May, C., *African All Stars: The Pop Music of a Continent*, Paladin, London, 1989.

Stone, R.M., *African Music and Oral Data: A Catalog of Field Recordings 1902–1975*, Indiana University Press, Bloomington, Ind., 1976.

Thieme, D.L., *African Music: A Briefly Annotated Bibliography*, Washington, 1964.

Tracey, H., *Ngoma*, Longmans, Capetown, 1948.

——, *The Sound of Africa Series of LP Records*, Catalogue, International Library of African Music, Capetown, 1949.

——, *African Dances of the Witswatersrand Gold Mines*, Johannesburg, 1952.

——, 'The Importance of African Music In The Present Day', *African Affairs*, Vol. 59, No. 239, 1961.

Trillo, R., *The Rough Guide to Kenya*, Harrap-Columbus, London, 1990.

Tshonga-Onyumbe, 'Les Problèmes Socio-Economiques dans La Chanson Zaïroise Moderne', *Zaïre-Afrique*, No. 205, 1986.

Vail, L., and White, L., 'Plantation Protest: The History of a Mozambican Song', *Journal of Southern African Studies*, Vol. 5, No. 1, 1978.

Van der Geest, S., and Asante-Darko, N.K., 'The Political Meaning of Highlife Songs in Ghana', *African Studies Review*, Vol. 25, No. 1, 1982.

Varley, D., *African Native Music: An Annotated Bibliography*, Royal Empire Society, London, 1936.

Wahome, J.K., *Musical Instruments: A Resource Book of Traditional Musical Instruments of Kenya*, Pupil's Book, Jemsik, Nairobi, 1986.

Waterman, C., *Juju: A Social History and Ethnography of an African Popular Music*, University of Chicago, Chicago, 1990.

Zindi, F., *Roots Rocking in Zimbabwe*, Mambo Press, Harare, 1985.

MAGAZINES

Africa Beat, 1986–8, London.
Africa Elite, 1988– , Paris.
Africa International, 1985– , Paris.
African Music, 1981–5, Lagos and London.
Afrika, 1986–8, Amsterdam.
Blues and Soul, London.
Folk Roots, 1985– , London.
Musical Traditions, 1986– , London.
Reggae and African Beat, 1983– , Los Angeles.
Straight No Chaser, 1987– , London.
Topical, 1991– , London.
Trade Wind, 1987 – , London.
West Africa, 1917– , London.
World Beat, 1990–1, London.

Index

INDEX

R E A L
S O U N D S

EARTHWORKS

MAKE LOVE TO YOUR EARS
WITH THE VERY BEST IN AFRICAN & LATIN SOUNDS!

THE INDESTRUCTIBLE BEAT OF SOWETO (VOL. 1)   (CDEWV-14/TCEWV-14)

Famous original compilation created by Earthworks featuring some of the very best mbaqanga music from South Africa. Mahlathini Nezintombi Zomgqashiyo, Amaswazi Emvelo, Ladysmith Black Mambazo, Moses Mchunu, Udokotela Shange Namajaha, etc.

THUNDER BEFORE DAWN   (CDEWV-1/TCEWV-1)

(The Indestructible Beat of Soweto, Vol. 2)

More blockbusters from the top township jive series. Mahlathini & The Mahotella Queens, Dilika, Moses Mchunu's Jozi, Malombo, Makgona Tsohle Band, etc.

FREEDOM FIRE   (CDEWV-17/TCEWV-17)

(The Indestructible Beat of Soweto, Vol. 3)

Mahlathini & The Mahotella Queens have never sounded better, plus gospel and Zulu-traditional sounds from Mahlathini, spectacular vocal harmonies from Amaswazi Emvelo, Shangaan disco from J.J. Chauke & The Tiyimeleni Young Sisters, accordion jive from Johnson Mkhalali, Inkunzi Emdaka's gripping traditional guitar music, Malombo. This is the big one.

THE KINGS & QUEENS OF TOWNSHIP JIVE   (CDEWV-20/TCEWV-20)

(Modern Roots Of The Indestructible Beat of Soweto)

The big hits 1968 – 1978. The music that won local fame for Mahlathini, The Mahotella Queens, The Soul Brothers, Abafana Baseqhudeni, and sax jive giants, Thomas Phale, West Nkosi, and Lulu Masilela. The finest roots music.

MAHLATHINI — THE LION OF SOWETO   (CDEWV-4/TCEWV-4)

Fierce township jive from The Man and the Mahlathini Guitar Band. Sparks fly from fiery guitars while Mahlathini growls and groans to awesome effect in this heavy selection from the mid 70s.

MAHLATHINI & THE MAHOTELLA QUEENS — THOKOZILE   (CDEWV-6/TCEWV-6)

Spectacular release from one of South Africa's greatest groups. The ultimate mix of Mahlathini's deep bass voice and the Mahotella Queens sweetly sweeping harmonies, driven by the compulsive mbaqanga jive rhythms of the Makgona Tsohle Band. Contains many songs featured in their shows.

THE SOUL BROTHERS — JIVE EXPLOSION   (CDEWV-8/TCEWV-8)

Top selling township jive band. Honey-dripping vocals, swirling Hammond organ, sparkling guitars, unstoppable rhythms, and the best horn section in South African mbaqanga. Will be featured on the forthcoming Indestructible Beat of Soweto (Vol. 4) with many other top artists.

MZWAKHE MBULI — RESISTANCE IS DEFENSE   (CDEWV-25/TCEWV-25)

Charismatic "People's Poet", Mzwakhe Mbuli and his first permanent band are the new successful phenomenon on the South African music scene. His uncompromising liberation lyrics and highly-charged township music have won ecstatic acclaim all over South Africa, and severe harrassment from the authorities. Hot guitar, pile-driving rhythms, sax, and female backup vocalists support Mzwakhe's singing, chanting, reciting, rapping. Performances feature Mzwakhe, together with his female vocalists, unleashing the finest traditionally-inspired dancing ever seen on stage. Recent tours abroad herald growing international success. This brand new recording marks an important step forward for Earthworks.

DUDU PUKWANA - IN THE TOWNSHIPS   (CDEWV-5/TCEWV-5)

The 70s township jazz classic. A fine memorial to the British/SA jazz scene stalwart.

THOMAS MAPFUMO - SHUMBA (Vital Hits of Zimbabwe)   (CDEWV-22/TCEWV-22)

The biggest hits of the giant of Zimbabwean mbira-style guitar music. Chimurenga songs of liberation and reconstruction. Thomas Mapfumo & The Blacks Unlimited are the main pioneers of modern Zimbabwean music. Hypnotic guitars and beat topped with Mapfumo's smokey traditionally-inspired vocals. Essential and incomparable selection.

JIT   (CDEWV-23/TCEWV-23)

(6 Essential Songs from Jit-The Movie plus 6 other Smash Hits)

Get Jitted! Great music from Zimbabwe's recent first commercial feature film. Husky-voiced Oliver Mutukudzi also stars in the movie; stunning guitar music from Robson Banda & The New Black Eagles; Jonah Sithole, Mapfumo's original guitarist, who helped invent mbira-style guitar playing; Leonard "Pickett' Chiyangwa, another Mapfumo protege, delivers a knockout blow with "Wapunza Musha". Other artists include John Chibadura, and Mandebvu. Not to be missed.

ZIMBABWE FRONTLINE   (CDEWV-9/TCEWV-9)

The hottest groups from Zimbabwe. Sparkling mbira-style guitars and a driving beat. There's no chance of standing still. Mapfumo, Robson Banda, The Four Brothers, Jonah Moyo & Devera Ngwena, Susan Mapfumo, Oliver Mutukudzi, Zexie Manatsa, Real Sounds, and Lovemore Majaivana.

SPIRIT OF THE EAGLE (Zimbabwe Frontline, Vol.2)   (CDEWV-18/TCEWV-18)

The ultimate selection of classic Zimbabwean guitar music. Thomas Mapfumo at his peak; Patrick Mkwamba and The Four Brothers, Nyami Nyami, Robson Banda & The New Black Eagles. A complete guitar feast. Jump, Jit and Jive to perfection.

KENYA DANCE MANIA   (CDEWV-24/TCEWV-24)

Devastating hip-grinding sensual sounds of East Africa rumba music and other styles. Earth-moving bass, the sweetest rumba guitars and saxes, breath-taking vocals and truly irresistible dance rhythms. Let yourself go! Tip top artists include the Maroon Commandos, Gabriel Omolo and his Apollo Komesha, Les Wanyika, H.O. Kabaselleh, Daniel Kamau, and Wanyika Super Les Les. It does not get better than this!

GUITAR PARADISE OF EAST AFRICA   (CDEWV-21/TCEWV-21)

Be good to your ears. Wonderful variety of Kenyan and East African guitar bands. The hard driving benga boogie of Daniel Kamau, the guitar heaven and soulful vocals of top benga music star – H.O. Kabaselleh, the earthy attacking sounds of Sukuma Bin Ongaro, the famous rumba guitars of Les Mangelepa, and a whole heap of treasures like Super Mazembe's "Shauri Yako".

SAMBA MAPANGALA & ORCHESTRE VIRUNGA   (CDEWV-16/TCEWV-16)
— VIRUNGA VOLCANO

Famous classic album by one of Africa's great groups. Astonishing rumba guitars, deep rippling bass, superb soulful horns, and awesome vocals from Samba Mapangala. Let the music take over your body and your mind. East Africa's number one band.

DANIEL OWINO MISIANI & SHIRATI BAND   (CDEWV-13/TCEWV-13)
— BENGA BLAST

All the heaviest tracks from one of the greatest benga music artists. Blistering guitars, mountainous bass, forceful vocals, some of the hardest and toughest rhythms in the world. Incomparable collection. Raw and melodic at the same time.

THE AFRICAN TYPIC COLLECTION   (CDEWV-12/TCEWV-12)

This compilation of the best dance classics from the Cameroun includes Sam Fan Thomas's groundbreaking celebration of dance, "African Typic Collection", Charlotte Mbango's "Dikom Lam La Mota", and Koko Ateba's "Nelson Mandela Will Never Give Up". Plus other hits.

HEARTBEAT SOUKOUS   (CDEWV-3/TCEWV-3)

Move and groove to the sounds of the top Paris-based Zairean soukous stars. Kanda Bongo Man, Nyboma and Pepe Kalle, Syran Mbenza, Bopol, Denis Loubassou, and Lokassa Ya Mbongo.

HURRICANE ZOUK   (CDEWV-2/TCEWV-2)

Modern hi-tech dance smash hits from Guadaloupe and Martinique. A mix of African and Caribbean sounds. Zouk Time featuring Kanda Bongo Man, naughty Francky Vincent, Gerard Hubert, and Kassav project, Soukoue Ko Ou, etc.

RAI REBELS   (CDEWV-7/TCEWV-7)

The modern sound of Algeria. Traditional Arabic music influences with synthesizers, guitars and a pop beat. All the top stars are included. Cheb Khaled, Chaba Fadela, Sahraoui, Zahouania, Hamid, and Houari Benchenet. Rai'n'roll to these atmospheric sounds.

POP-RAI & RACHID STYLE (Rai Rebels, Vol. 2)   (CDEWV-15/TCEWV-15)

Latest sounds of rai guru and top producer, Rachid Baba. Rai music's popularity has spread far beyond North Africa and the ex-patriot community in France. This compilation features superstars like Cheb Khaled, and top Chebs (guys) like Hamid, Zahouani, Sahraoui, Anouar and Houari Benchenet. Also included, the husky tones of female star, Chaba Zahouania.

HENRY FIOL — SONERO   (CDEWV-19/TCEWV-19)

Remarkable collection of the best of Henry Fiol, one of New York's hot Latin musicians. Traditional Afro-Cuban sounds updated with modern arrangements. Compelling dance music with a big sound, percussion, searing trumpet and sax, tres (type of guitar), and Henry's soaring vocals.

SABROSO (Havana Hits)   (CDEWV-11/TCEWV-11)

Hot and tasty collection of Cuban hits. Irresistible rhythms galore. Many top artists are included like Orquesta Chepin, Celina Gonzalez, Los Van Van, Irakere, Sierra Maestra, Orquesta Reve, and others.

YOUSSOU N'DOUR — IMMIGRES   (CDEWV-10/TCEWV-10)

This is the breakthrough album to international success for one of Africa's greatest artists, Senegalese superstar singer, Youssou N'Dour. First released in 1984, this classic album features Youssou's top sound with traditional mbalax percussion and the most powerful combination of guitars, horns and Youssou's unique stunning vocals. Live shows are not to be missed. The voice of Africa.

Earthworks is released by Virgin Records worldwide, except in the USA where it's by Cardiac Records. UK catalogue numbers are included in this advert. Consult your local Virgin catalogue for details in other countries; except USA.

WATCH OUT FOR NEW EXCITING RELEASES!!!
INCLUDING THE INDESTRUCTIBLE BEAT VOL. 4.

EARTHWORKS

*The Indestructible Beat Of Soweto (Vol. 1) is the only album not available on Earthworks in the USA, but is available in the rest of the world on Earthworks.

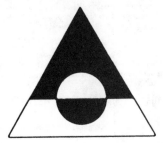

aster **a**weke
sona **d**iabate
cheb **k**haled
cheb **m**ami
m'mah **s**ylla
hukwe **z**awose

triple **e**arth
1-8 whitfield place
london w1p 5rw

tel: 071 380 0098
fax: 071 388 2756

RetroAfric

RETRO 1CD

E.T. MENSAH (GHANA)

RETRO 2CD

FRANCO (ZAIRE)

RETRO 3CD

E.T. MENSAH (GHANA)

RETRO 4CD

ALICK NKHATA (ZAMBIA)

THE AFRICAN ARCHIVE

RetroAfric
26 Gassiot Rd,
London SW17

Distribution: Sterns African Records
116 Whitfield St.,
London W1P 5RW